SHARED PLEASURES

WISCONSIN STUDIES IN FILM

General Editors

David Bordwell
Donald Crafton
Vance Kepley, Jr.
Kristin Thompson, *Supervising Editor*

*Shared Pleasures: A History of Movie Presentation
in the United States*
Douglas Gomery

*The Wages of Sin: Censorship and the Fallen Woman
Film, 1928–1942*
Lea Jacobs

Patterns of Time: Mizoguchi and the 1930s
Donald Kirihara

SHARED PLEASURES

A History of Movie Presentation in the United States

DOUGLAS GOMERY

FOREWORD BY DAVID BORDWELL

THE UNIVERSITY OF WISCONSIN PRESS

The University of Wisconsin Press
114 North Murray Street
Madison, Wisconsin 53715

Copyright © 1992
The Board of Regents of the University of Wisconsin System
All rights reserved

5   4   3   2   1

Printed in the United States of America

All photographs are from the author's collection.

Library of Congress Cataloging-in-Publication Data
Gomery, Douglas.
Shared pleasures: a history of movie presentation in
the United States / Douglas Gomery; foreword by David Bordwell.
408 pp.   cm. — (Wisconsin studies in film)
Includes bibliographical references and index.
ISBN 0-299-13210-2 (cloth) ISBN 0-299-13214-5 (paper)
1. Motion picture industry—United States—History.
2. Motion pictures—United States—Marketing.
3. Motion picture audiences—United States.
I. Title. II. Series.
PN1993.5.U6G59   1992
384'.8'0973   dc20   91-30618

Cover photo: Balaban and Katz's Chicago Movie Theatre, one of
America's great movie palaces, Summer 1948

CONTENTS

Part III / Technological Transformations

ILLUSTRATIONS

FOREWORD

Film studies, though often thought to be a maverick discipline, remains curiously respectful of boundaries separating the social sciences from the humanities. Film scholars pledged to traditional conceptions of humanistic inquiry often reject sociology, psychology, and other disciplines as irrelevant to the study of art. And the structuralist and post-structuralist thinkers of the 1960s and 1970s were obliged to invoke a realm of inquiry called the "human sciences," in order to rescue the sorts of (largely Continental) thought deemed appropriate to questions of text and discourse. Film scholars were eager to follow this lead, fencing off large bodies of exciting and rigorous theory and research and all too often castigating them as "empiricism."

It is therefore worth remembering that in the United States, film studies might have developed as a branch of social science. After World War II, academic inquiry into the media was largely the province of communications researchers, anthropologists (Ruth Benedict, Gregory Bateson), and social psychologists (David Manning White, Martha Wolfenstein, and Nathan Leites). For a variety of reasons, however, film studies emerged under the aegis of humanities departments.

Since then it has earned whatever intellectual respect it may have by allying itself principally with two trends in literary studies: the thematic interpretation of individual films, taken either as examplary works of art or as culturally revelatory artifacts; and the mounting of large-scale theories to explain how cinema creates meaning or pleasure. During the 1970s these two trends played an important role in introducing "symptomatic readings" and Grand Theory (drawn from the "human sciences" of semi-otics, psychoanalysis, neoMarxism, and feminism) into other areas of the humanities. The results, with all their strengths and weaknesses, are still very much with us.

It was not until the mid-1970s that empirical historical research, the *sine qua non* of most humanities disciplines, gained a firm purchase in American film studies. The most widely practiced approach treated films—usually Hollywood films—as reflecting cultural processes or as shaping audiences' ideological views. This approach offered a compromise between the intrinsic interpretation of films and an examination of the cultural context within which they were produced. Among the most important synoptic works in this vein were Robert Sklar's *Movie-Made America* (1975) and Garth Jowett's *Film: The Democratic Art* (1976).

By and large, the sociocultural historians were recognizably "human-istic," applying to cinema many assumptions already established in the field of American studies. It took a group—some would say a new gen-eration—of "revisionist" historians to displace the question of what this or that film might mean and to ask instead how modes of film production and consumption functioned.

At first this development might seem largely a matter of widening the range of data. The sociocultural researchers, like their colleagues in film criticism and theory, centered their inquiry upon the films themselves. The revisionists shifted the focus to the vast archives of primary materials generated by the film business. Trade journals such as *Variety* and *Moving Picture World*, court testimony, studio files, and other records offered a huge mine of resources. Partly, then, the revisionist impulse involved situating films within this network of business activity. But the revision-ists were not simply turning over new stacks of paper. They were impelled to ask new questions about the concrete practices of film production, dis-tribution, and consumption, and these cut across the lines that separated humanistic interpretation from more stringent explanation.

Start with the assumption that mass-market filmmaking and film ex-hibition, at least in most countries, is a business. What sort of business is it? According to what principles of structure and conduct does it oper-ate? What strategies of financing, organization, technical innovation, and growth does it follow? How have management policies changed over time, and how have they varied across firms? And what, finally, can the answers to such questions tell us about the look and sound of films, or about their functions in modern societies?

In the mid-1970s, a number of film scholars began posing such questions. Tino Balio's anthology *The American Film Industry* (first edition, 1976) became cinema studies' first book-length publication framing these issues. Robert C. Allen's research into early cinema exhibition (*Vaudeville and Film 1895–1915: A Study in Media Interaction*, Ph.D. thesis, 1977) proved to be another pioneering effort. At the same period, Douglas Gomery examined the same issues guided by the hypothesis that the American film industry could best be understood from the standpoint of economic principles.

Overall, it is not too much to say that Balio, Gomery, and Allen radically altered the way in which American film history is studied and taught. Today, a graduate student in film studies must know far more about the structure and conduct of the film industry than, say, a student of modern literature must know about publishing or a student of contemporary art must know about the economic dynamics of galleries and museology. Thanks largely to the work of the revisionist historians, film scholars have shown the crucial value of studying the industrial context if we want to explain the history of movies.

In this setting, Gomery's work quickly became the outstanding example of studying film history within a social-scientific frame of reference. Based in economic theory, self-consciously rigorous in its methodology, and exhaustive in its search for evidence, Gomery's research made an immediate impact in several domains. His Ph.D. thesis (*The Coming of Sound to the American Cinema: A History of the Transformation of the Industry*, 1975) treated technological history from an economic standpoint, producing what is still regarded as the most persuasive account of the causes for Hollywood's innovation of synchronized sound films. His use of economic models of technological change proved strikingly influential on other writers in film studies.

Informing this inquiry but coming to centrality in later work was a macrostructural inquiry into the economics of American film production. Gomery's ongoing research into this area was synthesized in *The Hollywood Studio System* (1986), a book which crisply delineates the structure and conduct of each firm and shows how certain phenomena of interest to more "humanistic" research (e. g., genres, cycles, and stars) can be explained within the framework of business practices.

The volume before you, based on over a decade of research, extends Gomery's inquiry into the domain of film exhibition. Drawing upon his earlier work and that of other scholars, *Shared Pleasures* is another demon-

stration of the explanatory power and sheer dramatic interest which an economic approach to film history can yield. By virtue of its subject, though,
the book represents something of a departure in its eagerness to address the
broader social functions of the film industry. By studying film exhibition,
Gomery shows how the Hollywood film industry adapted its business policies to diversity and change within American society. In this sense, *Shared
Pleasures* may represent a new synthesis between the sociocultural and the
"revisionist" approaches.

Gomery offers both an argument and a story. The argument shows, in
detail, that the American film business behaves as other businesses do.
It tends toward vertical integration, seeks to create a monopoly or an oli-
gopoly, and tries to control market forces through innovations and rational
conduct (centralized management, the run/ zone/ clearance system, and
other strategies). New entrepreneurs have to wriggle into the market place
by offering something different, such as drive-ins, shopping-center theatres, or discount theatres. While the protagonists of most film books are
directors, stars, or producers, here the major players are the Mastbaums,
Richard Smith of General Cinema, Nat Taylor of Cineplex Odeon, Ray
Dolby, Ted Turner, and above all Barney Balaban. Thus Gomery balances
his survey of large-scale structural forces with a consideration of those individuals whose decisions made film exhibition the enormous and profitable
enterprise it remains today.

The argument turns up new evidence and conclusions on almost every
page. One of the book's chief lessons is that the individual movie (the heart
of most scholars' inquiry) typically matters little to exhibition. (Again Balaban and Katz offer an exemplary case: "You don't need to know what's
playing in a Publix House.") In this framework the influential films turn
out to be items like *The Singing Fool* and *Brian's Song*, hardly the stuff of
poststructuralist exegeses. Another striking, but convincing, conclusion is
that in the future, contrary to conventional wisdom, American movies will
not decline as a form of entertainment. Factoring in cable and home video,
they are more prevalent than ever before; even considering only theatrical
venues, there are more screens for 35mm film projection in the US than at
any time in history.

Here Gomery's argument takes a frankly social turn. If his earlier work on
technological innovation and film production largely bracketed social factors, focusing on exhibition inevitably brings them in. So he shows how the
film industry adjusted to early waves of immigration, emerging urban culture, two world wars, and suburbanization. He shows how entrepreneurs
were able to exploit changing audiences, demographic shifts, and techno-

logical innovations in order to keep people coming to the movies. He out-lines how theatres functioned as popular concert halls, as temples to opu-lence or modernity, and as neighborhood gathering places. He traces the rise of specialized uses of theatres (children's matinees, midnight movies) as well as offering the first comprehensive overview of alternative venues that played important roles in American culture. Newsreel theatres and "art" cinemas are shown to have targeted audiences at the right moments to gain modest success. One of the most gripping chapters studies theatres for Afri-can Americans, which provides an unprecedented look at how segregation affected the film industry.

This argument, rich in detail and wide in its scope, is couched as a narrative—or rather, several narratives, since there is no one film history but only various question-motivated historical accounts. Gomery recounts a series of upheavals, from the nickelodeon boom to the rush to talkies and the new "sound revolution" of the 1970s. Theatres change from store-fronts to sumptuous palaces to sticky-floored mall crackerboxes and then to new palaces of postmodern multiplex luxury. Audiences change as well, expanding from working-class patrons to middle-class ones (still the indus-try's mainstay), from urban and small-town to suburban, but, strikingly enough, remaining largely young and relatively well-educated.

The story is vivid in its concern for particulars. We visit houses in Augusta, German-American theatres in Syracuse, the black-only Regal theatre in Chicago, and the Dent in Paris (Texas). Gomery's entrepreneurs weigh specific options. Where to show the first films—peepshow parlors or amusement parks? How could an exhibitor combine a film with a stage show? How might made-for-tv movies compete with broadcasts of theatri-cal releases? Despite the book's concern for broad trends, it keeps firmly before us the concrete experience of moviegoing. Gomery initiates us into the training of ushers in picture palaces, the tactics of games and giveaways during the Depression, and the business logic of 1950s kiddie matinees. We even learn the history of popcorn. Sidelights like these connect with the reader's memories and daily life in ways that academic research often fails to do.

Douglas Gomery was writing his dissertation when I joined the faculty of the University of Wisconsin–Madison in 1973. He and my colleague Tino Balio introduced me to the study of the American film industry and com-municated the intellectual excitement of what proved to be a significant phase in the maturing of our discipline. I think that this book conveys some of that excitement to the reader, and its influence should be no less robust.

For one thing, the book offers another demonstration of the explanatory power of the economic study of film history. Film is revealed to have intricate ties with other areas of life. In drawing on urban history, technological history, and demographic research, *Shared Pleasures* shows how the economic paradigm is open to theories and data from adjacent domains, all the while keeping its sights squarely upon the specificity of film as a business. Since scholarship is an ongoing activity, the book will probably trigger debate, but it will remain, I believe, an essential point of reference for studies of the history of American cinema. At the least, it should give the emerging study of filmic reception a firm historical point of departure.

This book also offers evidence that in the writing of film history, the distinction between the humanities and the social sciences can become fairly thin. *Shared Pleasures* shows that the most rewarding research is driven by imaginative questions, not fixed doctrines, and if one must cross hallowed boundaries to find answers—well, so much the worse for the boundaries.

DAVID BORDWELL

ACKNOWLEDGMENTS

Many persons helped me with research for this book. In particular I thank the employees who make the Library of Congress, my local resource, the best there is. Over the years I have spoken to many industry professionals, and I thank them, even though some might disagree with my conclusions. The Institute for the Humanities at the University of Michigan and the University of Utrecht in the Netherlands provided resources and useful forums. I thank Michael Budd and Charles Wolfe for their careful readings of the final manuscript. David Bordwell suggested this book might make a useful contribution. For his encouragement, valuable suggestions, and foreword I am grateful. In the end Marilyn Moon is responsible for the best parts of *Shared Pleasures*. I dedicate this book to her.

INTRODUCTION

Traditionally, a history of the American cinema concentrates on films and their creators. The locus of analytical "action" has long been that hub where art and commerce meet, Hollywood. Thus we have argument after argument focusing on the aesthetic history of film, supplemented by institutional analysis of the production constraints. Considerations of social, economic, and technological variables tend to be secondary to the analysis of the individual text.

I have long argued that film historians ought to examine and seek to understand the institutional economic apparatus.[1] In *Shared Pleasures* I seek to take up the challenge of David Bordwell: "Most people who study film still don't recognize the centrality of money."[2] To that end, *Shared Pleasures* offers a study of the economic, social, and technological history of film watching in the United States. It seeks to answer questions such as: How and where did Americans go to the movies? What corporations controlled the means of moviegoing? How did Hollywood control movie exhibition? Was there room for specialized theatres? How has the technological basis of movie presentation changed? What role has television played in the watching of motion pictures?

As a consequence *Shared Pleasures* concentrates on one part of the film industry—film exhibition. Simply put, as an economic entity, the film industry begins with the *production* of artifacts, followed by their *distribution*, followed by their *exhibition*. It is on this third level that the public takes on motion pictures. *Shared Pleasures* seeks to present a history of motion picture exhibition, in one nation, the United States. And it takes film exhibition as broadly defined—from the simple nickelodeon to the ornate movie palace, from the unpretentious neighborhood theatre to the orchestrated marketing of the multiplex in the shopping mall, from television's repetitive "Late Show" to vast selections available in the world of home video.[3]

Shared Pleasures takes as its central task economic questions and thus focuses on profit-making institutions. This book is a business history. As such it follows the outlines of work I have researched and written about for the past decade.[4] As a consequence readers seeking information and analysis of nonprofit institutions need look elsewhere. That is not to say that such sites for film presentation are not important. They are. But consideration of them would constitute a separate book, one not grounded in business history but in the social history of art.

My theory of the analysis of the economics of exhibition demands more than business history but also a grappling with technological change and social implications. That movie exhibition is based in technology is a commonplace idea. But that technology has always been changing, thus the economic history of movie exhibition is an economic history of technical change. Part III of *Shared Pleasures*, thus, addresses technical change directly.

But there is a second thrust of research in *Shared Pleasures*. I argue that the economic structure and behavior of an industry often leads to important social change. Such is the case with moviegoing. This can often lead to unexpected realms of research. Historian John F. Kasson has authored a book about manners in the nineteenth century. At the end of his *Rudeness & Civility* Kasson discusses behavior at theatrical events, analyzing how the rise of the nickelodeon precipitated a crisis in proper social behavior. But, as Kasson notes, this conflict between new and old Americans would never have come about without the rise of the movies as a mass entertainment industry. Although *Shared Pleasures* does not set out to fashion a social history of moviegoing, it will lay out the social implications of the industrial basis of moviegoing.[5]

Movie exhibition has only begun to inspire scholarly study. We lack a historical overview of the changing institution of theatrical exhibition in the United States; we have no survey of the activities of specialized theatres, from the newsreel theatres found in nearly every major city in the United States in the 1930s to the art houses of more recent decades; we lack systematic historical analysis of the technological transformation of the movie show, from the coming of sound, color, and wide-screen images to the dominance of television as the source of contemporary movie watching. *Shared Pleasures* seeks to fill these gaps.[6]

This statement of purpose needs to be qualified. This book is in no way offered as an encyclopedic history. To write about all phases of film exhibition would necessitate a series of vast tomes. I limit my scope in two ways. *Shared Pleasures* only examines the presentation of films in the United States. It is not meant to minimize the importance of viewers elsewhere, but histories of where and how people in other nations watched films will have to wait for another book. Studies of the exhibition of films in other countries around the world can and should be done. But this single volume begins with the United States, the largest cinema-watching nation in the world and home to the most forceful film industry in the world.

Shared Pleasures' focus on economic questions, while also considering technological and social matters, differs from one strand of important contemporary research. In recent years there has been a great deal of interest in the spectator and the cinema. A number of fine books and articles have reconsidered how one sees Hollywood cinema, principally from close analysis of the texts, employing sophisticated psychological theories. This book takes a different tack. I am interested in the history of changing material conditions of the exhibition of the movies that offer the beginning of a complete reexamination of the reception of cinema.[7]

The material history of the movie show in the United States provides a fascinating and stimulating look at a vast array of changes. How and where citizens of the United States watched films rarely remained static; such transformations were always affected by outside forces, ever since the earliest days of an exhibition business in the years immediately preceding the turn into the twentieth century.

Scholars have begun to appreciate the importance and influence of such economic changes. In one pioneering study, *The Classical Hollywood Cinema*, authors David Bordwell, Janet Staiger, and Kristin Thompson reevaluated the history of the Hollywood cinema and called for an additional work that would "examine the changing theatre situation, the history of publicity, and the role of social class, aesthetic tradition, and ideology in constituting the audience. This history, as yet unwritten, would require another book, probably as long as this."[8] *Shared Pleasures* takes up part of the call for action of Bordwell, Staiger, and Thompson—that aspect they have labeled the changing theatre scene. Indeed their formidable challenge, in part, inspired this present book.

THE BOOK'S STRUCTURE

Shared Pleasures offers an overview of how and where Americans watched feature films and analyzes the significant changes in the conditions and institutions for the presentation of feature films to audiences in the United States.

In particular, the initial part of *Shared Pleasures*, "Business History," in chapters 1 through 6, offers an economic history of *theatrical* movie exhibition in the United States. This history grapples with the creation of theatre corporations and the development of national theatre chains. To research and present such a history of any industry, the historian must examine changing conditions of supply and demand, industrial structure, and corporate behavior.

Shared Pleasures pays careful attention to understanding the factors that constitute the dynamics of corporate growth. That is, the development of the business of moviegoing in America mirrored the changes in other retailing institutions. First came the development of small, family run operations for the movie nickelodeons. But once a national strategy was developed, chain operations of commonly owned enterprises spread from coast to coast. Finally, to take advantage of economies of operation and control theatres were purchased by moviemaking corporations and thus the movies experienced vertical integration.

But moviegoing was also shaped and positioned by the larger forces of American history. Frequently historians observe that one can go to the movies to escape the realities of a harsh world outside. But the business of moviegoing could never stand separately. Throughout *Shared Pleasures* we shall see the effects of economic expansions associated with wars, the contractions caused by recessions and depressions, and the intrusions into economic activity by the powers of government. Indeed the economics of moviegoing brought on one of the most important and far reaching of antitrust sanctions in modern American economic history. Part I of *Shared Pleasures* is not purely a business and economic history; it also tackles the influences of outside economic forces. Social change has economic consequences.

For example, in the two decades following the Second World War the greatest boom in families in history took place in the United States. This forced movie theatres to select new sites and fashion new programming strategies, and in the end it reformed the institution of going to the movies. A number of important social factors, from the ever-changing configuration of urban America to the place of the movies as an art form, will be examined. In particular the influence of urban and suburban geography will be recognized for the significant roles they played.

Certainly social situations will be considered in detail. A separate chapter is devoted to understanding what factors gave rise to specialized theatres when an alternative to the business of moviegoing arose. Indeed theatres for what we might term "select audiences" have been available from almost the beginning of the cinema. Although marginal economic operations, all played an important role in the history of moviegoing and thus are treated in the second part of *Shared Pleasures*, entitled "Alternative Operations."

In chapters 7 through 9, specialized movie houses are examined, in particular newsreel theatres, segregated theatres demanded for African-Americans for the first two-thirds of this century, and ethnic and art cinemas offering movies, by and large, in non-English languages. These theatres are categorized by offering (newsreel and art theatres) and by audience composition (theatres for African-Americans and ethnic theatres). For example, for African-Americans legal separation in movie attendance lasted from the beginnings of the movie business until the desegregation of public institutions in the early 1960s.

In this second section the history of these institutions that filled special market niches is discussed. The concern is less with the size and development of the economic institution per se than with understanding how specialized institutions developed alongside the dominant Hollywood-linked operations.[9]

The third and final part of the book, "Technological Transformations," constitutes chapters 10 through 14. Here *Shared Pleasures* offers a history of the changing technology of theatrical film presentation and then details the introduction of television presentation of movies. Movie audiences in theatres in the United States experienced the addition of sound and color; television audiences have seen the coming of pay television, cable television, and home video.

Since movie presentation has always been largely a profit-maximizing industry, it is appropriate to examine technological change in terms of its invention, innovation, and diffusion. That is, for each new technology, the individual chapters will look at the creation of the necessary knowledge for presentation, then its introduction into the marketplace, and finally how it came into widespread utilization.

Let me stress that it is my purpose to blur the usual distinction made between film studies and television studies. The coming of television transformed the business and social practice of watching movies in the United States as did no other factor before or since. Television did not create a whole new industry, rather, television enveloped movie watching and gave rise to more persons watching more movies than any time before television became part of the very fabric of American life.

But factors of technological change are not simply internal to the film and television industries. The introduction of new technology in other phases of the American economy and society also often came to influence conditions of moviegoing. *Shared Pleasures* takes up the impact of urban rail transportation, the coming of air conditioning, and the overtaking of American culture by the automobile. Seemingly all phases of technical change have had some impact on the business of moviegoing.

To answer the research questions posed by concentrating on the factors of economics, technology, and sociology, *Shared Pleasures* takes up first dominant economic history, then the history of specialized niche markets, and then the economics of technical change. Thus, the arguments and analysis are not presented in a straightforward, chronological fashion. I hope this approach enables me to cast my view widely, and that *Shared Pleasures* will appeal not only to scholars of film but to students of business, urban, technological, cultural, and social history.

Shared Pleasures places its notes at the end to verify the sources of data used in the historical arguments and to offer specialized qualifications and asides. The bibliography presents "selected" further readings and does not function as a reorganization of the citations found in the detailed chapter notes.

PART I

Business History

ONE

The Movie Show Begins

Since the founding of the motion picture industry in the United States, showing movies has been organized as a business. Thus, at its base the history of motion picture presentation in the United States is an economic history. That is, since the innovation of motion pictures, presentation has been an economic institution, organized to maximize profits. Many movie pioneers considered and proposed alternative means of organization and goals; religious organizations and governmental agencies could have played a greater role, but they did not. This chapter, consequently, provides a history of the ways early entrepreneurs tried to use motion picture technology to find a formula to have the public regularly ante up to see motion pictures.

Surprisingly, during the first decade of innovation of the movie show, attempts to introduce a profit-making, movie-dominated programming strategy failed. No entrepreneur was able to provide a stable basis for the business of exhibiting movies in the United States. In retrospect we can learn a great deal about the beginnings of the motion picture industry through this initial set of failures. We must set aside the myth that Americans instantly embraced the movie show.

Instead, we must try to understand how entrepreneurs sought to fashion a profit-making entertainment strategy within a United States that was becoming more urban and more industrial. Numerous other inventions were competing for center stage, from the phonograph to the telephone, from the railroad to the automobile. Entrenched leaders of business, government, and education clung to traditional forms of entertainment, even as newspapers and magazines reached every home, as education past elementary school became a requirement, and as the incomes of the average family rose.[1]

As entrepreneurs sought a place for the movie show, they could see that business leaders in other retailing industries around the United States were making a place for themselves. Toward the end of the nineteenth century, with the completion of the railroad and telegraph, and the beginnings of the urban trolley system and the spread of the telephone network, the national market for goods and services saw a few firms—by taking full advantage of economies of scale—capture the marketplace. Successful business strategies involved finding a low-priced product (with a small profit margin per unit) sold by the thousands each day. The pioneer of movie theatre chains could appreciate the success of Sears, Montgomery Ward, A & P, and Walgreen stores.[2]

Entrepreneurs knew they approached a daunting task. The ideal of the new urban America called for order and civility. Yet, the staid world of the "refined" performing arts of opera, theatre, and European music contrasted with the rising tide of popular arts (called "cheap" and "vulgar") of vaudeville, popular music, and the circus. In "high-class" amusements, one behaved in a gentile manner; at Buffalo Bill's Wild West Show one was expected to whoop it up. Where would the movies fit in? Indeed, at the beginning the more important question was: Could the movie show attract business away from the smorgasbord of mass entertainments?[3]

THE MOVIES AS PEEP SHOW

Who organized the first true movie show is a question that has concerned many, but it is not the subject of this chapter.[4] Instead, I first seek to understand how entrepreneurs sought to innovate movies as mass entertainment. Initially, large-scale theatrical-like presentations were not the concern of entrepreneurs; the movies were to be shown to individual customers. The model for this philosophy was the recent success of the phonograph. During the 1880s the newly invented phonograph was set up in the arcades found in the heart of bustling cities. For a few cents customers could select various music and speeches, which they listened to through individual ear horns. These exhibits earned merchants a great deal of money in the years before phonographs became common in American homes.

Thomas Alva Edison sought to provide the same setup for moving pictures. Beginning in the late 1880s, Edison set his assistant, William Kennedy Laurie Dickson, to work mounting spirals of tiny photographic images on cylinders, which were to be viewed through a magnifying eyepiece while they revolved around a cylinder. Edison planned to exploit this latest invention as a novelty item in amusement parlors throughout the United States in the same manner he had made money from the invention and marketing of the phonograph. At this point Edison felt that the motion picture (accompanied with sounds from his phonograph machine) would function as a passing fad, and thus he did not create a system to project films onto a screen.[5]

By 1892 the vertical feed Kinetograph was ready. It was displayed a year later, and the first set of machines reached Broadway amusement arcades a year after that. The fifty-foot loops of Kinetoscope film moved through the machine in less than half a minute at forty-six frames per second. The loops were recordings of entertainers who were persuaded to journey across the Hudson to the West Orange, New Jersey, studio: denizens of Broadway vaudeville theatres, circus performers, trained animal acts, dancers, and comics. Early titles included *The Gaiety Girls Dancing*, *Trained Bears*, and *Highland Dance*. Vaudeville stars and celebrities of the day (for example, body builder Eugene Sandow, and Wild West stars Buffalo Bill Cody and Annie Oakley) all appeared before Edison's camera.

The date most accepted as the beginning of the peep show era is 14 April 1894, when Andrew Holland opened the first Kinetoscope parlor in a converted shoe store at 1155 Broadway in New York City. He charged twenty-five cents per person (later falling to a nickel) for access to a row of five Edison peep show viewers, each of which contained a single loop. Indeed Thomas Edison himself was part of the draw, with a plaster bust of the Wizard of Menlo Park adorning the entryway to the arcade.[6]

Edison's goal had been to exhibit the Kinetograph at the 1893 World's Fair, but that target was missed. But through these negotiations for that major event, Edison met Frank Gammon, secretary of the award's committee of the 1893 World's Fair. Gammon, with his rich brother-in-law Norman C. Raff, ordered twenty-five machines at one thousand dollars apiece. In time Gammon and Raff installed peep shows in penny arcades, hotel lobbies, and phonograph parlors in major cities across the United States. All presented motion picture shorts in the manner of a phonograph recording of a song. Edison sold not only equipment but also prints of films for ten to fifteen dollars.[7]

In Washington, D.C., on 6 October 1894, for example, Edison's Kinetoscope was first advertised by the Columbia Phonograph Musical Palace at 9th and Pennsylvania Avenue. That October five peep show devices were shipped to the nation's capital, with loops showing scenes of a barbershop, a barroom, a blacksmith at work, and a Scottish dance, among others. Columbia had long been the city's dealer for Edison's phonographs, and the company kept the Musical Palace open through the day and into the evening, awash with flowing air powered by mammoth electric fans and brilliantly lighted, mirrored walls. A second site opened on 8 November 1894 on Fifteenth Street near the Treasury Building. This was known as the Washington Kinetoscope Parlor, open from 8:30 A.M. until 11:30 P.M., and tendered five film subjects: a cock fight; an unnamed dancer; Eugene Sandow, the strongman; a prize fight; and a blacksmith at work. Each cost five cents to view.[8]

Entrepreneurs presented peep shows in cities large and small throughout the nation. The attempts in New York City are well known. But upstate New York also saw peep shows. For example, in Rochester, New York Edison's Kinetoscope opened in December 1894, when the store of Sibley, Lindsay & Curr installed four machines in the basement.[9] Yet the plan to make money showing movies in Kinetoscope parlors on the model of the phonographic parlor did not work. Why was this so?

An alternative to mass marketing of movie entertainment was already in the works, and that was the model of the theatre. Entrepreneurs believed they could make money by putting a crowd in a hall and projecting motion pictures onto a special surface. The impetus for this type of presentation did not, surprisingly, originate with Thomas Edison but came to the United States from Europe, principally from the efforts of the brothers Lumière of Lyons, France. They sought to develop what we think of today as the projector. After a thorough study of the Edison technology, the Lumières constructed their own version of a camera, printer, and projector. On 28 December 1895 the Lumières held the first public showing of ten short motion pictures—projected on a screen—in the basement of the Grand Café in Paris with their Cinématographe.[10]

Soon they brought this concept to the United States to rival Edison's business practice. Demonstrations of the new machine appeared in many cities. For example, in Washington, D.C., on New Year's Day of 1897 the Cinématographe was first used to project films for audiences in the capital of the United States. In Willard's Hall, at Fourteenth and "F" streets, in the heart of Washington's white downtown, for fifty cents (twenty-five cents for children) exhibitions were presented at 2:00 P.M., 4:00 P.M. and

8:00 P.M. [11] Whiting Allen delivered a short lecture and presented three short scenes of Washington itself plus scenes from abroad, which was the advertised feature of the Lumière attraction. [12]

The Lumières led the way to an exhibition system that would endure—projecting films onto a screen. They had seen the Kinetoscope in Paris and "corrected" its deficiencies, in particular its dimly illuminated images. Quickly Edison abandoned the peep show Kinetoscope for public presentation. These initial films were simplistic in their editing, camerawork and mise-en-scene. But the material recorded was fascinating. Indeed the Lumières took their cameras to parks, gardens, and many other public places to record everyday activities and, when possible, important events of the day. The titles of their early films reflect this: *Arrival of a Train at a Station, Baby's Lunch,* and *Workers Leaving the Factory.* [13]

By the year 1896 the movies were permanently on the screen. The Edison Vitascope projection system was exhibited to the press on 3 April 1896 and soon thereafter publically exhibited at Koster and Bial's Music Hall, a noted vaudeville theatre located near Herald Square in New York City. The Vitascope soon became part of the Koster and Bial's vaudeville show. On 29 June 1896 the Lumière Cinématographe was presented at Keith's Union Square Theatre in New York City. [14]

Quickly improvements were made. Raff & Gammon, for example, heard of the success of the Lumières' equipment, and so when in December of 1895 they learned of a projector designed by Americans C. Francis Jenkins and Thomas Armat which had been demonstrated at the Cotton States Exposition in Atlanta, they bought the exclusive marketing rights. In turn they arranged for Edison Manufacturing Works to build it. But the motivation was not to exhibit movies and make money. The plan was to use the movie show to convince others to buy the equipment. Raff & Gammon sought to franchise the Vitascope state by state; in turn that franchisee would subcontract rights to smaller regions, taking advantage of the name of America's most famous inventor. [15]

Quickly entrepreneurs set up halls in which to show Edison's films. For example, in late July 1896 the Vitascope Hall in New Orleans opened with a continuous program from 10 A.M. until 5 P.M., then from 7 P.M. until 11 P.M. Admission was set at ten cents. At the beginning business was good, with newspaper accounts noting opening crowds. From 29 August 1896 until 30 September 1896 the *New Orleans Daily Picayune* ran a promotion to admit any child under age ten for free. The programming at the Vitascope Hall included *The Cockfight at Babylon, Long Island, The Kiss, The*

Corbett-Courtney Prize Fight, and the locally produced *Bicycle Parade of New Orleans.*

As the entertainment season opened in September 1896, the newspapers of New Orleans listed Vitascope Hall under the regular mass entertainment offerings. (All the others were live performance attractions.) By the new year of 1897, a second "movie house" opened across the street, tendering Edison short subjects. At first crowds were large and curious, but neither operation lasted into the summer. A way was needed to harness the Edison miracle as more than the newest of novelties.[16]

New Orleans attractions were certainly typical of the day. In Washington, D.C., Vitascope Hall opened in the heart of downtown at the end of February 1897. Shows were presented at 2:30 P.M., 4:30 P.M., and 8:15 P.M. and cost twenty-five cents for adults and fifteen cents for children. But as elsewhere, even with favorable publicity from the top newspaper in town, the *Washington Star,* the Vitascope in the nation's capital lasted but a year. Remarkably it proved no permanent addition to the mass entertainment matrix of this thriving urban center.[17]

The Vitascope also made its way to more rural parts of the United States. Two months after Koster and Bial's premiere came the opening of the Vitascope at the Portland Theatre in Portland, Maine. Edison's "greatest wonder" cost twenty-five cents at night for adults and ten cents for children; matinees were only a dime for all ages. Rural America did not fall behind in experiencing the latest marvels of modern entertainment. And the Maine experience seems to be typical. By the end of 1896, within eight months of the initial Koster and Bial's exhibition, Lexington, Kentucky, had seen exhibitions of the movie technology of Thomas Edison and the brothers Lumière.[18]

MOVIES IN THE AMUSEMENT PARK

What was needed was a base for a permanent entertainment attraction. Entrepreneurs tried a variety of solutions. Late in the nineteenth century, amusement parks were built at the end of trolley lines in major cities in the United States to encourage riders to journey through the entire system. Amusement park entrepreneurs presented a variety of acts to attract audiences in the hot summer months. In that mix of contemporary popular culture, the movies would simply function as another addition.[19]

For example, in New Orleans a Vitascope Hall also opened in the West

End Amusement Park on 26 July 1896. This open air presentation was actually the first true movie show in New Orleans and undoubtedly the first in the South. Films were presented at night—at 8:30 P.M. and 10:00 P.M. They were not fillers for the regular band concerts but a major part of an evening's program. The movie shows ran for the summer season. This long-running presentation reduces somewhat the significance of the long singled-out 23 April 1896 debut of the movies at Koster and Bial's Music Hall in New York.[20]

The West End Amusement Park in New Orleans reopened in May 1897 and again advertised and presented Vitascope movie shows along with the usual vaudeville attractions and open air concert performances. The vaudeville attractions were classic circus acts: high-wire performers, tight-rope walkers, gymnasts, and clowns. The movies were frequently shown between sections of music and vaudeville entertainment. The local trolley car company ran trains continuously to West End Park, boosting its own business. Up to twelve different films would be shown each week, and often they were listed in advertisements in the local newspapers.[21]

New Orleans' West End Amusement Park was doing so well with its franchise of the Edison equipment and films that rival Athletic Amusement Park began to show motion pictures on the Lumières' Cinématographe beginning in June 1897. Newspaper advertisements stressed the exotic nature of these movies: *The Garden d'Acclimatation at Paris*; *Bathing in the Sea at Britannia*; *The Fete of a Millionaire at Budapest*; *The Swan's Park of the Goldenhead at Lyons, France*; *The Famous Mechanical Sausage Factory at Marsailles, France*; and *Shooting the Chutes at Geneva*. Both parks presented motion picture shows each summer, on a regular basis, through the remainder of the 1890s and into the twentieth century.[22]

Word spread of the success of entrepreneurs in New Orleans, and amusement park operators in other cities began showing films. For example, in Baltimore, Maryland, during the late 1890s and into the early years of the twentieth century, motion pictures were regularly shown at Riverview Park. This huge amusement park was located on the Patapsco River where the Broening Highway Plant of Western Electric Company would eventually stand. Riverview was one of the most popular mass cultural attractions in the Baltimore environs, famed for its three roller coasters and gigantic Ferris wheel. In particular, the park's casino presented films of the American Mutoscope and Biograph Company.[23]

In Lexington, Kentucky, the Woodland Park of the Lexington Chautauqua Society provided the location for summer screenings of films. Local businesses contributed so families would not take the train to Louisville or Cincinnati for weekend outings. The local street railway linked its routes to the entire community. From 1897 through 1903 the Chautauqua presented motion pictures in hopes of "moral uplifting." After the city purchased the park in 1904, motion pictures became a prime attraction at the Woodland Park Summer Theatre. Other activities were booked as well, including live theatre, circuslike acts, and uplifting sermons.[24]

Eventually amusement park entrepreneurs created a special attraction in order to convert motion pictures into a permanent attraction. All parks had some sort of rail ride, usually past painted scenic panorama, so entrepreneurs created a simulated railroad trip with movies. The Hale's Tour Car was created, consisting of a railroad coach rigged to sway gently from side to side as if it were moving, with movies providing the illusion of scenes flying by. The Hale's Tour Car craze lasted only from 1904 through 1906. Still, in its day, installations were found throughout the United States, from the White City Amusement Park in Syracuse, New York, to Riverview Park in Chicago, to Athletic Park in Montgomery, Alabama.[25]

Movies in amusement parks did not disappear with the coming of the nickelodeon. They continued as an attraction, playing off of what was first seen in nickelodeons of the era. For example, during the summer of 1906 Luna Park in Coney Island, New York, featured "The Great Train Robbery, a realistic reproduction of a moving picture series which caused much comment when shown in vaudeville houses on the screen." Movies also inspired new amusement park rides, the most famous of which was probably "A Trip to the Moon" at Luna Park in Coney Island, modeled after the famous Georges Melies' film of 1902.[26]

Many later exhibitors got their starts with movie shows at amusement parks. Harry Brandt, later the moving force behind the Trans-Lux newsreel chain, started in the picture business at age fourteen, with his brother William, in an abandoned lot behind a Coney Island hot-dog stand. By the early 1920s the Brandts had a successful independent chain in and around New York City, which they sold to William Fox. Similarly, Nicholas and Joseph Schenck started in show business in amusement parks, first showing movies at Paradise Park in upper Manhattan and then moving across the Hudson River to acquire Palisades Amusement Park in New Jersey. By two decades later, Joseph Schenck had built United Artists into a Hollywood power and was in the process of founding Twentieth Century-Fox. Brother Nicholas ruled at Loew's Theatres and its subsidiary, Metro-Goldwyn-Mayer.[27]

TRAVELING EXHIBITORS

Amusement parks were open only three to four months per year and hardly provided a permanent venue to exhibit motion pictures. Moreover, these parks were always located at the edge of America's expanding urban environs. But in 1900 the United States was still a rural nation, with most of the population living in communities of fewer than three thousand citizens and lacking any form of amusement park. Another solution was needed for the rural population, and the one that was inherited from the nineteenth century was the traveling exhibitor.[28]

By the middle of the nineteenth century there were two traditions of traveling entertainment that moved around rural America. One involved one-night bookings in small-town opera houses or other permanent venues that often doubled as the town hall or county courthouse. More common were the myriad of entrepreneurs who put on their shows under the stars or under a temporary canvas theatre. These individuals simply loaded a projector, films, and a sheet (for a screen) onto a wagon and took it from town to town. Or, as in rural Maine, they traveled from town to town by boat. Traveling exhibitors proved a popular means of early film exhibition, not only in the United States but elsewhere around the world.[29]

As the nineteenth century turned, film exhibition for rural Americans rested solely in the hands of traveling exhibitors. Itinerant exhibitors by the hundreds plied this trade; one famous entrepreneur of the traveling circuit was Lyman H. Howe, who began his career around the time of the World's Fair in Chicago in 1893. He began from his Wilkes-Barre, Pennsylvania, base in 1896 with a modified Edison projector. By 1900 Howe's programs were formulated into a two-hour program of shorts. To guarantee a flow of new and interesting motion pictures Howe frequently shot footage of local events and then showed the townfolk themselves on screen. Lyman Howe Attractions presented his shows well into the epoch of the movie palace, before his death in the early 1920s.[30]

Lyman Howe trained other traveling exhibitors, such as Edwin J. Hadley, who went out on his own circuit in upstate New York in 1897. From a base in Warrensburg—population about two thousand—Hadley moved about the rural northwest of what was then America's most populous state. In 1898 Hadley sought new territories, moving to the Midwest, using Chicago as a home base. Later he would return to the East and again work for Howe.

A typical Hadley show would be sponsored by a local civic organization, which provided an opera house, a YMCA hall, the basement of a library, or a school. The sponsor distributed advertising before Hadley arrived, promoted the event as a benefit, and then took a cut of the receipts. The show typically included sing-a-longs, motion pictures, and monologues by Hadley himself. The films were invariably of Edison origin. Footage of the Spanish-American War drew considerable commentary in 1898: "The pictures of the battleships in action were so real that every time a shot was fired the women would duck their heads to let the thirteen-inch shells pass over."[31]

Hadley and Howe have been singled out because business records of their activities have survived and made their way into archives. But they hardly operated alone; hundreds like them worked the byways of rural America. Cheap projectors and hundreds of short films were widely available by the late 1890s, often sold directly through the Sears-Roebuck catalog. At the opening of the 1896 entertainment season, in September, advertisements began to appear in the *New York Clipper*, the leading vaudeville trade paper, for Kineoptikon, Gyrographe, Zooscope, Edison, and Lumière equipment. Over the years the *New York Clipper* advertisements constituted a central clearinghouse for information about projectors, possible bookings, and an increasing number of films for sale.[32]

In the days before the nickelodeon, circuses also showed motion pictures as part of their eclectic mix of entertainment. For example, from 1897 through 1903 motion pictures were part of the regular show of the noted Ringling Brothers Circus. Exhibited in "black tents" and "black tops"— massive canvas structures constructed to keep the light out—the movie show was located directly opposite the main sideshow along the midway, preceding the entrance to the big top. A series of posters, each about fifteen feet high, lined the front of the black tent to promote this new show. A barker stood outside and hawked the moving pictures shown inside.[33]

As we shall see in the following chapter, ten thousand nickelodeons were in business by 1910. This number of permanent exhibition sites hurt the traveling exhibitor. More drastic threats to their livelihood came from the powerful social and economic forces that eradicated rural America. In particular the rise of the automobile made it easier to "go to town," where a permanent movie show was always available. And, the coming of talkies made the traveling show that much harder to mount.

Still, there were times when the business of the traveling exhibitor was helped by outside forces. The Great Depression in particular saw the closing of many theatres, and this reopened markets of "portable circuits." These markets seem to have thrived in the midwestern states, with their plethora of small towns at least twenty-five miles apart, as in Iowa or Kansas. Itinerant entrepreneurs would move by truck, often following irregular routes and showing films they owned, thus paying no rental fees to Hollywood. Their activities were hardly noticed, except for the all-too-frequent nitrate fire. The best season remained the summer and fall because of the regular schedule of fairs and carnivals. But shows were also set up in town halls, fraternal lodges, church basements, and school auditoria.[34]

The prosperity and wide adoption of the automobile after the Second World War ended the traveling movie show. Yet one golden era remained—the days of imposed restrictions during the Second World War. In many small towns across the midwestern United States, restrictions on auto travel, and limited availability of convenience goods and traditional entertainments, combined with the prosperity of the war economy to yield vast sums of spending money but little to do and few places to go. Traveling exhibitors secured aging equipment or the then-new 16 mm projectors, and they took to the road one final time. The "B" western proved a staple draw. Small-town merchants frequently sought out the itinerant exhibitor, in many cases putting up a guarantee so as to draw folks to town to shop. The rise of suburban America, with its ubiquitous cars, new houses, and later televisions in every room ended the need for even a permanent movie show in what was to remain of rural America.[35]

VAUDEVILLE THEATRES

If amusement parks had a limited season, and traveling exhibitors a limited market, the presentation of motion pictures in vaudeville theatres in the major cities of the United States hit at the very heart of mainstream mass entertainment. When movie technology was first innovated, there existed in the United States a complete matrix of commercialized, popular entertainment in vaudeville theatres in every major city from New York to San Francisco. Demonstrations of motion pictures were often held in vaudeville theatres. The Vitascope and the Cinématographe made their debuts in New York vaudeville theatres during the established vaudeville season of 1896–97 (September to May) as one fifteen-minute "act" among the eight others on the bill. Here was a theatrical base from which to introduce movies to millions of Americans.

The vaudeville exhibition of the late 1890s consisted of a typical show of eight variety acts running continuously throughout the day, aimed directly at a middle-class audience. The ten-to-twenty-minute acts were most often unrelated; there was no narrative or thematic relationship between one act and its predecessor. The vaudeville bill included tenors and sopranos of European origins, trained animal acts, inspirational readings, acrobats or other circus-inspired performers, comics, and "playlets"—condensed versions of popular theatre of the day. There was something for everyone; but vaudeville theatre owners did their best business in the emerging downtowns of America's major cities.[36]

The 1890s saw the building of vast chains of vaudeville theatres. There was the Keith's chain in major cities in the eastern part of the United States and the Pantages and Orpheum circuits west of the Mississippi. But the standards were set in New York City, then the largest and most dominant American city. To keep theatres filled, Keith's, Pantages, and Orpheum bookers sought newer acts. One source they looked to were visual spectacles such as puppetry, shadowgraphy (the making of shadows with one's hands), magic illusions, living pictures (famous scenes recreated by poses of live actors), and magic lantern presentations. The new motion pictures followed in this tradition.[37]

At first success seemed easily found; in the movies vaudeville found a wonderful new attraction. This latest marvel of the Edison factory could be marketed on the name of the greatest inventor in America. It could easily form a single vaudeville act. Indeed, with the restriction of the silent format, Edison created many of the studio's early films from recordings of vaudeville acts from across the river in New York City. As already discussed, the Lumières' Cinématographe made its American debut in June of 1896 at Keith's Union Square vaudeville theatre, a mere two months after the Edison Vitascope opened at Koster and Bial's vaudeville theatre. The Keith's chain, the major vaudeville power in the eastern United States, dropped its initial Vitascope contract and signed up the Lumières to service its theatres.

From their New York office the Lumières supplied the vaudeville theatres with a projector, technician, and films—a "complete package," in vaudeville parlance. The Lumières' act could ride the circuit just like a juggler, comic, or animal act. Unlike the Vitascope, the Cinématographe was hand cranked and so did not depend on the multitude of different electrical sources in American cities of the time. Finally, the Lumières cleverly coupled minidocumentaries of foreign lands (for example, France) with locally made footage, filmed by the traveling projectionist as the act moved from city to city.

By the end of the 1896–97 vaudeville season, a pattern of movie presentations as single acts in commercial vaudeville was established. This would endure until the coming of the nickelodeon a decade later. In vaudeville the movies found their greatest audience in the middle class. Indeed, vaudeville presented the forum in which many urban Americans were introduced to the movies.[38]

Many of the films of this era were aimed at vaudeville audiences. For example, "local actualities" presented audiences in city after city their "own home town" through images of local sporting teams in action, new buildings being constructed, or volunteer fire departments saving a family's home. In contrast travel films also presented moving images of exotic, faraway places.

The clearest indication of early moviemaking aimed at vaudeville audiences was the dramatic rise of the "coverage" of the Spanish-American War. Leading up to this war Americans were subjected to a constant barrage of public invective, especially from the newspapers of William Randolph Hearst. On 15 February 1898 the United States Navy's battleship *Maine* was sunk while at anchor in Havana's harbor; within two months the United States and Spain were at war. The actual incursion lasted only ten weeks, but vaudeville entrepreneurs, never missing a chance to take advantage of patriotic war frenzy, celebrated in song and dance and helped make Admiral Thomas Dewey and Theodore Roosevelt national heros.[39]

Vaudeville helped spread the fame and appeal of the movies throughout the United States. A typical case is New Orleans. The Auditorium Theatre initiated movies as part of its vaudeville entertainment in February 1897, with performances from 11 A.M. until 11 P.M., at ten cents admission for all. Business proved routine until the Spanish-American War offered an attraction few dared to miss. In May 1898 hundreds lined up to see images of the United States naval fleet engaged in the Battle of Manila, featuring the cruiser *New Orleans*. In August came the film *Roosevelt's Rough Riders at Tampa, Fla.* Films of returning troops, complete with pageants and parades, strung out the drawing power of the "Wargraph," a projector dedicated to war films, into 1899.[40]

New Orleans hardly seems exceptional. In city after city, where a facility existed for vaudeville, the movies were introduced on a regular basis in the years immediately before and after 1900. This proved the case in towns as small as Lexington, Kentucky, near the end of the line in terms of the various vaudeville circuits. Gregory Waller has found that the Lexington Opera House, the preeminent permanent venue for mass entertainment in Lexington, Kentucky, at the turn of the century, served as the most important site for the introduction of motion pictures.[41]

There seemed to be a pattern to the use of vaudeville as a means for bringing the movies into mainstream American popular culture. The popularity of motion pictures of the Spanish-American War provided a misleading indication that vaudeville theatres would serve as the permanent home for movie screenings. Looking at the attempted innovation of the movies through vaudeville, we can see that, based on a study of early movie exhibition in New York City, Chicago, and Rochester, New York, the success of Spanish-American War films offered but one of five stages in the attempted innovation of movies through vaudeville.

1. The period from April 1896 through the end of that year saw movies as simple novelties, principally in vaudeville situations. Properly the Koster and Bial's show is seen as being at the beginnings of the attempted innovation of the movies as a vaudeville attraction. Other vaudeville entrepreneurs recognized the value of a movie act, and Oscar Hammerstein, F. F. Proctor, and B. F. Keith all took on motion pictures for their influential vaudeville theatres. Theatre managers elsewhere quickly followed suit; the attempt to introduce movies to urban America would receive serious entrepreneurial energy.

2. The period commencing in 1897 and running into July 1899 saw films move into the forefront as acts in vaudeville theatres, boosted by the popularity of the Spanish-American War as variety entertainment. This era would prove to be the heyday of motion pictures in vaudeville theatres. At the time many thought movies would become a permanent part of the vaudeville show.

3. From midway into 1899 through late in 1900 vaudeville theatres scheduled movies that lauded the victory of the Spanish-American War and tried to keep this genre of programming at the center of scheduling. For a time this strategy seemed to work well, but the war was soon a part of the past and vaudeville audiences turned to other concerns. The ability of motion pictures to serve as a permanent part of vaudeville shows seemed to be fading.

4. From late 1900 through early 1903 it became clear that the movies were to function only as an intermittent part of the vaudeville industry. Movies became a specialty act at best. No genre of programming could be developed to match the consistent drawing power of the images of the Spanish-American War.

5. In the final years remaining before the innovation of the nickelodeon, there was a vacuum. Motion pictures had no permanent home. Amusement parks operated only in the summer months; traveling exhibitors sporadically serviced rural Americans; vaudeville theatres presented motion pictures only intermittently to urban Americans. Into this vacuum of interest would step nickelodeon pioneers whose behavior gave us the movie-only show, the nickelodeon, as is analyzed in detail in the following chapter.[42]

MOVING TOWARD THE NICKELODEON

The movie show was not unpopular during the late 1890s and into the early years of the twentieth century. Its innovation serves to define a crucial segment of the history of American vaudeville. Such theatres provided the key base to introduce the middle-class audience—the core of the twentieth-century movie audience in the United States—to the new entertainment form. The vaudeville industry provided a crucial laboratory for experimentation. The Adolph Zukors, Marcus Loews, and William Foxes, pioneers of the movie business, learned from their vaudeville predecessors.

Indeed the popular news films that fueled the hysteria associated with the Spanish-American War illustrate the essential problem of presenting movies through vaudeville. No one could predict when war—or news of that degree of interest—would happen. The movies were highly successful in vaudeville when a war was on, but otherwise there was not the demand relative to the live attractions that had long been the staple of vaudeville theatres.

The movie show in the amusement park and the traveling exhibitor hardly represented long-term solutions to a motion picture exhibition industry. They were important in introducing millions of Americans to the movies as mass entertainment but could not be the foundation of a business. A solution to struggles over basic patents was needed; alternative film forms needed to be perfected; and other problems such as a permanent apparatus for production and distribution needed to be worked out. Once these issues were settled, the stage was set for the innovation of a permanent solution—the movie-only theatre.

TWO

The Nickelodeon Era

Midway through the first decade of the twentieth century, many in the United States had seen the new motion pictures, but there existed no mass exhibition industry. This situation would change with the coming of the nickel theatre, transforming movie exhibition into a big business. The nickelodeon gave rise to a new sector of the American mass entertainment industry, an urban-based theatre situation that presented motion pictures as the core entertainment. The nickel show solved several problems: the seasonal limitations of the amusement park; the temporary, fly-by-night nature of the traveling show; and the high prices of vaudeville.

There had been nickelodeons from the start. Raff & Gammon, Edison's agents in the 1890s, franchised a number of business leaders, who in turn rented storefronts and showed movies there. These storefront theatres offered a brief program of films for a small admission charge. But this initial innovation never took off in the first decade of movies as an entertainment form. Acceptance—seemingly everywhere at once—would not come until 1905; by 1910 some astute observers counted almost ten thousand nickelodeons in cities from New York to San Francisco.

The nickelodeon functioned as a small and uncomfortable makeshift theatre, usually a converted cigar store, pawnshop, restaurant, or skating rink made over to look like a vaudeville theatre. In front large, hand-painted posters announced the movies for the day. Inside, the screening of news, documentary, comedy, fantasy, and dramatic shorts lasted about one hour. The show usually began with a song, a hit from the day illustrated with hand-painted, color magic lantern slides displaying the images and words of the song. Most entertainment, though, came from motion pictures.[1]

18

The front of the typical nickelodeon represented its most important and most costly feature. Nickel theatres sold their wares to a public walking by, and so soon they developed a myriad of lights with a prominent ticket booth, usually accompanied by a barker, to hawk their latest entertainments. Theatre owners attempted, for as little cost as possible, to emulate the legitimate theatre but in the end often had to settle for a simple selling window in the manner of an arcade or dime museum. Huge paintings might cost the operator hundreds of dollars. Wood gave way to pressed metal as the nickelodeon owners prospered.[2]

The name of the nickel theatre was spelled out prominently, and gaudy posters were standard to attract potential patrons walking by. Newspaper advertisement was infrequent. Instead melodramatic poster art, gaudy electric signs, and loud phonographs hawked the new photoplays and sparked the earliest set of complaints about this new mass entertainment. It was at this time that the box office, as a special architectural feature of the movie house, came into use. For a time the round box office became the very symbol of the new movie house, in the same way the striped pole had come to symbolize the barbershop. The box office often was ringed by electric lights flashing a multitude of colors, reminding passersby that this was a modern, marvelous movie marvel, all in an age when most citizens did not have electricity in their homes.[3]

The interior of the nickel show was more sedate, simple in design even when compared to plain, modern, multiplex standards. The auditorium, typically the only room inside, was little more than a converted screening room, long and narrow and darkly lit even when patrons were streaming in and out. Between fifty and three hundred simple wooden chairs or benches provided seating. A "stage" was usually no more than a simple platform positioned up front. The nine-by-twelve-foot screen was simply attached to the back wall. A piano accompanied the silent film, but in the better establishments there might be an ensemble including several stringed instruments. The projection booth was set off in the rear. Soon, with the passage of fire laws, a separate booth, lined with lead, was set up in the rear to safely house the potentially explosive film and often lethal projector.[4]

Once the wave of openings began to grow, the nickelodeon's rise in popularity expanded faster than anyone had anticipated. In 1907 *Variety* told its readers: "Three years ago [December of 1904] there was not a nickelodeon, or five-cent theatre devoted to moving-picture shows, in America."[5] By 1910 *Variety* reported more than one hundred in Chicago alone. The figure for the nation as a whole was estimated at five thousand; some placed the number over ten thousand.

In 1910 in Washington, D.C. one observer counted thirty-one movie houses. Some estimates put one hundred nickelodeons in St. Louis. These figures may be exaggerated, but as early as 1906 Harry Davis, the reputed "father" of the nickelodeon, was rumored to be thinking of starting a national chain from his headquarters city of Pittsburgh.[6] One estimate totaled some twenty-six million patrons each week at nickelodeons in 1910, then about one-fifth of America's population. Gross receipts for the year soon reached into the millions of dollars.[7]

Costs of day-to-day operation of the typical nickel theatre were low. Both *Moving Picture World* and *Variety* estimated that typical weekly expenses amounted to usually no more than two hundred dollars, requiring a cumulative attendance of four thousand every seven days (or about sixty per show) to break even. Little in the way of special training was required. Only the social stigma attached to this "fly-by-night" theatrical operation served to discourage potential entrants.

Consider the expenses for nickelodeons in Grand Rapids, Michigan:

1. Rent ranged from less than one hundred dollars per month for sites outside downtown to a top of four hundred dollars per month for certain prized, downtown locations.
2. Equipping the theatre was estimated to be in the three- to four-thousand-dollar range. As nickelodeons became fancier, this part of the basic cost rose considerably. This cost included woodwork, wall coverings, hiring a staff, seats, painting, and tile. Good opera chairs cost one and a half dollars. The projector and accessories cost four hundred dollars.
3. Film cost varied from ten to fifty dollars per week per reel. If the same reel was shown all week, the cost of that reel represented the sum of the charges, but if the reel was changed (for a new subject or for a new print of the old subject) the expense would increase accordingly.
4. Salaries were low since most of Grand Rapids' downtown operation employed at most ten persons. Specialists demanded and received the most: projectionists were paid from nine to twenty-one dollars per week, piano players four to twelve dollars. The total came to less than three hundred dollars per week.

And with these low costs, these Grand Rapids' theatres were constantly busy, earning far in excess of the aforementioned expenses. Midwestern nickel theatres did their best business on Saturdays and Sundays, with fewer people attending on weekdays. (In some areas, the Bible Belt in particular, Sunday shows were prohibited by law, but Saturday business compensated for this.) The Grand Rapids' nickel theatres, even then, depended on "repeaters" for the bulk of their receipts: "There are many persons who have moving picturitis and who visit the theatres day after day," wrote a reporter for the *Moving Picture World*.[8]

Governments at all levels required no special taxes or zoning requirements, save the rigid rules about fire safety. Theatrical fire laws, already on the books, were quickly amended to minimize the possibility of highly flammable nitrate film exploding into a death trap. The sole union problem arose in 1908, when it had to be decided whether the Brotherhood of Electrical Workers or the International Alliance of Stage and Theatrical Employees would organize the moving picture projectionists. The International Alliance earned the right and has continued to represent projectionists ever since.

The rewards for the right nickel theatre at the right location became the stuff of legend, spread by rumor through the burgeoning trade press and by word of mouth. One report in late 1907 claimed that the Golden Rule nickel theatre in New York City took in nearly two thousand dollars per week while having expenses of no more than five hundred dollars. The era of the nickelodeon represented a golden age for anyone willing to take a chance. The movie exhibition business would never be as open again.[9]

As early as October 1907 a report in *Moving Picture World* related: "Nickel madness is a term applied to the amazing popularity attained during the last year or so by five-cent moving picture theatres."[10] Suddenly there seemed to be a nickelodeon on every corner. By 1908 the nickelodeon had become the primary outlet; still vaudeville theatres, traveling exhibitors, and amusement parks, during the summer months, continued to show movies as a part of their regular entertainment.[11]

There were a number of additional reasons for the rise of the nickelodeon as a mass entertainment phenomenon. First, the United States economy had done reasonably well for the better part of a decade; popular entertainment as an industry was taking full advantage of "good times." The trade press of the time pointed out that as the number of nickelodeons seemed to double and then triple within the space of several months, so too was there a substantial increase in the number of vaudeville theatres and amusement parks. Second, the United States population was growing, chiefly from the unprecedented wave of immigrants flooding into America's larger cities. These poorer urban inhabitants embraced the cheap entertainment form, as we can see from the relative growth of the nickelodeon in city after city.[12]

The era of the nickel theatre was short-lived. The nickelodeon movement did not begin in earnest until 1905, but once it did, its rise in popularity was indeed rapid. In 1904 the vaudeville theatre functioned as the principal outlet for the movie show. By October 1906, a year into the nickelodeon era, *Variety* could report several dozen nickel shows in Chicago alone. Some pundits pegged the national figure at two thousand. By 1910 few industry experts doubted the national total had neared ten thousand. One early expert estimated that in 1910 gross receipts for that year reached into the millions of dollars. But by then the nickel show had become so successful that entrepreneurs began to look for ways to turn even greater profits. Such a strategy would come with the movie palace, but not before the nickelodeon had laid the foundation for theatrical moviegoing in the United States.[13]

CASE STUDIES

The remarkable aspect of the rise of the nickel theatre movement was its breadth and speed. In urban environs from the teeming metropolis of New York down to growing mid-sized cities such as Allentown, Pennsylvania, and Madison, Wisconsin, commentator after commentator was overwhelmed by the explosive growth. For example, by the spring of 1908 industry observers were not surprised to learn that according to one survey there were approximately one hundred nickel movie theatres in San Francisco alone, with attendance estimated at fifty thousand per day. Almost overnight movie industry receipts were moving toward a million-dollar figure in San Francisco alone.[14]

Through a series of case studies we can see and appreciate how quickly the nickelodeon craze spread across the United States, to the largest cities and the smallest towns. Most often the story of the rise of the nickelodeon is told only from the viewpoint of New York City. As a start, this approach is certainly appropriate. New York City stood as the center of the mass entertainment industry in the United States, and it set trends others across the nation were sure to follow. But by concentrating on New York City one fails to appreciate two remarkable facets of the nickelodeon craze.[15]

First, the nickelodeon was never the sole province of America's largest metropolis. So many "small-town" entrepreneurs followed suit that nearly all of America's urban communities of any size had permanent movie shows by 1910. Second, the nickelodeon movement spread across a vast nation very quickly. Naturally, entrepreneurs in other major cities learned quickly from the successes in New York. But what is surprising is that citizens of small-town America experienced their first nickelodeon within months of learning about it from newspaper and magazine accounts. In short, the following seven case studies show that the coming of the nickelodeon was remarkable because of its speed of adoption. By 1910 a permanent base for movie exhibition had been set up across the United States almost before anyone realized it.

The case studies move from large to small, from New York City to smaller, but certainly significant, metropolises including Baltimore, on the border between South and North, Milwaukee in the heartland of the Midwest, and New Orleans in the deep South. A study of a medium-sized eastern industrial city, Worcester, Massachusetts, leads to an analysis of the introduction of the nickelodeon in such rural America locations as in the state of Iowa and a typical small town in Kansas, Augusta. In all, we shall see extraordinary economic and social transformation.

New York City

The largest city and certainly the entertainment mecca of the United States at the turn of the century was New York. Although New York City had movies since the 1890s, it did not enter the nickelodeon era in earnest until the spring of 1906. But the number of storefront theatres grew rapidly after that, so fast that the then vaudeville-oriented trade paper *Variety* noted "they are increasing so rapidly that positive [concrete] figures are unobtainable."[16] Although more than a hundred theatres were in New York City by the end of 1907, nearly a third were located in the polyglot of immigrants on the Lower East Side, the most densely populated area of the nation. By 1911 one estimate placed the number of nickelodeons in Manhattan alone in excess of two hundred.[17]

One reporter, working for *Moving Picture World* in October 1907, found them everywhere: "[Nickel shows] are to be found with pretentious fronts in Broadway. In the Bowery and through the East Side they are almost omnipresent. Dozens of them are exceedingly popular in Brooklyn. They are springing up in the shady places of Queens, and down on Staten Island they are to be found in the most unexpected bosky dells, or rising in little rakish shacks on mosquito flats. They have even invaded nearby [New] Jersey cities."[18]

Entrepreneurs set up shop principally in the Bowery and Union Square sections of the city, which for prior decades had been the center of New

York City's popular amusements, including vaudeville, dime museums, saloons, and burlesque shows. Nickelodeon owners did not at first tred new ground but followed suit, setting up shop in already established entertainment centers. But during the first decade of the twentieth century New York City saw the development of many more centers of business and commerce. These developed neighborhood centers, often composed of ethnic concentrations such as "Little Italy" or "Jewish Harlem," serviced the immediate neighborhood. Here customers shopped every day on foot. Movie entrepreneurs set up shop where few theatres had ever been. For example, by 1910 the Germanic Yorkville section of Manhattan, the largely Jewish-populated areas of Brooklyn, and other teeming neighborhood centers in Queens, the Bronx, and Richmond contained dozens of the new nickel movie theatres.

In a city of neighborhoods, income class shaped the growth and distribution of the nickelodeon. For example, nickelodeons did not appear in wealthy neighborhoods. Rich New Yorkers already had a wide variety of established, respectable entertainments, from the legitimate theatre to "high-class" vaudeville, and could easily afford to patronize them.

Still, we must not assume that all nickel theatres were located only in poorer sections of New York City. The greatest concentration lay in areas of the city where the emerging middle class resided. For example, "in one street in [middle class] Harlem the writer [for *Moving Picture World*] counted as many as five [nickel shows] to a block." The poor may have had access to nickel shows, but they had precious little time and funds with which to attend. The emerging middle class had the time and money, and their neighborhoods became the preferable locations.[19]

Baltimore, Maryland

There were other thriving cities in the United States during the early part of the twentieth century, as the nation turned from a land based on agriculture to an urban, manufacturing country. At the turn of the century Baltimore constituted a major American city. Baltimoreans, like their neighbors to the north in New York City, were introduced to the movies in 1895 when Raff and Gammon opened a Kinetoscope parlor downtown. But, like other larger cities, in Baltimore movie presentation did not initially establish a permanent foothold, despite regular showings in vaudeville theatres and in amusement parks that ringed the city.

No one is sure when the first permanent nickel theatre opened in Baltimore, but it seems to have been the Amusea, opened for business during the spring of 1906 from 11 A.M. until 11 P.M., in the downtown area near the traditional entertainment district.

A year later the boom was on; some twenty-seven movie houses were opened in Baltimore in that year alone. A year later they seemed to be on every corner of this bustling port city. Most of these nickelodeon buildings were quite small, seating about three hundred or fewer. Theatre names were spelled across the front of the building facades above the entrance, and posters in glass cases or pasted to the wall advertised current attractions. (Regular newspaper advertisements did not arrive in Baltimore until 1913.) Baltimore may have been considered a provincial town near the Mason-Dixon line, but adjusting for its smaller population, its nickelodeon building boom rivaled New York City's.[20]

Milwaukee, Wisconsin

The coming of the nickelodeon was perceived as an overnight sensation in Milwaukee, Wisconsin, as well. This prosperous manufacturing city in the Midwest had been the site for the usual demonstrations of the Edison and Lumière equipment. For example, Thomas and John Saxe operated a Kinetoscope parlor downtown between September 1902 and May 1903. But they made little on this enterprise, and the brothers returned to their sign-painting business, often illustrating outdoor posters for the handful of vaudeville theatres clustered near the Milwaukee River.[21]

The Saxes returned to the movie business in 1905, when they established a Hale's Tours show downtown. A year later they set up the "Beer City's" first nickel show, the Theatorium, in a converted downtown store. Their initial investment was about three thousand dollars. On 10 November 1906 the movies permanently came to Milwaukee with a lecture, several sing-a-longs, and five short films. In 1906 the Saxe brothers had the lone permanent movie theatre; a year later there were ten. Indeed by the end of 1907 the trend was noticed by the *Milwaukee Sentinel*, which wrote: "The [nickelodeons] are not necessarily 'cheap and nasty.' At their best, they supply (not unprofitably) the demand for some form of inexpensive entertainment for those whose means are small."[22]

Soon nickelodeons began to appear in neighborhoods far from downtown. Among the first were the Imperial "5 Cents" Theatre at Fourth and Mitchell, in the heart of a Polish enclave of the city, and the Globe at Twelfth and Walnut in the more prosperous German section of the city.

Newly arrived Germans and Poles represented the largest immigrant groups in Milwaukee's melting pot. By 1908 nickelodeons served a half dozen outlying areas as well as the core of the city's downtown. Owners of legitimate theatres and vaudeville houses never set up shop outside the central business district of Milwaukee.[23]

A study of the recreation habits of the citizens of Milwaukee in 1911 estimated that more than two hundred thousand people went to the movies each week. Nearly thirty thousand were at the movies between eight and nine in the evening on a typical Saturday or Sunday night. (Milwaukee's population at the time was slightly less than four hundred thousand.) And this new movie audience was by and large a young one, with two-thirds of any typical evening's attendees under twenty-five years of age.[24]

New Orleans

In the United States the South is considered a unique region of the country. The Civil War was only forty years old as the nickelodeons began to appear. Southern cities were, by and large, not as prosperous as their northern counterparts. And, as we shall see in chapter 9, the South required separate institutions for black and white residents. Still, as with the experiences of New York City, Baltimore, and Milwaukee, the wave of nickelodeon building swept over the South.

Consider the situation in New Orleans. As seen in chapter 1, the citizens of New Orleans had regular screenings of movies in amusement parks and at vaudeville theatres through the early years of the twentieth century. But a movie-only theatre appeared in November 1906, when the Electric Theatre on Canal Street opened, running continuously from 10 A.M. to 11 P.M., with programs changed Wednesday and Sunday. The Electric Hall opened the nickelodeon era in New Orleans.[25]

The Electric Hall was not alone for very long. The Bijou opened in October 1907, with continuous shows from 6:30 P.M. to 11:30 P.M. Programs changed daily. Nearby the Penny Wonderland opened the same month, with shows priced at ten cents running from nine in the morning until eleven at night. Soon there were nickelodeons all over town. While some months "behind" New York, Baltimore, and Milwaukee, New Orleans proved the South was not so different. Nickel madness swept across the Gulf Bay port in as rapid a fashion as it had in the environs of its neighbors to the north.[26]

Worcester, Massachusetts

Worcester, industrial city in the northeast, was certainly an important city (possibly the most important in New England outside Boston), but it was hardly as big and important as New York City, Baltimore, Milwaukee, or New Orleans. But the pattern of the innovation and diffusion of the nickelodeon would prove altogether familiar. Prior to 1904 the movies were shown only on a sporadic basis, featured principally in two of the city's vaudeville theatres. In 1905 Nathan and Isaac Gordon converted a main street furniture store into a penny arcade, which failed. But the following year they opened a nickelodeon, which surpassed all their dreams.

The premiere of the Nickel Theatre came on 24 September 1906 and claimed some ten thousand patrons during its first week of operation. That may have been an exaggeration, but the competition that soon arose was real. The difference over the following years was that the nickel show in Worcester remained exclusively downtown. The city was small enough that downtown served the center of the city; outlying businesses were few in number. But that concentration was hardly unique. In smaller communities few nickelodeons were ever built outside the downtown area. All trolley lines led there, and business in the neighborhoods was simply not big enough to support a full-time theatre. This meant that nickel madness, in terms of the absolute number of theatres, was not as dramatic as in New York City or Milwaukee, with their dozens of outlying theatres. This does not mean that attendance or interest was any less, however.[27]

The State of Iowa

Iowa certainly represents the archetypal rural state, as far from New York City as one might venture in the United States. Without a major city or port of entry, Iowa's population was dispersed. In 1880, with nearly all the land under cultivation, more than seven-eighths of the population was classified as rural. And those cities that did exist were small, with fewer than thirty thousand people.[28]

But nickel theatres appeared as early as in the supposedly more sophisticated centers of the nation. Advertisements for nickel theatres began to appear in 1905, as expected in the bigger communities, including Waterloo's Electric and the Nickeldome in Des Moines. Then came the Radium, the Dreamland, the Mirror, and the Bijou. The Nickeldome offered "continuous motion pictures—come any time—12:15 to 6:00 P.M. and 7:30 P.M. to 11:00 P.M.—any seat five cents."[29]

In 1907 an explosion of nickelodeons came to Des Moines. *Variety* and *Moving Picture World* began to run separate stories about the growing movie business there. By the autumn of 1907 *Moving Picture World* declared a "moving picture war is on in Des Moines."[30] Popular in this early season were passion play films, which were widely advertised and patronized. *The Great Train Robbery* may be one's image of what drew fans, but in Iowa it was the biblical story of Jesus Christ brought to life. By 1909 the nickelodeon had spread through the state, with sites in Clinton, Davenport, Dubuque, Fort Dodge, Marshalltown, and Sioux City, as well as in Des Moines. In only two years, rural America had entered the age of the nickelodeon.[31]

Augusta, Kansas

The introduction to and embracing of the movies in America's heartland was hardly localized in Iowa. Augusta, Kansas, was a town of six thousand, located about fifteen miles due east of Wichita. The railroad arrived in Augusta in 1881 and pushed the town's population past one thousand. By the time movies were available, Augusta had grown to more than three thousand and functioned as a trading center for the farmers of the region. Prosperity would come to Augusta in 1914 with the discovery of oil. Two years later Butler County, of which Augusta is one of the two major trading centers, was producing some six million barrels per year, more than the rest of the state combined.[32]

Movies naturally found a place in this boom town. They were shown informally late in 1905 in temporary outdoor shows and on a permanent basis in 1907 with the first nickel theatre, appropriately called the Nickelodeon. In classic fashion two local merchants converted a storefront into a theatre. The enterprise, located in the heart of the five-block Augusta central business district, was a modest success. It would change names and even location once, but the Idle Hour, the theatre's second name, remained the sole outlet for movie shows for Augusta's citizens until 1916. The redoing of the Idle Hour represented the transformation of the nickelodeon into a fancier theatre.

The growth of Hollywood and the emergence of the feature film gave rise to the conditions for a second permanent theatre in 1916, the Isis, four doors up the street. With some four hundred seats this was much larger than the Idle Hour and was considered quite special in Augusta, although in New York City or Chicago it would have been simply another neighborhood movie house. But for Augusta here was a theatre district, a microcosm of the neighborhood theatre situations found in the bigger American cities. The movie show came slowly to Augusta, but come it did.

LEARNING FROM THE NICKELODEON

In small towns and large cities, the movie house had become a permanent part of the American scene by 1910. And the case studies hardly represent a biased sample. The selection was made on criteria of typicality, ranging from the nation's largest cities to smaller communities. But detailed studies exist for other diverse communities, including Reading, Pennsylvania; Muskogee, Oklahoma; Columbia, Missouri; Spencer, West Virginia; and Providence, Rhode Island.[33]

Because New York City is too often used as the sole vantage point, the nickelodeon is seen strictly as an urban phenomenon. It was more than that. The nickelodeon wave washed over small-town America within a couple of years of its urban influx. In all these diverse locales fans embraced the movies as they had no other popular art form. The nickelodeon was not simply a phenomenon of the teeming ghettos of the New Yorks and Philadelphias but a mass enterprise that swept across the United States in the years between 1905 and 1910.

With nickelodeon prices so much lower than a big-time vaudeville show, it is not surprising to learn that early devotees came from the poorer sections of the cities. This gave rise to the expression "democracy's theatre." But as can be seen from the case studies, a policy of catering to the poorer and lower middle-class (by income) patrons was not embraced by the theatre owners themselves. They could look down the street and see the monies being made by vaudeville entrepreneurs who sought out middle-class audiences. Movie entrepreneurs, once they felt safe with the nickelodeon formula, abandoned their original poorer patrons for a more selective audience, catering to a middle-class with more discretionary income and more time to spend in a movie house.[34]

Movie audiences were transformed. During the short span of the nickelodeon craze (from 1905 to 1909) moviegoers were less than affluent folks. But theatre owners who desired to make more money wanted a higher class of patrons (in terms of income). Moreover, less well-to-do audiences often contained rowdy youths who disrupted the shows and caused richer patrons to stay away. By 1910 movie theatre owners had taken direct aim on the emerging American urban middle class and with them would create the most profitable mass entertainment industry in the history of the United States to that time.[35]

Theatre owners succeeded, often beyond their wildest dreams. The movie show was no longer considered a fad that would go the way of bicycle races. The movie show, in more and more beautiful theatres, in better and better parts of town, became an accepted part of American show business during the 1910s. The nickelodeon would disappear within that decade, but not before it provided the platform that seduced a nation. Years later the movies' first home would be recalled with a nostalgic innocence celebrating a populist shrine.[36]

The nickelodeon provided the entryway into the new movie industry for nearly all the pioneers we now associate with the founding of Hollywood. For the entrepreneur the nickelodeon business proved easy to enter. The career of Carl Laemmle, founder of Universal Pictures, testified how simple the process of opening a nickelodeon actually was. In 1906, in the Polish Milwaukee Avenue neighborhood and the north side of Chicago, Laemmle launched his White Front Theatre, with fewer than two hundred seats rented from a nearby undertaker. Total capital needed came to thirty-six hundred dollars. Ten years later Laemmle presided over Universal City, then the largest movie production complex in the world.[37]

William Fox, for example, began by buying a failing Brooklyn nickelodeon with 146 seats. In 1908 he leased the Dewey Theatre on Union Square and turned it into a movie house. On Thanksgiving Day of that year more than ten thousand folks surged into the Dewey, a record that impressed impresarios throughout New York City, indeed the nation. By 1910 William Fox was operating fourteen theatres in the environs of New York City. A decade later he was the head of one of the leading studios in Hollywood, one bearing his name.[38]

Marcus Loew would gain national fame by forming Metro-Goldwyn-Mayer in 1924. He had begun twenty years before with penny arcades, then moved to nickelodeons and small-time theatres offering vaudeville and movies at prices only slightly higher than the nickel show. Loew, ever the sharp entrepreneur looking for an edge, sensed that vaudeville would be an advantage to his movie houses. In January 1908 he turned the Cozy Corner Burlesque Theatre in Brooklyn into the Royal Theatre, with vaudeville and movies. A year later he had a chain of twelve such operations around the city, and by 1910 Loew was beginning to expand to other major American cities.[39]

But Laemmle, Fox, and Loew were hardly alone. Adolph Zukor, the Warner brothers, Louis B. Mayer, and nearly all the other of Hollywood's original movie moguls began their careers in the era of the nickelodeon because little stood in their way. Other businesses discriminated against those foreign born (as all these moguls were) and Jews (as most were). The new nickelodeon movie business was wide open.

By the mid-1910s the matrix of nearly twenty thousand theatres was in place, supplemented by traveling rural operations. Yet the evidence from the day indicates that as early as 1907 there were just "too many" theatres chasing too many nickels: "Today there is cutthroat competition between the little nickelodeon owners, and they are beginning to compete each other out of existence." *Moving Picture World* penned an editorial arguing that the "craze is on the wane" and ran it in June 1907. Although it would be two years before everyone agreed that the nickelodeon era was to be short lived, the signs by 1907 were remarkably accurate.[40]

The original nickel price soon gave way to admission prices of ten cents and then more. Entrepreneurs seized the opportunity to increase their original prices. And with this new ten-cent price, still much less than the big-time vaudeville show, it is not surprising to learn that early devotees of the nickelodeon were keen to escape from average working days of ten hours or more, six days a week.

To lure the ideal family trade the nickelodeon owner looked to the "New American woman" and her children. On a shopping break or after school, the theatre owner set up special "tea hour" screenings; if women and children came, the owner had a stamp of respectability that could (and did) lead to more money and a more favorable image in the community. Thus women and children saw half-price afternoon specials. Stories in the movies catered to them. Filmmakers began to draw on respected authors such as Emile Zola, Edgar Allan Poe, Victor Hugo, Mark Twain, and even William Shakespeare for copyright-free inspiration for ten-minute capsulated versions of the classics. Owners of nickel shows saw that the popularity of such stories signaled the respectability that aspiring social climbers in the community sought.[41]

By 1911 the nickelodeon was often misnamed. Moreover newer theatres, designed as theatres and not made-over clothing stores, were rising. In the years preceding the second decade of the twentieth century, the trend was toward the movie show as a middle-class mass entertainment, held in a spacious theatre and costing as much as twenty-five cents. By 1909 *Moving Picture World* had predicted that nickelodeons would be soon part of the past, and movie theatres would take their place "seating five hundred to a thousand [patrons], most of them giving a mixed bill of vaudeville and motion pictures."[42]

The pundit writing for *Moving Picture World* proved correct, and the beginnings of change were reflected best in New York City, ever the leading edge of the mass entertainment industry. By 1908, two-hundred-seat converted storefronts were giving way to buildings that we would—until the mall cinemas of the 1960s—consider real movie theatres. In New York City, with so many theatre buildings available from the vaudeville era, it was possible to do this very quickly, without building a movie-only theatre. That is, entrepreneurs simply turned former live theatres into movie houses, theatres designed with the comforts of regular middle-class patronage.

In November 1907 William A. Brady turned the twelve-hundred-seat Alhambra Theatre on Union Square into an early version of the movie palace, featuring both movies and vaudeville. There always had been vaudeville with movies, as we saw in the previous chapter. The change here was found in the proportions; movies began, increasingly, to fill at least half of the show. Once the movie palace era began in the late 1910s, the movie show with vaudeville entertainment took on a special name—the stage show.[43]

For example, in Milwaukee, Wisconsin, the nickelodeon era came to an end through the efforts of two brothers. In December 1909 the Saxe brothers, slowly becoming Milwaukee's movie moguls, opened up the Princess Theatre downtown. Costing the staggering sum of fifty thousand dollars, the nine-hundred-seat Princess represented Milwaukee's first movie palace, albeit on a miniature scale. Thomas Saxe issued exclusive invitations to the premiere to members of Milwaukee's Merchants and Manufacturing Association and Citizen's League. Four ushers in cadet grey uniforms assisted the invited guests to elegant "opera" seats. Cut flowers and plants lined the lobby. Twelve hundred incandescent lamps ensured that the Princess's facade would be a highlight of the downtown environs. The Princess contained Milwaukee's first theatre organ and a seven-piece orchestra.

The Princess triggered a trend. The Butterfly Theatre, opened 2 September 1911, moved ever closer to the movie palace. With air "changed" every three minutes, a forty-foot ceiling, and a glowing butterfly electric sign (twenty-seven feet from tip to tip of the wings) above the marquee, no one confused the Butterfly with a nickelodeon built a few years earlier.

With the veins of the butterfly's wings studded with one thousand tiny electric lights, the Butterfly Theatre served as a beacon in the nightlife of Milwaukee. A ten-piece orchestra projected even to the balcony of the fifteen-hundred-seat house. The era of Milwaukee's nickelodeons was over; ornate, specially designed and decorated movie houses followed the models of the Princess and Butterfly and were even constructed in neighborhood shopping areas.[44]

But in its day, the lure of the new movie nickel show proved so successful that former filmmaking and manufacturing enemies—the Edisons, the American Mutoscope and Biograph Companies, the Lubins, and the Vitagraphs, among others—agreed temporarily to lay down their differences. They banded together to form a monopoly—one company to control the complete movie business in the United States: the Motion Picture Patents Company.

Although the company was vilified, it did little to impede the rise of the nickelodeon. (Indeed the Motion Pictures Patents Trust, as it was popularly called, ultimately failed, but not before it helped establish Hollywood as the center of the filmmaking world.) But during the rise of the nickelodeon, Hollywood as a center of filmmaking did not exist. Films were made in nearly every major city in the United States and thus freely circulated. Imports from France, England, and elsewhere in the industrialized world added to the stock of the film exhibitor's offerings.

The next step in the development of the movie industry was to take advantage of this national market. As was done with other types of mass selling, chains were organized to keep costs as low as possible. This was the case with the Woolworths Five-and-Ten Cent Store and the Sears-Roebuck department store chains. After the First World War, movies would adopt the same strategy. The mom-and-pop entrepreneurs of the nickelodeon era would give way to the age of mass merchandising. And because more and more of the spending power of the nation was concentrated in the largest cities, the first step toward the movie palace occurred there.

THREE

The Rise of National Theatre Chains

As we have seen, the age of the nickelodeon was short lived. In the decade after the First World War the forces of big business successfully monopolized the American film industry. On the production and distribution side, the Motion Picture Patents Company had failed to corner the market, but it set into play the forces that led to other monopolists, that is, the Hollywood studios, taking charge. On the level of exhibition, powerful, regionally based chains of movie houses assumed control of the business of American moviegoing.

Movie exhibitors followed the lead of department store and grocery chains, which had precipitated significant changes in mass selling in the United States in the years preceding the First World War. For example, a former vaudeville company, Loew's, Inc., based in New York City, was able to take over film exhibition in all five boroughs of America's largest market. One hundred miles to the south the Stanley Company of America seized power in and around America's third largest city, Philadelphia, Pennsylvania.

But the most successful regional movie chain was Chicago's Balaban & Katz, the chain that is the major focus of this chapter. Balaban & Katz's innovations proved so successful that all others simply followed its lead as best they could. When in 1925 Balaban & Katz merged with Hollywood's largest studio, Famous Players-Lasky, the most powerful movie company in the world was formed, and the United States film industry entered the age of big business.

But these three theatre chains, and those exhibitors around the nation

34

that would copy their successful methods, did not operate in a vacuum. Indeed selling movies as mass entertainment followed a national trend. Before the growth of powerful theatre chains—first on a regional and then a national basis—there was a considerable revolution in mass selling. In the latter part of the nineteenth century and during the first two decades of the twentieth century the United States economy was altered by the innovations of national wholesaling and chain store retailing. Both helped increase sales volume, speed delivery of service, standardize the product, and increase profits.[1]

It took an organized set of theatres, operated from a central office, to realize the benefits so well known to Sears-Roebuck, Woolworths, and A & P. Thus, from the nickelodeon to the movie palace, the leading exhibitors sought to learn the tenets of the ongoing chain store revolution. During the first two decades of the century, chain stores became a significant force in the United States economy. They emerged in the form of grocery stores (A & P, Grand Union, Krogers), variety stores (Woolworths, McCrory, Kresge), and then stores for drugs and sundries, auto parts, gasoline, and clothing.

The methods seemed simple. Chains kept costs low by taking advantage of economies of scale. Fixed costs were spread over more and more operations, so the cost per store was far lower than the competition across the street. For example, A & P had one central accounting department handle financial records and inventory control for their stores in a number of states. Store managers only made entries; others kept the books.

To take full advantage of this type of savings, chains relied on "scientific management." Owners hired university trained experts to study the situation and propose methods by which to minimize costs and maximize sales. Each department of the modern chain store enterprise was simply asked to perform its specialty at maximum speed and minimum cost. Only those tasks necessary to that goal need be learned. Owners and operators of single store outlets had to be jacks-of-all-trades. Masters of specialties could do the jobs faster and cheaper—and spread over hundreds of operations. There was no reason to think that "scientific management" could not be applied to the movie exhibition business.

The monopsony buying power of the chain organization also kept other operating costs low. Monopsony buying power refers to the economic advantage that results when a firm is one of a limited number of buyers of a necessary input. For example, as A & P grew to become the dominant grocery chain, it could seek and secure discounts from its suppliers, be they farmers or mass producers of household items. A & P would buy in bulk, at lower-than-normal unit prices. Sellers were happy to secure the sizable sale guaranteed by signing up with A & P. Movie chains would do the same by booking theatres with the same films or building several massive picture palaces based on the same design.[2]

During the first two decades of the century chain outlets, taking full advantage of these savings, increased dramatically. Grocery chains became the most ubiquitous. A & Ps red-fronted outlets came to represent the modern age of self-service grocery shopping, revolutionizing a major institution in the nation's economic life. In 1912 A & P had four hundred outlets; twenty years later the total exceeded fifteen thousand. By 1930, with sales topping one billion dollars per annum, A & P stores accounted for one-tenth of all food sold in the United States. The men and women who owned and operated movie chains around the country came late to the chain store revolution, but in the years between 1916 and 1924 all worked furiously to copy the efficiencies of their retail cousins down the street, to gain greater power within a city, to increase profits every year, and to become giants in the new industry of the movie show.[3]

LOEW'S AND THE STANLEY COMPANY OF AMERICA

In the period immediately after World War I, movie exhibition replaced big-time vaudeville as the mass entertainment form preferred by Americans. Pioneering exhibitors devised strategies that would cater to the largest possible audiences in the biggest cities. Thus it is not surprising that the two industry leaders of the late 1910s represented movie chains at the centers of the nation's largest and third largest cities. Early in the revolution of movie exhibition, the changes came most quickly in New York, from the Loew's Corporation, and in Philadelphia, from the Stanley Company of America.

The Loew's, Inc. used its position in vaudeville to fashion the dominant chain for movie exhibition in the nation's largest city. Loew's moved from the world of cut-rate vaudeville to being the owner and operator of a string of impressive movie palaces. This transformation proved so successful that Loew's was able to fashion the most renowned moviemaking company of its day—Metro-Goldwyn-Mayer. But MGM would have never come about if Loew's had not created a chain of theatres in need of more motion pictures.

Loew's began on its road to movie exhibition success in 1908, when it helped pioneer a form of motion picture exhibition that bridged the gap between the nickelodeon and the movie palace: small-time vaudeville. This entertainment form was characterized by a nearly equal mix of the old and new, vaudeville and film. Loew's offered its shows in thousand-seat theatres that nearly matched the beauty and flash of the big-time vaudeville theatres of Keith-Albee (east of the Mississippi) and Orpheum (west of the Mississippi) up the street. Marcus Loew sought to provide something better than the purely movie nickel show, but something not as expensive as the top talent mix of big-time vaudeville.[4]

Like many others, Marcus Loew had begun his career as a show-business entrepreneur with the opening of a nickelodeon. In 1903, Adolph Zukor persuaded Loew to invest in a New York City penny arcade. Liking the quick profits, Loew abandoned partnership with Zukor and formed his own nickelodeon operation. He made his move into small-time vaudeville when he bought a deserted burlesque theatre in Brooklyn and opened it as the Royal in January 1908. Two years later Loew's circuit covered the New York boroughs. By 1911 the now incorporated Loew's had forty small-time vaudeville theatres throughout New York.[5]

Despite this speed, Loew ran his empire with a conservative hand. He saw Loew's as a combination of two proven forms: vaudeville and movies. Loew then positioned his entertainment combination at a price lower than vaudeville and only slightly higher than the movie show. He ran the operation as a real estate business in which the show could fail but the land was still his. He did need a steady cash flow to make his mortgage payments, however. As a skillful manager, Loew was able to corner a new niche in the market. With the advent of the feature film in the mid-1910s, when a single, nearly two-hour film with a major star took center stage as the entertainment attraction, Marcus Loew stood as one of the largest owners of theatres in the United States.[6]

Through the late 1910s, Loew stuck to what he knew worked—well-situated theatres. George M. Cohan called him the "Henry Ford of show business," an appropriate term for an entrepreneur who sought to tender popular entertainment at low prices—as Ford did with simple, cheap automobiles. By the late 1910s Loew had begun to move his successful formula into other markets, usually one theatre per major city, from a base in the north in Montreal, Canada, to a southern outpost in New Orleans, Louisiana. By 1919 Loew's, Inc., backed by some of the top banks on Wall Street, had become one of the larger bookers of motion pictures in the United States.[7]

But the emergence of his new chain presented Marcus Loew with a problem. The stronger he grew in exhibition, the more he needed a *guaranteed* supply of quality films, especially those featuring top Hollywood stars. In 1919 Loew's fashioned a deal with Metro Pictures, owned by producer Louis B. Mayer. A decade later Marcus Loew noted: "I purchased Metro and determined to make pictures primarily to protect our own interests."[8] In 1924 Loew's purchased the ailing Goldwyn Pictures, and folded all its suppliers together as Metro-Goldwyn-Mayer.

Suddenly Hollywood had a new powerhouse studio and Loew had the films to fill the bills on its ever-expanding chain of theatres. MGM became the greatest Hollywood studio of the 1930s, but insiders knew that its power rested not at the studio in Culver City, California, but three thousand miles away at the offices of Loew's, Inc., atop the Loew's State Theatre, in Times Square, New York City, the heart of its theatrical market. Many came to know the name Louis B. Mayer, but the economic power rested with Marcus Loew.[9]

Loew's, Inc. was not the lone company crafting a movie exhibition empire within one region. It was just the most famous because of its location, New York City. Other entrepreneurs in smaller urban centers across the United States included the Saxe brothers in Milwaukee, the Skouras brothers in St. Louis, Harry Crandell in Washington, D.C., Finkelstein and Rubin in Minneapolis, the Blank circuit centered in Des Moines, Iowa, and John Kunsky in Detroit. Indeed, these chains became so successful that in 1917 they formed their own filmmaking cooperative—First National Exhibitors' Circuit.

Although First National has been hailed as a significant challenge to Loew's and other vertically integrated powers, it never was able to generate profits and ought to be remembered as a notable business failure. But the core of exhibitors that formed First National did demonstrate that in city after city scientific business management led to regional domination. No better case study can be examined than the leader of First National, the Stanley Company of America, based in Philadelphia.[10]

In Philadelphia, Pennsylvania, then America's third largest city, two local entrepreneurs fashioned a powerful regional chain with no vaudeville connections. They were so successful that by the mid-1920s, when their heirs sold out to Warner Bros., the Stanley Company of America held dominion from New Jersey south to Washington, D.C., and west to Pittsburgh, Pennsylvania. While his death in 1926 at age fifty-four prevented him from gaining the fame he deserves, Jules Mastbaum, founder and prime mover of the Stanley Company of America, developed one of the largest theatre chains in the United States. The Stanley Company of America opened as a single nickelodeon. But within twenty years it grew into a chain of 250 theatres through the width and breadth of the populous mid-Atlantic region and came to represent a prototype of the successful regional movie chain.[11]

Too often the successful movie exhibitor is portrayed as an unschooled immigrant who through skill and determination was able to turn a single rickety nickelodeon into a regional monopoly. This was certainly not the case with Jules Mastbaum and his brother Stanley. Jules Mastbaum attended the Wharton Business School at the University of Pennsylvania; he and his brother learned the methods of chain store retailing from a pioneer, the Gimbels department store. In 1901 Jules Mastbaum then went into the real estate business in Philadelphia and made a successful career. Through his sales he learned of the value of following the new public transportation lines to fame and fortune.[12]

The Mastbaum brothers began with a storefront theatre, near the heart of Philadelphia's bustling downtown, close to Gimbels department store. After this venture turned into a gold mine, they slowly acquired more theatres in and around Philadelphia. When pioneer Philadelphia-based moviemaker and exhibitor Sigmund Lubin decided to sell out, the Mastbaums won the bidding. The Mastbaums followed the trolley lines and began to build ornate theatres in developing Philadelphia. They also took over theatres in nearby cities.

By 1926 the Mastbaum operations had covered Philadelphia with twenty-three theatres downtown and fifty-one in outlying areas. Like Philadelphia-based restaurant chain Horn and Hardart, the Mastbaum theatres dominated the popular culture scene of the City of Brotherly Love, defining the city as much as the Phillies and Athletics did in professional baseball. One could go to a Stanley theatre for a full afternoon or evening of vaudeville and motion picture entertainment, for like Loew's, the Stanley Company of America presented top-flight stage shows as well as fifty-piece orchestras.[13]

Like Marcus Loew, early on the Mastbaums were concerned about a consistent supply of films. Thus in 1916 they founded a production company with Herbert Brenon and Lewis Selznick, father of the more famous David O. Selznick, producer of *Gone With the Wind*. But they proved to be poor producers. Thereafter the Mastbaums sought another solution and in 1917, with twenty-five powerful exhibitors, formed the First National Exhibitors' Circuit. But, as with their earlier experience, the Mastbaums could not transfer their skills in managing a chain of theatres to similar success in making and distributing motion pictures. That is, First National had managers of considerable skill but not in making movies or setting up a national system of production, distribution, and exhibition. That would await Sam Katz and Paramount Publix.[14]

The Mastbaums stuck to trying to dominate their region. For the Philadelphia theatres they owned and for other "independents," the Mastbaums created a booking combine in order to secure the best films Hollywood had to offer. In time, through its administration of the booking combine, the Mastbaums dictated the bookings of nearly all Philadelphia theatres, even ones they did not own directly. Here was another example of chain store style economies of scale. The Mastbaums proved so successful that their actions led to a suit by the Federal Trade Commission accusing them of intimidating exhibitors who refused to deal with their combine, and by 1920 they had to give up this phase of their operations.[15]

After Stanley Mastbaum's death in 1918 and in the wake of the troubles with the Federal Trade Commission, Jules Mastbaum reorganized the theatres into the Stanley Corporation of America, named in honor of his late brother. In the years immediately following the First World War, the company concentrated on acquiring theatre chains in the mid-Atlantic region. By early in 1927 it had taken over the Crandell chain, the dominant one in Washington, D.C., the Mark-Strand houses in New York City, the Fabian organization of northern New Jersey, and the Rowland-Clark chain of Pittsburgh and western Pennsylvania. Jules Mastbaum was a skilled businessman, but his premature death robbed the company of its driving force. Thus, few industry observers were surprised that in 1928, with the monies it had made from pioneering talkies, Warner Bros. bought the Stanley Company of America for $200 million.[16]

BALABAN & KATZ

The successes of Loew's in New York and the achievements of the Stanley Company in Philadelphia tell us much about the development of *regional* theatre chains. Neither, however, established the standard for running a *national* theatre chain. A strategy for a national chain had its origins in the second largest city in the United States, Chicago, Illinois, with the extraordinary accomplishments of Balaban & Katz. By 1924 this one company was making more money than any other theatre chain in the United States and was being copied from coast to coast.

In retrospect this must be considered somewhat surprising. Balaban & Katz entered the exhibition game late. While other regional chains had established their presence by 1920, Balaban & Katz was just beginning its rise. Indeed, as late as 1919 Balaban & Katz owned just six theatres, of which only two were large, formidable movie palaces. What makes the growth of this company so remarkable is that its ascent took place over the course of a mere five years. Balaban & Katz went beyond simply combining vaudeville and movies and forming a company such as MGM, beyond skillful real estate dealings, and beyond careful use of economies of scale. To understand Balaban & Katz is to learn how the movie show captured its place as the dominant mass entertainment form in the United States.

Balaban & Katz started with a single nickelodeon. The Balaban side came first. Oldest brother Barney and second in line Abraham Joseph (simply known as A. J.) and their parents set up a nickelodeon theatre in Chicago's west-side ghetto in 1908. The Balabans did better than many and opened their second theatre in 1909 and a third in 1914. They moved into local film distribution, peddling cheaply made features and shorts to fellow theatre owners. For a time the brothers even operated a restaurant, the Movie Inn, located downtown in the heart of film-sellers row. The Movie Inn served as a meeting place for exhibitors, distributors, and visiting movie folk, and although the restaurant never made much money, it did serve a vital function for their owners. It was there that the Balaban brothers met the dynamic Samuel Katz.[17]

Samuel Katz, "Sam" to one and all, followed a more traditional route toward success, graduating from high school and even attending college. He supported his education with a series of part-time jobs, one of which found him playing piano for a nickelodeon located in Chicago's south side. There Katz fell in love with the movies, and he set his sights on becoming an industry leader. In 1912 Katz acquired the Wallace theatre, next door to his father's barbershop; by 1915 he owned three theatres and was in the movie business full time.

In 1916 Sam Katz and the Balaban brothers teamed up and decided to follow the model of Samuel Rothapfel's New York City Rivoli and Rialto theatres. They would open a large theatre, one that could take advantage of the continually growing interest in moviegoing they saw in Chicago. They sought to become giants like Loew's in New York or the Mastbaums in Philadelphia. For their first major theatre they chose the North Lawndale neighborhood of Chicago.[18]

Sam Katz went to work. He approached Julius Rosenwald, president of Sears-Roebuck, the neighborhood's largest employer. Rosenwald put Katz in touch with S. W. Straus, a Chicago mortgage company. On 16 August 1916 Straus granted the Central Park Building Corporation a $125,000 mortgage. Sam Katz and the Balabans put up their theatres as collateral.

Balaban & Katz's Central Park Theatre opened on schedule on Saturday, 27 October 1917. This mighty picture palace was an immediate success and Sam Katz, as corporate planner and president, began to draw up plans for a second picture palace in the fashionable Uptown district of Chicago's far north side. Katz thought big. He proposed and built a three-thousand-seat picture palace, the Riveria.[19]

At this point Sam Katz assembled a syndicate of backers who all were doing so well in their own Chicago-based businesses that they had some extra cash to invest.

Julius Rosenwald had seen Sears-Roebuck grow into America's most important mail-order retailer. During the 1920s Sears would move to the top position in retail sales in the United States, with stores often found just across the street from movie palaces.

William Wrigley, Jr.'s sales were expanding at a furious rate as a nation acquired the chewing-gum habit. In the 1930s his confectionery treat would become a staple in concession stands in movie houses.

John Hertz had become Chicago's taxi king. His yellow cabs made his fortune; the rental car business would come later. And many a taxi took passengers to a night at the movies. Rosenwald, Wrigley, and Hertz added to their fortunes through their backing of Balaban & Katz.[20]

Balaban & Katz opened the Riveria on 2 October 1918 and again had a major success. Katz knew what his next steps must be: open a picture palace on Chicago's south side and then in the downtown Loop area. He moved quickly, although strikes and shortages that remained after the end of the First World War limited rapid expansion. The south side's Tivoli opened 16 February 1921; the Chicago Theatre in downtown's north Loop area opened 26 October 1921. Now Balaban & Katz could offer their brand of movie entertainment to Chicago's west-, north-, and south-siders as well as crowds in the central city. All were hugely profitable from the start.[21]

At the same time Sam Katz began to solidify Balaban & Katz's place in the Chicago moviegoing marketplace. He furiously began to buy theatres, simply with the excess monies produced by his four movie palaces. Balaban & Katz's four remarkable Chicago picture palaces were so successful that excess profits permitted future expansion from internal cash flow. The five-thousand-seat Uptown Theatre, the three-thousand-seat Norshore, and the four-thousand-seat Oriental opened in the mid-1920s and provided Balaban & Katz with total domination of the cinema in Chicago.[22]

From this base of power in Chicago Katz began to seek theatres in the surrounding states. In May 1924 Balaban & Katz acquired Midwest Theatres, a chain in Illinois and Wisconsin. By 1925 Hollywood came to Sam Katz. Skillfully Katz played one studio off another, but in the end he chose to affiliate with the largest Hollywood movie company, Famous Players-Lasky. This alliance guaranteed Balaban & Katz access to Hollywood's top films and secured for Famous Players-Lasky a top manager for its own expanding theatre chain. Thus, in October 1925, Sam Katz moved to New York to run what would be known as the Publix theatre chain.[23]

Balaban & Katz's rise to power symbolized the rise of the theatre chain in the American movie business. Twenty years earlier, in 1905, the field of film exhibition had been one of entrepreneurs who could enter the motion picture exhibition business with a few hundred dollars. In 1925, with the Balaban & Katz/Famous Players-Lasky alliance, the field of movie exhibition became a part of the pantheon of American big business. By examining why Balaban & Katz was able to expand so rapidly and successfully, we can understand why the movie exhibition business moved from a marginal leisure-time industry to center stage in the business of entertainment.

Remarkably, one of the variables that did *not* count in Balaban & Katz's rise to power and control was the movies themselves. Indeed the company grew and prospered despite having little access to Hollywood's top films. Balaban & Katz's competitors may have been able to book the films that proved most popular elsewhere, but it did not pose a significant obstacle to Balaban & Katz's rise. Indeed, Balaban & Katz took the films others did not want. Only after 1925, with the alliance with Famous Players-Lasky, did Balaban & Katz gain access to the top Hollywood feature films. By then Balaban & Katz used this extra advantage to wipe out the competition.

Indeed Balaban & Katz knew it could never depend too much on films to form the foundation of its theatrical empire. Barney Balaban and Sam Katz argued: "We cannot afford to build up a patronage depending entirely upon the drawing power of our feature films as we display them. We must build in the minds of our audience the feeling that we represent an institution taking a vital part in the formation of the character of the community."[24] Balaban & Katz carefully formed this institution by taking advantage of certain factors where it did hold advantage over the competition. By differentiating its corporate product through five important factors—location, the theatre building, service, stage shows, and air conditioning—Balaban & Katz was able to transform itself, and the film industry as a whole, from a small-time operation into a part of the growing chain store revolution.

Location

Possibly the most important factor in differentiating theatres was one recognized by Loew and the Mastbaums, and even more thoroughly by Balaban & Katz, that is, location. Previously, owners of motion picture houses had followed the prevailing tendencies of entertainment districts and sought the ideal location downtown. Balaban & Katz established the locus of their power by going to new audiences who lived in what were then the suburbs of America's biggest cities, with easy access to mass transit. Balaban & Katz demonstrated that it was not enough simply to seek the middle class by happenstance; one had to take the movie show to their neighborhoods.

What gave Balaban & Katz their opening was Chicago's construction of a mass transit trolley and elevated lines. As in other cities, rapid mass transit enabled the middle class and rich to move to the edge of the city to the first true suburbs (although many were actually within city boundaries). Thus, as late as the year 1900, Chicago was a compact city, with most citizens living three miles from the Loop; two decades later that distance had doubled. Balaban & Katz took advantage of this revolution in mass transit. The firm built its first three theatres, the Central Park, the Riveria, and the Tivoli, in the heart of *outlying* business and recreational centers of Chicago. Only then did it construct a theatre, the Chicago, downtown in the north Loop area.[25]

The Central Park Theatre came first and was located in an area of Chicago the Balabans and Katzes knew well, North Lawndale. On what was then the far west side of the city, North Lawndale was where immigrant Jewish families like the Balabans and Katzes moved to in order to prove they had "made it." The elevated line had reached North Lawndale in 1902, and within two decades this lightly populated outpost had grown into a teeming neighborhood of Jews who had left Maxwell Street. Indeed, the 1920 census determined that three-quarters of the population of this particular neighborhood were Russian Jews who had come to America in the 1880s and 1890s, settled in the neighborhood around Hull House (Maxwell Street), and then resettled in North Lawndale.[26]

Louis Wirth's classic sociological study *The Ghetto* documented this transformation. Wirth found that the children pushed their parents to move to North Lawndale to achieve higher status in life. In turn, these children had acquired a strong desire for upward mobility from education in public school, from reformers such as Jane Addams, and from newly acquired gentile friends and co-workers. This new generation ate non-Kosher food, attended synagogue less frequently, shopped outside the neighborhood, and spoke Yiddish only at home. And as part of this cultural assimilation they also embraced the movie show. The Central Park made its fortune catering to the very people Louis Wirth had studied.[27]

For Balaban & Katz's second picture palace the firms' leaders chose a site in the thriving outlying center of the prosperous north-side neighborhood of Uptown. The "bright-light" center of this streetcar transfer point was already filling up with dance halls, cabarets, and arcades. In the early 1920s Uptown stood as the largest outlying center in Chicago, with more than 100,000 prosperous residents living in apartment buildings only a walk from the neighborhood center. Since Balaban & Katz came late to this center, the Riveria was initially several blocks from the "el" station. But because the crowds became so big with the opening of Balaban & Katz's Uptown Theatre in 1924, across the street from the Riveria, the city of Chicago opened up a new station. Uptown became the "hottest" of the hot spots in Chicago in the Roaring Twenties.[28]

The Central Park and the Riveria, because of their location near the terminus of the "el" lines, were able to attract patrons from all parts of the west and north sides of Chicago—all the new middle-class patrons who had moved to the periphery of the city. The Tivoli performed the same function for the south side. Again, it was located near the center of an outlying business and recreational center at Sixty-Third and Cottage Grove avenues. The "el" was nearby, as were thousands who worked or attended the University of Chicago. Indeed "Sixty-Third and Cottage" was the south side's equivalent of Uptown.[29]

The matrix of theatres appealing to all sectors of the city was complete. The Chicago Theatre downtown in the Loop was almost an afterthought, built with the profits made from the suburban theatres. The Chicago Theatre stood as a symbol of the success of the outlying theatres, not the central movie house that had vaulted the company to the top of the exhibition business. After the outlying theatres were established, it only made sense to construct a theatre for the thousands who journeyed downtown to shop and have fun.

Once these four theatres—the Central Park, the Riveria, the Tivoli, and the Chicago—were in place, Balaban & Katz could advertise that no one need travel more than a half-hour to reach one of its wonder theatres. Acquiring more theatres, as the company did with the millions pouring in, simply reduced the maximum required travel time to fifteen minutes. Sam Katz had leveraged four theatres into an empire, and so by 1924 all power in the theatrical market for movie exhibition in Chicago flowed through his office atop the Chicago Theatre on North State Street.[30]

Balaban & Katz proved that the movie entertainment business was not one of simple *mass* market appeal. Middle-class patrons who had recently settled on the edges of the city went to the movies far more often and were willing to pay more than other citizens of Chicago, New York, Philadelphia, or any other major metropolis. It is crucial to recognize that in the 1920s young, middle-class, upwardly mobile apartment dwellers living in the better parts of the city did not find it in their best interest to acknowledge this love for the movie show. Nonetheless they did go to the movies, as the lines in front of Balaban & Katz's Tivoli, Central Park, or Riveria theatres indicated. (The queues began in earnest at ten in the morning.)

Depending on the shape of the city, theatre owners built most of their movie palaces outside the center city. Chicago is typical of what urban geographers call a fan-shaped city. Built on a body of water, the city spread in the 1920s, with increasing mass transit, in the shape of a fan away from downtown. In other cities there was similar pressure to build theatres on the edges of the fan. The theatre owners in Detroit (John Kunsky), St. Louis (the Skouras brothers), and Milwaukee (the Saxe brothers), to name only three examples of large fan-shaped cities, copied the Balaban & Katz example, and we can still see the three-thousand-seat St. Louis theatre (now Powell Hall) in St. Louis and the two-thousand seat Modjeska in Milwaukee, both miles from their city's central business and recreation areas.

The fan-shaped city saw the greatest development of the outlying theatre. Square-shaped cities had less development per capita. Growth in these square (or circular) urban areas exploded in the 1920s in all directions, not constrained by mountains and/or large bodies of water. Indianapolis had outlying picture palaces in the north, west, south, and eastern parts of the city. Outlying theatres also were more likely in cities where growth was limited by mountains and/or bodies of water spread. Thus the expansion of Madison, Wisconsin, was defined by its lakes.

Or, consider the long, narrow island of Manhattan. Certainly there were more than a dozen movie places in Times Square, all easy to travel to by a variety of mass transit. But if one looked closely at the only section of Manhattan Island that saw population growth in the 1920s, that area north of 145th Street, it can be seen that entrepreneurs built movie palaces far exceeding any section of the island outside Times Square. The area north of 145th Street had one-twentieth of the population but one-fifth of the movie palaces. This area was the only part of the island that in the 1920s offered a high-quality life-style at affordable prices.

In northern Manhattan the newly admitted middle class and upper middle class Americans flocked to just-built apartment buildings. Second- and third-generation Americans, educated far in excess of the norm and holding well-paying jobs, had the time and money to spend on the new movie entertainment. But they stayed home, so when Loew's, Inc. decided to expand in 1930 it opened the Loew's 175th Street, a Hindu-Indochinese temple, to this group of movie fans.[31]

The Theatre Building

It was not enough to select the optimal crossroads to locate a theatre. A motion picture exhibition company had to offer an attractive building. The entertainment commenced with the building, which was a palace for the motion pictures. Balaban & Katz surpassed the splendor of the vaudeville and legitimate theatre by making their buildings attractions unto themselves. With the pride associated with the opening of a world's fair or new skyscraper, Chicagoans of the 1920s proclaimed and heralded their movie palaces as the finest in the world.

Consider the evocative memory composed by novelist Meyer Levin writing in *The Old Bunch*. He has his characters go to the Chicago theatre in the 1920s:

> As [they] turned into State Street, the Chicago sign blazed at them. Boy, was that a sign! It made daylight of the whole block. Eight stories high. Three thousand bulbs spelled CHICAGO!

> After a wait of forty-five minutes they got inside the lobby. Everything white and gold and mirrored.

> Up on the promenade was a grand piano, all in white . . .

> And overhead, a magnificent chandelier! The largest in the world! Six tons![32]

All Balaban & Katz theatres spelled opulence to the average Chicago moviegoer. It was a special treat to go to these theatres.[33]

The architects for the Balaban & Katz empire came from the Chicago architectural firm headed by the brothers George and C. W. Rapp. The Rapps began with the Central Park Theatre and from that day until 1932 their drawing boards had underway at least one major project for first Balaban & Katz and then Sam Katz's Publix theatres. Katz was their patron for a set of theatres that stretched from New York's Paramount to the Ambassador in St. Louis to the Paramount in Portland, Oregon. Since others, like the Skourases in St. Louis with their Rapp & Rapp Ambassador Theatre, sought to do in their community what Balaban & Katz had done in Chicago. The Rapps became rich men designing movie theatres from one coast to the other.[34]

The Rapps were among the leading architects of the movie palace, establishing a style and look fundamental to the industry. Their opulent designs dazzled patrons with images from Spain, Italy, or France and into the 1930s with art deco renderings. Throughout the 1920s fans marveled at the triumphal arches overhead as they entered the theatre, the monumental staircase (inspired by the Paris Opera House) found in the typical lobby, and the ornate designs filling the sidewall of the auditorium.[35]

The expense of outfitting a theatre was considerable. Consider the Uptown Theatre, opened in 1924. For this five-thousand-seat monument to movie entertainment, Balaban & Katz spent nearly twenty-five thousand dollars on furniture and double that on drapes and carpets. The restrooms, hidden in the basement or in the balcony foyers, were more splendid than many private houses. They were spacious, clean, and decorated with their own sets of drapes, furniture, paintings, and mirrors. The patron could only wonder if the well-to-do had such facilities in their country clubs or boardrooms.

But these overpowering spaces were also highly functional. Everyone had a perfect view of the screen. In vaudeville theatres often there were posts in the way or the angle for viewing the stage was awkward. Acoustical planning for Balaban & Katz movie palaces ensured the orchestral accompaniment to the silent films could be heard even in the furthest reaches of the balcony. Lighting played a key role throughout the performances. Auditoriums were lamped with thousands of bulbs, often in three primary colors. Thus a silent film with live music could also be accompanied by changing light motifs through the show. In general the lights were kept low and patrons kept their seats throughout the show. Too much light invited patrons to move about, and that would have become chaotic with full houses of four thousand or more. This was a dignified setting and patrons responded accordingly.[36]

Since there always seemed to be a line to get into a theatre, keeping the waiting customers happy was as important as entertaining those already in the auditorium. Indeed the rule of thumb was that a Rapp and Rapp lobby ought comfortably to hold ticket holders equal to the number of seats in the auditorium. Indeed one of the main functions of the building was to make sure thousands could enter and exit quickly and safely so the maximum number of shows could be tendered each day. Massive enclosed passageways speeded exit and entry.

Service

Balaban & Katz had a stated policy of treating the movie patron as a king or queen. Theatres offered free child care, attendant smoking rooms, foyers and lobbies lined with paintings and sculpture, and organ music for those waiting in line. Ushers were at the center of this strategy, and they maintained a quiet decorum in the theatre that went along with, and even underlined, the upper-class atmosphere so sought after by suburbanite patrons.

In the basement of each movie palace was a complete playground that included slides, sandboxes, and other objects of fun. For no extra cost children were left in the care of nurses and attendants while families attended the show upstairs. There were afternoon tea shows for women who went shopping with small children and infants. Balaban & Katz advertised that one could come to their movie palace, drop off the children, and enjoy the show. A nurse with complete medical equipment was nearby.

The centerpiece of the special Balaban & Katz service was the corps of ushers. They guided patrons through the maze of halls and foyers, assisted the elderly and small children, and handled any emergencies that might arise in a crowd of four thousand in the auditorium and four thousand waiting for the next show. A picture palace had twenty to forty ushers and doorkeepers in attendance for all shows. Indeed, there was a regular changing of the guard throughout the day.

Balaban & Katz recruited its corps from male college students, dressed them in red uniforms with white gloves and yellow epaulets, and demanded they be obediently polite even to the rudest of patrons. The ushers responded to patrons with "yes, sir," or "no, ma'am" and all requests had to end with a "thank you." Even the rowdy were led away with propriety and sensitivity to emphasize that if they opted to be well behaved they were welcome to return. Balaban & Katz emphasized that it was an honor to be selected for the special job of usher.

Ushers worked hard. They used "spill-cards" to record how full each section of the theatre was at any one moment so patrons could be ushered in to empty areas and not run into each other. Phones and early calculating machines also helped in filling every possible seat. (These data were collected and forwarded to the main office and used to plan future programs.)

Ushers received a free week's "vacation": a special camp during the summer that offered more training and created a special esprit de corps. Any usher who accepted a tip was immediately fired. The special treatment ushers provided was "free," a part of the price of admission.[37]

But there were more than nurses, baby-sitters, and ushers who worked in a movie palace. Aside from the manager and direct assistants, there were cashiers, projectionists, maintenance staff, electricians, and others backstage. Musicians and stagehands helped mount the live stage show. Balaban & Katz demanded strict standards to qualify for employment. Ushers had to be white males, seventeen to twenty-one years of age, five feet seven inches tall, 125 to 145 pounds, and enrolled in a local college. In contrast, messenger boys had to be "the smaller type of negro boy, not over five feet four, of slight, or slender build, well formed and in good proportion, not markedly of negro type with heavy features."[38] Balaban & Katz regulated its labor to effect a special image and to keep costs to a minimum. Acceptable white males out front in uniform guaranteed an image that most patrons associated with a fine hotel, country club, or bank.

And labor costs were not high. Hollywood may have paid its stars thousands of dollars a week, but the minimum wage of the day was accepted for the privilege to work in a Balaban & Katz theatre. Indeed, most employees, from maintenance and cleaning staff to ushers and even managers, were either young, female, and/or black. None save the musicians, stagehands, and projectionists belonged to a union. All were given specific routine tasks so the management of the chain could regulate their actions like an assembly line. Janitors filled out charts to tell how long it took to clean a certain area of floor. Ushers were of a given size so uniforms could be passed down. These operations were run with an efficiency Henry Ford surely admired.[39]

Stage Shows

The purpose of the location, theatre building, and service was to lead to the entertainment inside the auditorium. In the beginning Balaban & Katz could not offer its patrons at the Riveria, Central Park, Tivoli, and Chicago theatres anything close to the best films coming out of Hollywood. Rival circuits had exclusive booking contracts with the major studios. Balaban & Katz took what was left over. Since they could not offer superior movie entertainment, Balaban & Katz filled the well-located, architecturally splendid, and well-serviced movie houses by producing live stage shows.

As we have seen in the previous two chapters, mixtures of vaudeville and movies were not new. Samuel Rothapfel and Sid Grauman made big names for themselves in New York City and Los Angeles, respectively, with their stage shows. Grauman's prologues were known from coast to coast; Roxy's "Rockettes" were hits long before Radio City Music Hall opened in 1932. Balaban & Katz can hardly be credited for the invention or even innovation of the stage show.[40]

But Balaban & Katz carefully exploited the stage show, melding live presentations into a "product mix" that generated fabulous profits. The company nurtured and developed local talent into stars who would play Chicago exclusively. Balaban & Katz knew that if it could mount popular but tasteful shows, it could solidify its appeal to a middle-class audience so long wedded to vaudeville theatrical entertainment. Moreover, local stars guaranteed that Balaban & Katz would not suffer swings in revenues. The strategy worked. In time Balaban & Katz became more famous for its impressive stage attractions, orchestras, and organists than for any movies it presented.[41]

Consistently Balaban & Katz divided their 150-minute shows between movies and live stage shows. (Often feature films would be shortened to fit the required formula.) The stage show was an elaborate minimusical, with spectacular settings and intricate lighting effects. Much like the stage shows at Radio City Music Hall in recent years, the stage show stood as a separate package of entertainment, emphasizing its theme rather than individual stars. There were shows to celebrate holidays, fads of the day, and heroic adventures, including all the highlights of the Roaring Twenties from the Charleston dance craze to Lucky Lindbergh's solo flight across the Atlantic to the new electronic phenomenon radio. In the entertainment trade, this strategy was known as the "pure presentation," as opposed to Sid Grauman's prologues linked dramatically and thematically to the movie that followed or to the Loew's chain strategy for its theatres of putting on a typical vaudeville show with big-name stars.

Typical was "Jazz and Opera" week. In an era when jazz was looked down upon in the same way rock-and-roll was during the 1950s, the theatre would play one off against the other. It was a "battle of the sounds," and jazz always won. By 1925 jazz shows or evenings of syncopation were staged regularly throughout the year. Classical music was reserved exclusively for free Sunday morning concerts by the star organists and orchestras, in order to appease the reformers and city fathers and mothers. It is hard to overestimate how popular these shows were. One night the Chicago Theatre's curtain would not rise, and although the movie could still be presented, the stage show could not. More than half the audience walked out and demanded their money back.[42]

Brother A. J. Balaban was in charge of these stage attractions. He, his assistant Frank Cambria (who had trained under David Belasco), and their staff put together a new show each week. The talent was initially drawn from bookers at the Western Vaudeville Association. Later Balaban & Katz signed up a stable of talented performers and stage designers of their own. Some would go on to international fame. Noted Hollywood director Vincente Minnelli, the man behind the camera for many of the best Hollywood musicals (*Meet Me in St. Louis* and *The Band Wagon*), began as a set designer in the Balaban & Katz shop.[43]

Such shows were quite expensive. An average presentation cost between three and five thousand dollars to mount and run for a week. A special show around a holiday might cost more than ten thousand dollars to mount. Consequently Balaban & Katz had the shows play the circuit in true vaudeville fashion. They began downtown at the Chicago Theatre and were reviewed at this venue. Then they played a week at the Riveria, then the Tivoli, and ended at the Central Park. Expenses to create the show thus could be spread over four (and later more) theatres. This repetition did not seem to hurt grosses of outlying theatres and effectively spread the audiences around to all theatres. Again it was a device to wed neighborhood theatregoers to the movie palace entertainment in their community.[44]

For its orchestras and organists who provided music for the silent films and occasional concerts, Balaban & Katz depended on the star system. The company tried any number of musicians until it hit upon two stars. The organist Jesse Crawford became an organist as well known as any Chicagoan of the 1920s. Balaban & Katz had hired him away from Sid Grauman in 1921 to open the Tivoli Theatre and then to open the Chicago eight months later. A year later he commenced his free Sunday morning concerts, with equal parts classical and popular music. By 1923 Crawford's wedding to fellow organist Helen Anderson was the talk of Chicago's tabloids. The couple began to perform together and by 1925 were a Chicago institution, complete with a radio show and a recording contract. When Sam Katz took the pair to New York when he moved to head the complete Paramount theatre circuit, the newspapers mourned the loss in the same way as for a star who had left the Bears, Cubs, or White Sox.[45]

The other music star was a red-haired, flamboyant band leader brought in from the West Coast. Paul Ash may be a footnote in the history of popular music of the 1920s, but in Chicago he was a star unmatched by any band leader of his era. He ran into the audience and conducted sing-alongs, and his hokum-filled vaudeville act, leading what most conceded was an ordinary jazz band (dressed in a new set of costumes each week), was a smash. During the mid-1920s the lines stretched around the corner to see Ash and his "Merry, Mad Musical Gang" first at the McVickers and then the new Oriental, which some said was designed with Ash in mind. Sam Katz, again paying him the highest possible compliment, took Ash with him to New York to Paramount's theatre on Times Square.[46]

Air Conditioning

Balaban & Katz's Central Park Theatre, opened in 1917, was the first me-chanically air cooled theatre in the world. Other theatre entrepreneurs had tried crude experiments with blowing air across blocks of ice to cool audi-toria, but these never functioned without severe breakdown. Prior to the Central Park, most movie houses in the Midwest, South, and far West simply closed during the summer or opened to small crowds. Great progress toward safe mechanical cooling was made during the first two decades of the twentieth century. Technological change centered in Chicago, because firms in that city still slaughtered and processed most of the meat in the United States. The Kroeschell Bros. Ice Machine Company of Chicago developed a carbon dioxide system that efficiently cooled large spaces but required an investment of thousands of dollars as well as a room full of equipment. Thus Kroeschell Bros. sold it only to industries with a cash flow to justify the expense. Customers remained mainly meat packers, although a carbon dioxide system was installed to cool the banquet hall of Chicago's Congress Hotel.[47]

Before Barney Balaban entered the movie business he worked in the office of the Western Cold Storage Company. He knew firsthand of the ad-vances in the art of air cooling. Consequently as Balaban & Katz planned the Central Park Theatre, they convinced Kroeschell Bros.' chief engi-neer and inventor to work up a system specifically designed to cool movie patrons. Wittenmeyer adapted a carbon dioxide system first for the Central Park and then an improved system for the Riveria a year later. Both only *cooled* the air, by forcing it through vents in the floor. The air then ex-hausted through ducts in the ceiling. Chicago movie fans became, for the first time, patrons of the movies year round.

But these early systems had two distinct disadvantages. First, the cool air on the floor bothered patrons, especially women with long skirts. Second, the air remained too dry or too moist. So a method of dehumidification to perfect true air conditioning was needed. Wittenmeyer worked on both problems and the improved system for the Tivoli and Chicago theatres solved them. The air entered from the side and was dehumidified.[48]

These air conditioners were no window units. The apparatus took up a vast basement room. For the Chicago Theatre the equipment included more than fifteen thousand feet of heavy duty pipe, a 240-horsepower electric motor, and two all-steel, seven-foot flywheels, each weighing seven thousand pounds. An engineer was always on duty to watch over the equipment and effect necessary repairs.[49]

Once in place, these air cooled fantasy worlds became famous as summertime escapes from the brutal Chicago summers. Balaban & Katz's publicity constantly reminded Chicagoans of the rare treat in store inside. Icicles were hung from all newspaper advertisements. Announcements were made, in an almost public service fashion, that the Balaban & Katz theatre was a marvel of modern-day engineering and comfort. Others helped. The Public Health Commissioner of the city of Chicago proclaimed that Balaban & Katz theatres had purer air than Pike's Peak and that anyone with a lung disease or women in the final trimester of pregnancy ought to regularly spend time "at the movies." In their advertisements the Chicago Chamber of Commerce heralded Chicago as a wonderland of summer fun, in part because of the pleasures inside a Balaban & Katz movie palace.[50]

The results of Balaban & Katz's pioneering efforts in building a movie theatre chain were nothing short of phenomenal. Movie trade papers noted the consistently high grosses during the summer months and could find no better explanation than the comfort inside. Indeed, box-office receipts in the summer regularly exceeded those during the normally peak months during the winter. The location, architecture, service, stage shows, and indeed the movies themselves simply did not matter. Movie palaces provided relief from the heat that no other institution in the city could provide from May through September. No wonder millions embraced Balaban & Katz's unique brand of movie show in the years just after the First World War.[51]

BALABAN & KATZ'S INFLUENCE

With its five-point strategy of mass entertainment, Balaban & Katz changed the movie business by keeping houses full and costs low. Workers were not paid much, since many wanted to work in the movies and there were no unions, except for the projectionists and certain musicians. The buildings were expensive, but they were filled from morning to night, nearly every day of the week. Prices were higher than the usual five and ten cents and sometimes reached a dollar for the best seats on the best nights of the week for the top attractions.

The Balaban & Katz experience proved, despite the oft-asserted claims, that the profits from the movie exhibition business were not found in the "common man and woman" but in those striving for the riches offered in twentieth-century urban America. Smaller neighborhood theatres, without a stage show, with limited service, and in less-than-optimal surroundings, were cheaper and thus the province of the working family.[52]

By following the Balaban & Katz strategy, exhibitors around the United States created carefully crafted packages of pleasure that consistently generated high profits. Movies per se were never the sole driving force to attract audiences to ante up their quarters, fifty-cent pieces, and, at times, dollar bills. Instead Balaban & Katz's strategy depended first on finding the location that could appeal to most riders of mass transit. Then the building was made so spectacular that it served as an attraction on its own. There was nothing like the lobby of the Uptown or the exterior of the Chicago Theatre. Once inside you were waited on, led to your seat, and made to feel comfortable—and in the summer cool.

Only then can we properly focus on the Balaban & Katz entertainment show. Its music and stage shows were reviewed, followed, and debated in the 1920s. Many patrons, at times, did not care what was actually playing on the screen. But the movies were there, and they fueled a special brand of entertainment in this well-located, entertainment paradise. Balaban & Katz's multi-media package of pleasure kept audiences enthralled and they looked forward to queing up for the next show.

It is no wonder the major Hollywood companies scrambled to ally themselves with Balaban & Katz, and few were surprised when in 1925 Famous Players-Lasky, the largest movie company in the world, formally merged with the Chicago exhibitor. Sam Katz moved to New York, and during the late 1920s he successfully transferred the Balaban & Katz system to Paramount's theatres. Soon the newly christened Publix chain was the world's largest, most profitable, and most imitated. Immediately Katz set in motion on a national scale the five-part strategy that had worked so well in Chicago. The centralization of the movie business would become the standard that Hollywood would employ in the next twenty years.[53]

The successes of the Loew's, the Stanley Company of America, and the

Balaban & Katz chain operations were soon copied around the country. Indeed these three became the bases of three of the largest Hollywood movies companies—Loew's and MGM, Stanley and Warner Bros., and Balaban & Katz and Paramount. By the late 1920s, as sound was apparently transforming the movie business, major regional chains in every city made sure that little was disrupted. They had control, and when Hollywood came to bid and buy, the founders of these great operations sold out. Based on this foundation, the coming of sound would lead to profits unprecedented in the history of Hollywood. From New York and Hollywood offices the chief operating officers and presidents of the five major studios—with their powerful theatre chains—ruled the mainstream movie industry and set up the conditions for filmgoing in what is now labeled the golden age of the movies.

FOUR

Hollywood Control

The 1930s and 1940s represent an age of moviegoing in America dominated by chains organized and controlled by five Hollywood companies. By owning and operating the most profitable theatres in the United States, five firms held sway in the American film industry: Paramount, Loew's Inc., owner of MGM, Warner Bros., Twentieth Century-Fox, and Radio-Keith-Orpheum (RKO). All of them produced, distributed, and exhibited films. This amounted to coordinated national power, based upon movie exhibition.

These Hollywood chains were not created overnight. Sam Katz led the way. His Paramount Publix theatre chain, begun in 1925 when he moved to New York as a consequence of the Balaban & Katz plus Famous Players-Lasky merger, spread Balaban & Katz's methods across the United States. Sam Katz's newly christened Publix theatre chain stretched from North Carolina to Texas and from Michigan to Iowa. The locus of power remained the Midwest, centered in Chicago. Through Famous Players Canadian, Publix also dominated movie exhibition north of the United States border. An estimated two million patrons streamed into Publix theatres each day.

At the acme of the silent film, Publix employed more musicians than any other organization in the world. And at the head of this operation Sam Katz centralized power in his New York City office, high atop the Paramount Building on Times Square. Katz and his assistants decided on everything from the patterns of the carpets to the appropriate music, from the curtains to be hung to the booking of films. Katz ranked, from 1925 through the early years of the Great Depression, as the most powerful executive in the movie exhibition business.[1]

Because of his method of centralized management, Katz probably had more power than any figure in the history of American movie exhibition. During the nickelodeon era the house manager was also, in most cases, the owner of the theatre, and so the whole family helped operate the enterprise. In the Balaban & Katz era, control had rested in a central office in the city that headquartered the regional chain. Sam Katz, Jules Mastbaum, and Marcus Loew worked not far from most of their theatres.

But with the coming of Paramount Publix the theatre chain became a national operation, and most corporate central offices were moved to New York City. All decisions were made in New York based on information passed up the line. This was scientific management and economies of scale taken to a higher plane. Movie shows were now just another chain store, found invariably next door to a Woolworths five-and-dime, the A & P grocery store, and the Sears department store.[2]

Although Katz and his assistants gave preference to Paramount films when booking movies, they made deals directly with all the major Holly-wood studios. Stage shows were staffed, assembled, designed, and sent on the road from New York. All major employees were hired by the New York office; for a time one Publix division even set up a school to train managers. The local manager received instructions about selling the show, stories prewritten for the press, and a tight budget in which to do every-thing. Scientific movie exhibition brought a standardized product to the United States. Paramount Publix's slogan summed it up: "You don't need to know what's playing at a Publix House. It's bound to be the best show in town."[3]

The coming of sound caused hardly a ripple in Sam Katz's efficient scheme. Filmed stage shows—short recordings of the top vaudeville acts of the day—were substituted for the far more expensive live stage shows in all but the largest theatres. In the months during the spring of 1928, just prior to the film industry's collective selection of a sound system, the Publix stage show circuit reached its acme. Each of these minispectacles toured the Paramount circuit for thirty-three weeks plus four weeks of guaranteed vacation. Then the cycle began again.

The coming of sound enabled Katz to order films of hundreds of vaude-ville players and musicians and substitute short films of Al Jolson, Weber and Fields, Eddie Cantor, and Else Janis for live stage shows. Paramount Publix saved thousands of dollars with no decrease in demand at the box office. Not surprisingly Sam Katz lobbied hard for Paramount to switch to talkies. By 1929 Publix theatres, save a handful in New York, Chicago, and other very large cities, offered only films, an even more standardized, easily monitored, and controlled product. Profits soared.[4]

There seemed no end in sight; the Balaban & Katz system could have gone on for years—as long as attendance kept increasing. Growth had certainly been the order of the day since the nickelodeons first opened in 1905. But then came the Great Depression. Since Katz had borrowed extensively to open more and more theatres, Paramount Publix was thirty million dollars in debt. By 1932 debt rose into the hundreds of millions and Katz was eased out. The first great era in the history of the American movies had come to an end. Nonetheless every city had a dozen or more movie palaces, and these buildings lived on to remind us of the "golden age" of the Balaban & Katz–inspired movie palace.[5]

AN INDUSTRY OF MOVIE PALACES

Sam Katz did far more than teach an industry scientific and centralized management. He and his staff showed an industry that power lay in ownership of certain movie houses: the large, well-situated movie places built in America's largest cities during the 1920s. began Hollywood moguls Adolph Zukor and Sam Katz wanted to own a measure of control in the exhibition market and so began to acquire the best regional theatre chains. Hollywood did not have to own all the movie theatres to exercise effective control, only the two thousand select few.

Although there were relatively few large theatres (two thousand seats or more) in the United States during the 1930s and 1940s, they held more patrons than all the smaller (five hundred seats or less) theatres in the nation. Most of the smaller theatres were situated in less well-off neighborhoods of big cities or in small towns. The smaller-sized neighborhood theatres in large cities often had to compete with a picture palace down the street, with its air conditioning, stage shows, and grand service and architecture. Larger theatres, the movie palaces, were found only in higher-income, outlying shopping districts or in the downtowns of the largest cities.

The five major Hollywood companies—Paramount, Loew's/MGM, Warner Bros., Fox (after 1935, Twentieth Century-Fox), and RKO—made it their business during the late 1920s to acquire ownership of the circuits that had built these large theatres. By doing this they gained access to approximately three-quarters of the average box office of Hollywood's films.[6]

The so-called Big Five controlled the vast majority of all first-run movie palace theatres in the ninety-two largest cities in the United States, those cities with populations exceeding 100,000 citizens. The Big Five was thus able to dictate the terms of the marketplace for movie exhibition in the United States during the 1930s and 1940s, often appropriately labeled the "golden age" of Hollywood. A brief look at each company shows that these vital theatre chains, through a wave of mergers in the late 1920s, formed during the 1930s and 1940s the core of each of the major Hollywood companies.[7]

Paramount

In its day the Paramount Publix theatre chain ranked as the largest movie theatre operator in the world. And its merger with Balaban & Katz was only one measure of its power. Through dozens of acquisitions Paramount, through the 1930s and 1940s, dominated moviegoing in the South, in New England, and in Illinois, Michigan, and Indiana.[8]

This leading movie company was known as Famous Players-Lasky until 1925, Paramount Publix for the next decade, and simply Paramount Pictures thereafter. The firm was directed in its early years by Adolph Zukor. By 1920, through a series of adroit mergers, Zukor had taken Famous Players-Lasky to the acme of Hollywood production and world-wide distribution. In 1920 Zukor acquired a ten-million-dollar line of credit from the Wall Street banking house of Kuhn Loeb, and he began to purchase theatre chains to control access to the markets for his films. In a short time Famous Players-Lasky had purchased Lynch Enterprises, with its hundreds of theatres throughout eleven southern states; two fine first-run houses in Times Square (the Rialto and Rivoli); small circuits with theatres throughout New England; and a controlling interest in one of the two major theatre chains in Canada.

By the mid-1920s Famous Players-Lasky held interest in nearly four hundred theatres in the United States and Canada. The 1925 deal with Balaban & Katz provided Famous Players-Lasky not only with domination of moviegoing in America's second largest city but also Balaban & Katz's management team. In November 1925 Sam Katz, the driving force behind the Balaban & Katz empire, moved nearly his entire staff to New York City and instituted the Balaban & Katz system in the five-hundred-theatre, newly named Publix chain. In five years Publix grew to control more than one thousand theatres, making it the largest theatre chain in movie history up to that point.

The Great Depression struck at the heart of the assumptions on which these expansionary schemes were based. With decreasing attendance, it became impossible to meet mortgage payments. Wall Street's Lehman Brothers, under partner John Hertz, stepped in "to help" in 1931, but the company went into receivership because of mounting theatre debt. Katz and his assistants were forced out. A plan for reorganization was formulated in July 1935, and the "new" Paramount Pictures, Inc. emerged with a movie studio, a network for world-wide distribution, and more than one thousand theatres. Only Adolph Zukor survived from the salad days.

After a period under an interim management team, Barney Balaban, Sam Katz's former partner, was made president of the whole company. As a former theatre man, he paid particularly close attention to the regional theatre chains that made up the base of Paramount. With the help of his old cronies, such as Abe Blank in Iowa and his brother John, then running Balaban & Katz in Chicago, Balaban had Paramount on the road to greater and greater profits. Barney Balaban even placed fellow theatre man Y. Frank Freeman from Atlanta in charge of film production at the West Coast studio. Of the great Hollywood studios of the 1930s and 1940s, none had stronger ties to the world of theatre exhibition than Paramount.

Loew's/MGM

With its merger with MGM in 1924, Loew's, Inc. ranked second in power based on its integrated production, distribution, and exhibition. But through the remainder of the 1920s Loew's actually expanded very little, and so by the end of the decade its chain fell to fifth in size of the Big Five. Nonetheless Loew's always kept its domination of New York City and thus the ranking by size masked its true power base.[9]

Loew's had nearly two hundred theatres, which were managed with fiscal care and prudence. When the Great Depression came, the company needed little belt tightening and never needed to reorganize like its four rivals. A few well-placed, well-managed theatres in the largest city in the nation made sense during the lean days of the early 1930s. However, the conservative practices of Loew's came back to haunt the company in the 1940s. During the Second World War, record numbers flocked to the movies. Those with the largest chains—Paramount, Fox, and Warner

Bros.—had the theatres to take advantage of the surge in moviegoing. Loew's did not. The company did well, but not as well as it might have had it developed a chain of five or six hundred theatres.

The Loew's empire had its origins in the vaudeville empire of Marcus Loew. Although it turned to movies, Loew's stuck to a base in the five boroughs of New York City. Expansion only took place into the big cities east of the Mississippi. Loew's opened its flagship house in New York City's Times Square in 1921, the 3,500-seat Loew's State. By mid-decade Loew's had added more than fifty additional theatres to bring the circuit total well in excess of one hundred, but it never increased to two hundred theatres.

With the death of Marcus Loew in 1927 and the ascent of his longtime lieutenant Nicholas M. Schenck, the company began to operate more aggressively. Schenck considered several options and then, to the surprise of many, sold the Loew's empire to William Fox—only temporarily, as it turned out. The coming of the Great Depression and Fox's inability to meet debt requirements threw the theatres back to Loew's control. Nicholas M. Schenck and a small set of trusted advisors then ran this theatre empire for the next twenty-five years.

During the 1930s Loew's owned and operated about 150 theatres, principally in New York City and with strong but hardly dominating positions in Cleveland, Boston, Toronto, Jersey City, Los Angeles, Washington, D.C., and a handful of smaller cities in the state of Connecticut. Unlike Paramount, Loew's "stayed at home" and sought to establish a stronghold. Single theatres in Kansas City, Houston, and Los Angeles, however profitable, provided the lone exceptions to the rule. They were three reminders of the glory days of the late 1920s.

Warner Bros.

Only with the millions made from pioneering movie sound was Warner Bros., a formerly obscure family enterprise, able to take a significant position in the movie theatre world. The profits from talkies gave the brothers Warner the capital necessary to take over the Stanley Company of America. This mid-Atlantic chain thereafter provided the core of the Warner Bros.' theatre empire, stretching its power from the plethora of New Jersey cities adjacent to New York City to a huge concentration of theatres in Philadelphia, Baltimore, Washington, D.C., and Pittsburgh, Pennsylvania.[10]

Warner Bros. represented Hollywood's lone family enterprise, with Harry Warner, as eldest brother, running the complete show from New

York, including closely monitoring where the monies came in—the five-hundred-house theatre chain. Jack Warner may have gotten the bulk of the publicity from his Hollywood base, but all industry insiders knew that Harry Warner held the keys to the company's powerful set of well-located theatres.

At the time of its expansion into sound in 1925, Warner Bros., backed by the Wall Street finances of Goldman Sachs, purchased ten first-run houses, including Broadway's Piccadilly Theatre. Warner Bros. vertically integrated in 1928 when in the fall it formally took over the Stanley Company of America. Often lost in the descriptions of that important deal is the fact that Warner Bros. also acquired what remained from First National, including more theatres and a production facility in California. In 1929 Warner Bros. added more theatres, including the former St. Louis theatres of Spyros Skouras, to bring the number in the chain to nearly seven hundred at its peak. This number was about equal to what Fox had gathered but far below Paramount's thousand-plus movie houses.

The Great Depression assaulted Warner Bros.' balance sheets; the company suffered severe losses. As the red ink accumulated, the brothers Warner only had to deal with themselves as controlling stockholders. They stubbornly refused to go to court to reorganize. Instead theatres were sold and leases terminated. In the process, by the mid-1930s the company's circuit was trimmed from about seven hundred movie theatres to four hundred concentrated in Pennsylvania, Maryland, New Jersey, and Washington, D.C., with smaller, scattered outposts in Chicago (the far south side), Los Angeles, Cleveland, and Milwaukee. Looking back from 1935, the chain resembled its 1928 genesis; the locus of corporate power rested with the regional theatre chain built up by Jules Mastbaum that was known to all as the Stanley Company of America.

Fox

Although a pioneer in the movie theatre business, William Fox was able to lay claim to a theatre empire because of the riches he reaped from investments during the development of movie sound. Although Fox Theatres always counted as its base its acquisition of the former West Coast Theatres chain, founder William Fox had grander plans. He wanted a national chain and during the mid-1920s set out to build or acquire the greatest movie palace in "every" major city. Indeed in its heyday Fox Theatres owned and operated ornate, massive, four-thousand-seat theatres in

Detroit, Philadelphia, San Francisco, Atlanta, St. Louis, and New York City (the fabulous Roxy).[11]

The origins of the company lay in William Fox's entry into the entertainment business in New York City. He was Marcus Loew's principal rival in the small-time vaudeville business of the first two decades of the twentieth century. But Loew always seemed to get the best corners, and the Fox chain of theatres grew rather slowly. By 1920 Fox Metropolitan Theatres consisted of only twenty-five houses, all located within the New York City environs. At that point William Fox redirected his energies into producing films.

In the early 1920s his chief rivals, Famous Players-Lasky and Loew's, Inc., were vertically integrating. Quickly Fox's meager theatre holdings paled beside the power of Famous Players-Lasky's national theatre enterprise and the ever-growing power of Loew's, Inc. in New York City. Trapped on both sides, Fox initiated a major theatre building program in the mid-1920s. In July 1925 he began his acquisition of West Coast Theatres, a regional chain with the leading position in California and other western states. At the same time Fox set out to build his wonder theatres from coast to coast. By 1927 Fox Theatres had fabulous theatres from Brooklyn on one coast to San Francisco on the other. Every major city west of the Rockies was covered. The Fox flagship became the Roxy in New York.

The coming of sound fueled William Fox's ambition and borrowing power. Fox assistants inked deals to take over small theatre chains in New England, New York, New Jersey, California, Wisconsin, and the Pacific Northwest. At the pinnacle of its power, Fox Theatres, the company division in charge of movie houses, held an estimated seven hundred theatres, equal to Warner Bros. and second only to Paramount Publix. Acquisitions seemed to come daily, and in the nine months before the stock market crash Fox was constantly in *Variety*'s headlines for buying a theatre or opening a new picture palace.

By the time the Great Depression crippled Fox's rivals (save the frugal Loew's, Inc.), the stock market crash had already demolished William Fox's movie empire. Fox's stock dealings left him badly overextended and made it impossible to meet debt payments. He had borrowed heavily from American Telephone and Telegraph, the supplier of sound equipment to his theatres, and they called in their loans in 1930. William Fox was out, and a series of executives from outside the film industry were brought in to repair the ailing Fox corporation.

They failed. The temporary takeover of Loew's was canceled. Fox's core theatre chain, Wesco (the former West Coast Theatres), went into court-supervised receivership in 1933; it was reorganized a year later into National Theatres. Fox nearly went under during the early 1930s, but mid-decade the management of Joseph M. Schenck, brother of the president of Loew's, and Darryl F. Zanuck came aboard and merged their operation, Twentieth Century Pictures, with Fox. Twentieth Century-Fox was formed. Twentieth Century-Fox originally held less than a controlling share in National Theatres, but in the midst of the prosperity of World War II, Twentieth Century-Fox took majority control. What remained was an empire that stretched from Denver to Los Angeles, north to San Francisco and the Pacific Northwest. Isolated outposts could be found in Kansas, western Nebraska, Missouri, and Wisconsin.

Former St. Louis theatre executive Spyros Skouras took over the presidency of Twentieth Century-Fox in 1941. Skouras by then had become head of what remained of Fox Metropolitan Theatres. Indeed for a time Skouras seemed to be working for everybody; in the 1930s he became a specialist in "saving" theatre chains, for Paramount and then eventually Fox. In 1932 Skouras and his brothers Charles and George teamed up to save the Wesco chain. The trio took charge of all Fox theatres in the early 1940s, and after 1941, as Spyros Skouras sat in the presidency of the company, his younger brother ran the theatre division, National Theatres. The Skourases became rich as millions streamed to southern California to work in the war industries and spent part of their newfound wealth in a Fox theatre near their new homes.

Radio-Keith-Orpheum (RKO)

RKO held the smallest of the Hollywood affiliated theatre chains. Unlike the four others, which were fashioned from the base of regional theatre chains, the RKO circuit was already a single national entity made up of the theatres left from the old Keith-Albee vaudeville chain and the Orpheum vaudeville chain. RKO took its initial creative impetus from the Radio Corporation of America; the Keith-Albee Orpheum amalgamated vaudeville theatre chains were abbreviated "KO." The well-placed vaudeville theatres provided the core of the more than one hundred theatres; in 1929, RKO added more theatres, often taking over theatres that owed RCA for installed sound equipment and could not pay for it.[12]

It was not surprising that the Great Depression would hit RKO the hardest. Like Fox and Paramount, RKO plunged into debt. Beginning in 1933, it needed to be formally reorganized by the United States federal court because it could not meet its mortgages on the theatre buildings. RKO was tied up in court for more than six years, emerging only in 1940, just in time to benefit from the industry-wide prosperity associated with the boom times of the Second World War. Americans had money to spend and RKO theatres, however ragged and old fashioned, were one place where fun did not require a ration coupon.

At the peak of its power, in the late 1920s, RKO held nearly two hundred theatres, a few more than Loew's but far fewer than Paramount, Twentieth Century-Fox, or Warner Bros. Although the chain had a theatre in nearly every major city in the United States, the bulk of RKO's houses, because of late-1920s deals, were concentrated in the New York City environs. Undoubtedly the RKO circuit's most famous movie house was Radio City Music Hall, leased from Rockefeller Center, Inc. Radio City provided a national showcase for the premieres of all the famous RKO films of the 1930s and 1940s, from the Fred Astaire–Ginger Rogers musicals to Orson Welles' *Citizen Kane* to John Ford's *Fort Apache*.

But in the end, the RKO chain stood as the weakest of the Big Five. It did not dominate any single area of the United States the way that Warner Bros. controlled the mid-Atlantic region, Fox the western states, Loew's the East, and Paramount the Midwest and the South. RKO had to split the New York City market with Loew's, and indeed in that huge market it was at best a second cousin. RKO always represented the weakest of the vertically integrated Hollywood companies. The history of RKO reached an apex only during the heyday of the Second World War, providing a vivid example of how the theatre chains of the Big Five dictated the corporate bottom line to a far greater degree than the ebb and flow of Hollywood hits.

THEATRE POWER, HOLLYWOOD STYLE

The control of key theatres by the Big Five had far-reaching consequences. All other Hollywood film companies had to accede to the dictates of the Big Five in order to place films in vital first-run sites, a necessity if profits were ever to be made. Independent, nonaffiliated exhibitors had to conform and wait their turn as a third-, fourth-, or fifth-run house or risk that the Big Five corporations would not rent to them at all. Alternately, the independent exhibitor could turn only to Republic and Monogram for poor-quality features, knowing these films never made much money.[13]

To make sure they extracted the most from their ownership and control of the theatre chains, the Big Five developed a complex set of practices to sell films to theatres. By carefully manipulating trade arrangements for the booking of films, the Big Five were able to reduce risk, ensure continuity of operation, and almost guarantee regular profits. Proper exploitation led to their ability to wring out the maximum amount of revenues from each film through what was known as the run-zone-clearance system of distribution and exhibition.

The Big Five set up a series of runs for a particular film, establishing gradually lower admissions. If a fan wanted to see the film featuring a favorite star as soon as it came out, he or she paid the maximum. If the fan was willing to wait, the price of admission at a second-run house was less, and so on down the line. Admission to final runs was no more than a quarter and often only a dime.

To protect these runs, the Big Five enforced the run status of each theatre within a certain zone (or geographical territory). The run status of the theatre was changed only when the Big Five decided a change would be in their best interest. Then the Big Five bookers and theatre managers fixed a certain period of time between runs, known as the "clearance" period. Movie patrons knew they had to wait if they wanted to pay less.

The distribution exchanges of the Big Five cooperated to set and maintain runs, zones, and clearances for all cities and towns in the United States. All first-runs (usually at Hollywood-owned downtown picture palaces) were followed by a period of thirty or more days before a film would appear in a second-run, neighborhood picture palace. Then there came another thirty-day wait, and so on. In New York City or Chicago there might be more than a dozen runs, and it could take nearly two years for a film to work its way down to the final-run cinema. In smaller towns there might be a first-run theatre downtown, a second-run house across the street, and a third-run house around the corner.[14]

Actual bargaining for bookings by the theatre owner followed a strict seasonal pattern. If owned by the Big Five, the theatre manager simply took orders from "the office in New York," since negotiating was done within a tightly knit set of distribution executives. The Big Five company first booked their own films; for example, Loew's, Inc. scheduled MGM films. Then the firm worked in the best films offered by the other four. Independent theatre owners were given a spot in the run-zone-clearance status and "minimum" admission price (always "the" admission price stipulated within the contracts issued by the Big Five producers). In short, the Big Five operated collectively to ensure maximum profits.

Within those constraints a theatre sought to somehow line up the best films possible for its local market. The independent theatre took the left-overs. If times were good (such as in the Second World War era), the Big Five might permit an independent theatre to book major studio features relatively early in the cycle of runs. When times were bad (as in 1933) the Big Five squeezed every possible dime from their films in their theatres before permitting an independent theatre to book at all.

Films were booked sight unseen—so-called blind buying—and little information was available on the films. This did not matter to the bookers of Big Five–owned theatres. The independent theatre owner was visited by a Big Five sales representative in the spring preceding the opening of the movie season (Labor Day through Memorial Day). The independent theatre owner had to choose from vague descriptions of films not yet completed. If the theatre owner passed on a selection, an independent theatre across the street might grab it. The independent theatre owner thus attempted to secure as good a deal as possible (the maximum number of "Gables" and "Garlands") at the lowest percentage of the box office given to the distributor.

The Big Five sales force attempted to sell independent theatre owners a complete package for the year—so-called block booking. Since a studio produced only fifty or so films per annum, and since most exhibitors changed bills twice a week, through one calendar year a theatre owner needed the whole output of two studios. Adventuresome independent theatre owners bargained as best they could, seeking the best of each studio. Those taking less of a risk simply booked the product of the best two studios and then spent their energies promoting the product on the local level.

The Big Five preferred to book films in independent theatres in blocks since this kept the number of prints needed low (prints were recycled from run to run), kept sales costs low, and guaranteed a steady flow of revenue. The Big Five embraced block booking and blind buying in order to maximize revenues through a system of price discrimination. If done properly, fans would tender as much as they were willing at each run, revenues would be maximized, and the Big Five would make the most possible money from their investment.[15]

In sum, based within a zone, and given the clearance periods, different prices were charged for the "same" film. The most anxious fans saw a film first and paid the most. Less interested but still habitual movie watchers would pay less, but only after months had elapsed. Keen fans might advance more than a dollar to see their favorites; patient and casual fans could expect to hand over as little as a dime. Wide-scale advertising encouraged everyone to see the first-run showing. Hollywood distribution executives (from offices in New York) juggled run, zone, and clearances as well as admission prices in an attempt to milk the most from the continuous flow of films. They used a trial-and-error method, adjusting for shifts in the population, booms in the economy, or other outside factors not within their control.

To maximize box-office returns for first-run movies the Hollywood studios finely tuned the art of motion picture publicity. Invariably the publicity campaigns were planned by departments of the major studios. A cooperative, the National Screen Service, handled the distribution of materials, from large posters to lobby cards. As the film industry emerged from World War I, the standardization of publicity accompanied the consolidation of the ownership of theatres. At that time the "pressbook" package was formulated and sent to the theatre with the reels of the film. By the 1930s, studio staffs were constructing one-hundred-page pressbooks. Among the poster choices were "one-sheets" (a poster twenty-seven by forty-one inches), with runs of twenty thousand commonplace.[16]

The allocated budgets for publicity art were a direct function of the amount spent on the film. The top, first-run features were often heralded by advance one-sheets (and some posters double or triple that size) months before the film ever arrived. On rare occasions a forty-eight sheet (really twenty-four one-sheets) stretched twenty-four feet long and rose nine feet in height. Historians have catalogued the style of posters by studio and auteur. Indeed at one time in the 1940s Twentieth Century-Fox hired Norman Rockwell to craft poster art for *The Razor's Edge*.[17]

The coming of sound gave rise to a publicity vehicle for the auditorium—the preview or (in industry talk) the trailer. Although previews had been used since the 1910s, the addition of sound moved them to the front of the program. But there were any number of publicity stunts that defined the 1940s Hollywood cinema. In September 1941 Twentieth Century-Fox sent snowballs to critics in Boston and Washington, D. C., to promote the opening of *Sun Valley Serenade*. Universal redressed ushers as cowboys for *The Lady from Cheyenne*. The age of the silly promotion was when the studios owned the major theatres and held their greatest vertical power. Earlier or later there simply was not the excess money.[18]

Games and Giveaways

The system of Hollywood theatre ownership and control worked well through the 1930s and 1940s. Complaints came constantly and consistently from independent theatre owners who, properly, protested that they were being denied access to maximum profits. But the Big Five owned the key theatres, and so the independents could only complain. With the studio system the Big Five had the films everyone wanted. Only "outside" factors—those not under the control of the motion picture industry—truly modified the profits the Big Five could take from their ownership of theatres.

As has been noted, the major movie chains could do little to counter the decrease in demand for film entertainment caused by a decline in purchasing power during the Great Depression. Although accurate statistics are hard to come by, from 1930 to 1932 box-office revenues declined by at least 25 percent. Recovery began in 1934, and in fits and starts the movie business improved through 1940. Still, in the 1930s customers abandoned the movie show for cheaper entertainment substitutes; one might pay twenty dollars for a radio knowing that it would supply free programs for the foreseeable future.[19]

All movie exhibitors had to solve the problem of fewer patrons lining up outside. At first they adopted several familiar retailing tactics. Many independents began giving away premiums (for example, dishes), holding gaming contests (for example, SCREENO, a form of bingo), or both. Retailers of all ilk initiated giveaways and games in reaction to the Great Depression. One estimate had the amount in prizes surging over three million dollars in 1937. Items at the movie house usually included chinaware, glasses, linens, cooking utensils, and even groceries. One theatre instituted a program of giveaways, then the competition had to follow, looking for different prizes.[20]

One special giveaway scheme, called Bank Night, was popular because it offered the prize everyone wanted during the Great Depression—hard cash. Indeed by 1937 Bank Night had become something of an American obsession. After four years on the scene, the event functioned in five thousand theatres, with an estimated one million dollars given away per year. One industry observer noted: "It's got to the point where nobody can schedule a basketball game, a church social or a contract [bridge] party on Tuesday night, because everybody is down at the Gem hoping to cop a cash prize—usually standing in the street beyond the marquee because the theatre is too small."[21]

Bank Night was by and large a small-town phenomenon. Charles Yaeger of an independent theatre chain based in Colorado and New Mexico and his Affiliated Enterprises, Inc. were behind Bank Night. For his small chain, as elsewhere, the nadir had come during the winter of 1932–33.

To drum up business Yaeger staged beauty contests and gave away Christmas trees, but the effects on long-term attendance proved nil. Bank Night changed all that. Yaeger copyrighted the name and registered fourteen possible different titles at the United States Patent Office in Washington, D.C. (Ironically it was noted that at the acme of its popularity Bank Night proved a hit everywhere save Washington, D.C., where New Deal government jobs gave residents plenty of cash.) Patrons at theatres around the United States registered at their local theatre for free, but they had to be at the theatre the night of the drawing to win.

Bank Night evaded the antilottery laws then on the books because patrons did not have to pay for their lucky number, and theoretically they could wait outside the theatre to learn if they had won.[22] On a Monday or Tuesday night—the slowest of the week—the manager would appear on stage and call a child from the audience. The child would be blindfolded and then draw the winning number from a revolving drum. Bank Night kept many a small-town theatre open during the worst days of the Great Depression.[23]

The world of noncash giveaways—from china and silk stockings to simple door prizes—began in 1931. Two nights of the week were targeted: Mondays, always the slowest night of the week, and Fridays, when the Big Five theatres presented premieres of the latest Hollywood fare. Quickly entrepreneurs set up shop, offering the theatre owners giveaway premiums in large lots at discounted rates. They helped with the attendant financing and instructed rural single-house owners in the art of the giveaway. The secret, they claimed, was to attract females, who then, the theory went, brought along the rest of the family. On average each prize cost the exhibitor a dime. If, on a slow night, the movie house usually took in fifty dollars, and if an investment in one thousand pieces of china (cost: one hundred dollars) boosted the box office take to three hundred dollars, the theatre owner was far ahead.[24]

In a common variation the theatre owner staged a game that ended in giving away prizes. For example, SCREENO was simply a patented name for a system of Bingo wherein the cards were punched out by player-patrons as the numbers were called by the theatre manager from the stage. As the numbers were called, they were flashed onto the movie screen using a slide projector. SCREENO reached its apex during the winter of 1936–37 with one thousand theatres. But if antigambling forces had trouble convincing judges to reign in Bank Night, they had more success with SCREENO, particularly in New York City under progressive Mayor

Fiorello La Guardia. Thus by the beginning of the boom preceding the Second World war, SCREENO and other games in movie theatres had all but disappeared.[25]

Less Service, Big Bands, and Art Deco Theatres

Giveaways and games represented the most noticeable reaction to the greatest economic downturn of the twentieth century. But theatre owners went beyond gimmicks. They also began to cut costs. In the 1920s lavish service had been at the core of the Balaban & Katz system. By the late 1920s it represented the industry standard: a score of door attendants, ushers, and nurses scurrying around. By 1932 all, save the minimum number of ushers, had been fired. The ushers who were spared saw their positions transformed from crowd assistance to crowd control. High school students, paid the minimum wage, replaced more expensive university students as ushers. Several chains recruited out-of-work women to save even more. But male managers also had sexist reasons in mind as well as represented in a recommendation made in a manual for theatre managers:

> In [theatres] where carpets, draperies, and furnishings are worn, and some of the luster has faded, beautiful young usherettes, attractively costumed, help keep the public's eye off the shabby spots. In small operations, usherettes can also save the management the expense of a maid.[26]

The major circuits, led by Paramount-Publix, eliminated stage shows. Indeed this began in the heady days of the coming of sound. By September of 1928, for example, four months after the contracts for sound were signed, Publix had pulled stage shows from theatres in Texas, Alabama, and Louisiana. But with the onslaught of the Great Depression, only the top movie palaces in the largest American cities still booked acts. Stars such as Benny Goodman or Frank Sinatra were the top attractions of the day. The days of a Balaban & Katz developing local stars like Jesse Crawford and Paul Ash would never be revived again. If the coming of sound caused the end of the stage show, the Great Depression buried it. Orchestra pits were covered up; paint in the dressing rooms began to peel; and backstage became another storage room.[27]

The Great Depression did not wholly signal the end of the presentation of live attractions in movie theatres. Indeed, the history of popular music during the 1930s and 1940s, for example, is intertwined with performers playing movie houses at the peak of their fame. In 1937, for example, Benny Goodman's band had thousands of young people lined up in front of the Paramount Theatre before the sun had risen at six in the morning. Another noted example is Frank Sinatra's famed appearances at the same theatre six years later.

Top theatres became showcases for the best musical attractions. Consider what treats Chicagoans had in 1941. At a trio of downtown Paramount-owned theatres—the Chicago, the State Lake, and the Oriental—added attractions appeared regularly. Many have long been forgotten, including the orchestras of Will Bradley and Joe Sanders. But between January and November of 1942 a patron in a theatre in downtown Chicago could have heard (each booked for a week) Fats Waller, the Andrews Sisters, Louis Armstrong's Red Hot Revue, the Eddy Duchin Orchestra, the Glenn Miller Orchestra, the Lionel Hampton Orchestra, the Artie Shaw Orchestra, the Jimmy Dorsey Orchestra, or the Nicholas Brothers. Throughout the war years, the stage show would thrive in Chicago, New York, and other major American cities. Indeed, the war years proved a miniresurgence for the stage show.[28]

Mainstream pop acts hardly constituted the sole source of programming for movie theatres in the 1930s and 1940s. For example, in the southwestern area of the United States during the late 1930s there existed no more popular star than Gene Autry of radio, phonograph records, and movie fame. Autry's "Melody Ranch" radio show featured Gene, Champion (his horse), a female singer, a male trio, comics, Indian dancers, and backup musicians. When Republic Pictures geared up to release a new Autry feature, Gene Autry took this package on the road and played movie houses throughout Oklahoma and Texas. He presented a version of the radio show on stage as part of the film's premiere.[29]

But a limited stage show was not the only way the movie palace formula of the 1920s was transformed. The fundamental style of the building took on a new look, reflecting the changes that were taking place in the world of architectural design. The few hundred theatres built between 1932 (the end of the movie palace era) and 1954 (the coming of television) were planned and constructed in a stripped-down version of the international style, at a cost far less per square foot than a 1920s movie palace.

For example, during the 1920s John Eberson pioneered the atmospheric movie palace—"stars-and-clouds" theatres featuring interiors designed to remind viewers of European gardens. During the 1930s, however, Eberson sought a less expensive style. He abandoned ornamental plaster work, resulting in tremendous labor-saving cost reductions. Low-price fabrics decorated the sidewalls. His all-too-rare commissions of the 1930s wasted no space and were efficient in cost, construction, and operation.[30]

Often the only construction was a part of new suburban complexes. John Eberson's Silver Theatre, designed for Warner Bros., was built in the heart of downtown Silver Spring, Maryland, adjacent to Washington, D.C. In the late 1930s Silver Spring grew from a quiet residential suburb to the second largest business community in the state of Maryland. Over sixty stores opened their doors, and statisticians counted an average of fifteen thousand cars passing through the heart of this suburban shopping center every twenty-four hours. The shopping center plus theatre complex offered a careful blend of art deco and sweeping streamline modern. The Silver Theatre, built as part of the overall shopping center, was constructed in glazed brick with bands of red vitrolite, an opaque glass. Several hundred other such theatres, often part of larger complexes, were built before the restrictions of the Second World War set in.[31]

Although architects showing in the Paris Exposition of Decorative Art suggested the elements of the art deco style in 1925, it was not until the mid-1930s that the owners and operators of the American film industry, needing a differentiated, new look, adopted the machine-inspired design. It was only in selected parts of the United States, particularly in growing California, that art deco theatres were ever built in any number. Among the major architects of the movie palace era, John Eberson, already noted, and Rapp & Rapp were the most successful at incorporating the elements of the new style. Indeed the Rapps' Theatre in Milwaukee, Wisconsin, offered a silver-lined and mirrored art deco lobby leading to a classically French baroque auditorium.[32]

Although the largest movie theatre in the United States was of art deco design, the Radio City Music Hall, the style was used far more for the few hundred neighborhood theatres built in the 1930s and the small number built in the decade after World War II. Some were newsreel theatres; for example, the Trans-Lux Theatre in Washington, D. C., was one of the most handsome in the nation's capital. The Apex, six miles from the White House in the growing suburbs, was more typical. Opened in 1940, the Apex included a circular aluminum ticket booth placed between two glass doors (lined in aluminum) and set beneath a streamlined marquee lined with lights. Inside the lines were clean and simple. Gone was the constant decoration of the downtown palaces, instead replaced by clean simple lines and deeper-set colors.[33]

The Apex was typical because of at least two factors. It was not designed by a nationally famous architect. John Zink was known for a number of movie palaces in Washington, D.C., and Baltimore, Maryland, but none outside this mid-Atlantic region.[34] Indeed the reason Zink, not Eberson or Rapp & Rapp, was hired was because the theatre was opened by an independent company, KB Theatres, not one of the major circuits. Washington, D.C., in the 1930s was a Warner Bros.' town; KB Theatres, one of Warner Bros.' independent rivals, used the art deco style to differentiate the look of its theatres from the picture palaces of the 1920s.[35]

AIR CONDITIONING

All was not simple cost cutting and trimming back during the 1930s. There were positive moves made in movie exhibition amidst the gloom of the Great Depression. The 1930s were not simply an era of stripping away the glories built up in the 1920s. Exhibitors were willing to spend money installing one new piece of technology they reasoned would help business—air conditioning. Balaban & Katz had proven this a draw, but who outside the great movie palaces owned by the major chains could afford the extra thousands of dollars for investment and upkeep?

Before 1917 theatres in the United States of all types employed extensive systems of fans or simply closed their doors during the summer months. By 1925 air conditioned theatres, especially those in Chicago, were the talk of the film industry. The apparatus was so large and so expensive that only picture palaces of two thousand or more seats could afford installation. Neighborhood theatre owners glared down the street at the competing movie palaces that not only had the best Hollywood films but also were air cooled in the summer.[36]

This changed in the 1930s, when Willis Carrier produced a more compact, less expensive system costing from ten to fifty thousand dollars. The 1933 World's Fair generated favorable publicity, and during the bleak years of the Great Depression air conditioning sales to movie theatres grew, not fell. At first, the new Carrier units were principally installed for the convenience of the rich in luxury Pullman cars, fancy hotels, expensive restaurants, and large estates. As the movie business began to pick up in 1935 and 1936, hundreds, then thousands of movie theatres scraped together the necessary investment and installed air cooling. During the 1930s owners of movie theatres throughout the United States, especially in the South and

West, installed air conditioning apparatus. They pushed sales of air conditioning equipment to a record fifty million dollars in 1936; sales doubled to one hundred million dollars by 1941. Movie theatres were one of the few public institutions in which the middle-class and poor citizens of the United States could indulge in cool, dehumidified comfort until well into the 1950s.[37]

Installations ceased during the Second World War because war restrictions did not permit the manufacture of air conditioning equipment. But technological needs of the military in the Second World War prompted even greater development of air conditioning equipment. The United States federal government insisted that crowded factories install air cooling to increase productivity, especially within shipbuilding plants. One year after the war's end, installations picked up again, and by 1950 nearly three-quarters of movie theatres had air conditioning.

This comparative advantage held throughout the 1950s, and only in the 1960s and 1970s did America see the rise of totally air conditioned cultures in the Sun Belt. The Texas cities of Dallas and Houston could hardly exist in their present form without air conditioned buildings. The comparative advantage of air conditioning to movie exhibition in the United States during the 1930s and 1940s cannot be overestimated. A Watergate journalist, in his memoir of growing up in Washington, D. C., remembered:

> My most pervasive memory of those two summers [1951 and 1952] is of the heat. That oppressive Washington heat. This was before air-conditioning, or at least before anyone I knew had air-conditioning at home. . . . [But] the Trans-Lux [movie house] had air-conditioning. Next to the ticket window a big sign announced in shimmering blue-tinsel-icicle lettering, "It's Kool Inside." Some evenings, after trying to get served in the restaurants on F Street, my mother and I would go to a movie to cool off.[38]

The innovation of air conditioning made going to the movies a year-round treat. Indoor entertainment could provide welcome relief from the heat and humidity whether or not the feature films were entertaining. This turned the summer into the prime moviegoing season and drew children out of school in greater numbers to the movies. With more children and fewer ushers, unruly crowds again became a problem in the movie houses to a degree unreported since the nickelodeon day some twenty-five years earlier.[39]

DOUBLE FEATURES

One trend in movie exhibition, from the days of the nickelodeon to the movie palace, was the constant increase of admission fees. The Great Depression reversed that trend; theatres began to offer the customer a bargain. In 1930, more and more movie houses began to tender "two-movies-for-the-price-of-one," or double features. As the Great Depression worsened, theatre owners regularly scheduled double and even triple features. At first such discounting occurred only at small neighborhood theatres, which desperately sought some method of competing with the movie palaces that regularly scheduled first-run showings of the latest Big Five attractions.

Double features were not something new. Once the feature film was established as the dominant movie form, exhibitors in New England tried the idea. But during the 1920s, only a handful of small neighborhood theatre owners, unable to obtain attractive films from the major companies, dared to resort to regular double features. Moviegoers in the United States came to expect one feature, a couple of shorts, a newsreel, and possibly a stage show for their entrance fee of fifteen to seventy-five cents (equivalent to about one to five dollars today).

In 1933 federal government of the United States gave double features a temporary boost. That year the National Recovery Act became law. As part of the motion picture code of fair conduct, giveaways and games of chance were outlawed (for only eighteen months it turned out) as "unfair competition." With these lures unavailable, nearly all movie theatres in the United States turned to double features.[40]

The widespread adoption of what were then known in the trade as "duals" resulted in a new formula for movie shows. A complete show became longer and longer, and so a theatre would turn over its audience fewer times each day. Initially this loss of revenue from fewer shows was offset by increased attendance. For example, there might be four instead of five shows a day, but if attendance per show rose by 30 percent, the theatre owner would come out ahead. But as more and more theatres began to "double," any single theatre's relative advantage lessened.[41]

Initially, public opinion (as expressed through random sample surveys) seemed decidedly anti–double features, despite the fact millions attended them each day. For example, one poll taken in 1937 reported that only one-fifth of those surveyed would attend a double feature when given the opportunity to go to a single feature. Children preferred duals; adults did not. The poor wanted more for their money, they told survey takers; the rich held onto the tradition of the single feature, a fixture of moviegoing in the United States for nearly a generation. Opponents provided three objections to double features:

1. Their excessive length caused eye strain and fatigue.
2. "Good" films were too often paired with "poor" films.
3. Fewer quality short subjects were being presented.[42]

For a time during the late 1930s antimovie forces proposed laws banning or restricting double features. This political controversy climaxed in 1938 in Chicago. Since this city had one of the strongest traditions of stage shows accompanying movies, Paramount, the dominant theatre chain, had long resisted completely switching to double features. But with profits declining, in 1938 Paramount instituted double features throughout the second largest city in the United States. Two hundred members of the local Parent Teachers Association marched on City Hall. Independent exhibitors appealed to the Chicago City Council to pass laws restricting double features. Health hazards to children were the reasons opponents cited when pressing for the new law.[43]

But Paramount represented a powerful corporate presence in Chicago and was able to get the city council to table the issue. Thwarted by city politics, opponents turned to the state legislature of Illinois. Rural exhibitors cooperated with the owners of small neighborhood houses from Chicago, and this coalition pushed a bill restricting double features through the General Assembly of Illinois. The proposed law would have limited all film shows in the state of Illinois to two hours and fifteen minutes, thus in effect outlawing double features (save serials or "B" films from small studios such as Republic and Monogram). Fines and prison sentences were established. But before this measure could become law, the governor of Illinois had to sign it. He refused, and there the matter stalled. Thereafter through the 1940s the double feature functioned as the standard in movie exhibition.[44]

Indeed through the 1940s double features enabled lower-run theatres to create some choice in their shows. They could mix and match various combinations of films depending on the interest of their specific neighborhoods. Entire bills did not move in lockstep from one theatre to the next, from third run to fourth run to fifth run and so on. Instead as the films moved from run to run, new combinations were tried to entice patrons. Sometimes two Bette Davis or Spencer Tracy films were paired; or features were moved from the top to the bottom of the bill.[45]

Into this came the production of so-called B films in the 1930s, from studios such as Republic, Monogram, Grand National, and Producer's Releasing Corporation. The Hollywood majors also had B film production units as well, so in the run-zone-clearance distribution system they favored the B films as "duals" in their owned and operated houses. Independent theatres preferred subsequent-run high-budget films and took them if they could get favorable terms (that is, a run not too far down the line and a clearance not too many months from the film's actual premiere.) But there were theatres that took the products of Republic and Monogram and crafted profitable (albeit smaller than with top feature films) existences from their showings.[46]

POPCORN AND OTHER TREATS

The Great Depression also pushed movie exhibitors to seek a new source of revenue—to collect monies for something besides admission to the show. The answer lay outside their doors. Rather than let patrons buy snacks from confectionery stores within a few steps of the cashier's booth, exhibitors ignored the associations with "lower-class" amusements and began to sell candy, then soft drinks, and finally popcorn in their lobbies.

This transformation represented a radical break from the development of movie exhibition over the previous thirty years. The selling of food had long been associated with carnivals, burlesque shows, and cheaper-class entertainment from whose image the new movie theatre owners sought to disassociate themselves; they sought a "higher-class" tone. During the 1920s movie palace owners steadfastly refused to sell food.

But moviegoing in the United States had always been accompanied by snack treats. Patrons in small-town theatres or in informal neighborhood houses simply purchased their candy, popcorn, and soda before or after the show from a nearby shop. Pictures of movie theatres taken during the 1920s invariably display a confectionery store adjacent to a movie house. During the 1920s some small neighborhood theatres did sell candy in the lobby because it was prepackaged and thus easily handled, it required little investment, and with their lower-run status, it often meant the difference between profit and loss. But the norm dictated that the higher-class theatre did not need the added revenues from the sales of sweets.[47]

During the Great Depression such assumptions were swept aside. The introduction of selling snacks came in three steps. First came the candy stand. A simple wooden stand, staffed by a high school student, could generate hundreds of dollars of pure profit that did not have to be shared with any greedy Hollywood company. This instant success prompted exhibitors, particularly independent exhibitors not affiliated with Hollywood, to expand the base of revenue creation. They wanted a source of profit less dependent on the popularity of the feature films.[48]

To use the economist's terminology, the movie theatre owner internalized the sales of a complementary good that had long been associated with going to the movies. Through the 1930s concession stands opened in nearly every movie theatre in the United States. By 1936, sales of candy in movie houses topped ten million dollars. This may have paled beside the estimated one billion dollars taken in at the box office, but to the average exhibitor who kept half the receipts at the concession stand as profit, this may have represented the only profit he or she had.[49]

Then came popcorn. For decades, vendors had sold this snack to movie patrons from the nearby confectionery store or from wagons positioned outside theatres. During the late 1930s theatres owners simply moved the popcorn stand into the lobby. Popcorn, easy to manufacture, spread its aroma to waiting customers. Theatre owners learned that popcorn was one food that Americans ate more, not less, of during bad economic times. With popcorn, which is relatively cheap, consumers bought more (and less of more expensive treats) as their incomes fell. And once the habit took, Americans seemed to be hooked.[50]

It may be hard to realize, but eating popcorn, at the movies or at home, is an acquired taste. Vassily Aksyonov, a Soviet emigre, reminds us of this when he noted in a memoir about adapting to life in the United States: "I too keep catching myself reacting spontaneously in ways I know to be American. Yet at first all kinds of things irritated me. The smell of popcorn in movie theatres, for instance."[51]

During the late 1930s exhibitors overcame the negative associations with popcorn and began to pop corn by the bushel. The aging movie palaces, owned by the Big Five chains, negotiated to purchase popcorn in bulk and thus effected considerable cost savings. Consequently they could produce a fifteen-cent box for three cents and a nickel bag for about a penny. Even with the other associated costs (wages to salespersons, costs of containers, and popping apparatus) profit rates for the sale of the average bag of popcorn frequently exceeded 100 percent.[52]

The movie theatre industry made popcorn into an important farm crop in the United States. The popcorn harvest grew from 5 million pounds in 1934 to more than 100 million pounds in 1940. By the boom times of the Second World War popcorn became a fixture at theatres. And farmers responded. Even with acre after acre devoted to growing wheat and other staples for the troops, the popcorn harvest still soared beyond 400 million pounds per year. That represented more than 4 pounds of popcorn for every person in the United States.[53]

The third phase in the introduction of the sale of snacks in the movie house had to await the end of the war. During World War II sugar was rationed; moreover, Coca-Cola and Pepsi-Cola, the nation's two leading soft drink companies, sent most of their product to the fighting men and women in Europe and the Pacific. After the war, the Coca-Cola Corporation pushed to open new markets and led the way for the introduction of soft drinks into movie houses. In conjunction with Morton's salt (sprinkled on the popcorn to create thirst), Coke pushed to have theatre owners create virtual confectionery supermarkets in the lobbies of their theatres. By 1950 the red Coke fountain symbol stood in nearly every theatre, at least those in which Pepsi had not beaten Coke to the punch.[54]

During these years immediately after World War II, movie theatre owners ritualized the intermission in order to provide two chances to sell snack foods to a captured audience. To many theatre owners movies became secondary to the sales of food. The feature film and air conditioned environment may have pulled patrons into the theatre, but sales of popcorn, Coca-Cola, and candy provided exhibitors with real, live profits. The word around film industry conventions became: find a good location for a popcorn stand and build a movie theatre around it.[55]

But there were problems associated with bringing a snack food counter into the movie house and permitting patrons to consume while they watched their favorite movie stars. Soft drinks plus candy and popcorn led to the sticky floors that many of us associate with the contemporary movie-going experience. Audiences at first did not seem to mind. Bathed in cool air, going to the double feature and having a Coke and a bag of popcorn had become part of the fabric of American life.[56]

Later events in the history of American movie exhibition would build on the basis of the sale of candy, soft drinks, and popcorn. The drive-in theatre of the 1950s simply expanded the concession stand, making the snack bars into the size of small cafeterias. Drive-in theatre owners sold not only an assortment of candy and soft drinks and fresh popcorn but also hot dogs, coffee, milk shakes, ice cream, taffy apples, steak sandwiches, hamburgers, pizza, and potato chips. By the 1960s the concession stand had become a cornerstone of the theatrical film business. In the mid-1980s the average sale at the concession stand had risen to nearly three dollars. The profitability of the snack treats ran thusly: (1) popcorn, (2) beverages, (3) hot dogs, (4) ice cream, and (5) candy. Prices in a 1987 survey saw single soft drinks and bags of popcorn ranging from one to two dollars and beyond; candy was a relative bargain at fifty cents to two dollars.[57]

LOOKING TO THE FUTURE

The increased spending at movie houses associated with the coming of the Second World War ended the innovations in movie exhibition brought about by the Great Depression. From 1941 through 1945 movie exhibitors experienced a golden age, one never since repeated. Indeed, as hostilities spread throughout Europe and the Orient, the American public turned to the movie theatre in record numbers. Business, especially in large cities with war-related industries such as Detroit and Washington, D.C., boomed beyond any records set during the coming of sound. Revenues at the theatrical box office crested in the spring of 1946 at the highest per capita levels in history.

The era from 1930 to 1950 did not represent an unchanging period of theatrical movie exhibition in the United States. While it certainly was true that filmgoing in the United States reached its apex during the 1940s, popularity should not be equated with the lack of change. The moviegoing institution reached a new acme because exhibitors were willing to change. The coming of giveaways, international style theatre design, air conditioning, double features, and confectionery sales significantly altered the way Americans experienced moviegoing. Popularity of the classic Hollywood movies of the period never assured enough business to guarantee consistent profits. And that change would continue, sparked by massive shifts in American society, during the 1950s and 1960s.

FIVE

New National Chains

Important social and economic forces led to the breakup of the hegemony of the Big Five. Two causes are usually adduced: the United States federal government antitrust suit that forced the major Hollywood corporations to sell their theatre chains; and the emergence of television. But the fundamental changes that transformed movie exhibition in the United States were of a far more basic origin: mass migration and population growth. When middle-class Americans moved to the suburbs in record numbers after the Second World War, they also abandoned propinquity to the matrix of downtown and neighborhood movie theatres. In addition, these young adults, previously the most loyal of movie fans, concentrated on raising families. This unprecedented population spurt has been called the baby boom.

Although limited television broadcasting commenced before the Second World War, it was not until after that war that television as a mass entertainment industry began. By the turn into the 1950s, there were still only one million sets in use. The rapid innovation of over-the-air television in the United States, however, took place years after the initiation of the decline in the attendance at motion picture theatres. The coming of television might have further exacerbated the decline of theatrical moviegoing, but it surely did not initiate it.[1]

Theoretically the "blame television" account rests on the assumption of the economics of the substitution effect. The analysis goes something like this. What television as a mass entertainment vehicle did was provide a far cheaper substitute for watching narratives composed of visual images and sounds. Television was not a perfect substitute, but surely it was cheaper. At this point the argument points to the real costs of attending a movie from the suburbs by adding in transportation costs, parking fees, and frequently baby-sitting expenses. As television became more widely available during the late 1940s and early 1950s more and more people, the argument goes, turned from the relatively more expensive movie show to the relatively cheap night with television.

Substitution forms an important principle of demand analysis in microeconomic theory. It takes no great leap in logic to theorize that if viable substitutes exist for a good or service, and they exist at a cheaper price than the original, then consumers will demand more of the new good or service and less of the original. But one sizable problem with using the substitution effect to explain the coming of television's effect on the movie industry is that movie attendance—by any measure—began its decline five years before anyone can reasonably argue there was a significant "substitute" available in the form of television. As measured in dollars presented at the box office, and/or estimated annual attendance (the most reliable data available), the fall in theatrical moviegoing in the United States began in the latter months of 1946 and continued steadily downward through the 1940s and into the 1950s.[2]

Even zealots will not try to press the point that television had much of an impact in the marketplace for mass entertainment before 1950. Some would reasonably point to a time as late as 1952, for it was only then that the NBC and CBS television networks actually began to make profits. And it was really only in 1954 and 1955 that the heartland of the United States was finally flooded with television stations, following the ending of the FCC's freeze on granting licenses. But the decline in admissions at the theatrical box office was greater for the 1946 to 1950 period than from 1950 to 1960. If the substitution effect is pointed to as the cause of the loss of the movie audience, then what happened before 1950 must be explained.[3]

Comprehensive data indicate that United States television stations accumulated losses until 1951 and only then began to make profits. Still profits proved few and far between until 1954. By 1955, they broke into double-digit profit percentages. Indeed until the mid-1950s not enough Americans had television sets to matter much. The penetration rate did not exceed one-half of all American homes until 1954. Less than a quarter of homes had sets in 1952. One should not confuse rapid growth with the availability of the necessary absolute size and profit base to effect a true substitute. Only from 1955 on did a surge in audiences and profits occur, and thus from

1955 on we can consider television a business strong enough to provide a true substitute for American movie theatres.[4]

To learn why movie attendance began to decline immediately after the Second World War, one needs to return to demand theory, of which the substitution effect is only a part. There are two other factors that economic theory raises that can play as important a role as the substitution effect: the income effect and the effect of complements. Each of these principles can help explain why moviegoing declined after World War II and must be applied more broadly than looking only at motion picture and television entertainment.

First consider the income effect. If nothing else changes and one's income goes up, then one ought to demand more of a particular product or service. After the Second World War, incomes first fell and then rose, so that by 1950 they were back to 1946 levels. But something curious regarding the income effect happened after World War II. With incomes flat, overall personal consumption rose in spectacular fashion between 1946 and 1950. People cashed in their savings. During the war there was much money to be made, but precious little on which to spend it.

Wages and salaries had doubled during the war while personal saving rates tripled. What people did was take wealth held in one form (savings bonds) and spend it on long-unavailable cars, refrigerators, and home washers and dryers. In the years after World War II sales of these and other consumer durable goods soared. With the reduced output of military goods, the United States economy could begin to turn out these civilian goods.[5]

Many types of goods were consumed in record numbers after World War II, but one stood out historically for its unprecedented growth—housing. After the Second World War Americans accelerated a trek that they had begun at the turn of the century, a movement to single-family dwellings in the suburbs of America's cities. To appreciate the scope of this internal migration compare it to the more famous transatlantic movement from Europe to the United States around the turn of the century. In 1907, when this migration was at its peak, more than one million Europeans landed in the United States. This was precisely the magnitude of the suburban migration of the late 1940s and early 1950s.[6]

The settling of the suburbs was one of the great postwar historical phenomena. Nearly all of the increase in new population growth in the United States after the war took place in the suburban rings around America's cities. United States suburbs grew at a rate fifteen times faster than any other segment of the country. Once the movement to the suburbs began, more than one million acres of farmland were plowed under each year. To keep the move within the family budget, to get the biggest possible house, and to be near the "best" schools, American families sought houses where land prices were low and relatively spacious homes were affordable. Supported by Veterans Administration and Farmers Home Administration mortgages, home ownership in the United States increased by nearly 50 percent from 1945 to 1950, and it went up another 50 percent in the decade after that. By 1960, for the first time in the history of the United States, more Americans owned houses than rented.[7]

Coupled with this massive move to the suburbs was a historically important increase in family size—the baby boom. The two-child family so common since the turn of the century gave way to families with four, five, and even six children. Somewhat cynically, economists fit children into their models as durable goods "consumed" by the parents. Durable (versus nondurable) goods provide a stream of long-term (versus short-term) benefits. A child certainly generates costs in terms of doctor's care, clothes, food, education, and so on. The benefits are traditionally explained in terms of increased labor value from children (as in work around the house or in a family business) and in terms of increased psychic benefits to the parents, what some might call the "make-us-proud-of-you" effect.

This historical rise in the "consumption" of children represents both an income effect and a substitution effect (during the Great Depression the birth rate went down). After the Second World War, the "consumption" of this particular durable good—like others that had been postponed during the war period (and the depression era)—rose dramatically when income rose.

Indeed, during 1946 the birth rate increased steadily each month. By the end of that year an all-time record of nearly three and a half million babies were born in the United States, some 20 percent more than the previous year. The usual precursor to having children, marriage, took place at twice the rate as the year before. The year 1946 set a nuptial record not topped for thirty-three years. This baby boom would continue until 1964, uniquely in the United States.

Many factors helped cause this incredible increase in the "consumption" of children. First, the marriage boom continued through the 1950s. And not only were more Americans marrying, they were doing it at a younger age. The change was startlingly rapid. As recently as 1940 as many as 15 percent of all women who reached their early thirties had never been married. By 1960 that number had been halved. This meant that more and more married people were preparing to have children. After the war the median age at which women married fell from the early twenties almost into the teens. Indeed more than half of brides were still in their teens, and more than half had their first child before the age of twenty.

The baby boom in the United States proved remarkable because it was a mass movement in which all segments of society participated. Bachelors and spinsters, childless couples, and couples with only one child all but vanished. But on the other end, the odds of a mother with four children having a fifth or sixth actually declined. What was left was an unprecedented concentration of families with two or three children. That is, like other consumer durable goods, families went out and acquired children as fast as they could, but not in numbers greater than they could afford. With the pent-up demand for this good, put off during a Great Depression and a World War, the key point is that nearly everyone of child-bearing age had children.

The other stunning reversal of long-term historical trends was in the characteristics of the families who were having more children. Demographers usually have led us to conclude that modernization leads to fewer children. The baby boom should have seen the lowest participation among the urban, educated, and rich. In an unexpected population explosion these groups actually led the baby boom. Families with high school–and college-educated parents, upper middle class in terms of income, had larger and larger families. For example, lawyers, doctors, and executives contributed more proportionally to the baby boom than did factory workers and farmers, usually thought to be the creators of the biggest families. Likewise, and unexpectedly, families in urban and suburban areas contributed more than rural Americans.[8]

In sum, a full analysis of the income effect shows us why there was a decline in movie attendance. Americans had little new personal income to spend on movies. What they had saved they chose to spend on housing and children, making up for what they had missed during the Great Depression and the Second World War. Suburbanization located more and more families away from the downtown location of the movie palaces. It cost more (in terms of time and money) to travel to the picture palace. Finally, the baby boom took away the time and interest of the very demographic heart of the moviegoing audience—a different type of substitution effect. Robert Sklar has accurately summarized what the typical audience of the 1940s was like:

> Contrary to received wisdom, researchers found that the more education a person had, the more often he or she went to the movies; people at

higher income levels attended movies more frequently than people in lower brackets; . . . young people went to the movies more than older people.[9]

So by having families at younger ages and producing more children, the very group of educated, urban, and well-off persons who most frequently went to the movies had other demands. They chose the psychic benefits of having children over other forms of consumption. Since there were so few people of the prime age of eighteen to thirty *not* having families and children, it would seem to follow, ceteris paribus, that attendance at movie theatres should have gone down after the Second World War.

But to complete an analysis of what happened to recreation after World War II, one ought to consider a third factor in any demand analysis, the effect of complements. Many goods and services are consumed in pairs and thus serve as complementary goods. If goods are complements, and if the price of one goes up, the consumer consumes less of *both*, other things being equal. Imagine the case of tea and cream in the United Kingdom. All other things being equal, if the price of tea goes up, the consumption of tea ought to go down, and since cream is a complementary good, the consumption of cream ought to go down as well.[10]

During the late 1940s growing families in the suburbs, confined by their children, began to look for entertainment activities that could be consumed at home. The first complement they chose was radio. Radio advertising expenditures and profits increased steadily after the war, peaking in 1952. The late 1940s, in terms of making profits, proved to be the golden era for the radio business.[11]

But audiences deserted radio as television began to present itself as a viable entertainment substitute in the home. Television proved to be a complementary entertainment good for the families already in the suburbs with young children to keep occupied. So we have a direct *substitution* between two complementary goods as television replaced radio (not the movies per se) as *the* mass entertainment for new baby boom families in their suburban homes. This substitution took place exactly from 1953 thereafter. Thus radio properly saw television as the enemy; the motion picture theatre owner had to blame more basic causes—suburbanization and the baby boom.[12]

THE FILM INDUSTRY REACTS

Executives in the film industry were not wholly oblivious to the economic consequences of these social factors. But first the chief operating officers of the Big Five had to grapple with a legacy of the past—the antitrust suit filed by the federal government in the late 1930s. They lost their antitrust struggle and in 1948 commenced to sell their theatre chains. The factors of suburbanization and the baby boom would have led to change in any case, but the negative decision of the *Paramount* case forced a more radical break. In the first week of May 1948, that decision brought to an abrupt end two decades of direct Hollywood control. The subsequent decrees by the court ended restrictive trade practices and permitted, for the first time in a generation, the possibility of new chains entering the marketplace and seeking control.[13]

The five successor corporations that acquired the theatre chains of the five major *Paramount* defendants—Loew's, Inc., Paramount, RKO, Twentieth Century-Fox, and Warner Bros.—tried as best they could to deal with the changing face of the moviegoing audience. They could acquire theatres but first had to convince the Southern District of Manhattan Court that this acquisition would not unduly restrain trade. Each petition required a formal hearing, often with stiff opposition by attorneys representing the Department of Justice.

Significantly, the closing of a downtown movie palace and the purchasing of one in the suburbs was, repeatedly, *not* considered equivalent. It was not until 1974 that the supervising judge in the district court agreed to let one of the surviving former Big Five theatre chains go into the suburbs of a city in which they formerly had held sway.[14]

Indeed by 1979, only one of the five former circuits, Loew's, Inc., was still being operated by its original successor corporation. In 1959, once Loew's had fully complied with the court's decrees, the new corporation, no longer affiliated with MGM at all, operated fewer than one hundred theatres. By 1978, Loew's had sold most of its original picture palaces and had transformed itself into a small chain of multiplexes—sixty theatres with 125 screens. The corporation's principal business had become hotels, insurance, and cigarette manufacturing. In the mid-1980s Loew's sold its theatre chain to Columbia Pictures Corporation.[15]

The former Paramount theatres were purchased by American Broadcasting Companies, Inc.—ABC television and radio—in 1953. In 1949, the year of the *Paramount* decree that effected the selling of the theatre chain, this was the largest of the then Hollywood-owned circuits with nearly fifteen hundred theatres. But after the specific divestitures ordered by the court, ABC's Paramount division had just over five hundred theatres by 1957. Thirteen years later, the circuit numbered slightly more than four hundred. But the Paramount chain still generated millions of dollars in revenues and should be credited with providing the monies that kept ABC television going in the hard times of the 1950s and 1960s.[16]

In the 1970s ABC was a successful television network and so sold—in two stages—its theatres to one of its former employees, Henry Plitt. In 1974, the northern division of 123 theatres was sold to Plitt for twenty-five million dollars. Four years later ABC exited the theatre business entirely, selling the remainder of the theatres (its southern division) to Plitt Theatres, Inc., for approximately fifty million dollars. By then theatre revenues of more than eight million dollars per year constituted only one-twentieth of ABC's total business.[17]

The successor to Twentieth Century-Fox's theatres, the National General Corporation, controlled nearly 550 theatres at the time of the 1951 divorcement and divestiture. Six years later, by court direction, the number had nearly been halved. The company struggled, trying to deal with the new world of film exhibition, but grew little. Thus it surprised no one that in 1973 National General, controlling some 240 theatres, was sold to its former employee, Ted Mann, who did well running a chain that concentrated activities in the Los Angeles area. In 1985 Mann sold his chain to Paramount. Two years later Paramount merged them into the Cineamerica chain it owned and operated with Warner Communication. Thus the former Fox theatres became the core of a nationwide chain that is controlled by Paramount and Warner Bros., long two of Fox's chief rivals. Ownership once again returned to major Hollywood moviemaking powers.[18]

The fates of the final two of the successor companies—RKO and Warner Bros.—would become intertwined. RKO Theatres had only 124 theatres at the time of its divorcement in 1948. The chain was sold twice, and when in 1967 Glen Alden Corporation surfaced as owner, only 32 theatres were left. Meanwhile, the former Warner Bros. Theatres became the core of the Stanley Warner Theatre chain, beginning with more than 400 theatres at the time of the 1951 consent decree. But under court directives that forced sales, the number that Stanley Warner controlled fell to 300 by 1957, to about 200 by 1960, and to approximately 150 by 1967. In 1967 Glen Alden merged what remained into RKO-Stanley Warner, but the chain hardly thrived, and yet another company, Cinerama, purchased them in the 1970s.[19]

THE DRIVE-IN THEATRE

Breakup of the Big Five circuits provided openings in the theatre business, and responding to suburbanization, new entrepreneurs built "auto-theatres" at the edges of all United States cities. Drive-ins had, in fact, been around in small numbers since the mid-1930s. Once the necessary building materials became available after the Second World War, thousands of drive-in theatres opened in paved-over farmer's fields. Sitting in parked cars, movie fans watched double and triple features on massive screens. The development of the drive-in was an American phenomenon because of the huge demand for auto-convenient movie exhibition by the millions of new suburbanites from coast to coast.[20]

But the origins of the drive-in were in the Great Depression. Indeed most credit the first drive-in from June 1933 in Camden, New Jersey, just across the river from Philadelphia. This initial effort contained seven semi-circular rows of parking spaces accommodating four hundred cars. Richard Hollingshead correctly anticipated that patrons "would enjoy movies where they could dress as they please, smoke, talk, and eat supper at the same time." Although he did not know it, he was describing the modern movie-watching experience.[21]

With little suburban growth during the 1930s, and none during the Second World War, the number of drive-ins in 1945 stood at less than twenty-five theatres. By the early 1950s about a quarter of box-office grosses was attributable to drive-ins. Indisputable was their growth in number from the handful after the war to more than eight hundred by 1948, to more than two thousand in 1950, and to more than four thousand six years later. One exhibitor noted in 1950 that "the exhibition plant has seen no such expansion since the rise of the nickelodeon."[22] (He forgot the picture palace of the 1920s, but the point was one still worth making.)

By 1952 the average attendance at drive-ins had grown to nearly four million patrons per week. One estimate had the public spending more at drive-ins, which had not existed a mere decade before, than at live theatre, opera, and professional and college football combined. By the early 1960s, drive-ins accommodated one out of every five movie viewers. For the first time, during one week in June 1956, more people attended drive-ins than went to traditional "hard-top" theatres. Moviegoing attendance peaked when the weather was the most pleasant out-of-doors, during the summer, a trend that has continued to the present day.[23]

By the mid-1950s the deluxe drive-in typically included space for more than two thousand cars, a cafeteria with snack bar, and a playground for the tots, the baby boomer children. Indeed by 1955 drive-ins sold about four times as much popcorn, candy, and soft drinks as the average indoor theatre. But many drive-ins offered far more, from pizza to barbecued turkeys, from french fries to onion rings. Carhops often traveled from car to car.

Some drive-ins took direct aim at the suburban family with an ever-growing number of young children by tendering free passes to parents of newborns up to three months of age. A New Orleans drive-in installed a special indoor theatre—equipped with 16mm—for children in high chairs. Many drive-ins passed out free milk. Children age twelve and below nearly always were admitted free. Exhibitors knew children could not drive themselves to movies under the stars.

But the additional services and treats went far beyond drawing families with small children. One Tennessee drive-in installed a while-you-wait laundry service. Others tendered shuffleboard, horseshoes, miniature golf, wading pools, baby bottle warmers, firework exhibitions, petting zoos, facilities for the family cat or dog, and even free pony rides.[24]

From a design standpoint, the "interior" of the drive-in represented an extension of the stars-and-clouds atmospheric theatres of John Eberson. The exterior presented a more perplexing problem for it functioned as a twenty-four-hour-a-day advertisement. Many drive-ins borrowed from strategies of the movie palace. Screen tower backs were enlivened with flamboyant neon displays. The Rodeo Drive-in in Tucson, Arizona, featured a cowgirl twirling a neon lasso. A moon floated across the sky to lure patrons into the New Moon Drive-in in Lake Charles, Louisiana. A giant cheerleader adorned the Campus Drive-in in San Diego, California. Appropriately the Florence Drive-in in Kentucky refigured the rear of the screen to resemble a colonial mansion. In general, neon signs lit up the evening sky, letting customers know that here was a movie show.[25]

But the drive-in, even with CinemaScope or Panavision, could not provide a permanent solution to serving suburban America or even in the long run a viable alternative to the basic comfort of the suburban television room. If the movie palace had been the grandest of arenas in which to enjoy watching films, the family car was not. What fantasies it held—for teens desperate for a little privacy or for a family hungry for a cheap night of fun—had little to do with the movie-viewing experience.

The lone attraction of the drive-in seemed to be that it was cheap entertainment for baby boom families wanting the occasional night out—two dollars a car for whoever could squeeze in. The slogan for Pacific Theatres' Southern California customers became: "Come as you are in the family car." Still, price, convenience, and informality could not clear the foggy windshield or improve the sounds from the tinny loudspeaker hooked to the car window, frequently falling off as someone climbed out to run to the restroom or buy more popcorn.[26]

Drive-ins had further potential problems that too often turned acute. Sound systems, however good, never proved reliable. Those drive-ins located north of the Mason-Dixon line, for instance, offered free in-car heaters for winter viewing. Noise and fuss from "wild teens" led to special zoning ordinances. As the drive-in craze hit its peak during the 1950s, some owners even built motels nearby so mom and dad could escape the kids. (In coming decades chain motel complexes would offer indoor pools, restaurants, video game parlors, and pay-per-view room service.)

Most important, the land at the edge of town in the early 1950s became by the 1970s too valuable to remain the site of a drive-in. Suburbanization continued unabated, and the acres required for a drive-in could be more profitably employed as space for a score of new homes. Even drive-ins offering inexpensive fun with triple features like *Nashville Girl, Blazing Stewardesses,* and *Dirty Mary, Crazy Larry* failed to make money. As the receipts of drive-ins ebbed, exhibitors sought some sort of longer-term and more permanent response to the suburbanization of America—to the television-in-every-household life. Ironically, they found it near their drive-in theatres.[27]

SHOPPING CENTER THEATRES

The new suburban theatre emerged from a radical transformation in American retailing, from the modern shopping center in the 1960s to the shopping mall in the 1970s. The motion picture industry followed, and thereafter came the familiar multiplex theatres and mall cinemas ubiquitous in the latter quarter of the twentieth century. By 1980, to most Americans going to the movies meant going to the mall. To the exhibition industry the movement to the mall completed the transition from the downtown-oriented, run-zone-clearance system.

Downtowns dominated the retailing scene in the United States as the first movie houses were built. Outlying centers grew at the intersections of transportation lines, but these centers were accessed by public transportation and surrounded by apartment buildings. Postwar suburbia was based on the automobile and the single-family dwelling. Thus, without these conditions, few shopping centers were built in the 1920s or 1930s: Upper Darby in Philadelphia (1927), Highland Park in Dallas (1931), and River Oaks in Houston (1937) offer rare examples.

The most famous shopping center of all was J. C. Nichols's Country Club Plaza, opened in 1925. This is usually considered the archetype for the modern, preplanned shopping center because it was auto-oriented, it had extensive homogeneous landscaping, and it offered acres of free parking. But the Great Depression and World War II called a halt to cloning these centers, and as of 1945, there were only eight shopping centers in the United States.[28]

The suburbanization of the late 1940s gave rise to the shopping center as we know it today. The number of shopping centers grew from a few hundred in 1950 to nearly three thousand in 1958 to more than seven thousand in 1963. Extraordinary growth took place in the 1960s and 1970s. By 1980 the United States had twenty-two thousand shopping centers. The bulk of retail trade moved to the edge of the city, even in New York City, Chicago, and San Francisco. New regional centers emerged at the intersections of the major new highways built with funds from the 1956 Federal Highway Act. All shopping centers had acres of parking; more and more were enclosed from the elements. Special services included piped-in soothing music, nurseries, band concerts, fashion shows, and, of course, movie theatres.[29]

The concept of the enclosed, climate-controlled shopping center or mall was first introduced at Minneapolis's Southdale Shopping Center in 1956. Malls required large tracts of land and multimillion dollar financing, so it took time and planning before many were built. The mall-building movement commenced in the late 1960s. Soon, the Paramus Mall in northern New Jersey, Tyson's Corner Shopping Center outside Washington, D.C., Northridge near Milwaukee, Sun Valley in Concord, California, and Woodfield Mall in Shaumburg, Illinois, near Chicago's O'Hare airport provided the shopping hubs for their respective communities. "Superregional" malls were intended to draw from several states, not simply the metropolitan area. These malls contained hundreds of stores, with at least four department store hubs, restaurants, hotels, ice skating rinks, and, of course, a handful of movie "screens."[30]

The idea of an enclosed place to shop and play became one of the defining icons of the 1970s. Whether it be the Olde Mistick Village in Mystic, Connecticut (a whole shopping center representing a New England village); plain-vanilla Towne East in Wichita, Kansas; or the self-proclaimed world's largest mall in Edmonton, Alberta, Canada, the mall was defined by its uniformity, not its differences. Everywhere a Sears, J. C. Penney, or Gimbels stood alongside a B. Dalton or Waldenbooks and a Limited clothing store. Malls are among the most meticulously planned structures of the late twentieth century, brightly lit to promote a safe image, enclosed to keep out the elements, and convenient to the highway to make a car trip seemingly effortless. Here was one-stop shopping superior to what any aging downtown could offer. Thus, by the late 1970s, reports claimed that Americans spent more time in shopping malls than anywhere outside their jobs or homes.[31]

The look of the shopping center was pure international style. Function dictated. Stylistic considerations were set aside. For the movie theatre this meant stripping all the art deco decoration that had made theatres of the 1930s and 1940s so attractive. Little survived. There was a necessary marquee to announce the films. The lobby consisted of a place to wait, a department store concession stand, and restrooms. The auditorium was a minimalist box with a screen at one end and seats in front. It was as if one had come into a picture palace and stripped it of all possible decoration.

The *Paramount* case opened up the market for new shopping mall theatres; the shopping center offered the locus for new power and profits. And from these initial operations would come new theatre chains, those that still dominate the final decade of the twentieth century. Consider the case of General Cinema, a company that grew to become one of the largest national chains of the 1970s. When Phillip Smith, the founder of General Cinema, built his first drive-in outside Detroit in 1935, the downtown movie palace was still king. Indeed in Detroit he faced the most powerful of theatre chains, the Paramount Publix circuit. A drive-in was the only way he could enter the market because Paramount did not care about this venue.

After the end of the Second World War, Paramount signed a consent decree in 1949, and suddenly Detroit was an open market for the movies. Smith, the pioneer drive-in exhibitor, had a step on the competition, and he prospered by building many drive-ins. By 1949 the chain had twenty-odd sites. Smith and his associates booked first-run films, admitting children free as long as their parents paid full fare. Smith sought to attract the suburban family, emphasizing vast concession stands enclosed within self-service, cafeteria style cinder-block buildings, which often included the projection booth and the manager's office. General Cinema takes credit for the introduction of the folding tray for cars, the extra-large-sized (and more profitable) drinking cups, the barbecue hamburger, the pizza pie craze, and even the wooden stirrer for coffee. Whether or not they were first does not matter. General Cinema prided itself on the concessions and the enormous profitability of this area of the business.[32]

Philip Smith died in 1961 just as the drive-in industry was reaching its zenith. His son, Richard Smith, a thirty-six-year-old Harvard-educated assistant to the president, went one step further than his father and moved General Cinema into the new suburban shopping centers being built across the United States. By the late 1960s the company owned nearly one hundred shopping center theatres, the largest such collection in the United States at the time.

In 1967, General Cinema, with shopping center theatres providing more than half its revenues, earned more than two million dollars in profits on more than forty million dollars in revenues. Little of the company's growth was due to purchases of existing theatres. In 1967 it had 150 theatres in twenty-six states. By 1970 the number of theatres topped 200, with more than 250 screens. By mid-decade of the 1970s the numbers had doubled, with the number of drive-ins declining from thirty-eight in 1966 to ten in 1978.[33]

As profits rose, General Cinema diversified in 1968 into the allied soft drink business. The company knew this business well from its concession stands, first in drive-ins and then in suburban shopping center theatres. General Cinema bought a Pepsi-Cola bottler with four plants in Florida and Ohio. Smith stated at the time that the young people of the country were the best movie customers as well as the best soft drink customers. Moreover he noted that the two businesses operated in similar fashion; both were decentralized. By the 1980s General Cinema would be one of the largest soft drink bottlers in the United States, far better known for this segment of the company than its theatres.[34]

But by the 1960s many more exhibitors than Richard Smith had come to realize that the shopping center cinema would soon define moviegoing. During the 1960s, with preplanned malls opening in record numbers around the United States, innovative theatre chains worked with shopping center developers to jam a half-dozen multiplexes of prefab, indistinguishable design into malls across the nation. With acres of free parking, and easy access by superhighways, the movies in the shopping center grew to accommodate the majority of the nation's indoor screens and became the locus of Hollywood's attentions.

No company symbolized the growth of the multiplex more than the Kansas City–based American Multi-Cinema. As the shopping center world expanded to take over retailing in the United States, it became possible to operate a half-dozen average indoor theatres of a few hundred seats each with one concession counter with two high-school students, one projectionist, and one manager who doubled as a ticket taker. Like the fast-food operations across the nation, labor in the movie theatre had been reduced to low-cost, untrained servers and button pushers. With costs so low, it only required a few "boffo" box-office films a year to guarantee a profitable venture.[35]

The multicinema concept certainly was not invented by American Multi-Cinema, but the company took it to its logical extension by opening hundreds of similar operations from coast to coast. In July 1963 the predecessor company to American Multi-Cinema opened the Parkway Twin, reputedly the nation's first twin screen theatre in a shopping center. Significantly, the Parkway, the first theatre constructed in the Kansas City area since the late 1930s, presented first-run films. Parkway One was four hundred seats; Parkway Two had three hundred seats. But they had a common ticket booth and a single concession stand. The Parkway cost around $400,000 and was seen from the beginning as a closely watched test case in the movie trade. It succeeded beyond all expectations.[36]

The Metro Plaza Complex, which American Multi-Cinema opened in December 1966 in Kansas City, was acclaimed as the world's first planned fourplex. The "first" sixplex came in January 1969 in Omaha, Nebraska. The "first" eightplex came in 1974 in the Omni International Complex in Atlanta with a total of 1,175 seats, nearly in sum the size of a picture palace. The Omni International Complex contained auditoria ranging from 200 to 100 seats; the complex shared a common concession stand, box office, and restrooms.[37]

It is not clear whether these actually were the first multiplexes of their size in the United States, but they were among the first. Durwood Enterprises, in business since 1920 (and as late as 1959 had but a dozen theatres, including a handful of drive-ins), had found a way to prosper in the movie theatre business. When company patriarch Edward Durwood died in 1960, Stanley, his son, expanded the company. In 1969 it became American Multi-Cinema, a name more descriptive of its operation. As shopping centers were being built, this company in the heart of the United States took advantage of the opening. It was not a franchise system; rather it owned and operated all its screens.[38]

Through the 1960s Stanley Durwood, the owner, with architect Stanley Staas (of Nearing and Staas), designed and built the Empire-4, the Midland-3, and the Brywood-6, all in the Kansas City area. American Multi-Cinema duplicated this experience throughout the nation so that by 1972 it owned more than 160 screens in nearly thirty cities in thirteen states. Durwood noted: "Four theatres [later six or more] enable us to provide a variety of entertainment in one location. We can present films for children, general audience, and adults, all at the same time." American Multi-Cinema would extend the concept so new complexes in the late 1970s handled a dozen or more screens.[39]

The corporate triumphs of General Cinema and American Multi-Cinema led them and two others to develop national chains of hundreds of theatres each. These were the successors to the chains of the Big Five. The difference lay not only in the size of the auditoria (about two hundred seats) and the number in any location (multiplexes of up to twenty screens), but in the fact that these chains did not concentrate in single regions of the country. They were spread the length and breadth of the United States. By the early 1980s, according to Variety, four dominated the United States.[40] First in line was General Cinema, with one thousand screens in some 350 locations in nearly all forty-eight continental states. Few of the original drive-ins were left by 1980; this was a multiplex operation pure and simple.

Second place was occupied by United Artists Communications, with slightly less than one thousand screens in nearly 350 locations, with one in twenty being drive-ins. United Artists Theatre Circuit, Inc., grew to become one of the largest theatre circuits in the nation, ironically more powerful than its more famous Hollywood producer of a similar name. United Artist Theatres had been a leader through the 1960s and 1970s in building multiscreen theatre complexes in suburban shopping centers.

United Artists had begun as an adjunct of Joseph M. Schenck's interest when he was head of the United Artists moviemaking company in the late 1920s and early 1930s. Although the two companies operated closely when Schenck was on top, he owned the theatre chain outright and kept it separate from the moviemaking company. Thus, when Schenck parted with United Artists to form Twentieth Century-Fox, he and his partners retained their hold on the theatre chain. United Artists Theatres represented a chain of top movie palaces in such cities as Detroit, Chicago, and Los Angeles and, in partnership with others (including Sid Grauman), in Pittsburgh, Baltimore, Louisville, and New York City and in Los Angeles with the famous Grauman's Chinese and Egyptian.[41]

Upon Schenck's death in 1961, Michael Naify of United California Theatres took charge, with Salah Hassanein as the top executive. With steady acquisition of mall cinemas and drive-ins the company grew into one of the industry giants, with major concentrations of screens in California, New York, and Texas. It also was an early entrant into the cable television business.[42]

The company remained an unknown player (save to industry insiders) until in 1986 Tele-Communications, Inc., the largest cable company in the United States, purchased control of United Artists Communications, later renamed United Artists Entertainment. Thus in the late 1980s one of the largest movie theatre chains in the United States, a dominant participant by any reckoning, was owned and operated by the largest cable television enterprise in the world. Indeed Tele-Communications, Inc. expanded United Artists so that by the close of the decade it controlled 2,700 screens in thirty-four states—some 10 percent of all the movie theatre outlets.[43]

Third in size was American Multi-Cinema, with nearly seven hundred screens in only 130 locations across the United States. None were drive-ins.

Fourth place was taken by Plitt Theatres, then based in Los Angeles, having moved from the former headquarters in Chicago, with six hundred screens in nearly three hundred sites. Again none were drive-ins. The history of this chain, the only one of the top four that had been associated with one of the former Hollywood chains of the 1930s and 1940s, has been discussed earlier. In the 1980s, Plitt sold most of its theatres to Cineplex Odeon; that history is treated in the following chapter.

No other chain had more than 350 screens. The smaller circuits, with a couple of hundred theatre screens, included the midwestern-based Commonwealth chain, the southern-based Martin Theatres, the Boston-based National Amusements, the Southern Cobb circuit, Kerasotes of Illinois, and Pacific of Southern California.

NEW-STYLE MOVIEGOING

What movie patrons received for their entertainment dollar in mall theatres, save locational centrality, proved as far from the golden days of the movie palace as one could imagine. A cluster of unadorned screening rooms offered only feature films and concession stands. Space was at a premium, and screens were often sandwiched in the basement. It was as if, having realized they had "lost" the battle with television and the living room, the movie theatre gave up all pretense of struggle at the level of architectural fantasy and the viewing experience and actually produced interiors with *less* to offer than at home.[44]

Taking their cues from the dominant trend in architecture, the new movie chains seemed to push the slogan of the international style to a new low of literalness: only function should dictate building form. The function, in the age of television, was clear: show blockbuster feature films and nothing else. Gone was the architectural ambience of the movie palace; any decoration on the sidewalls or around the screen was considered irrelevant. The movies had become self-service; ushers were rarely sighted. The idea of live entertainment plus movies was something only grandmother and grandfather talked about. Only air conditioning continued to add a measure of pleasure. The movies offered minimalist moviegoing.

Viewing conditions reached an all-time low. By shoehorning as many auditoria (rarely more than 250 seats each) as possible into a corner of a shopping center, projection booths rarely lined up with the screen. That is, one booth served two or more spaces, so the image invariably came out with one-half of the movie larger than the other (a phenomenon called "keystoning"). To further skimp on costs, theatre owners inadequately padded walls between auditoria. Thus, as one tried to catch a quiet moment of *Annie Hall* (1978), more often than not the rousing battle sounds of *Star Wars* (1977) poured through the wall, drowning out lines and distracting attention.

Ironically, part of the sound problem resulted from one of the few improvements in the viewing experience. Dolby sound systems attempted to outdo the television set by eliminating all extraneous noises. Six-foot speakers were placed in every corner of the auditorium and behind the screen. The sound in two-hundred-seat auditoria was so good that it could have only been properly accommodated in a three-thousand-seat movie palace of the 1920s.

Such sound systems, for a generation trained on home stereos and portable stereos, made music in the movies—or almost any noise—far superior to all but the best home stereo systems. A four-inch television speaker was simply no match. Now, finally, the images of Panavision were coupled with new, clear sound, ratchetted to levels that offered the audiences of the 1980s a new, totally enveloping technological experience.

Unfortunately, this improved sound seemed to encourage television-trained viewers to talk during the screening. Television had trained movie fans at home to accept constant conversation as part of the standard viewing experience. By the 1980s, talking and constant commotion had become the order of the movies in the mall.

Other interior amenities, once taken for granted by film fans, disappeared in the age of the multiplex. Waiting in the lobby of a movie palace designed to hold as many folks as could sit in the auditorium was a wonder-filled experience. In the multiplex, lines often spilled out into the mall, getting tangled with shoppers. What space there was in the lobby was invariably taken up by the popcorn stand, which in some cases also hawked tee-shirts and posters, while attendants made change for the video games tucked into any corner adaptable as a "profit center."

Going to the movies in many ways was reduced to the equivalent of standing in line at the K-Mart to buy a tire or lawn furniture. The physical viewing conditions of the multiplex, save its advantage of superior sound, were a throwback to the nickelodeon era. Indeed, a live projectionist was rarely in the booth to deal with a torn film. The social experience of vast crowds in an auditorium seating thousands had been fragmented into screening rooms typically holding no more than two hundred patrons—albeit noisy ones.

The suburbs and television had changed the nature of film in any number of ways, none more important than this fragmentation of viewing conditions. Indeed, to draw folks away from their television sets and living rooms, one needed a diverse set of attractions, all hoping to create *the* blockbuster. That is, so much money could be made on a single film, such as a *Star Wars* or *E. T.*, that fashioning blockbusters became the single purpose of the contemporary film industry. But no one could predict which film would become a blockbuster. So theatre owners tended to construct one large auditorium (about five hundred seats) surrounded by a half-dozen of one hundred seats each. Films were then tested in the smaller auditoria and only the true blockbusters moved into the more spacious auditorium.

The multiplex put an end to people over thirty-five going to the movies regularly. By the late 1970s there were too many sticky floors, too many noisy patrons, and too many films that seemed alike. Yet there was a reaction. Despite predictions of the demise of the movie theatre as a cinema experience, during the 1980s theatres got better. They also grew in number, making more screens available than existed in the peak period of the late 1940s. A new theatre circuit would not take advantage of openings provided by suburbanization or the *Paramount* case. Cineplex Odeon was set to offer a better moviegoing experience.

SIX

Contemporary Moviegoing

As we entered the final quarter of the twentieth century, many pundits predicted the end of moviegoing. Critics claimed fans would go out on occasion to watch their favorites, but the burgeoning set of television channels that showed movies at home would kill the theatrical movie show. The image of the movie fan would shift from the darkened theatre to the home equipped with cable television, a video cassette recorder, a satellite dish, and a giant fifty-inch screen. Pundits were again tempted by the argument of a substitution effect. They were proven wrong during the 1980s, as theatrical moviegoing remained a vital part of the movie exhibition scene in the United States.

This melancholy scenario of a stagnant theatre industry, with little growth and change because of television, never came true. In fact, through the final quarter of the twentieth century there has been renewed interest and more change in the movie theatre business than any time since the age of the picture palace. As of the close of the 1980s the number of "hardtop" screens in the United States stood at nearly twenty-three thousand, with fewer than two thousand drive-ins.[1]

Not surprisingly California in the late 1980s led the nation in the number of indoor and outdoor screens, followed by Texas, Florida, and New York. Yet as of 1988, it was surprising which cities had the most screens per capita: Grand Forks, North Dakota; Killeen-Temple, Texas; Des Moines, Iowa; Charlottesville, Virginia; and San Francisco led the way. New York City did not even make the top ten, but college towns did—for example, the aforementioned Charlottesville, Virginia, and Iowa City, Iowa. The old

Northeast led the way with the fewest screens per capita: Utica, New York; Scranton, Pennsylvania; Pittsfield, Massachusetts; Lowell, Massachusetts; and Niagara Falls, New York.[2]

In recent decades the film exhibition end of the industry has undergone a significant transformation. As the 1980s came to a close, there were more and more screens, but the number of tickets sold remained static at around one billion per year. That meant that each screen averaged fewer admissions. But with ever-rising ticket prices, there was more money to be fought over.

The battle, consequently, was for market share, and it was led by chains that controlled 40 percent of movie screens in the United States: United Artists Theatres, Cineplex Odeon, American Multi-Cinema, and General Cinema. Those four film exhibition giants of the 1980s prospered in the shopping mall. Indeed, with the construction of new multiplexes in the 1980s, by the end of the decade there existed more new screens available for movies than at any time since the 1940s. But they were multiplexes in malls and not traditional single-screen operations.[3]

And multiplex complexes have gotten bigger. On 20 May 1988, the Michigan-based Jacks Loeks circuit opened the Studio 28 in Grand Rapids. This complex of twenty screens (named 28 because of its route location) opened as a drive-in in 1948 but evolved into a gigantic multiplex. (The drive-in is now gone, its space offering some twenty acres of free parking.) Spread over 125,000 square feet of property, Studio 28 had been a twelve-screen operation since 1983. Management has a simple goal: "To handle *all* of the commercial films from *all* the major movie companies *on* their release dates." Therefore, they had a better chance of capturing and capitalizing on any blockbusters.

Studio 28 has nearly 6,000 seats, an average of 300 per screen. At the center is a 1,000-seat auditorium, which is the original enclosed cinema added to the adjacent drive-in. Screen sizes range from 45 feet diagonally in the smallest house (120 seats) to 120 feet in the 1,000-seat auditorium. The complex's lobby is fully 40,000 square feet with three traditional concession stands and a "Reel Sweets" bar offering fresh baked cookies, cinnamon rolls, ice cream, frozen Coca-Cola, pizza, and hot pretzels.[4]

The move to the multiplex cinema caused a fundamental change in release of films. As late as the early 1970s, Hollywood feature films were released regularly throughout the year, with the big hits saved for Christmas. In the world of the shopping mall, the summer, defined as beginning at Memorial Day and ending with the Labor Day weekend, denotes the season when the Hollywood majors unleash their hoped-for hits. Block-busters then can hang on for months thereafter, sometimes even a year. The summer movie season accounts for nearly 50 percent of the domestic box-office take. New films open almost daily throughout the summer as well as during the Christmas and Easter vacation periods to draw upon cinema's most reliable audience, teens out of school.[5]

THE RISE OF CINEPLEX ODEON

Yet all was not upbeat as the movie exhibition business entered the 1980s. The mall moviegoing experience left some complaining about sticky floors, closet-sized auditoria, sounds spilling from adjacent auditoria, and all too few creature comforts. One corporation, Cineplex Odeon, set out to change all that. During the 1980s this Canadian enterprise significantly altered the standards by which North Americans judged "going out to the movies." Following the economic logic of product differentiation, Cineplex Odeon's executives replaced the dominant mode of showing films in drab "cookie-cutter" multiplexes. Cineplex offered vast complexes of whimsical, postmodern "picture palaces" offering a seemingly boundless number of different cinematic choices to the public. And in the process, this company, founded in Toronto, Ontario, Canada, in 1979, became one of the giants of the movie business in North America.[6]

Cineplex (the name of the company comes from *cin*ema plus com*plex*) startled the world in 1979 with its original Toronto complex of eighteen different auditoria under one roof, generally agreed to be the largest multiplex at that time. In mid-April the complex opened in Toronto's new *downtown* billion-dollar Eaton Centre shopping complex. Its auditoria, ranging from 60 to 130 seats, had a central, computerized box office. The complex featured a combination of contemporary foreign films, second runs of recent Hollywood hits, and repertory favorites from the past.

A staff of fifty-eight ran the whole operation, including all projection equipment by way of an electronic remote control. The estimated cost of construction and start-up came to just over two million dollars. Cineplex was the brainchild of long-time Canadian film exhibitor Nat Taylor and a twenty-nine-year-old Canadian entertainment lawyer, Garth Drabinsky. Taylor claimed at the opening that "I'm happy to say that twins, triples, quartets, sixplexes and others have helped save the motion picture industry."[7]

Cineplex tried to go beyond the usual mall cinema complex. Screening times were staggered in fifteen-minute intervals; auditoria were color-coded to guide patrons to the attraction they had chosen. Showings were also sold on a reserved seat basis with advanced sale on the day of the show only. No tickets were sold after the start of the show in order to prevent latecomers from disturbing the audience. Patrons could purchase tickets, shop, and return in time for the movie. The lobby included rotating art exhibitions and a medium-sized cafe for snacks. During the Christmas and Easter school holidays, Cineplex set up a free baby-sitting service, enabling parents to buy tickets for their children for a Disney reissue, for example, while they were free to go shopping in the adjoining mall. The Eaton Centre, with three hundred stores, was easily accessed by subway and also had a massive adjacent parking garage. The whole complex was designed by Mandel Sprachman, a distinguished Canadian theatre architect.[8]

The first few months proved troublesome, but by the summer months and the first big hit, *The Marriage of Maria Braun* (1978), Taylor and Drabinsky began their plan to construct a chain across Canada. The plan was to take the model of the Toronto Cineplex to Vancouver, Calgary, Edmonton, Montreal, and Winnipeg. By late 1981 Cineplex was operating 124 screens in sixteen locations; the firm's box office had risen to twenty million dollars (Canadian). Yet Wall Street pundits saw only doom and gloom. For example, in 1981 Tony Hoffman of A. G. Becker, Inc. argued that Cineplex "seems to be going in exactly the wrong direction in terms of trends in the motion picture business." At that point all Wall Street observers believed that pay television and video discs would kill Cineplex. They would prove incorrect on both counts.[9]

Cineplex targeted its early audiences. Reggae movies were played to Toronto's Caribbean audience, and Yiddish movies aimed at the city's sizable Jewish population. But Cineplex did its best business in those early days by finding "move-overs," which were subrun product that still had an audience and could make money because of the low overhead in the Cineplex complexes. *Midnight Express* (1978) ran for sixty-eight weeks after its first run and *Life of Brian* (1979) even longer. Minimizing operating costs proved the key. At the Eaton Centre a maximum of three employees were needed to sell tickets for all two thousand seats; two projectionists handled all the platters. Since the products of the baby boom, patrons under thirty years old, made up three-quarters of the Cineplex audience, future expansion focused not only on major cities but also on college campus towns such as Peterborough with its Trent University.[10]

Taylor and Drabinsky concentrated on filling all possible seats. They reasoned that it was better to have a seventy-five-seat house turn away twenty-five than have one hundred patrons spread out in a four-hundred-seat auditorium. Drabinsky and Taylor employed an analogy to the airline industry. In 1981 Drabinsky pontificated: "When the movie starts or the plane takes off, the income from any empty seats is lost forever."[11]

After scouting several sites in the United States, Drabinsky and Taylor brought their Cineplex formula to Los Angeles; on 16 July of 1982 they opened a three-million-dollar, fourteen-screen Cineplex inside the chic new upright mall, the Beverly Center. At the time it provided the largest number of screens in any one complex in the United States. The fourteen screens (totaling more than sixteen hundred seats) were tucked away on the eighth floor; the largest auditorium held about two hundred persons, the smallest seventy-five. Three projectionists ran the fourteen projectors, which were all platter systems with a single continuous loop. The concession stand offered the usual popcorn, soft drinks, and candy but also bottled Perrier water and Cadbury's Fruit and Nut Bars. Since surveyed movie audiences pointed to "dirty theatres" as their biggest complaint, Cineplex hired extra cleaners; the company prided itself on a comfortable, albeit confined, atmosphere to watch films.[12]

With the Beverly Center, Cineplex began booking first-run Hollywood films and developed a formula: open a popular, well-advertised film on three or four of its screens, and then slowly cut back the number of auditoria as the popularity of the film waned. Maneuvering auditoria was perfected to a science. What Taylor and Drabinsky hoped, however, was for the opposite problem. If an *E.T.* or *Top Gun* came along, they would move it into a half-dozen of their largest auditoria, accommodate the surging crowds, and not miss a single possible customer. This defined the Beverly Center during the summer months, Christmas, and Easter. Other times of the year its screens were used for revivals and foreign films, making it a haven for the specialized film fan.[13]

Based on this success, Taylor and Drabinsky decided to make over Cineplex into one of the world's largest chains of movie houses. They wanted to be major players. Their initial move came in Canada. Two big companies had long dominated that market: the Famous Players chain owned directly by Paramount Pictures and the Odeon chain. In May of 1984 Cineplex bought Odeon's 164 sites—with 297 screens—for forty million Canadian dollars. The newly named Cineplex Odeon suddenly had 446 screens and ranked in the top-ten largest circuits in North America. *Variety* called it a case of "mighty Mouse swallowing an elephant."

Almost overnight, Drabinsky, who had for the previous two years battled the major Hollywood companies for rights to book films, had become one of the two major forces in the film exhibition sector within his own country. Famous Players still had slightly more screens (thirty-four more) in slightly more locations (twenty-seven more), but the yearly box-office take of the two companies was virtually equal.[14]

Drabinsky moved to keep expanding his company. In April 1985 Cineplex Odeon took over three theatres in posh neighborhoods of Los Angeles: the Fairfax (three screens with more than one thousand seats), the Gordon (one screen, nine hundred seats) and the Brentwood (two screens, nine hundred seats). The Gordon was extensively remodeled into the Cineplex Showcase Cinema. The house got a new 70mm screen and a new Dolby sound system. Many of the original 1938 art deco features were retained in the remodeling, including the classic ticket booth, the neon-encrusted marquee, and the ceiling murals in the auditorium. This gave Cineplex Odeon twenty screens in the best parts of movie-mad Los Angeles.[15]

Cineplex Odeon would startle the world in August 1985 by taking over the huge Plitt Theatre chain for $136 million. As noted in chapter 5, Plitt had in turn taken over the theatres spun from Paramount Pictures in the early 1950s. When Cineplex Odeon took over Plitt, it suddenly became the fourth largest theatre chain in the United States, with over six hundred screens in more than two hundred locations, with significant presence in Texas, Illinois, North Carolina, South Carolina, Minnesota, Florida, Utah, and Georgia. Plitt's largest concentrations of screens could be found in Texas, especially the Houston and Dallas-Fort Worth areas (with 158 screens), metropolitan Chicago (with 100-plus screens), and the state of Florida, particularly in Jacksonville, Orlando, and Tampa.[16]

Four months later yet another important deal came to pass. It was announced that MCA, parent company of Universal Studios, and Cineplex Odeon would build and jointly operate the world's largest cinema complex in the Universal Studio's parking lot in California. The estimated cost, ten million dollars, would be shared equally. For this the pair would construct eighteen screens, accommodating six thousand patrons. The deal seemed a natural at the time: "During the final stages of the discussions with respect to the Universal theatre complex, it became apparent that Cineplex Odeon and MCA (the world's leading producer of leisure time entertainment) held a common approach to the exhibition of motion pictures in North America."[17]

Drabinsky was now playing with the "Hollywood grown-ups." At the time, MCA was taking in two billion dollars in revenues annually. It was among the largest producers of movies and television shows as well as recorded music in the world. But Cineplex Odeon proved no shrinking violet. Cineplex Odeon then operated more than 1,100 movie screens in the United States and Canada, recently dislodging General Cinema from its long-held position as the industry's largest. The deal cleared the United States Department of Justice during the spring of 1986 and in the process set a precedent. The Reagan administration wanted to encourage mergers and thus would not invoke the *Paramount* decrees.[18]

Throughout this period of takeover and deal making, Cineplex Odeon continued to build new theatre complexes. In 1985 alone it opened or substantially refurbished eight complexes across Canada, from the Oakridge Centre in Vancouver to the vast West Edmonton Mall (reputed to be the world's largest) to home base in the Royale Theatre in Toronto. So much activity was underway that in 1985 Cineplex Odeon established its own in-house professional design firm, directed by architect David Mesbur and engineer Peter Kofman. Working closely with other Cineplex Odeon personnel, the design division assigned each geographical region of the vast chain its own theme and color. Carpets were custom designed and imported from England. The aim was to be "reminiscent of the movie palaces of the 1920s." Elegant inlaid marble flows through the lobbies in an art deco inspired design. The motifs of the carpets are carried forward in the ceilings, columns, and archways, with often a touch of neon.[19]

Cineplex Odeon commissioned new works of art for the lobby and waiting areas of its theatre complexes. In November 1984 Drabinsky hired David Burnett, then curator of contemporary Canadian art at the Art Gallery of Ontario, as a consultant. With his advice, Cineplex Odeon signed Alan Wood to paint *The Movies*, for the Oakridge Mall, Vancouver; Phil Richard to paint *Once Upon a Time*, for the Woodbine Centre in Toronto; Phil Darrah to paint *Western Projections*, for the West Edmonton Mall; and Doug Haynes to paint *Forty Heroes and Wide, Wide Fifties*, for the Westmount Shopping Centre, Edmonton. The designs ranged from high realism to color-field abstraction, from painting to mixed-media constructions.

Cineplex Odeon executives established criteria for its artistic commissions. First, the artists had to be from the area where the commission would hang. Second, they were chosen because of strong reputations. Third, they were asked to relate the theme to the movies in a broad fashion. Cineplex Odeon took pride in its Art Commission Program to foster Canadian art.[20]

In the mid-1980s the operations of Cineplex Odeon represented a throwback to the centralized control of the Big Five theatre circuits, which in turn had been modeled on the management techniques Sam Katz developed in Chicago. Drabinsky required weekly managers' reports and district supervisor's summaries; he even appeared for spot inspections. All information had to cross his massive desk at the Toronto headquarters. One centralized purchasing department acquired all supplies and services, including hundreds of pounds of popcorn each year. Each theatre's inventories were monitored weekly to eliminate shortages, overstocking, spoilage, and waste. Records were computerized; the aim was for optimal control to keep costs low and profits high.[21]

Concessions had moved to the heart of the new Cineplex Odeon. The company prided itself on its clear, attractive, and massive concession stands, which featured ultramodern equipment designed to eliminate all unnecessary procedures on the part of servers. This allowed the company to hire cheap, inexperienced workers at low wages along the lines of the fast-food industry. Through rigorous testing and experimentation, company experts evolved what they thought to be the ideal assortment of offerings. Cineplex Odeon pioneered selling Diet Coke in movie theatres; in 1984 it purchased Kernels Popcorn Limited to supply needed franchise food and also to manufacture the required bags of sugar-glazed gourmet popcorn. Several Cineplex Odeon complexes were set up with cafes in their lobbies, serving capuccino and espresso coffees, fine pastries, and upscale sandwiches.[22]

Through 1986 and into 1987 Cineplex Odeon purchased several smaller circuits to extend its control of several key markets. The Atlanta-based Septum Theatre circuit, with forty-eight screens in twelve locations, gave the company more power in the growing Sun Belt. In May of 1986 Cineplex Odeon acquired the Essaness Theatres Corporation, with forty-one screens in thirteen locations, all based in greater metropolitan Chicago. Now Cineplex Odeon controlled moviegoing in Chicago to an extent that rivaled Balaban & Katz sixty years earlier.[23]

On 31 July 1986 Cineplex Odeon announced it was moving in on New York City. The company agreed to acquire the RKO Century Warner Theatre chain. This was a major operator of theatres in the New York City area, and Cineplex Odeon payed nearly $180 million for the ninety-seven screens in forty-two locations in Manhattan, Queens, and Brooklyn, as well as Long Island, posh Westchester County, and northern New Jersey. There were flagship theatres in the prestigious Cinema Five Theatres located on Manhattan's East Side, for many years the center of movie releases in the largest movie market in the world. On 19 March 1987 Cineplex Odeon acquired all the outstanding shares of The Walter Reade Organization, Inc., which operated eleven screens in New York City for $32 million. This deal included the flagship Ziegfeld House in the heart of Times Square and made Cineplex the major player in the New York moviegoing market. Suddenly the upstart Drabinsky acquired the nickname "Grab"insky.[24]

The final piece of the Cineplex Odeon empire came through deals in metropolitan Washington, D.C. It was not the largest city in the United States (eighth largest in size as a metropolitan area), but it was one of the wealthiest per capita and one of the best moviegoing towns per capita in the world. Two days before the announcement of the RKO Century Warner deal, Cineplex Odeon told the world it had purchased the seventy-five screens of Neighborhood Theatres of Virginia for twenty-one million dollars. In December 1987 Drabinsky completed his domination of the Washington, D.C., market with a fifty-one-million-dollar buy out of Circle Theatres, an eighty-screen outfit.[25]

The climax to the company's growth came with the construction of the eighteenplex in the parking lot of Universal Studios in Southern California. The Universal Studios complex opened to massive crowds over the Fourth of July weekend in 1987. With eighteen theatres, ranging from two hundred to eight hundred seats, the 120,000-square-foot complex featured marble floors, vast glassed-in spaces, a floral garden, stars and clouds in the ceiling of the lobby, two football-field-length concession stands, and even balconies in two of the auditoria.

Pundits in Hollywood said Los Angeles was overbuilt in terms of the number of theatres. They claimed no one would drive all the way out to Universal City for a movie. They were wrong. The Universal Studios complex proved an instant success with some thirty-eight thousand patrons showing up during the first weekend alone. Set smack in the middle of a parking lot, the complex lacked adequate parking that first weekend! For top prices of six dollars one saw a wide selection of films in "clean and comfortable" surroundings, noted the *Los Angeles Times*. Schedules had to be readjusted that summer to handle the overflow traffic.[26]

On 26 March 1987 Cineplex Odeon filed to sell stock on the New York Stock Exchange. The initial sale of common stock was underwritten by Merrill Lynch Capital Markets and Allen & Company. The gross proceeds generated forty million dollars. On 14 May 1987, the journey begun nearly ten years before ended as Cineplex Odeon stock was listed on the New York Stock Exchange for the first time.[27]

During the final month of 1986 Cineplex Odeon's holdings rose to more than fifteen hundred screens in nearly five hundred locations. Most had come through the acquisition of the Plitt chain. But during 1986, even outside the Plitt deal, Cineplex Odeon had taken over nearly four hundred new screens in the best movie markets in North America. At the end of 1986 the company employed 12,500 workers in twenty American states and six Canadian provinces, the largest employer in the movie business. By the end of 1987 the eight-year-old company's statistics were nothing less than staggering. Cineplex Odeon controlled nearly five hundred multiplexes in twenty states plus the District of Columbia and six Canadian provinces.[28]

But as its buying spree reached its acme, those who followed the string of successes of Cineplex Odeon noticed cracks in the armor of this new movie theatre giant. Drabinsky, insiders for once correctly argued, too often seemed willing to pay far above prevailing prices for multiplexes he considered vital to his vision of a national chain. Where would the additional revenues and profits come from to cover this ever accumulating debt?

At times corporate difficulties spilled over from the pages of the business section into the world of entertainment news. In late 1987 and into the first months of 1988, Cineplex Odeon began to raise prices to meet expenses. Moviegoers balked but soon realized they had no choice. Seemingly overnight in community after community across North America Cineplex Odeon had become the only game in town. In New York City during the prime Christmas moviegoing season of 1987 Cineplex Odeon increased ticket prices from six to seven dollars. New York mayor Edward Koch proposed a boycott. Cineplex Odeon claimed that the increase was necessary, and with no alternative, fans soon agreed to pay the necessary amount.[29]

But Cineplex Odeon's problems always came back to the nearly two-thirds of a billion dollars debt it had taken on during the heady days of expansion. Wall Street wanted to make sure Cineplex Odeon could and would meet its payments. So did partner MCA. From the heights of 1987 the fall was far and fast. By the spring of 1989 Cineplex Odeon, innovator of so much during the remarkable past ten years, was up for grabs.[30]

Early in December 1989, an eight-month struggle ended as Garth Drabinsky resigned, after failing to take full control of Cineplex Odeon. Unable to raise the necessary millions to buy Cineplex Odeon outright, Drabinsky had to settle for a multimillion-dollar buyout and control of Toronto's Pantages Theatre. MCA had forced him out. Allen Karp, who had headed the chain's North American theatres, was named president.

The plan, as the company entered the 1990s, was to sell off subsidiaries and concentrate on making money from movie theatres located in the top markets. Moving into the 1990s, Cineplex did begin to sell theatres, but with the continued backing of MCA, few doubted that Cineplex Odeon would continue to be a power in the movie business well into the next century.[31]

Whatever its future in the 1990s and beyond, during the 1980s Cineplex Odeon introduced significant long-run changes in the movie theatre business in the United States and Canada. This company should be praised for bringing elegance back to North American moviegoing. Before Cineplex Odeon the multiplex cinemagoing experience was characterized by drab, ill-kept auditoria lacking any architectural elegance. The feature film provided the sole attraction. People went to the movies in spite of the theatre, not because of it.

Cineplex Odeon's complexes were carefully crafted, postmodern Xanadus of pleasure, reminding film buffs of the glories of the 1920s movie palace era. Auditoria were built with the creature comforts of the patrons in mind and maintained by a staff with pride in being part of the fastest-growing theatre chain in the world. Costs of operation were kept low through large-scale operations of ten to twenty auditoria under one roof. Concession areas the size of basketball arenas only made the experience of going out to the movies that much more special.

In the 1980s, when many thought the movie theatre business would be killed off by cable television and home video, Drabinsky and company taught the world that architectural splendor, careful monitoring of costs, a multitude of films, and restaurant-like concession stands with trendy snack foods, all in convenient locations, would lure millions away from their television sets to the fun of going out to the movies.

Cineplex Odeon tapped into the market of grown-up baby boomers. As those Americans born between 1945 and 1964 reached moviegoing age, the question became: Would they continue to go out to the movies past age thirty or abandon the theatre for the television set? Doomsayers predicted no movie theatres would be necessary by 1990 as baby boomers stayed home. Cineplex Odeon proved them wrong. During the economic expansion of the 1980s, young upwardly mobile Americans continued to go to the movie house. Although the baby boomers had by and large graduated from college by the late 1980s, they kept on going to the movies. Their relatively smaller families and relatively greater disposable incomes (than their parents, who had to spread monies over more children) enabled them to keep up the moviegoing habit. Cineplex Odeon pioneered business strategies to draw this very group. By 1990 Cineplex Odeon's methods had become common industry practice.[32]

MOVIEGOING—AS IT MOVES TOWARD THE TWENTIETH CENTURY

In the 1990s, the movie theatre business is thriving.[33] It remains a core social activity for the young. Fully seven out of eight of the admissions in recent years come from persons under forty, with the bulk of these being teens, half of whom tell researchers they go to the movies at least once a month. Yet an urban-based, college-educated audience of adults into their forties will go out to see such features as *Shirley Valentine* and *Driving Miss Daisy*, both released in 1989. This trend toward moviegoing at all ages should maintain itself well into the twenty-first century.[34]

The major chains discussed in the previous chapter remained in command of the marketplace: United Artists Theatres, Cineplex Odeon (owner of Plitt), American Multi-Cinema, and General Cinema. These were the Big Four; they control more than fourteen hundred screens each, with United Artists' total well in excess of twenty-five hundred. But there were others: Number 5, Loew's, owned by Columbia Pictures of Hollywood, with more than eight hundred screens; Number 6, Carmike of Columbus, Georgia, a power in the South, with more than seven hundred screens; Number 7, Hoyts of Boston, controlled by an Australian corporation, with five hundred screens in ten states plus Australia and New Zealand; and Number 8, National Amusements of Dedham, Massachusetts, a subsidiary of the giant media conglomerate, Viacom, Inc., and owner of more than five hundred screens.[35]

In large and small chains alike, concession stands continued to produce millions of dollars in profits. And no wonder: in Washington, D.C., as the decade of the 1980s ended, a bucket of popcorn ranged in price from a dollar and a half to nearly four dollars. The soft drink was a little cheaper (nearly three dollars for an extralarge cup) and candy came in as a relative bargain at only a dollar or two. Action films sold the most popcorn; contemplative films the least. Popcorn remained tops in consumption, providing nearly half the sales. The consumption of popcorn in the United States increased by 50 percent through the 1980s.[36]

Contrary to the doomsayers, moviegoing will remain a province of college-educated folks. This is not only because of film courses taught at most universities in the United States; it was the case even before television converted movies from a mass media into a specialized medium. Indeed in any "average" multiplex, the typical patron has three times the chance of sitting next to someone who graduated from college as a high school dropout. Skeptics who assert that the average Hollywood movie is aimed at the mind of a twelve-year-old must have a bright preteen in mind. The average patron also drove to a multiplex not too far from his or her suburban home and attended a recently released feature based on advice from a friend or an advertisement seen on television.[37]

The final decade of the twentieth century signaled a crest in the construction of multiplexes, climaxing a thirty-year growth phase. Yet the state of the moviegoing audience in the American theatres was healthier than it had been since the early 1950s. In the 1990s theatre owners will seek ways to differentiate their offerings from videotapes. Paradoxically, more new movie screens have been constructed in the 1980s than anytime since the 1920s. This is so because consumers want easy access to the latest in first-run Hollywood product. Summer blockbusters open in two thousand screens at one time, a figure likely to increase to more than three thousand screens before the end of the twentieth century.[38]

As entrepreneurs look to the future, change must always be considered. It is hard to predict how moviegoing will differ in the year 2000, but consider several examples.

Architectural Design

Theatre chains will continue to look for new styles of architectural design for theatre complexes while containing costs of construction and operation. Melissa MacDonald and Tina Warner of Corporate Design, a firm based in the Dallas suburb of Irving, Texas, seek to make the average multiplex cinema interior more elegant. Working with the United Artists theatre chain they are helping refurbish complexes with new carpeting, concession stands, wall coverings, and bathroom tiles. These two designers strive to add excitement to the moviegoing experience. Like their competitors at Cineplex Odeon, Corporate Design will seek a postmodern look for movie spaces in the future. Some go further and propose that we return to mini–movie palaces.[39]

The New Concession Stand

Entrepreneurs will continue to look for new temptations to sell at concession stands. Barney Danzinsky, heir to the fortune of Giant Food Corporation, began a business to sell "healthy snacks" to movie patrons accustomed to popcorn, candy, and soft drinks. His goal was to convince folks to munch on blue corn chips, honey-wheat pretzels with sesame seeds, and cookies sweetened with fruit juices. In the fall of 1989 the twenty-one-year-old named his upstart company Movie Munchies. While most chains were properly skeptical, a local Washington, D.C., chain, KB Theatres, and the giant American Multi-Cinema agreed to a trial study during the final two months of the 1980s. Sales were slow in the beginning, but the ever-hopeful entrepreneur remained confident. Whatever turns out, Danzinsky properly recognizes the high-income, discretionary nature of the modern theatrical moviegoing experience. The movie theatre is the place for a fun night out, not the day-to-day fare that the modern television set serves.[40]

More promising on the concession front was the 1988 debut of the self-service concession stand. In a high-tech twist, patrons can serve themselves the usual soft drinks, popcorn, and candy as well as hot snacks including hot dogs and nachos. One cashier handles all sales, and so this Coca-Cola innovation (in conjunction with United Artists Theatres) cuts down waiting in line, reduces labor costs, and does not require training—every three months or so—a new crew of concession-stand workers. The various Cinema 'N' Drafthouses, Cinema Plus, and Cinema and Pizza function as restaurants with movies as an added attraction.[41]

Discount Theatres

During the 1980s "dollar" cinema houses arose, presenting feature films after their successful first-runs, preferably (but not always) before the video came out. The key was the concession stand. The rental for the films was low, but the 300 such "dollar houses" across the United States, led by the Dallas-based Cinemark, which ran more than 150 houses itself, organized in September of 1989 into their own trade association, the National Association of Discount Theatres. The theatrical experience was still a draw, even when the home video was in two-thirds of America's home. Dollar houses, looked down on by many, seem to indicate that the theatrical film business will be with us well into the next century.[42]

Advertising

Presenting advertisements along with feature films in theatres will probably continue. Service and product providers from many industries seek to sell their wares in front of a captive, educated, relatively well-off, young adult audience. Screenvision Cinema Network is an example. Research shows that an audience will sit through up to five advertisements as part of the slot that used to be filled with only cartoons and advertisements for forthcoming movies (or trailers). In 1990 the theatre services charged about a 25 percent premium versus what an ad would cost on prime-time television. The alternative is cinema billboards, where ten-second slides are shown before the movie begins. As of the end of the 1980s only one theatre in three did *not* show some sort of advertisement, whether a thirty-second filmed spot or a ten-second slide, although the Disney Company had begun to prod theatre owners not to use advertisements with Disney films.[43]

Catering to Families

In 1989 Cineamerica's Mann Theatres of California opened two soundproof viewing rooms for children (and parents) in a new eightplex in Laguna Niguel, California. The glass-fronted rooms are fashioned at the rear of two four-hundred-seat auditoria, where parents can sit with young children and not worry about disturbing other patrons. These rooms had been used in the 1930s but were abandoned. Each room holds six strollers.[44]

Audience Behavior

Possibly change will come in the behavior of theatrical film audiences. Can audiences be quiet? During the age of the movie palace this was not a problem. The theatres had been kept so dark during the show and so controlled by ushers that quiet was the expected decorum. But that all changed with the double-feature cinema of the 1930s, when seating oneself became the norm. Noise in theatres has become so much of an issue that in 1989 in Washington, D.C.'s renovated Union Station the American Multi-Cinema complex issued a policy of "two shushes and you're history." Noisy patrons are issued one warning and then asked to leave without a refund. Ushers make the rounds of the nine auditoria every twenty minutes. One complaint and the usher remains through the rest of the program. Managers open half the shows with a simple welcome and a reminder of the "no talking" policy. Also offered is a policy prohibiting children younger than age six after six in the evening, except for G-rated films. American Multi-Cinema advertises its services for adult movie lovers.[45]

New theatre designs, concessions, pricing schemes, revenue sources, and conditions for viewing all should serve to differentiate the moviegoing experience in theatre complexes as the industry moves through the 1990s. Coupled with fresh locations and films, the institution of the movie theatre will make money, and thus it will continue to be with us well into the foreseeable future. Entrepreneurs will adapt to the changing face of America's cities, to demographic transformations, and to other transfigurations of the economy and society.

Theatrical movie screenings aimed at the masses have not always provided the only vehicle to make profits. Throughout the history of the movie show there have been theatres that served specialized functions. The institution of the profit-seeking but alternative theatre is the subject of Part II of *Shared Pleasures*.

1. *The Loew's Vaudeville Theatre in Kansas City*

2. *An open-air movie theatre (upper right). Taken in 1904 at the Fourth of July Celebration in Huron, South Dakota*

3. *An early big-city nickelodeon*

4. *A small-town nickelodeon, the Lounge Theatre in Huron, South Dakota*

5. *The interior of one of the first true movie palaces in the United States, Balaban & Katz's Central Park Theatre in Chicago*

6.   Part of the vast interior of Balaban & Katz's Uptown Theatre, in the fashionable north side of Chicago

7. *The crowd streaming to New York's Roxy Theatre in 1941*

8.   *The stage of the New York Paramount—note the lighted organ to the left*

9. *The massive lobby of the Fox Theatre in St. Louis, October 1933*

10. *The exterior of one of the first air conditioned theatres in the world, Balaban &*
Katz's massive 4,000-seat Tivoli

11.   The crowd listening to the organist at New York's Paramount Theatre

12.   *Advertising air conditioning at Chicago's Roosevelt Theatre*

13. A *"dream palace"* in the middle of Brooklyn, New York

14. *Inside the most beautiful theatre in America's playground for the rich, the Paramount in Palm Beach, Florida*

15.   *The movies in small-town America—the opening of Cecil B. DeMille's* King of Kings *in South Bend, Indiana*

16.   *The end of the movie palace; the Paramount in Des Moines, Iowa, is destroyed*

PART II

Alternative Operations

SEVEN

Specialized Theatres

Not all theatres were movie palaces or multiplexes, programming strictly Hollywood fare. The history laid out so far has dealt with an industry aimed at the mass audience; the next three chapters deal with specialized movie theatres. Such theatres came in all variations. Consider the craze for cartoons in 1934 set off by the popularity of Disney's shorts in Technicolor. To exploit that interest, in October 1934 Robert Schirmer opened an all-cartoon theatre, a half block off Times Square, modeled after one he had seen in France. He leased a legitimate theatre and during the first week drew nearly one thousand admirers of Mickey Mouse and friends at a quarter for an hour show. The theatre was short lived but proved that with the right material a specialized theatre could make money.[1]

Or consider how one keen exhibitor was able to fashion a specialized niche in the world's largest movie market. Arthur Mayer made the Rialto, formerly a staid movie palace on New York's Times Square, into a mecca for fans of action movies of the 1930s. In 1936 he took what had opened as Oscar Hammerstein's Victoria Theatre, a pioneering vaudeville house, and made it into a cinema "action" house, catering almost exclusively to a male audience. Mayer's theatre was accessible directly by subway and was amidst the hustle and bustle of New York City's "main street" on the mend from the Great Depression. Sailors and soldiers on leave and young males from all five boroughs made this specialized theatre profitable.[2]

Arthur Mayer ballyhooed promotion was reminiscent of a carnival or burlesque theatre. He recalled that when he booked the film *The Jungle Princess* (1936), he had his assistants recreate a tropical jungle in the lobby full of mangy lions, moth-eaten tigers, stuffed birds, and an occasional live monkey swinging from a papier-mâché tree. With sound effects (lions roaring, tigers bellowing) this was a new form of the stage show but hardly with the class and dignity his former boss, Sam Katz, would have approved.

Mayer would change the titles of the "B" films he would play. *A Son Comes Home* (1936) became *From Gangland a Son Comes Home*. Newspaper advertisements screamed: "How would you like to see your own burial?" Popular hits were brought back and teamed, such as *Dracula* (1931) and *Frankenstein* (1931). There were few imitators, but in the 1930s and 1940s there were few cities like New York. Mayer, a well-known figure in the film exhibition business from his days as one of Sam Katz's innumerable assistants at Paramount-Publix, became a celebrated figure for proving that picture palace style film exhibition was not the only way to run a major movie theatre.[3]

Rural America in the 1940s had its equivalent specialized cinemas: small-town movie houses that showed only westerns. Typically the oldest (and often smallest theatre) in downtown would be reopened to an all-western program, featuring first-run "B" westerns from the factories of Republic, Monogram, and Columbia plus comedy shorts and newsreels. The show would change frequently (often Monday, Wednesday, and Friday) and the theatre would be redecorated in a western motif.[4]

Indeed after the Second World War, as the western genre reached its peak of production and popularity, there was even a chain of such houses in California. Known as the Hitching Post Theatres, the first was built where Gower Gulch meets Hollywood Boulevard. By 1947 the chain had reached five, including one in Beverly Hills. While these theatres appealed largely to children, they also were populated by adults. The owners claimed director Mervyn LeRoy and actor Randolph Scott were frequent habitués. But it was the kids, at five shows on Saturdays and Sundays, who filled the seats—and their stomachs with candy and popcorn.[5]

The children's matinee constituted the most common specialized use of traditional theatre. The movement for this children's programming actually began in the 1910s, as women's clubs pushed exhibitors to present "clean" shows. Thus in 1916 the Collegiate Alumnae Association of Kansas City, Missouri, persuaded a house manager to allow their committee to book films one night per week. Thus for a short time they took over a night at the Alamo in one of the better sections of the city to appeal to upper-income audiences. In the era of the talkies, Parent-Teacher Associations and YWCAs regularly rented theatres, particularly on Saturday mornings, when children were out of school, to present uplifting, family programs. Theatre owners agreed because they wanted to appease the women's groups, and they felt that if children attended, the parent was sure to follow.[6]

But the film industry's real push to Saturday matinees began in the 1930s. The cause was the Great Depression. If normal methods would not keep marginal theatres open, then operators tried something new. Through women's clubs and schools, parents were notified of clubs with names like "Junior Matinees" or "Junior Motion Picture Clubs." Theatres had special Saturday morning and early afternoon shows for these groups (before 4 P.M., which was considered, especially in the summer, a weak box-office time). The low-priced neighborhood houses could pack them in.

In the fall of 1931 this movement began to spread across the country. The Fox West Coast Theatre, cooperating with the Better Films Association and the local Parent-Teachers Association, established a series of "Mickey Mouse Clubs" throughout the state of Washington. All theatres played the same program: a Mickey Mouse cartoon, a serial, and a feature chosen for children aged six to sixteen, all for a dime.

The programs opened with a community sing and a salute to the flag. They elected officers and had a creed:

I will be a square shooter in my home, in school, on the playgrounds, or wherever I may be. I will be truthful and honorable and strive always to make myself a better and more useful little citizen. I will respect my elders, help the aged, the helpless and children smaller than myself. In short, *I will be a good American!*

In Riverside, California, children had the "Krazy Kat Klub." Each child had a club pin, and during the summer there were picnics, a pet parade, prizes, and a fund for tubercular children in a local sanitarium. Chicago's Balaban & Katz had a "Radio Patrol" tie-in with a local newspaper with a cartoon strip of the same name. Eighteen theatres around the city had chapters and held meetings at Saturday matinees. The Glendale, California, Alexander Theatre organized a "Brownie Club" and increased Saturday revenues by 100 percent. All appealed to the "uplifters" in the community, concerned there was not enough in the way of wholesome movies for children.[7]

THEATRES FOR THE RICH

By the late 1920s going to the movies had become so popular that all classes of Americans clamored to see them. Even the wealthy embraced the movies. Expectedly, the rich preferred special theatres that catered only to "their own." The extravagant built in-home screening rooms. But in rare instances there were theatres built with the rich in mind. For example, the Paramount Theatre in the exclusive vacation hideaway of Palm Beach, Florida, opened in January 1927. The Palm Beach Paramount presented films only from January through April, the vacation season. The Paramount's tickets were by subscription only—at one thousand dollars![8]

In the 1920s Palm Beach was *the* winter playground for America's rich. So respectable and popular had the movie show become by the mid-1920s that the Palm Beach Paramount was personally financed by E. F. Hutton, the founder of the noted Wall Street investment house. The Palm Beach Paramount thrived in its exclusive policy as long as the resort remained an exclusive retreat. No middle-class folks or blacks were allowed in and no "B" films or low-budget westerns were shown. But during the 1950s, once Palm Beach (and southern Florida) was opened up through easy air travel, the Palm Beach Paramount reverted to standard first-run movie house programming and prices.[9]

Movie theatres for the rich also could be found on luxury trains and fancy ocean liners. On trains, fifty-seat theatres in air conditioned dining cars provided viewing conditions similar to screening rooms. Projection was done with 16 mm equipment. The seven-day ocean liner trip across the Atlantic had always had live entertainment for its top-paying passengers; in the 1920s luxury liners added movie theatres. Remember, this was an era when everyone who could afford it crossed the ocean by boat, with segmentation by income class.

By the 1930s first-run screenings were a regular attraction in the luxury-class passage across the Atlantic. For example, the liner *Queen Elizabeth I* carried two thousand passengers in the 1940s and contained a cinema—modern and tasteful in an art deco design—that held 380 viewers. This floating movie house was principally for the first-class passengers; those traveling cabin classes used it only during restricted hours. This cinema was, of course, air conditioned. The cinema on the S.S. *France* held more than six hundred patrons.[10]

The 1960s equivalent of movies with luxury travel was screenings on lengthy airplane flights. This has long been an upscale audience and was even more so in the days before airline deregulation. In the early 1980s, three-quarters of the captured audience was traveling on business, with median income twice the national average; most owned their own homes; and two-thirds were managers or professionals. Although there had been experiments in showing movies in flight beginning as early as 1925, regular long-distance air travel by jet provided the showcase. TWA's screening of *By Love Possessed*, on a regular New York to Los Angeles flight on 19 July 1961, for first-class passengers only, signaled the beginning of movies in the air.

The company in charge of the project for TWA, Inflight Motion Pictures, Inc., would become the dominant firm in the business. The initial show went over so well that it was quickly set up as a regular operation. The Hollywood companies loved Inflight because of the millions of dollars in extra rentals it created. Union projectionists were originally employed to change films at terminals, but soon flight personnel handled the operations. Special events were arranged. For example, in 1970 Paramount held a world premiere of *The Adventurers* on TWA's inaugural 747 flight from New York to Los Angeles to two members of the press, assorted executives, and stars Ernest Borgnine and Leigh Taylor-Young. By the early 1980s video had replaced 16 mm for in-plane screenings.[11]

NEWSREEL THEATRES

Throughout the 1930s and 1940s, only one type of specialized theatre was able to survive within the matrix of Big-Five-owned theatres: newsreel houses. Three chains developed in that era, which specialized in showing newsreels in theatres found only in America's largest cities. Newsreel theatres provided Americans with visual images of many of the most important news events through the Great Depression and the Second World War. Well-educated adults kept these newsreel theatres flourishing until they went out of business with the advent of regular television news broadcasts.

The newsreel played a significant role in the American cinema, beginning during the late 1910s. They formed an important genre throughout the golden age of Hollywood. The coming of sound gave a particular boost to interest in newsreels. Since radio news was only beginning, and newspapers most often provided the sole source of news, motion picture newsreel scenes from around the world became a significant attraction within the commercial American film industry. The newsreel was Hollywood's bow to reality cinema.

But the Hollywood-produced newsreel had to entertain as well as in-

142 / Part II. Alternative Operations

form. The typical newsreel was a ten-minute potpourri of recorded news footage, released twice a week to theatres from 1911 on. It was a photographic news source that inherited the mantle of the actualities that had been so popular with vaudeville audiences in the first decade of the history of cinema.

Indeed the newsreel—a regular compilation of news footage organized as stories as in a magazine—began in France and England. It was the French Pathé Company that introduced the idea into the United States as part of the service of the Motion Picture Patents Company. In 1911 came Pathé's Weekly, a reel of international news scenes issued every Tuesday. The model was straightforward enough. Pathé strived to produce an illustrated magazine on film. Promised (and delivered) were shots of Queen Victoria from London, marching troops in France and Germany, navy battleships, horse shows, sailing regattas, sporting events, funerals of the famous, and the exploits of early aviators. These subjects would become standard items, and they proved so popular that Pathé increased issues frequently to twice a week.

By 1914 Pathé had thirty-seven full-time photographers in North America alone. Around the world the company maintained sixty offices, from which enough footage for two features was sent to its headquarters in Jersey City, New Jersey, to be edited into one gripping reel. Demand was so strong that in 1914 Pathé introduced a daily newsreel service.

Pathé was hardly alone in the newsreel market during the 1910s. Vitagraph had long produced actualities, but not until 1911 did it begin a regular news service. The Vitagraph Monthly of Current Events focused on the sensational, even to the point of buying old locomotive engines and staging crashes for the "news"reel cameras. In 1913 the newspaper organization of the wide-flung Hearst newspaper chain began its own newsreel with the inauguration of President Woodrow Wilson. Joining in 1914 with William Selig, the movie producer, the Hearst-Selig News Pictorial became a twice-a-week offering. Hearst provided the reporters to hunt out exclusives; Selig provided the experience in the moviemaking field. But in 1918, after several other attempted alliances, Hearst ventured on its own and became the International Newsreel. Hearst released its product first through Universal and then Metro-Goldwyn-Mayer.

Slowly during the 1910s a number of major services appeared to rival Pathé and International. In 1913 Universal introduced The Universal Animated Weekly. During the fall of 1919 came Fox News issued on Wednesdays and Saturdays. To offset the advantages Hearst had, Fox affiliated with the United News Service. By 1922 Fox had more than a thousand photographers around the world. Scoops included unique footage of Mexican revolutionary Pancho Villa, exclusives of the Ku Klux Klan, and aerial shots of the Grand Canyon.

A significant boost to interest in newsreels came with America's entry into the First World War. In April 1917 the United States declared war on Germany, and American photographers covering the war were replaced by the United States Army Signal Corps. The administration of President Woodrow Wilson wanted to sell the American public on the war, and so it produced all the battle footage for the newsreel companies. It even edited and compiled a final product to be sent out. Unflattering footage was simply shelved. But what film made it through was well received and created more interest in newsreels.

In the mid-1920s, just before the introduction of sound, the newsreel was standard fare in nearly every theatre in the country. Picture palaces, in fact, subscribed to a number of services (including local ones) and compiled their own "topical specials." Theatres paid according to their size, with picture palaces getting exclusive first-runs and then passing down the footage to lower-rung competitors. The newsreel followed the tenets of classical Hollywood continuity storytelling, although its "characters" were selected from public popularity. It was best to get exclusive footage of the important, interesting actions of a major popular figure such as Charles Lindbergh, Babe Ruth, or the king and queen of England. From the 1920s on newsreels were shown in nearly all theatres as part of the package that constituted the show. Outside events of historical importance, such as interest in the Second World War, made theatres hubs in their communities.[12]

The coming of sound made newsreels even more popular. During those first months of 1928, at the height of the innovation of sound, the Fox Film Company provided Warner Bros. its sole competition. Fox had adapted a version of AT&T's pioneering technology to record sound on film. (In the 1930s sound on film would become the industry standard.) In 1926 William Fox signed with AT&T to use this technology to improve his company's newsreel business. Like the brothers Warner, William Fox did not believe there was a future for feature-length talkies, but the veteran showman reasoned that the public might prefer newsreels with sound to silent offerings.

William Fox never made a better business decision in his career. Fox Film engineers labored to integrate sound on film with accepted silent newsreel techniques. On the final day of April 1927, five months before the opening of *The Jazz Singer*, Fox Film presented its first sound newsreels at the ornate, five-thousand seat Roxy Theatre located at the crossroads of the entertainment world on Times Square. Less than a month later, Fox stumbled across the publicity coup of the decade when it presented the only footage *with sound* of the takeoff and triumphant return of aviator Charles Lindbergh.

The enormous popularity of Lindbergh's hop across the Atlantic undoubtedly contributed handily to Fox's success with sound newsreels. Fox newsreel photographers soon spread to all parts of the globe in search of stories "with a voice." Theatre owners queued up to have their houses wired simply to be able to show Fox Movietone newsreels. To movie fans of the day, Movietone newsreels offered as big an attraction as any movie star.

In the end, Fox Film would adroitly use the coming of sound to boost its newsreel (retitled Fox Movietone News) into first place among the various competitors. Its success was so great that it forced the largest movie company in the world at the time, Paramount, to begin its own news service rather than buy from Fox. With Paramount's introduction (guaranteed a success because of its ownership of so many important movie theatres), by 1930 the following companies produced and distributed newsreels: Pathé (distributing through RKO), Hearst (through MGM), Universal, Paramount, and Fox. There were also a number of local services that operated on the fringe of the industry.[13]

These national services were supplemented by local newsreels that consisted of silent footage of key local events, crafted into gripping stories through the use of a simple voice-over narration. Local newsreel production existed throughout the United States, usually sponsored by a newspaper to gain an edge on the competition. Such local newsreel operations were sporadic in delivery, but they did provide more material from which theatre owners could choose.[14]

With the coming of the various outlets for newsreels with sound emerged the possibility for a theatre that specialized in presenting *only* newsreels. Enough newsreels were made each week, and all that was needed were locations in which the street traffic was large enough that a "new" audience would be available all day long. That obvious location was New York City, and in particular Times Square, the heart of the city in the late 1920s.

Thus on 2 November 1929, as part of its growing chain of theatres, Fox Film opened the Embassy Theatre at Broadway and Forty-sixth Street and devoted it exclusively to newsreels. The theatre opened with standing-room-only crowds and promised eleven shows per day. There were only six hundred seats, but crowds reached nearly seven thousand per day in toto. The political problems of Europe and the feats of aviators were the star attractions. The Embassy opened at ten in the morning, ran newsreels until midnight, and cost the patron only a quarter per hour show.[15]

In the heyday of the newsreel theatre during the 1930s and 1940s fully one-third of them could be found in Manhattan; few other cities could support more than one. The idea of a theatre devoted to newsreels seems lost in the past of film history. Sources suggest that such a theatre showing early Pathé newsreels existed in Paris during the first decade of the twentieth century. Some claim the first was in London in 1906. Indeed it seems there were many more in London than ever were present in the United States. They were principally located near and within rail stations. By the mid-1930s London had fourteen, Paris eight, and fewer in other capitals. Europeans seemed more interested in the events in flux around them.[16]

Such rail theatres existed in the United States as well. In 1937 one opened opposite track seventeen on the Upper level of Grand Central Station. The 250-seat house was an independent operation, costing about $125,000 to construct. Air conditioned, the walls of the auditorium were of simple knotted pine, splayed out every third board to eliminate echoes. The theatre was open from nine in the morning until midnight and existed for passengers who were waiting for trains or had missed one.[17]

CHAINS OF NEWSREEL THEATRES

Like their much larger feature film cousins, newsreel theatres realized economies of scale and joined together as chains. Indeed save for the period in the Second World War, when the newsreel theatre business prospered, nearly all such theatres were part of one of three chains: Trans-Lux, Newsreel Theatres, Inc., and Telenews.

Trans-Lux

The Trans-Lux Corporation started with a simple idea: to project information (slides, movies, etc.) in a lighted room. The solution was a rear projector plus a finely wrought translucent screen, and in 1923 the Trans-Lux Daylight Picture Screen Corporation was set up to exploit the first movie screen with silk as a base. Its initial breakthrough in the marketplace was as a "Movie Ticker" at the New York Stock Exchange. Thus, instead of swarming to glimpse at a ticker tape, one could sit and watch as the tape ran by. In the rapid expansion of the stock markets of the 1920s, this proved to be a very successful product.[18]

Looking for a new market, Trans-Lux thought about the movie business, also an expanding industry in the 1920s. But it needed much larger screens (fifteen by twenty feet) with no seams. After a year and half of experimentation, Trans-Lux developed a marketable, commercial-sized theatre screen with no seams. It also developed a special wide-angle lens so the distance between the screen and projector was equal to one to one: this meant the projector would not have to be more than twenty feet behind the screen for a twenty-foot-wide screen, which was average for a small theatre.

Trans-Lux needed a way to innovate this new invention for projection. It had arranged a demonstration of a short film at the opening of the Roxy Theatre on 11 March 1927 as a novelty, but the International Alliance of Theatrical and Stage Employees and Moving Picture Operators, the projectionist's union, demanded extra operators, and the novelty was dropped in favor of normal programming of the day.

In June of 1930, just as the boom of theatre building of the 1920s was coming to a close, Trans-Lux and RKO, a major owner of movie houses in New York City, established the Trans-Lux Movies Corporation as equal partners. (Both contributed a quarter of a million dollars.) Courtland Smith, operations manager of RKO's theatres, knew the drawing power of the newsreel, for it was he who masterminded the innovation of newsreels with sound when he was with Fox Film Company. Smith became the head of the new Trans-Lux Movie Company.[19]

On 14 March 1931 the Trans-Lux Newsreel Theatre opened in New York, managed by Smith. The theatre, at Fifty-eighth and Madison avenues, soon rivaled the Embassy in popularity. Close to sixty thousand patrons attended the first month alone. The theatre offered several advantages to its upper middle-class customers in this posh section of New York. Its seats were larger than normal, with more leg room and wider aisles than the average theatre of the day. This made movement without ushers the rule, since customers could come and go without bothering each other.[20]

For the company, the costs of such an operation were low. Since rear projection eliminated the need for an elaborate balcony projection booth, the needed space requirements were minimal. Indeed Trans-Lux could create a "theatre" in almost any small, one-story commercial building. If the investment at one site did not work out, it could easily be dismantled and moved, making it easy to cut any losses.

Trans-Lux employed a number of innovations to keep costs down. They used rented space, few seats (160), rear screen projection, and turnstile admittance, and they kept house lights high to minimize the need for ushers. Prices were low (twenty-five cents), and a complete show ran for about forty-five minutes. The shows ran continuously, as in the early days of vaudeville, from ten in the morning (Sundays and holidays: noon to midnight). One could come in at any point and then leave when the show had run full cycle. The audiences were committed shoppers and "news junkies" who wanted to see and hear the news rather than simply read the newspaper.

Programs at the Trans-Lux were changed twice a week (every Wednesday and Saturday) and offered compilations of the best material from Pathé, Universal, Fox-Movietone, MGM-Hearst, and Paramount services. There were daily inserts of major breaking stories, shipped cross town from the headquarters of the newsreel services in Manhattan. They also offered popular short subjects, cartoons, and occasional two-reel revivals of a Charlie Chaplin or Buster Keaton silent short, now with a sound track added. Indeed during 1933 Disney's *The Three Little Pigs* ran a record-breaking eight weeks. The shows lasted under an hour and ran continuously from morning to midnight. For a time there was even talk of running newsreels twenty-four hours per day.[21]

A Trans-Lux Theatre was meant to symbolize the modern and attract a higher class of trade. The art deco design was black and silver on the outside and gray and blue inside. The auditorium was twenty-eight feet wide and seventy-two feet deep and had a ceiling height of a little more than eleven feet. The *New Yorker* magazine called it "most refined," and a ticket only costs a quarter. The Trans-Lux became such a symbol of upper-class New York that Peter Arno made use of it in a *New Yorker* cartoon—a group of well-heeled matrons and elderly gentlemen in tuxedos asking their friends: "Come along. We're going to the Trans-Lux to hiss Roosevelt."

During the early 1930s Trans-Lux opened new "theatres" at Forty-ninth and Broadway and moved the Fifty-eighth Street house to a theatre of 450 seats at Sixtieth and Madison. By 1934 Trans-Lux had opened two newsreel theatres in Brooklyn and one in Philadelphia. By 1937 there was another at Fifty-second and Lexington and at Eighty-fifth and Madison, plus one more in New York City and another Washington, D.C.[22]

The Washington, D.C., Trans-Lux Theatre offers an exemplary case study. This theatre was one of the most elegant buildings in the nation's capital. The theatre and its accompanying office building swept down the block like an ocean liner, with a prismatic mirror tower of aluminum and a finish of etched glass. At one end colored lights shone through at night; the other end bore an RCA radio transmitter insignia, complete with thunderbolt. Architect Thomas Lamb, who had designed many of the most famous movie palaces of the 1920s, added an illuminated glass tower over the marquee. At least one critic has called it "among the finest art deco buildings in Washington."[23]

Four blocks from the White House in the heart of Washington's downtown, the Trans-Lux was designed to show newsreels with an assortment of comedy shorts, travelogues, and other shorts thrown in when the news was slow. The block-long building extended two stories on the theatre side and three stories in the rear. A dozen commercial shops (People's Drug Store, a shoe store, insurance agents, etc.) occupied the first floor, while on the second was the National Broadcasting Company radio studio for WRC, its locally owned and operated station. (Indeed old timers tell of radio newsmen sneaking down to cool off in the theatre and then, inspired by the newsreels of foreign events, vastly embellishing their radio news broadcasts.) This made sense since RKO was at that point linked to NBC radio as part of the RCA Corporation.

The patron paid a quarter for a program that lasted about an hour in a six-hundred-seat auditorium. Adjacent to the screen were carved and painted murals depicting various scenes of sport (polo, rodeo, skiing, and boxing) and military scenes of battleships and tanks. The theatre had well-spaced, blue leather chairs, indirect lighting, rear screen projection, wall-to-wall carpeting, and air conditioning. The balcony contained a glass-enclosed box that was frequently used to seat private parties; in the afternoon, mothers could leave their infants there in the care of a nurse. The translucent screen material allowed daylight projection of movies, so lights were kept up and patrons, used to ushers in the big movie palaces, seated themselves. The screen cost some fifty thousand dollars and used an extreme wide-angle lens to minimize the throw distance behind the stage. Patrons found no traditional ticket sellers or ticket takers; after they paid a quarter, they entered through an automatic turnstile.

Washington's Trans-Lux opened on 13 March 1937 as a special benefit for the local Children's Hospital. Although President Roosevelt was not there, much of his administration was. Vice-President James Nance Garner pulled the switch to begin the first show. In the audience were the wives of the secretary of the navy, Mrs. Claude Swanson, the wife of the secretary of state, Mrs. Cordell Hull, and a smattering of members of the House of Representatives, Senators, and other dignitaries. The program for this first week was typical. It included as subjects the Spanish Civil War, President Roosevelt's fireside chat on the future of the Supreme Court, the Academy Award Ceremonies from Hollywood, loggers in cypress swamps in Louisiana, the British Royal family meeting ordinary Americans, the boxing Golden Gloves finals, horse racing, baseball spring training, and a travelogue about Yellowstone National Park.[24]

The Great Depression hit all movie theatre operations hard, but Trans-Lux survived and indeed in 1936 began to turn a profit. But by then RKO had ceased to be a major player in the operations, struggling to survive a corporate reorganization of its own. The theatres in Times Square and at Sixtieth and Madison consistently made money, while others did not. Thus by 1938 Trans-Lux began to show subsequent-run films in some of its theatres, for example, at the Eighty-fifth and Madison theatre and at the Fifty-second and Lexington theatre. But Trans-Lux prospered in the newsreel theatre business during the Second World War. Postwar suburbanization and other associated socioeconomic changes forced the company into the subsequent-run feature film business. By 1949 only the Times Square Trans-Lux was still showing newsreels, and indeed it survived into the 1960s as the sole remaining newsreel theatre in the United States, a reminder of what Times Square had once been.[25]

Newsreel Theatres, Inc.

Newsreel Theatres, Inc. traces its origins to the opening of the first newsreel theatre—the Embassy in Times Square. Within two years of the premiere at the Embassy, Fox Film ran into significant financial problems as a movie company, and by 1933 it was closing theatres. (The company would eventually merge into the smaller Twentieth Century Company, and as Twentieth Century-Fox, after May 1935, it prospered.) As part of its retrenchment, Fox closed the Embassy in December 1933 and looked to sell the house. In its heyday the theatre drew as many as thirty thousand admissions per week, but business had slipped badly as the Great Depression took more and more money from the pockets of middle-class Americans.[26]

W. French Githens had been an editor for Fox Movietone News and later managing editor for Pathé News. He and his partner, Carter Wood, Jr., organized Newsreel Theatres, Inc. to reopen the Embassy in 1935. As an independent, the Embassy then took the best of the newsreels from all the major companies and spliced them together to draw the largest audiences.

They also controlled the Newsreel Theatre in Newark. In the mid-1930s they expanded into three more houses in New York, the first at Seventy-second and Broadway.[27]

Newsreel Theatres, Inc. even used a form of the star system to attract audiences. They found that Franklin D. Roosevelt was their best draw. Millions of Democrats lived in New York City and Newark, New Jersey, and they loved to see their champion giving a speech or opening a new dam. But Franklin Roosevelt was also the president Republicans loved to hate. These prosperous moviegoers also came to the Embassy and other theatres to hiss and boo—as they did at the Trans-Lux as well. Foreign leaders also played the role of "the man you love to hate," but they never became full-fledged villains until America's entry in World War II had become inevitable.[28]

In 1939 the company carved out space in Rockefeller Center to open the 450-seat Newsreel Theatre. The theatre, designed by noted architect John Eberson, was tiny next to the nearby Radio City Music Hall (sixty-two hundred seats) and the Center Theatre (thirty-six hundred seats). This elaborate operation had a doorman stationed in front of stainless steel doors of modern design. Normal projection was used, with a tiny lobby and lounge done in the same design of the Music Hall. This was another elegant operation. In 1949 Newsreel Theatres, Inc. had five theatres, four in New York City and one across the water in Newark, New Jersey.

Telenews

The Telenews chain began in the late 1930s. A syndicate of New York business leaders, led by Alfred A. Burger and Herbert L. Sheftel, announced this direct creation of Wall Street in 1938. Paul Felix Warburg, a millionaire banker, and Angier Biddle Duke, of the tobacco fortune, supplied the money; former reporter and then real estate speculator Burger handled the day-to-day operations. There were only eight newsreel theatres operating at the time of the announcement; still, this was a business enterprise that did not emerge from the brains within the movie industry (as had Newsreel Theatres, Inc.) or from the technology side (as had Trans-Lux). This was a pure and simple investment.

The worst part of the Great Depression was over, and the time seemed right for investment. Telenews signed up consultants, who formulated mathematical models to find the optimal location in San Francisco with the "heaviest traffic flow in the city over a period of eighteen hours a day."

The chain would be vertically integrated, with its own photographers, editors, sound technicians, and distribution staff. The Telenews Theatre, the first in San Francisco, opened on 1 September 1939 with a program of newsreels on the German invasion of Poland.[29]

The second Telenews house was in Chicago, and gradually for the next twenty years Telenews operated a chain of thirteen newsreel theatres across the United States and even set up an operation to create newsreels for its houses as well as other independent theatre operators. Its theatres were built from the west to the east, with operations from San Francisco to Denver to Detriot to Cleveland, with one operation in New York.[30]

A representative house was the Telenews in Chicago, opened 23 December 1939. The company remodeled the venerable Capitol Building, a store and office complex at the busy corner of State and Randolph streets, to bring the nation's second largest city its first newsreel theatre. With lounges in the basement, the auditorium (of four hundred, with two hundred seats in the balcony), lobby, projection booth, usher's dressing room, and film storage room occupied two floors. Open from nine in the morning until midnight for twenty-five cents, it had a turnstile entrance but used ushers. This was a more expensive operation than the Trans-Lux theatres. The theatre did fantastic business during the boom period of the Second World War.[31]

Telenews expanded at the right time when it opened theatres in 1941. This can best be seen in the example of the Telenews in Seattle. It opened the very month of the attack on Pearl Harbor, in what had been the Capital Theatre. The films of the war were of special interest to this port city. Sports newsreels, running from noon to midnight, also proved attractive to an overwhelmingly male audience at twenty-five cents a show.

The case of the Telenews Theatre in Milwaukee, Wisconsin, illustrates the troubles the chain would have at the end. This was a medium-sized city in the United States with a population in 1940 of nearly six hundred thousand people. With the boom of the war Alfred Burger saw Milwaukee as a market he could enter. He announced the "newsreel theatre of tomorrow," complete with a radio-television lounge. Construction of the theatre began in March 1946, as soon as the necessary materials could be acquired, and would cost a mere seventy-five thousand dollars. Unfortunately materials in the days immediately after World War II were hard to come by, and the new theatre was not ready until 11 July 1947, two years after it was announced and a year after the construction permit was issued. By completion the cost rose to nearly a quarter of a million dollars.

The Friday opening ceremony was widely covered. Milwaukee's Telenews would operate from ten in the morning until midnight, with each show lasting about an hour and covering up to forty subjects. Burger, a former *New York Times* reporter, was there for the grand opening with one thousand invited guests. (The theatre actually held only 480 persons.) Milwaukee's first television station came on line six months later, and although WTMJ-TV would be the city's lone television station until 1953, the Telenews still suffered. Thus, few were surprised when on 28 May 1952, less than five years after its opening, the Telenews switched to an art house mode, showing the British comedy *The Man in the White Suit* (1951). When asked by the local newspaper, the management had a simple answer; even art movies would make more money than newsreels in Milwaukee.[32]

THE RISE AND FALL OF THE NEWSREEL THEATRE

The golden age of the newsreel theatre came during the Second World War. As members of the armed forces moved around the United States, and workers filled their pockets with wages from defense factories, downtown America prospered. Millions stopped by a Telenews or Trans-Lux to catch up on the latest news from the front. The draw of the latest war footage was so strong that many chose not to sit through a feature and so the newsreel theatre became the theatre of choice. Who knows how many Americans sought out a newsreel theatre in hopes of catching a glimpse of a friend or relative in action. Newsreel-only houses were opened in Seattle, Portland, Oregon, Buffalo, Denver, Minneapolis, Sacramento, Los Angeles, and Houston. Nearly all were conversions of former second-run theatres, located downtown.[33]

The desire for instant information brought the newsreel theatres a direct tie to radio and press sources. Most newsreel theatres subscribed to a news ticker, and the management would stop the show to read the latest war news. Then the items would be posted in the lobby. Trans-Lux theatres had radio news broadcast through loudspeakers set up in the auditorium. One theatre in Louisville, which opened in 1942, called the Scoop, was directly allied to a radio studio. The newsreel theatre companies began to advertise widely in newspapers, announcing their superior coverage of the war news. So when footage from a battle that the Allies had won arrived, it was advertised in the morning paper and then premiered that day.[34]

By America's formal entry into the war in December 1941, there were some twenty-five newsreel theatres in operation in America's biggest cities.

Radio provided the real sounds of the war through on-the-spot coverage, but the newsreels offered much more: moving pictures as well as sounds. Telenews and Newsreel Theatres, Inc. formed a subsidiary, Newsreel Productions, to produce special attractions for their customers. One operator commented: "Our patrons like pictures of actual combat filmed under fire. This is evidenced by the increased business we enjoy when we are able to present such scenes instead of ordinary war clips." [35]

But the era of prosperity was short-lived. By 1950 many newsreel theatres had closed down across the nation. Two events caused the closings. The first was the coming of suburbanization. What this meant for the newsreel theatres, even in New York City, was a lack of the critical mass necessary to turn over the audience hourly. But suburbs were not the sole culprit. In time television stations also drew away vital street traffic, and initial versions of television news simply offered viewers televised newsreels. On 5 August 1945 NBC premiered the weekly "NBC Tele-Newsreel" with film supplied by various newsreel companies.

Beginning in 1947 the various newsreel companies were setting up separate organizations to serve television broadcasters. When R. J. Reynolds combined with Fox Movietone News to produce a ten-minute daily "newsreel" on NBC called "Camel Newsreel Theatre," it was clear that early television viewers could and would get significant doses of newsreels at home. In 1948 Telenews even began to supply film to television stations. A year later CBS was receiving the bulk of its footage from Telenews. Telenews still released newsreel films on the same day to theatres. At first no one seemed to mind, and Telenews certainly liked the extra monies. [36]

Thus, few who paid close attention to the newsreel business were surprised when on 6 November 1949, twenty years to the week of its opening, the Embassy Theatre on Times Square switched to feature films. An estimated eleven million patrons had been accommodated in that 550-seat house. The management blamed one specific television event: sports highlights. In the past the theatre had done a phenomenal business as fans streamed in to see the highlights of the local games filmed that very afternoon. By 1949, though, many were broadcast on television in the New York City area. W. French Githens, manager of the Embassy, noted: "Business has been slipping since the end of the war. Lately we've been doing only about 60 percent of our old volume." [37] By the summer of 1949 Trans-Lux had only one operating newsreel house. As the 1950s passed the newsreel theatre would quickly become a distant memory, the relic of another age. [38]

It should not be forgotten that newsreel theatres offered a generation of

America's city dwellers specialized theatres that gave them doses of what would become later so familiar as television news. The pictorial impact, the star celebrities, and the entertainment fluff were all there. Television news, as we know it today, surely had its antecedents in radio news, but its most immediate predecessor was the hour programs offered to millions around the clock in America's newsreel theatres that survived—and during World War II prospered—through the 1930s and 1940s, the golden age of Hollywood.

EIGHT

Movie Theatres for Black Americans

African-Americans frequently were not welcome in mainstream movie theatres prior to 1965. Often they had to go to special theatres or make do with special accommodations. In particular, to be black in the South in the United States during the early part of the twentieth century was to fall victim daily to white oppression.[1] "Jim Crow" laws throughout the South, during the first two thirds of the twentieth century, caused nothing less than total humiliation.[2] Blacks from the North were stunned. Paul Warfield, the noted football player, recalled the first time he visited relatives in Tennessee in the early 1950s at age eleven: "Inside a movie theater, striding toward the front row center, [I] had [my] arm gently tugged by a cousin. We must go this way, I was told. Upstairs."[3]

The South of the early days of the movies was a legally segregated society. Various court decisions of the 1880s limited the scope of the Fourteenth and Fifteenth amendments of the United States Constitution. In addition, state statutes deemed separation of race a reasonable regulation, well within the power of the state. In Virginia, for example, the law held that races must be segregated. If not the law then segregation was the accepted custom.[4]

The law that would govern the movie theatre came from legal precedents concerning live theatre. Massachusetts passed a civil rights law that prohibited discrimination on account of race in a public place of amusement or theatre immediately after the Civil War; most other states followed. By 1875 there were similar laws even in the Deep South. But in that year a counteroffensive commensed. In Delaware a law was passed that relieved theatre owners from the obligation to present shows to "any person whose presence

155

there would be offensive to the major parts of his spectators or patrons, and thereby ruin his business." The crushing blow came in 1883, when the United States Supreme Court approved the possibility of any state passing legislation to permit theatre owners to exclude blacks. Southern state legislatures and governors moved quickly, and so when the movie shows were opened laws governing theatre attendence were on the books.[5]

In some southern states, theatre owners could decide where a patron must sit even though the common law held that once a ticket was sold that patron could decide where he or she wanted to sit as long as the seat was available. In Virginia, for example, the law was as follows:

> It shall be the duty of any person . . . operating . . . [a] motion picture show . . . which is attended by both black and colored persons, to separate the white and the colored races, and to set apart and designate in each . . . theatre, certain seats therein to be occupied by colored persons.

The penalty for failure was a misdemeanor, carrying fines of one hundred to five hundred dollars. Patrons who failed to obey the instructions of the theatre manager could also be fined.

In the states of the North and West with civil rights laws on the books, a person was entitled to any available seat. Thus most black houses in northern cities were segregated by residential patterns of use, while in the South local custom dictated specified customs to follow or the theatre would not be permitted to open. Door attendants and ushers were instructed to insist that blacks sit in certain parts of the theatre.[6]

THE COMING OF SEGREGATED MOVIE SHOWS

From the early days of the nickelodeon era exhibitors in the South grappled with legal and social segregation. One Louisiana exhibitor wrote the leading motion picture trade paper, *Moving Picture World*, in 1910 to ask the best way to project films while keeping blacks on one side of the theatre and whites on the other. He contemplated the use of back projection so a wall could be erected between the races. Probably he settled for a small barrier and the effective use of social pressure. *Moving Picture World*'s editors answered: "Of, course, we in the North are not so keen on race prejudice, but we should imagine that reserving one side for each race would be sufficient segregation."[7]

Robert C. Allen, in a fine case study of the theatres of Durham, North Carolina, has laid out the typical exhibition practices of a southern town.[8] This small North Carolina community (only twenty-six thousand citizens in 1910) was one-third black at the turn of the century, with a section of a segregated six-block separate downtown called "Hayti." As with the rest of the largely rural South, movies came to Durham in 1907 and 1908—for white citizens. It was not until 1913 that a theatre was opened for blacks. The original Durham movie theatres either excluded blacks altogether or only allowed them in the balcony. Once available, blacks began attending their "own" theatres (nearly always owned by whites).

Gregory Waller examined the moviegoing experience for blacks in Lexington, Kentucky, in particular, and the nation as a whole, for the same period.[9] He found that black-oriented theatres were quite common by 1909, with one estimate placing the national total at more than one hundred (with ten thousand theatres then operating in the United States). But many of these first theatres were black-oriented vaudeville theatres that presented motion pictures.

In general, by the mid-1920s, there seemed to be three basic ways that blacks were kept "in their place" within the movie theatres of the South. Durham illustrates the first example. Blacks lived in one part of town and attended "their own" theatre(s). This segregation by neighborhood was common in larger towns and was nearly always the operating principle in northern cities. These black-only houses ranked at the bottom of the moviegoing scale. Invariably, they occupied the final runs in the area, showing films seen months, sometimes years, earlier by white audiences in the same city. Owners of black-only theatres never expected to make much money with these operations and so invested little in their upkeep and equipment.[10]

In the North where segregation was against the law, discrimination still existed. In mixed neighborhoods one could sit more or less where one wanted, but a black patron had to be careful not to cause any commotion. One former moviegoer remembered it this way: "My mother made sure my appearance and that of my sisters was acceptable. We were told not to argue with the ticket taker, who would act as if he didn't want us there, and we weren't to say anything uncalled for."[11]

There were two other possibilities for blacks when there were a limited number of theatres in a southern community. One was segregation by time. Blacks could use "white" theatres but at specific times of the day (usually after the theatre had closed for whites) or, less commonly, on special days of the week. For example, community after community had midnight shows for blacks, after whites had finished "their" screenings throughout the day and evening.[12]

But such were the laws and customs of the day that even midnight shows could cause problems. In one case in High Point, North Carolina, a manager of a white theatre arranged for a black midnight show. Two thousand blacks showed up, but so did fourteen whites. The law stated that the fourteen whites were able to claim the several hundred seats in the auditorium, while the manager scrambled to rent other theatres to accommodate the overflow of the balcony. By bicycling reels, the manager was able to present the show to all but not in the original, single theatre that could have held everyone but for "Jim Crow" laws.[13]

A second tool of theatrical segregation was to provide a separate entrance leading to a blacks-only balcony. In South Carolina these segregated balconies were called "buzzard roosts" or "peanut galleries." Whites went in through the front doors and had their choice of orchestra seats. Waller found two examples of this segregation format in Lexington, Kentucky, in the 1910s.[14]

Another possibility was far rarer; a curtain or some other type of barrier was set up down the center aisle of a theatre with no balcony. Blacks sat on one side, whites on the other.[15]

However it was accomplished, millions remember the experience of the segregated moviegoing experience. One longtime resident of Nashville, Tennessee, summed up the humiliation this way: "[The ticket taker] would say in a voice above a whisper, 'Upstairs for you,' as if we didn't know their rules. Once we reached the Jim Crow section we ran the risk of not finding a seat in this area, which was very limited. We could see very well there were many seats in other parts of the theatre."[16]

By the 1920s, as the movies were being fully enveloped into the dominant social pattern of white America, the pattern of segregation was firmly established. Even the nicest black theatres paled beside the magnificent picture palaces. White residents of Nashville, Tennessee, could attend the Loew's Palace (two thousand seats) and the Loew's State (twenty-five hundred seats); black Nashvillians had to settle for white hand-me-downs. The Bijou in Nashville was white-owned and originally intended for white touring shows, but "since the Negro business section has been drawn toward this locality, the [Bijou] theatre became more properly adapted for a first class movie picture house for Negroes." The Bijou booked Hollywood films, focusing on westerns and serials. Its silent film orchestra was small; more often than not a pipe organ was played to keep costs down. Still the thousand-seat house had once been first class, with a balcony and even boxes. Blacks had to make do, for in a city with nearly fifty thousand black citizens there were only four black theatres, and the Bijou was certainly the best.[17]

Not surprisingly, one study found that in the late 1920s, at the height of the popularity of the movies in America, southern cities had fewer motion picture theatres catering to blacks than simple population needs would have indicated. In Atlanta, for example, with a population of ninety thousand blacks in 1930, there were only five black movie houses. In Birmingham, Alabama, also with a black population of ninety thousand, there were only four. And in the former capital of the Confederacy, Richmond, Virginia, with more than fifty thousand black citizens, only two movie houses operated exclusively for blacks.

The outcome of such "underseating" was expected: "A much smaller percentage of Negroes of all [economic] classes attend the [motion picture] theatre than is true of whites." Blacks, the study found, center their recreational and social life in their churches, clubs, and lodges. The study found blacks in the South tended to rely on radio, because they were sometimes unable to secure access to theatres and radio provided a solution to the embarrassment associated with going out to the movies.[18]

During the 1920s and 1930s in the North, segregation was handled more by residential propinquity. As cities became more and more segregated by residence, blacks went to theatres in "their" neighborhoods, and whites to theatres in "their" parts of town. Indeed in some states progressive reformers passed laws to prohibit theatres from refusing admission to blacks. But usually social convention took over. The state of Iowa, for example, passed such a law in 1923. There were several test cases in Des Moines and Council Bluffs. In the latter city a white woman sought her money back because an usher seated her next to a black woman. The manager returned her money even though he was under no legal obligation to do so.

Motion Picture News summed up the situation this way: "The colored people are generally considerate of their privileges and occupy the section especially reserved for them. The manager has the privilege of trying to seat his patrons." In Harlem, even into the 1930s, the Loew's theatre managers had their ushers seat blacks in one part of the theatre and whites in another.[19]

Racial segregation dictated an unequal moviegoing experience. Consider the situation in Washington, D.C., in the days immediately after the coming of sound. Whites had a vast array of movie theatres from which to choose, thirty-eight in all. These included three deluxe presentation houses with an average of more than twenty-five hundred seats, five more downtown movie houses without stage shows with an average of fifteen hundred seats, and five smaller downtown theatres with an average of three hundred seats. There were eleven neighborhood houses averaging more than one thousand seats and twelve more neighborhood houses of four hundred seats each.

Blacks had only twelve theatres from which to select. The twelve black theatres included only five first-class theatres in the black downtown, which averaged only eight hundred seats or roughly equivalent to white-only neighborhood houses. The seven neighborhood theatres averaged three hundred seats, about three-quarters of their white counterparts. Thus, the black theatres were far fewer in number and smaller in size. Black theatres had fewer ushers and door attendants, who were paid far less than their white counterparts. Laborers were paid from half to two-thirds their precise counterparts in white theatres.

But the greatest contrast could be seen in the number of musicians employed. The three deluxe downtown theatres for whites employed seventy-eight musicians in 1930, inclusive of leaders and organists. These were not large orchestras but rather had twenty or so members. The smaller downtown theatres had orchestras of about ten members before 1930. All the other white downtown theatres relied on organists alone. In the black-only theatres the five deluxe theatres had a total of seventeen musicians or "orchestras" averaging about three members each. All were immediately dropped during the transition to sound, while the three white-only houses retained orchestras of only slightly smaller sizes than before. That is, whites always had greater orchestras and major stage show talent. The lone exception for blacks was the Howard Theatre, famous for its stage shows in the 1930s spotlighting great African-American jazz musicians.[20]

By the mid-1930s, as the movies for whites entered the golden age of the studio system, there were some eight hundred theatres serving blacks in thirty-two states and the District of Columbia. As estimated in the *Motion Picture Herald*, these included some four hundred to six hundred black-only movie houses and two hundred more that opened to blacks at certain parts of the day. The largest concentration of black-only theatres was in the Deep South. The states with the highest populations and the largest numbers of movie theatres open, were, in order, North Carolina, Florida,

Virginia, Georgia, West Virginia, South Carolina, Alabama, Kentucky, Louisiana, Mississippi, Texas, and Arkansas. But New York, Illinois, and Ohio also had substantial numbers of black-only theatres, principally found in New York City, Chicago, Cleveland, and Cincinnati.[21]

Black-oriented films did well in these theatres but so did major Hollywood products. In the early 1930s the greatest box-office grosser in black theatres was a Hollywood product with a black theme and black star, *Imitation of Life* (1934), starring Claudette Colbert and Louise Beavers. This film, in part about the daughter of a black woman who passes for white, played return engagements in black theatres during the money-starved Great Depression. Black films encountered few censorship problems because white censorship boards simply never took the time to screen black films.[22]

Advertising for black theatres took one of two routes. First the theatre owner could use posters. Since most African-Americans lived in small towns, they could see the changes in films during daily shopping trips. Theatre owners used a limited amount of newspaper advertising. Frequently, distributors of black-oriented films advertised in black-oriented newspapers for films they felt had an elevated box-office potential. Since most communities did not have their own black newspapers, most newspaper advertising appeared in a few prominent black newspapers from selected big cities: the Baltimore *Afro-American*, the Chicago *Defender*, the Pittsburgh *Courier*, and the New York *Amsterdam News*. Copies of these papers would circulate throughout the South and thus the publicity about upcoming films was spread.

The major change in black moviegoing in 1930s America took place in northern cities. During the 1920s, blacks had begun to stream up from the South to northern cities such as industrial Chicago, Detroit, and Milwaukee. As these cities changed so did the sociology of movie theatres. For example, the Regal was built during the teens in a Germanic enclave in a north-side Milwaukee neighborhood. When the German immigrants began to move to the edge of Milwaukee during the prosperous 1920s, they were replaced by Jewish immigrants. The Jews, by the late 1920s, also began to move to the suburbs on the northwest side of town, and during the 1930s blacks replaced them. Thus the Regal Theatre, which was built for Germanic whites, "turned" black in the late 1930s. The change was gradual, but once the neighborhood had changed, so did the theatre. The Regal remained Milwaukee's black theatre well into the 1950s.[23]

In the mecca for southern blacks in the North, Chicago, East Forty-seventh Street represented the "Magnificent Mile" for the expanding black community of the 1930s and 1940s. And, as in white neighborhoods of that movie-palace-laden metropolis, East Forty-seventh had its wonder theatre—the three-thousand-seat, Spanish-baroque Regal. Like the more noted Apollo in New York, and the Howard in Washington, D.C., the Chicago Regal played movies but was more famous for its great black musical stage shows, including performances by talents of the caliber of Duke Ellington, Count Basie, Louis Armstrong, Billie Holiday, and Lena Horne. It is reputed that Nat "King" Cole got his start on the stage of the Regal in an amateur night contest. Down the street was the Metropolitan Theatre and next door was the Savoy Ballroom. Like its outlying neighborhood counterparts that Balaban & Katz had developed for white Chicago in the 1920s, this area of the south side was the hub of movie entertainment throughout Hollywood's golden age of the movies.[24]

The apex of the segregation era for moviegoing, both in the North and the South, came during the late 1940s. While states bordering the South and the District of Columbia ran black-only theatres, a number of northern states did have civil rights statues prohibiting exclusion by race: California, Colorado, Illinois, Indiana, Kansas, Michigan, Nebraska, New Jersey, New York, Ohio, Pennsylvania, and Wisconsin. Despite this, of course, the *Film Daily Yearbook* listed "black" theatres in all of them: California (Los Angeles), Colorado (Denver), Illinois (Chicago, East St. Louis, Cairo), Indiana (Indianapolis), Kansas (Topeka), Michigan (Detroit), Nebraska (Omaha), New Jersey (Newark, Atlantic City, Trenton), New York (Manhattan, Brooklyn, Bronx, Long Island, Buffalo), Ohio (Columbus, Dayton, Cincinnati, Cleveland), Pennsylvania (Philadelphia), and Wisconsin (Milwaukee).[25]

During the 1940s the black-oriented movie theatre reached its acme. That is because for the first time in history the American black man and woman had money to spend due to the prosperity associated with the Second World War. And with so few things to spend the money on, blacks, even more than their white counterparts, went to the movies. Federal government spending on the Second World War brought the American economy out of its doldrums and began an expansion in industrial activity that would draw blacks from the South to northern cities. In 1942 *Motion Picture Herald* celebrated the prosperity of the thirteen million black members of United States' population, leading to an increase in the number of all-black movie theatres. In a survey, the *Motion Picture Herald* found that 90 percent of all-black theatres were owned by whites, with prices up to forty cents in the North but topping out at a quarter in the South.[26]

In all cases the black theatres, however prosperous, received feature films in their final runs. In big cities such as Chicago and New York this could be months, and at times more than a year, after the major white theatres in the Loop or on Broadway had played the same film. In the rural South, the runs rarely exceeded two or three months and the wait would be less than six months. Thus, blacks in the northern cities, although theoretically better off because legally they could go to white theatres, by de facto segregation saw movies in their neighborhood theatres months after their counterparts in the South. And although blacks in the South saw Hollywood releases earlier, they were humiliated by seating patterns. In each case blacks were clearly second-class moviegoing citizens.[27]

Because of such an expanding black market (in terms of both population and wealth) a handful of new theatres were built. But a new theatre was rare; it took exceptional circumstances such as the case of the Carver Theatre in New Orleans for a new theatre to be built. Blacks in that city had new wealth since the war and their numbers dictated the need for a new theatre. That pent-up spending power caused the one-thousand-seat Carver to open on 29 September 1950. Named in honor of George Washington Carver, as were many black theatres, the theatre prospered for only a decade, until the civil rights movement caused white theatres in New Orleans to be opened to all citizens.[28]

MOVIE THEATRE CIVIL RIGHTS

The pattern of theatre segregation did begin to change for the better after World War II. Although the civil rights movement would not make headlines until the late 1950s, the system of legal segregation began to break down far earlier than that. In 1949, *Pinky*, a Twentieth Century-Fox film starring Jeanne Crain and Ethel Waters dealing with racial conflict, was shown with an unprecedented advertising campaign in the black press. Although other Hollywood films with themes sympathetic to integration were made, in the late 1940s southern customs regarding movie theatres held fast. *Pinky* premiered at the Roxy in downtown Atlanta because it was considered the theatre with the most extensive balcony "where Negroes spectators may sit." [29]

The beginnings of desegregation of theatres began in the legitimate theatre. For example, in a test case the National Association for the Advancement of Colored People (NAACP) fought for six years to desegregate the Ford Theatre in Baltimore in 1952. A more famous case was fought in

Washington, D.C. In the summer of 1948, thirty-three playwrights, composers, and lyricists in the Dramatists Guild announced that they would not permit their productions to play the National Theatre unless race discrimination ended. This action was backed by civic leaders and the *Washington Post*. But the management of the National refused and during the fall of 1948 switched to movies when actors also refused to perform there.[30]

In 1953 the United States Supreme Court outlawed all segregation in theatres in the nation's capital. Quickly the movie houses of the District of Columbia moved into line. That is, they began to rely on de facto segregation by neighborhood rather than outright discrimination. The Loew's theatre chain lifted the ban on sales of tickets to blacks in the fall of 1953 as did the Stanley-Warner chain (the former Warner Bros. theatre chain had long dominated the Washington movie market). The Trans-Lux Newsreel Theatre and the KB chain followed suit. But by then a majority of whites lived in the suburbs and would attend theatres in Maryland and Virginia.[31]

The impetus for changing the system of segregated movie houses came from economic pressure. In 1954 *Variety* headlined on page one (read by every movie exhibitor in the country) the "sensational ten-year upsurge of Negro Market; Worth 15-Billion-$ Yearly." It concluded: "While the Negro goes struggling for equal rights in schools and colleges and public transportation, he is increasingly courted by those with goods and services to sell." In this terrible year for the movie theatre business in the United States, many observers noted that black-only theatres, especially in major cities, were experiencing gains at the box office, not losses. Whites were fleeing to the suburbs and abandoning urban theatres, while blacks remained city dwellers and began to frequent former movie palaces.[32]

While de facto segregation continued to work in northern black theatres and those downtown theatres increasingly being abandoned by whites, the battle lines were drawn in the South's cities. Racial segregation was getting in the way of profits. Films such as *The Joe Louis Story* (1953), starring Coley Wallace and Paul Stewart, and *Go, Man, Go* (1954), a film about the Harlem Globetrotters directed by famed cinematographer James Wong Howe and starring Dane Clark and a youthful Sidney Poitier, did well in the North but were not played in the South. No one wanted to stir up problems. There was picketing for *Carmen Jones* (1954), directed by Otto Preminger and starring Dorothy Dandridge, Harry Belafonte, and Pearl Baily, in San Antonio, Texas, to protest the segregated seating for the film in the Texas Theatre downtown. *Variety* noted the "progress" since "heretofore [the Texas] has not admitted Negroes." In New Orleans, despite premieres at an all-white theatre and all-black one, the American Legion objected to "creating friction between the races" with *Island in the Sun*, a 1957 film directed by Robert Rossen and starring Dorothy Dandridge, Harry Belafonte, and James Mason.[33]

Even attempts at technological change to attract bigger audiences caused controversy when confronted with traditional segregation patterns of the South. When the special widescreen process Cinerama turned downtown theatres into special attractions, there was no problem in the North. But Cinerama had to limit its growth to fourteen of twenty planned sites because in the South, with half the population banned from the theatres, it was feared that "potential drawing power will not be as great for long runs required." To deal with this issue, the Cinerama Corporation used mobile equipment set up in tents and municipal auditoriums. Another solution, used in Dallas, was to have a special night reserved for black-only screenings.[34]

Still the struggle continued. There were victories by the NAACP in Kansas City in 1960, when the dominant National theatre chain opened up its movie houses to blacks. But in San Francisco in the summer of 1960 there were small-scale racial fights in downtown theatres as blacks ventured into the white-dominated, first-run movie palaces. Black-oriented subsequent-run theatres closed, and blacks turned to downtown theatres in record numbers. This was good for business but aroused the potential for violence.[35]

As the movement for greater civil rights picked up steam in the early 1960s, more and more sit-ins included movie theatre lobbies. Citizen committees working with the NAACP to avoid problems were formed in earnest in 1961. In what is considered a liberal bastion of the South, Chapel Hill, North Carolina, the NAACP sought to integrate the Varsity Theatre. The group Citizens for Open Movies picketed for three weeks in February 1961. The largest theatre in Chapel Hill, the Carolina, saw picketing in November of the same year. By the beginning of 1962 an accommodation was reached and in this liberal southern university town, the movie theatres were fully integrated—without violence.[36]

The pressure for change was building. In part this came with the ever-increasing economic clout of black men and women. A study undertaken for *Ebony* magazine in 1961 found that blacks had moved in increasing numbers to the major cities and attended movies more often than any other group in the population. Exhibitors by 1960 had come to realize that the population of Washington, D.C., was one-half black; one-third of the citizens of Philadelphia and Chicago were black.

Hollywood prepared advertising aimed directly at these black, urban audiences. For example, for *All the Young Men* (1960), starring Alan Ladd and Sidney Poitier, Columbia Pictures prepared two separate advertising campaigns, one for whites and one for blacks. To reach potential black patrons Columbia Pictures used black radio and newspapers and contacted black groups such as the NAACP.[37]

Upwardly mobile blacks, like their whites counterparts, were abandoning the movie theatre for the new world of television. As one historian noted, television held an advantage because it was entertainment at home. With rising expectations of the late 1950s and early 1960s, blacks could view movies as well as variety shows, situation comedies, westerns, and all that television offered, without undergoing the indignities long associated with Jim Crow nests.[38]

But change did not come quickly. The battle over integrating the southern movie house continued in city after city. The transformation to integrated movie theatres took place in Nashville in May 1961. Miami and Atlanta concluded desegregation of their downtown theatres in the spring of 1962, while Memphis accomplished this in September of 1962. In downtown New Orleans a picket line was maintained in front of the Loew's State, the Joy, and the Saenger from November 1963 until March 1964 by members of the Congress of Racial Equality. Only then were blacks admitted to these movie palaces.[39]

The Atlanta case was held up as model by many. In May of 1962, with the cooperation of the NAACP and other civic groups, a limited number of blacks were admitted to theatres. All was quiet. By June, the theatres, all first-run, were fully desegregated. *Motion Picture Herald* noted that desegregation proved good for business and that other theatre owners not facing up to the problem ought to be aware of the monies they could lose. The trade paper stated that the issue had to be faced, and theatre owners ought to do it with an eye toward positive public relations.[40]

In the world of national politics, desegregation of movie theatres would climax with the civil rights legislation that President John Kennedy sent to the United States Congress on 19 June 1963. To facilitate passage of the bill Robert Kennedy, the president's brother and attorney general, proposed that Kennedy invite influential groups to the White House and personally persuade them to support the legislation. These groups included lawyers, educators, clergy, and traditional business and labor leaders, but much publicity was garnered from invitations to movie theatre owners. Theatres were highly visible institutions in their communities—especially in small southern towns—and if Kennedy could convince these leaders, the favorable publicity might spill over into other arenas. It also presented the image of an active president, something not lost on Kennedy.[41]

Kennedy's push began in late May of 1963 when Attorney General Robert Kennedy formally asked the remaining segregated theatres in the South to remove restrictions and not give blacks more reason to demonstrate. Kennedy wanted to deny more radical members of the civil rights movement reason to picket and perhaps even riot. The focus fell on southern theatres with separate sections or complete bans on black attendance. On 22 May 1963 Robert Kennedy called in forty theatre executives to press for voluntary action. The chain owners agreed but stalled. They knew of the pickets at theatres from North and South Carolina to Georgia, Texas, and Tennessee. But the theatre owners did not want to lead: "We don't want to assume the leadership in desegregation when the problem more broadly concerns transportation, hotels, department stores, and eating places." The most prominent leaders to meet with Robert Kennedy and then a week later with President Kennedy included Democrats Arthur Krim and Robert Benjamin, the heads of Hollywood's United Artists, and Leonard Goldenson, head of ABC-Paramount Theatres, the largest chain in the South. Krim, Benjamin, and Goldenson were active supporters of Kennedy's presidency.[42]

Even while talks continued, leaders in Richmond, Virginia, Houston, and El Paso, Texas, were already working out solutions through less formal negotiations. Reports indicated that once big-city southern theatres opened their doors for blacks, nothing out of the ordinary happened. The higher ticket prices for first-run films kept attendance by blacks small in the beginning, but still there were incidents. Problems arose when white college students joined with blacks to staff the picket lines. Sit-ins in lobbies and rotating queues outside (blacks queuing up in line time after time) became common tactics of the day. For example, in 1961 students began to picket the local Hiser Theatre in Bethesda, Maryland, just outside the nation's capital, to force the owner to admit black patrons. In Thomasville, North Carolina, the local chapter of the NAACP organized a protest at the Davidson Theatre, the town's only movie house.[43]

In the end, as an outcome of the civil rights movement, as a result of economic pressures, and as a result of direct intervention by the Kennedy administration, the theatrical movie exhibition market began its move to desegregate fully during the latter half of 1963. Kennedy was singled out specifically for his efforts to get the industry to cease discriminatory admission policies voluntarily. At the time of Kennedy's death, in late November

1963, hundreds of theatres had taken the president's advice and hundreds more would do so within a year of his assassination. Indeed, in an article in December 1963 the *Motion Picture Herald* praised the late president as a "friend of the industry." But it had not been easy. On 28 October 1963, a month before President Kennedy's death, Robert Kennedy had explained the administration's view on racial desegregation to a Theatre Owners of America dinner and a "minority booed." At a Texas Drive-in's convention in 1961 one spokesman proclaimed that the problem would be solved by "killing them all." [44]

The end of legally segregated movie theatres came in the summer of 1964 with the passage of the new civil rights law. In July 1964, the Congress of Racial Equality reported no theatre owner not abiding by the law. There had been a couple of minor incidents in Georgia and South Carolina but no major problems. In many communities there was partial desegregation so that blacks had access to some but not all theatres. Full compliance came in the summer. [45]

What remained then were black theatres based on segregation by location. These were mainly in black ghettos in the North. Chicago in 1967 had some twenty houses classified as black only, all on the south side and west side. These were theatres in neighborhoods that had "turned"; the owners kept the theatres open to service a black clientele. Such de facto segregation expanded as the legal segregation policies ceased in 1964. It was legal for blacks to go to downtown first-run theatres in the South, but that was precisely when whites began to go exclusively to suburban theatres in their "own" neighborhoods. [46]

The urban riots of the 1960s in Detroit, Los Angeles, Milwaukee, Washington, D.C., and elsewhere signaled the end of first-run theatres in the downtowns of the United States. Most whites had their own theatres by now in the suburbs, as we have seen, and blacks were ceded the sites downtown. This was true in city after city. Rochester, New York, and Tampa, Florida, illustrate the general principle.

On Friday, 24 July 1964, the city of Rochester had a race riot. Two days later a thousand National Guard troops were brought in. A curfew was declared, with theatres closing before dark. Calm was restored within a few days, but the downtown theatre business would never be the same again. Before the end of the decade the city's fifteen first-run downtown sites would be relocated in suburban shopping malls. The shopping center movie house movement, detailed earlier, was not race-neutral but accommodated itself to the patterns of housing. [47]

In Tampa, Florida, the riots came in June of 1967. They started in front of the Lincoln Theatre in the heart of the black portion of Tampa's downtown. The theatre shut down for three days. Ironically the film playing there was *To Kill a Mockingbird* (1962), a sympathetic tale of a southern jury's racism, starring an outspoken white liberal, Gregory Peck. Although most Tampa theatres had long since integrated, the Lincoln continued to play to a predominantly black audience due to its location. Outside downtown Tampa, things remained remarkably normal. General Cinema's major shopping center theatre, the Britton, reported good business playing a current Disney double bill. Business in drive-ins was off because many stayed home rather than venture out to theatres accessible to both black and white. The downtown theatres reported major drops in business although they did stay open even at night.[48]

By the late 1960s the black-only theatre—by law—was a thing of the past. However, as downtown and inner-city theatres in large cities were abandoned by whites, a large number of blacks patronized the theatres. *Variety* reported that although blacks were only 10 to 15 percent of the population, they represented a third of movie ticket buyers, especially in major cities. Columbia Pictures hired a special public relations firm to deal with the black press and cater to black patrons. Indeed part of the success of *To Sir, With Love* (1967), starring Sidney Poitier, and *Guess Who's Coming to Dinner* (1967), also with Poitier and Katharine Hepburn and Spencer Tracy, stemmed from an extensive screening program in major cities for the black press and opinion makers.[49]

By the early 1970s, the former picture palaces and neighborhood houses that during the 1930s and 1940s had provided Hollywood with all its gold were servicing only African-Americans. Chicago was typical. In the early 1970s the former picture palaces in Chicago's Loop programmed action films exclusively. The changeover in Chicago took place in the years after that city's urban riot. The owners of the theatres actually welcomed the transformation because targeting black teens precipitated the first boost in patronage since the flight to the suburbs had begun in earnest two decades earlier. A few theatre owners did try to attract a white audience, with disappointing results. So during the Christmas season of 1972 the marquees of Chicago's Loop picture palaces lit up with *Black Gunn*, *Tricky Baby*, *Sounder*, and *Dirty Harry*. Family fare of that Christmas season, such as the musicals *1776* and *Man of La Mancha* (1972), opened in shopping mall theatres.[50]

Chicago was certainly not alone in its abandonment of the downtown picture palaces to action films for black audiences during the early 1970s. In Boston, exhibitors in the downtown celebrated the return of the family audience, but as in Chicago, the interest was in black films or action products. Blacks in Boston even appeared to be better spenders at the concession stands than the whites they replaced. One exhibitor noted a pattern: "On Sundays whole families come, the kids, the wives, husbands, and even babies. That's their day out for the family." [51]

Thus the change from a nation of two kinds of theatres—one for blacks and one for whites by law and custom—had come to movie theatres segregated only by the "normal" patterns of de facto living spaces. That is, much of America's cities had been given over to African-Americans, while the suburbs had been taken by whites. But the issue of segregation in movie houses had hardly disappeared in the 1980s. In South Africa, Hollywood took a stand that it would not book films to theatres that remained segregated. In 1986 nearly all theatre owners agreed; they did not want to lose the profits Hollywood films promised and integrated their theatres. The movie theatres had long been segregated under a law called the Group Areas Act, forbidding races to mix. But throughout South Africa, theatres are in areas segregated by housing. Television and home video solved the problem somewhat, creating a movie show in the home. As long as South Africa remains a two-tiered society, home entertainment will have to be the solution. [52]

The memory of the days of separate theatres in the United States did not go away fully, nor does custom. In 1989 came the movie *Mississippi Burning*, about the civil rights workers who journeyed to Philadelphia, Mississippi, in 1964 and were murdered by members of the Ku Klux Klan. The film graphically depicted the murders and their impact on the frightened, embittered, segregated community. The owner of the local movie house in tiny Philadelphia, Mississippi, when interviewed by *Newsweek* late in 1988, was trying to decide whether to book the film or not, for few wanted to relive that memory. Ironically she noted that if she did, local custom would surely be followed with "most blacks still [sitting] in the balcony at the Ellis Theatre and whites still [sitting] downstairs." [53]

NINE

Ethnic Theatres and Art Cinemas

Black Americans were not the only social group to patronize specialized theatres; however, they were the only group forced to have their own theatres. More numerous were the movie theatres aimed at Americans interested in the films from foreign countries. From the beginning of the movies as a business non-English speakers sought out films in French, Spanish, German, and Italian. Regularly, theatres offered films from foreign countries as well as films from Hollywood dubbed into a foreign tongue. These began in the 1910s with translated titles but became a bigger issue in the early 1930s with the coming of sound.

It must be remembered that the United States was, even as talkies came in during the late 1920s, a nation of first-generation immigrants. Two of every three Americans consciously claimed membership in an ethnic community, either as foreign born or their descendants. While the experience of African-Americans has been discussed in the previous chapter, there were other ethnic groups in the United States as well:

The Mexican-American community had grown to be an influence in the Southwest, with several million Spanish speakers.
More than a half million Asian-Americans lived primarily on the West Coast, particularly in Los Angeles.
German-Americans numbered near twenty million.
More than nine million Slavs lived in America's industrial cities.
Five million Jews supported a Yiddish culture in the biggest cities.
Approximately six million Italian-Americans, largely working-class citizens, lived in the northeastern states.

In the 1930s and 1940s American cities were collections of ghetto communities inhabited by European and Asian immigrants. These ghettos had two dimensions: cultural and residential. These were not walled in, escape-proof communities; new Americans lived there because of the emotional security they offered. They provided havens for adjustment, easing the transition into the new society.

In these ghettos—the Chinatowns, the Little Tokyos, the Little Italys—immigrants spoke their native tongue and lived near friends and relatives from the old country. On New York City's Lower East Side, it was not simply Italian-Americans but the Genoese, Calabrians, and Sicilians; Jews broke down by the land of their emigration.

The institutions of these enclaves helped ease the transition. The buildings often had an old world flavor. There were Greek coffee shops and Irish pubs. In New York City Jews sat in cafes on Hester Street and debated religion and politics. Germans in St. Louis and Milwaukee had their beer gardens. There were ethnic holidays and special societies and clubs.

Mass communications reflected and fit into these needs. New Americans often learned to read their native language to keep in touch with distant friends and to get news from the old country. And because many European languages had been suppressed—such as Polish by the Germans and Bulgarian by the Greeks—the ethnic newspaper offered a perfect medium for open and free expression in the new land of the United States. By 1920 there were more than one thousand ethnic newspapers, from the *Staats-Zeitung* for Germans to the *Japanese American News* and the *Franco American*. It was not surprising that when talkies became the rage in the United States and then the rest of the world, ethnic Americans would want to see the newest film from "back home."[1]

FOREIGN LANGUAGE MOVIE THEATRES

In the 1920s, some Americans became interested in foreign films. At first it was thought that a circuit of cinemas showing films imported from Europe could be made into a viable concern. That would not prove the case until after the Second World War with the art house cinemas. But this does not mean there were not scattered successes during the 1920s. Mostly these successes came from distributing films to specialized audiences rather than tendering an art house policy to educated citizens. In the 1920s it took time to determine the appropriate policy, particularly in face of the coming of talkies.

An important example came after the First World war with the importation of the first European imported hit, German Ernst Lubitsch's *Passion* (often titled *Madame DuBarry* in the United States). *Passion* opened at the Capitol Theatre in New York City late in 1920 and did well. Then the highly experimental *The Cabinet of Dr. Caligari*, another German film, was distributed in the United States by Samuel Goldwyn. Goldwyn had muscle in the industry and was able to get a booking at the five-thousand-seat Capitol Theatre, beginning the first week of April 1921. After doing well at this initial test screening situation, Goldwyn picked selected bookings in theatres in the major cities across the United States. Goldwyn sold *The Cabinet of Dr. Caligari* as an exotic attraction to Americans with backgrounds in Europe. He consciously followed the model of opera.[2]

The appeal of *Passion* was its European novelty, but this film also caused a controversy that surely contributed to its take at the box office. The American Legion branch in Los Angeles objected to its German origins and later, when *The Cabinet of Dr. Caligari* opened at the Miller's Theatre in early May 1921, veterans of World War I were there to picket. By the evening of 7 May the streets in front of the theatre were clogged with protesters and onlookers. Eventually the film was pulled, but the publicity surely helped it and *Passion*, the most noted European motion pictures of their day in the United States.[3]

But *The Cabinet of Dr. Caligari* proved a failure at the box office. Mainstream audiences wanted classical Hollywood fare, not experimental European cinema. But the fame of *Passion*, *The Cabinet of Dr. Caligari*, and other movies from Europe gave rise to the "little cinema" movement. American exhibitors took their inspiration from the cine-clubs in Paris and London, which specialized in bringing the best of the foreign cinema into these European capitals as an alternative to the Hollywood films that seemed to be everywhere. (By the close of World War I Hollywood had developed a dominant position in the international distribution of motion pictures.)[4]

Symon Gould, for example, founded the International Film Arts Guild in October 1925 and organized Sunday screenings at the George M. Cohan and Central theatres in New York City. These foreign films played in these legitimate theatres in the dark time between the matinee and evening show. Gould tendered a subscription series to add prestige; he offered something not available at a normal motion picture theatre. In 1926 Gould had competition. The International Film Arts Guild inaugurated regular screenings at the Cameo Theatre on Forty-second Street in New York's Times Square. In 1927 Gould expanded his operation to include a second site in New York (at the Greenwich Village Theatre); in 1929 he opened a branch in a Philadelphia theatre.[5]

Gould only demonstrated how marginal a film-as-art policy was in the 1920s movie business. The failure of the Philadelphia theatre provides a case study of the problems of programming European films during the 1920s. Gould took over what had been the Regent Theatre in a better part of downtown Philadelphia, near City Hall. The four-hundred-seat house had opened some years earlier as a subsequent-run silent film house. Gould argued he could make more money with first-run European films. In 1929 he transformed the theatre to art films and changed its name twice. It opened as the Film Guild Cinema, playing on the reputation of the New York theatre.[6]

Business proved slack and so Gould changed the name to Cinema Art. He also removed seats from the back of the house to create a coffee lounge. None of these strategies worked. Philadelphians in 1929, at the peak of the prosperity of the Roaring Twenties, would not support an art theatre. In part this was because of the immense popularity of the new talkies from Hollywood. It seemed any film from Hollywood with sound was preferable to any silent film, whatever its origins. By the Great Depression the theatre played subsequent-run Hollywood movies.[7]

Other entrepreneurs learned from Gould's experience and fashioned movie house programming strategies that combined an appeal to more faithful ethnic audiences with fares that might lure intellectuals as well. For example, Michael Mindlin, a former producer of legitimate plays, founded the Fifth Avenue Playhouse on 9 October 1926; in time he developed a "subway circuit," with the 55th Street Playhouse, the Europa, and the St. George Theatre in Brooklyn. Leo Brecker opened his Little Carnegie Playhouse on Fifty-seventh Street in New York City on 2 November 1928 with Sergei Eisenstein's *October* (1928). Brecker had long been part of the New York exhibition scene trying to make a go of theatres in specialized situations. But his operation in the Bronx was more typical, where far away from midtown Manhattan Brecker operated the Verona, in the heart of the Bronx's Little Italy. First- and second-generation Italian-Americans flocked to the Italian films Brecker presented.[8]

Case after case seems to indicate that it was just not possible to establish a foreign language theatre outside a teeming ethnic neighborhood.

Hollywood, particularly after talkies, seemed all too powerful a lure. For example, Nathan Machet's Motion Picture Guild opened as the first art theatre in the nation's capital at the Wardman Park Theatre in 1926. It would survive only three years. At the premiere the appeal was high-toned. Special armchair seats (similar to captain's seats) were installed in the six-hundred-seat theatre with a faintly Spanish design. The theatre was located in one of the city's highest income neighborhoods. Three years later the Wardman Park ceased to be a movie house and was used only for meetings and recitals.[9]

Keeping the theatre small and operating on a shoestring helped. Being one of a handful of foreign language theatres in a city with a multitude of ethnic neighborhoods enabled the Little Theatre in Baltimore, for example, to limp along. Opened in downtown in December 1927, the Little was appropriately named, for it held only two hundred patrons, making it one of the smallest theatres in the city. The opening show initiated a high-class, art house policy: the German film *Tartuffe*, directed by F. W. Murnau and starring Emil Jannings, played, accompanied by a small string orchestra. But by the late 1920s the Little was offering an eclectic mixture of foreign fare to appeal to all clusters of ethnic interest in Baltimore. As the lone entrant in the field, the Little Theatre of Baltimore proved a rare example of the art house theatre (if only part of its schedule) able to survive through the 1930s into the heyday of the art cinema.[10]

By far the greatest success for a foreign language cinema came when the theatre owner took direct aim at the varied interests of the masses of ethnic Americans in the neighborhoods of his or her particular city. This policy worked so well that during the depressed 1930s, movie house entrepreneurs were able to open and eke out profits at an estimated five hundred theatres across the United States. Transcontinental Pictures Inc., for example, took direct aim at the millions of Italian-Americans. Corporate heads Paul Rinaudo De Ville and Leandro Forno played a flexible game by booking Italian language films into some fifty theatres from Boston to Washington, D.C., principally in New York City. They anticipated the policy of "four-walling," whereby they rented a theatre in the Italian section of town, splashed posters on every black wall, and reaped the rewards.[11]

The ethnic makeup of various parts of the United States dictated special types of theatres. Honolulu, in the territory of Hawaii, before air travel, was a melting pot, based on its importance as a seaport. Thus, the makeup of its population featured a bit of Japanese, Filipino, and Chinese. Intermingled were smaller numbers of Samoans, Hawaiians, Koreans, French, German, and British. As a consequence the theatres of Honolulu were booked with films from all over the world. The Japanese theatres even retained, well into the 1930s, their benshi (interpreters standing by the side of the screen to offer sound effects and dialogue). Indeed Japanese films were still being played as the Japanese attacked Hawaii on 7 December 1941.[12]

Surprisingly, once Japanese hysteria ceased during the decade after World War II, Honolulu theatres again played Japanese films. Indeed in 1964 the twelve-hundred-seat picture palace was remodeled and converted to a theatre that played Japanese films and live theatre. For a time the theatre was a success. When it was twinned in the 1970s, it became an Asian duplex with the Nippon Theatre for Japanese films on one side and on the other the Golden Harvest for Chinese films. The ethnic audience continued to be served.[13]

The apex for foreign film screenings during the golden age of Hollywood came for a brief moment early in the 1930s. There was a time in 1931 when it was thought that foreign language cinemas would become a regular, indeed a major, part of the exhibition scene in the United States. In 1930 patronage in foreign language theatres was reported up some 20 percent and growing. Audiences in ethnic theatres seemed to enjoy the first early talkies from native countries over the new talkers from Hollywood. As a consequence the Hollywood movie moguls ordered their production staffs to convert popular English-language feature films and shorts into "foreign language films." The original film was made in English and then, often with different stars, a version in Spanish, German, and/or French was made.

These "foreign versions" could then be targeted for a specific European country and its colonies as well as the theatres in the United States that catered to non-English speakers.[14] Metro-Goldwyn-Mayer took the lead. In November 1929 the studio embarked on a two-million-dollar program to replicate its features in at least three languages. Several of its imported stars, who came to the United States in the silent era when language was no problem, were helped by this transition. For example, MGM cast Swedish star Greta Garbo as a woman who spoke broken German in one film, which directly matched the star's ability in that language.[15]

Paramount followed during the winter of 1929–30, when it set up producer Robert T. Kane in a studio outside Paris and gave him ten million dollars to produce films in five languages. By March 1930 Kane's Joinville facility had created nearly sixty shorts and had ten features in production. Movie mogul Adolph Zukor even made a special trip to Paris to check on this new investment and declared that this seemed to be the way to handle the foreign language problem for the talkies. He ordered the production stepped up to a new film per week, a production schedule equal to the Hollywood studio itself. Hollywood would handle English and Spanish versions, while films in all other languages would be made at Joinville.[16]

Hollywood's experiment in making foreign films for foreign-speaking enclaves in the United States (and then to export) proved short-lived. By the beginning of the following year, 1931, it was clear to all involved that the revenues from foreign versions did not match their costs. This was probably due as much to the impact of the world-wide influences of the Great Depression as anything else. Specifically, the promised box-office take in the United States foreign language theatres generated the greatest disappointments. Only the Spanish community in the southwestern United States, from Texas to California, ever added any sizable revenues.[17]

MGM called off the production and distribution of foreign versions in April 1932; Paramount followed soon thereafter and converted Joinville into a center for dubbing American films. Indeed dubbing would prove a much less costly solution to developing films for special markets, a practice that seems to satisfy foreign languages audiences to this day. Only Fox Film, desperate for any revenues in its near-bankrupt state, bravely continued on, creating Spanish versions of some of its feature films and short subjects until 1935. With expiration of Fox's unit as the company merged with Twentieth Century Films, Hollywood ended its experiment with the production of special foreign language films.[18]

Hollywood's terminus hardly called a halt to interest in foreign films in the United States. Through the 1930s, an estimated two hundred theatres regularly presented foreign films—about 1 percent of all movie theatres operating in the United States at the time. Of this total, however, only half showed foreign films exclusively. Moreover, on occasion the major circuits, then owned by Hollywood companies, showed certain important foreign films. For example, Jean Renoir's *The Grand Illusion* (1938) played the RKO, Paramount, and Warner Bros. circuits in 1940. But this was a rare occurrence at best.[19]

New York City continued to be the center for theatres with regular foreign film screenings. Fans of foreign language films could count on twenty-five theatres to present feature films in a staggering array of languages. The situation in 1939 is summarized in Table 1. This sampling was taken at the high tide of filmgoing, in the days immediately before the Second World War closed the most important production centers of filmmaking.

Table 1 New York City Foreign Language Theatres, 1939

French films: Ascot, Eighth Street Playhouse, Fifth Avenue Playhouse,
    Fifty-fifth Street Playhouse, Filmart, Plaza (occasional),
    Roosevelt, Sixty-eighth Street Playhouse, Thalia, and World
German films: Eighty-sixth Street Casino, Eighty-sixth Street Garden,
    Europa, Ninety-sixth Street Theatre, Roosevelt, World, and Irving
Polish films: Chopin
Irish films: Irish/Miami (split policy)
Italian films: Cine Roman
Russian films: Cameo and Radio
Greek films: Irish/Miami (split policy)
Hungarian films: Modern Playhouse
Chinese films: New Chaham (occasional)
Yiddish films: Radio and People's Cinema

*Source: *Motion Picture Herald*, 15 July 1939, pp. 39–40.

Four other cities rivaled New York in their importance as foreign film markets. Philadelphia and Chicago possessed a diverse immigrant population approaching that of New York City. In the world of foreign film theatres of the 1930s and 1940s the "Big Three" were New York City, Chicago, and Philadelphia, in that order. In Chicago, for example, there were three theatres that programmed a variety of foreign films (the World, the Cinema, and the Europa) as well as three exclusively Yiddish language theatres, two Polish language movie houses, and the Sonotone, which occasionally presented Russian films, and the Julian Theatre, which occasionally showed Swedish films. Likewise Philadelphia had three multi-ethnic theatres (the Arcadia, Cinema Art, and Studio) as well as cinema houses that showed exclusively Italian, Yiddish, Russian, and Polish films.[20]

Smaller in size than the Big Three but nearly as rich in diverse immigrant populations were San Francisco and Milwaukee. In the mid-1930s San Francisco had nine theatres that regularly showed foreign films, principally to Hispanic and Italian audiences. San Francisco stood as the leading Italian movie center in the United States, with some seven theatres regularly presenting films made in Italy. The counterpart to Italian San Francisco were the massive Polish and German communities in Milwaukee, Wisconsin. Before World War II Milwaukee contained three theatres that regularly presented German films; four Milwaukee movie theatres programmed Polish films.

No other cities could approach the size and diversity that rivaled New York, Chicago, Philadelphia, San Francisco, and Milwaukee. The southwestern states did, however, contain cities with concentrations of Spanish language movie houses. In particular, Denver, Colorado; Dallas, Texas; Laredo, Texas; Los Angeles, California; and San Antonio, Texas all contained at least two theatres that regularly played films from Spain, Mexico, and South America. Indeed throughout Texas there were theatres that regularly played Spanish films in such relatively small towns as Asherton (population 1,538 in 1940), Austin (population 87,930), Brownsville (population 22,083), Cotulla (population 3,633), Crystal City (population 6,529), Eagle Pass (population 6,459), Flatonia (population 1,024), Fredericksburg (population 3,544), Halletsville (population 1,581), La Grange (population 2,531), McAllen (population 11,877), Moulton (population 643), New Braunfels (population 6,976), Rio Grande City (population 2,283), Roma (population 1,414), San Diego (population 2,674), Schulenburg (population 1,970), and Zapata (population 1,041). In many cases the Spanish theatre operated on a split policy, programming mainstream Hollywood films one part of the week and Spanish films another.[21]

In smaller cities it took an enterprising entrepreneur to be successful. In Syracuse, New York, for example, there existed a sizable population of some twenty thousand German-Americans. On any number of occasions theatre owners tried to program a German theatre. Yet no theatre was ever consistently available for German films. Syracuse's population of Polish-Americans was far smaller than the German enclave, but for years the Liberty Theatre played Polish films on a regular basis.[22]

Economic success seemed to come when the theatre owner could mix what would later become known as art house policy with a specific ethnic appeal. Throughout the United States, in major cities, a handful of such hybrid operations were able to make a go of it during the 1930s. Consider the case of the Fine Arts Theatre in Boston. This six-hundred-seat house charged fifty cents in the afternoon and seventy-five cents in the evening, and weekly it took in five hundred to five thousand dollars. It had its greatest success in the 1930s with a film that appealed to Boston's sizable intellectual and Irish communities: Robert Flaherty's *Man of Aran* (1935). Operating such a theatre required skill and cunning. The theatre owner could not, for example, piggyback on a national advertising campaign. Thus, the owner had to cultivate contacts in the ethnic community and hope to pass the word.[23]

World War II forever transformed the foreign language cinemas of the United States. On one hand many theatre owners opted to change their programming and become a subsequent-run house. Showing Hollywood movies had become so lucrative that everyone was making money, even at the tenth and eleventh runs. The marginal theatre that had turned to foreign films in the 1930s now could make far more money showing anything from Hollywood. Moreover, the production centers of the filmmaking world, outside Hollywood, were closing down. In Europe and Asia, in particular, it was very difficult to make movies in war economies. Of course, German, Japanese, and Italian films were forbidden for reasons of patriotism. Theatres that during the 1930s had showed movies from all parts of the world turned to westerns and war films. The World War II era was the nadir for viewers interested in foreign films.[24]

THE ART CINEMA

After World War II, interest again resurfaced for screenings of films from Europe, Japan, India, and other nations with long filmmaking traditions. But this interest came not in ethnic enclaves, which were dispursing to the suburbs, but in the form of specialized art house theatres (located in major cities). High-income, well-educated Americans attended these art theatres, embracing film as more than "mere entertainment." As more and more filmmakers outside the United States formulated a vision of film as art, movie house entrepreneurs pitched this "product" as an addition to the traditional modes of "high art"—literature, music, and drama.

The rise of the art house was precipitated by forces from the outside. Gradually through the 1950s and 1960s film took on the characteristics of an accepted art form. That is not to say the predominance of the classical Hollywood film in Europe lessened. Hollywood still pulled in millions of dollars from distribution in Europe with films in new wide-screen and color formats. But increasingly Europeans gave up trying to best Hollywood and sought alternative styles and forms. During the 1950s and early 1960s a resurgence in world cinema took place in Europe with films like Ingmar Bergman's *The Seventh Seal* (1957), Federico Fellini's *La Dolce Vita* (1960), and Michelangelo Antonioni's *L'Eclisse* (1962). These were labeled art films and shown in specialized theatres in the United States and elsewhere. They provided a distinct alternative to the look and narrative formula continuously coming from Hollywood.

In time European directors became international stars. Alain Resnais, François Truffaut, and Jean-Luc Godard, the key members of the French new wave, emerged as "names-above-the-title" on the art house circuit. In the 1960s, in Europe and increasingly in the United States, it was *de rigueur* in university circles to have seen the latest Fellini or Bergman film and to be able to discuss it intelligently. Directors became so famous they even became known by a single name. "I'm going to see Tati's latest film," or "I hear the new Buñuel is in town."[25]

The genesis of the art theatre as a separate category—aimed at educated filmgoers, not recent immigrants seeking motion pictures in their native language—came in the late 1940s. Approximately one hundred foreign films opened in New York in 1947, many of which made their way to theatres across the United States. Much of the interest came because of the publicity of a single film, Roberto Rossellini's *Open City* (1946). One source placed the gross revenues at American box offices for this movie at almost one million dollars. *Paisan* (1946), Rossellini's second neorealist feature, grossed more than a million dollars, breaking all previous records for a foreign film in the United States.[26]

In the United States, through the late 1940s and the entire 1950s, many a theatre owner began to seek an alternative to closing. These entrepreneurs rarely espoused film as art, but they did provide sites for showing European art cinema in every major American city and at universities and colleges across the nation. Millions of new college students—the first to attend college in their family because of the G.I. bill—embraced these serious films. By 1956 the number of art cinemas had reached two hundred; ten years later it was five hundred; by the late 1960s (including film societies presenting the best of the European art cinema) the total exceeded one thousand.

Changes in the mainstream theatrical film industry in the United States also helped develop this art house movement. After the *Paramount* decision, independent theatre owners, long under the thumb of the power of the Hollywood circuits, struggled to find profitable niches in the new postwar filmgoing culture. Moreover, after World War II there grew greater interest in foreign culture and art forms, particularly European, as many members of the service returned home after living in England, France, and Italy.[27]

In November of 1945, only months after the hostilities were over and indeed before many members of the service had actually come home, Metro-Goldwyn-Mayer announced that it would distribute some twenty foreign films annually, dubbed in English. MGM would provide these foreign films the national publicity usually accorded only MGM's Hollywood products. Foreign films would play the estimated two hundred theatres in America's largest cities, university communities, and enclaves of the rich and educated that existed before the war. Distributors noted that a foreign film could be killed by film critics, principally those in New York, who usually had little power to influence the public who went to Hollywood films. In this case foreign films were after the same audience as the Broadway theatre.[28]

Much of the pressure of an MGM to import foreign films originated because of incentives provided by the governments of European nations. Many countries, seeking hard currency after the war, pressured Hollywood to open the theatres it still then controlled to foreign films in return for letting Hollywood back into their countries. The Second World War had temporarily crippled Hollywood's ability to export films to lucrative markets in Europe and Asia. As the Second World War drew to a close, the major Hollywood companies formed the Motion Picture Export Association (MPEA) to present a united front to foreign markets. The MPEA, which operated as the sole bargaining agent for members by setting prices and terms of trade, became the center of Hollywood's renewed thrust in a postwar world. Since the United States government used Hollywood films to help project America's best face around the world, the Department of State and succeeding presidents supported Hollywood's continuation as the world's dominant film seller.

But after the Second World War, foreign governments faced problems that required immediate solutions and that impinged on Hollywood's ability to trade. For example, if a nation let Hollywood take out precious currency, it severely upset that country's balance of payments. A country literally could not afford the luxury that Hollywood wished to provide. As a result, the Department of State (assisted by the MPEA) signed treaties with a number of countries (Britain and France, to name but two) that allowed Hollywood to draw out some currency but take the bulk only in credits toward filmmaking in that country. That is, a film with an American cast, director, and producer would be shot overseas with monies made at foreign theatres showing American films. Films featuring exotic locations as well as certain types of genre films (in particular westerns) were often shot in Europe through the 1950s and 1960s. Hollywood soon learned the value of "runaway" productions, the shooting of films outside the confines of their studio backlots.

The development of faster film stocks, better and more portable sound recording, and techniques that facilitated location shooting made it cheaper to shoot a film in England, Spain, or Italy than to recreate sets in the studio.

Audiences, probably reacting against television's crude studio production qualities, came to prefer features shot on location. There were also significant cost savings since the expenses of making a feature in Hollywood rose dramatically after World War II as craft unions asserted their demands and actors and directors used their leverage to extract greater payments. It simply became easier and cheaper to shoot a film anywhere but Hollywood. Foreign governments cooperated, supplying armies (sometimes literally) of extras to people spectacles. For example, it was widely rumored in the 1960s that the Spanish army was a profit-making enterprise because of its frequent use in Hollywood movies.

By the mid-1960s coproductions had become a fact of moviemaking. Since all Western countries had some form of governmental assistance scheme in place to encourage "native" production, a coproduction deal enabled a Hollywood company to gain a governmental partner to share the financing risk. A good example is Bernardo Bertolucci's *Last Tango in Paris* (1972), starring Marlon Brando and Maria Schneider. This film was an Italian-French coproduction, on paper 60 percent Italian and 40 percent French. In reality it was an Italian-Hollywood coproduction. The "French" partner was in fact Productions Artistes Associes, a subsidiary of United Artists, one of the major Hollywood movie companies. Many a "foreign" art film was actually a Hollywood-sponsored cross-bred work.[29]

THE BEGINNINGS OF THE ART HOUSE THEATRE

Exhibitors around the United States, anticipating this increased flow of foreign films, began to plan new theatres and convert others. Martin J. Lewis, director of the long-running "little cinema," the Little Carnegie Playhouse, was said to be scouting houses in Atlanta. The South had never had much interest in the cinema of other nations during the 1930s; this seemed to be an open market. The fifteen-hundred-seat Mayan Theatre in downtown Los Angeles and the soon to be opened Las Palmas in Hollywood were said to be aimed at a foreign art film policy. These were the two newest entries in the art house field in what was then the nation's fastest growing city. The Varsity and Uptown in Seattle, Washington, converted to an art house policy just as the 1947–48 movie season commenced. The Varsity drew from the community that ringed the seventeen-thousand-student University of Washington and the Uptown from a relatively prosperous part of town.[30]

By the winter of 1947–48 it was clear to many observers of the film business that, to quote the *New York Times*, "While Hollywood's motion pictures are finding the going rough in foreign lands, bucking up against currency exchange restrictions, political censorship, quotas and other import restrictions . . . , imported films on the other hand currently are being greeted with open arms by American moviegoers and enjoying unprecedented popularity." [31]

The upsurge in patronage at art houses was indeed very profitable. One estimate placed the national gross take at the box offices of art houses in 1947 at over fifteen million dollars. This can be compared to the two-and-a-half-billion-dollar gross (one-and-a-half billion in the United States) Hollywood took in at the world box office in 1947, only a year from the peak year in Hollywood's history. [32]

But the beginnings of the art house movement centered in New York City. In the 1940s approximately 60 percent of the revenue of a typical art film came from theatres in Manhattan. Thereafter the movement did begin to spread, but even so, approximately 40 percent of the nation's more than two hundred art houses were in the New York City environs alone before 1950. The art house would always do its best business in major cities (such as New York) and certain specialized college towns (such as Ann Arbor, Michigan, or Madison, Wisconsin).

The art house proved a different affair from mainstream Hollywood-fed theatres. Runs lasted weeks, even months. The Sutton on New York's trendy East Side ran the British *Quartet* (1949) for more than six months in 1949. The Selznick Releasing organization waited to premiere Carol Reed's *The Fallen Idol* (1948) for the Sutton rather than book it first in Radio City Music Hall. It ran more than twenty-nine weeks at the top prices for any theatre in New York. *Motion Picture Herald* found that it was filled with the "cream of the carriage trade" from the surrounding neighborhood. [33]

Another good example is the case of the Paris Theatre, which opened in September of 1948. Located at the posh corner where Fifth Avenue meets Central Park, it was opened and operated by the Pathé group, which operated theatres in the major capitals of Europe. The lounge of the new Paris, placed beneath the foyer-lobby area, was a simply appointed home-like room of modern furnishings. Tea, coffee, bouillon, and little cakes were served at no extra charge. Patrons were also encouraged to use the room to play bridge, chess, or backgammon or to inspect the products of French industry in glass-enclosed cases.

The auditorium of the new Paris was gray in tone, exuding a tasteful Bauhaus style not to be confused with the garishness of the Roxy or

Paramount movie palaces only blocks away. This was a posh house—the entrance vestibule was set into a limestone facade with a marble base—set in one of the most upscale locations in New York City. The motto seemed to be: sell the art films to the rich and well educated and a sizable group of the middle class might follow. Such films as *Symphonie Pastorale* (1948) attracted large audiences, holding over for several months late in 1948. The Paris Theatre was one of the top art houses through the 1950s in New York City and later the site for a dispute that would provide the movies with free expression equal to printed books, newspapers, and magazines.[34]

Other New York theatres also were able to make the successful conversion to an art house policy. Probably the most famous and widely reported was the conversion of the original newsreel theatre in the United States, the Embassy Theatre at Broadway and Forty-sixth on Times Square, in November 1949. It temporarily closed early that November and opened in time for Christmas, playing two British imports: *The Gay Lady* (1949), a musical in Technicolor, and *The Hidden Room* (1949), a mystery thriller from the J. Arthur Rank Organization. This was typical around the country in the late 1940s: specialized newsreel theatres lost their function in a suburbanized world and quickly converted to an art theatre policy.[35]

Interest in art films was apparent throughout the United States. Surprisingly, after New York City the locale with the next greatest earnings was Hollywood itself. Other cities followed in terms of city size and interest in international events: Chicago, Washington, and Boston. Theatres everywhere, if well situated, did well. The two aforementioned Seattle theatres, the Varsity and Uptown, opened with foreign films exclusively and business jumped dramatically. Indeed at the Varsity box office, the take doubled from the previous season. Plans were being made to open art theatres in such unexpected places as Salt Lake City, San Diego, and Denver. By the close of the 1940s even *Time* magazine had discovered and praised this new trend. The number of art theatres had increased to nearly three hundred, still a small portion of the twenty thousand United States theatres.[36]

The specific case of the Esquire on the near North Side of Chicago illustrates the transformation of a subsequent-run theatre into an art theatre. Located just off the trendy shopping street of Michigan Avenue, the Esquire needed to fashion a new business strategy as movie attendance declined everywhere in Chicago. In 1949, a particularly bad year in the Chicago film business, the eleven-hundred-seat art house reached all-time record attendance. (The theatre was opened in 1938.) The Esquire was constantly filled, despite an increase in ticket prices. Its films were a combination of Hollywood sophistication (Bette Davis and Cary Grant were popular in the late 1940s) and foreign fare, principally from Great Britain. The theatre had no posters, publicity photographs, or on-screen previews. Only a simple card outside gave the name of the film and its stars. Indeed the theatre was popular in the film trade and was used by distributors for trade screenings on a regular basis.

The Esquire, like many art houses, used a mailing list of regular customers. Each week in the late 1940s the Esquire sent out seven thousand announcements. Every Christmas it mailed regular customers two free tickets, inserted in a discreet folder. To maintain its image it paid its ushers 50 percent more than the competition in order to get college students who appeared clean-cut in their simple tan uniforms. In the lobby one could read Chicago's "Townsfolk," a social newsletter, or the *New Yorker* in mammoth leather easy chairs while muted classical music was piped in. An art gallery off the mezzanine presented shows of local talents and was reviewed in the major local papers.

By the mid-1950s the Esquire was the lone house in the Windy City, doing a booming business because of its switch to an art house policy. The Esquire became the prestige house of Chicago, drawing from all parts of the city, in particular the northern suburbs, based on its supposed snob appeal. The Esquire began to compete for "patrons" with the nearby Art Institute and Symphony Hall. Properly situated on Chicago's Gold Coast, a combination of New York's Beekman Place, Sutton Place, Park Avenue, and the East Fifties, it was located in an area of old homes and gold-plated restaurants, a stone's throw from the fashionable Drake Hotel.[37]

The art house of the late 1940s differed considerably from its mainstream competitors, even beyond the difference in the source of films. Art houses presented a single feature, while Hollywood theatres continued with the double feature began a decade earlier. Art houses did not hawk popcorn; if any food was sold it was coffee, tea, cakes, or light sandwiches. The seats were new and the ushers stressed politeness and seriousness; no talking was permitted during the screening of a serious art film. And for this art theatres charged the highest prices of any movie theatre; often in New York City their admission fee exceeded two dollars, prices equal to (and sometimes higher) than those found on Broadway. The wealthy patrons of the average art theatre could easily afford it.[38]

Encouraged by the widely reported successes of the Paris and Sutton, a number of new art houses were built in Manhattan on Fifty-seventh and Fifty-eighth streets, from Second Avenue to Seventh Avenue, while the

Little Carnegie was remodeled. With the new openings early in the 1950s there were no fewer than ten art theatres in the Fifty-seventh to Fifty-eighth streets corridor, along with fine shops and restaurants. The total seating for foreign films was in excess of five thousand, a bit less than the total available seats in Radio City Music Hall.

One new theatre was the Fine Arts, a five-hundred-seat house at 130 East Fifty-eighth on the prior site of the Cafe Society Uptown, a nightclub. Costing $150,000 to construct, it had a playroom, a gallery for experimental paintings, and a television room. The Fine Arts offered first-run French and British films. Built by Michael Hyams and Joseph Green, who operated the Little Cine Met, the City Theatre, and the Irving Place, all in New York, it stressed relaxed comfort. With 385 orchestra seats and 100 more in the mezzanine, the theatre opened with *The Lavender Hill Mob* (1951), which did fine business. The house was equipped with wide reclining state-of-the-art chairs and would have a long run as an art house.[39]

The Weinstock brothers, who operated another theatre on East Fifty-third in New York, opened the Normandie at 110 East Fifty-seventh on the site of the old Lotus Club. (Obviously since these theatres were small, a reasonable tract of land could be purchased; this was never the case for the massive picture palaces of the 1920s, which required several tracts of land.) Seating six hundred, it was included in a modern six-story building, and it too would have a long run as an art house.[40]

One of the first of the art cinemas in New York, opened in the 1920s, was the Little Carnegie on Fifty-seventh Street, near its more famous cousin, *the* Carnegie Hall. In the winter of 1951–52, because of the boom in art houses in New York City, it was enlarged and refurbished after twenty-five years in business. An adjoining building was acquired to shift the foyer and thus make room for a larger auditorium. Capacity was increased from less than four hundred seats to more than five hundred. The lounge area was expanded to include a television area so patrons could watch one of the local stations (which was common at the time). The colors were muted grays and browns. Redecoration cost four hundred thousand dollars.[41]

In 1952 the Baronet opened at Third Avenue and Fifty-ninth to be operated by the Walter Reade circuit, which already ran the Park Avenue. Formerly the Arcadia, it was refurbished and provided with a new marquee, lobby, lounge, and carpeting throughout for its 430 seats. In time the Reade organization not only became a force in running art theatres (as well as mainstream cinemas) but also a force in the distribution of offbeat films.[42]

In May of 1952 came the Beekman at Second Avenue and Sixtieth, a six-hundred-seat theatre operated by Edward Rugoff. The opening of this new luxurious house, free of offensive popcorn smells and boasting the latest taste in modern architecture and design, was celebrated. Located in an apartment building, it was meant to enhance this prestigious neighborhood. The Beekman was fashioned mainly from stainless steel and glass, and it was an expression of the modern architecture sweeping the nation at the time.[43]

Edward Rugoff passed away soon after the opening of the Beekman, so his son, Donald Rugoff, became the theatre's operator and later a major force in the art theatre business. Rugoff's father had founded the family business in 1921 with Edward Becker. In 1959, with support from Mrs. David Rockefeller, the younger Rugoff took over the Paris Theatre. Also in 1959 the circuit opened the Murray Hill Theatre on Thirty-fourth at Third Avenue as a traditional first-run house. In 1959 Rugoff also operated other art houses: the Sutton, the Beekman, the Fifth Avenue Cinema, and the Art in Greenwich Village. In 1962 Rugoff opened the Cinema I and Cinema II, the first two new theatres opened in New York City in a decade. Thereafter the Upper East Side of New York became the major releasing location of art cinema in the United States.[44]

THE GOLDEN AGE OF THE ART THEATRE

By 1952, with the art house movement being hailed in the New York press and by various opinion leaders, the movement became the biggest news in the film exhibition business. Art house theatres represented the first increase in filmgoing since the apex of the war years. The art house, 300 to 750 seats in size, presented foreign as well as select, older, "sophisticated" Hollywood films. There were an estimated 470 art houses in January 1952, and the number was growing. In addition some 1,500 theatres were booking foreign films at some point in their schedules. Although these could—at the most generous counting—account for one-twentieth of the total theatrical business, they were heralded because they represented a rare trend upward in movie attendance during the early 1950s.[45]

Art theatre owners tried anything to draw an audience. When the theatres were still new, miniature television screening rooms were planned. But in general the art house movement suffered during Hollywood's experiments with 3-D, CinemaScope, and VistaVision. Temporarily there was a stagnation in attendance in art theatres. One film ended that and restarted momentum: Roger Vadim's *And God Created Woman* (1956). This film earned four million dollars in the United States in 1957, a year in which all other French films shown in the United States combined took in four million. Theatre owners, who thus far had looked askance at art films, scrambled to book "offbeat" French films. Thereafter such films as Federico Fellini's *La Dolce Vita* (1960) were hawked to highly educated Americans for themes that were taboo to the Hollywood cinema of the day.[46]

Generally, audience studies found that art theatres attracted persons of above-average education, more men than women, and many solitary movie-goers. This was the crowd who attended the opera, theatre, lectures, and ballet. They continued to listen to radio for its classical music, while not even purchasing a television set. They read the *New Yorker*, *Harpers*, the *Atlantic*, and the *Reporter* as well as many newspapers and publications devoted to fine arts and literature. Their favorite paper was the *New York Times*, even if they did not live in New York. These were professionals, managers, or aspiring "eggheads." Indeed one of the constants of the art cinema of the 1950s was the painting gallery in the lobby.[47]

During the late 1950s and early 1960s the international art cinema reached an apogee. In just five years celebrated efforts included Federico Fellini's *Nights of Cabiria* (1957), Ingmar Bergman's *Wild Strawberries* (1957), Michelangelo Antonioni's *L'Avventura* (1959), Alain Resnais' *Hiroshima mon amour* (1959), Francois Truffaut's *The 400 Blows* (1959), Jean-Luc Godard's *Breathless* (1960), and Luis Buñuel's *Viridiana* (1961). The European film director rose to the status of international celebrity and was talked about in the same breath with noted novelists or composers. Fellini, Antonioni, Bergman, Truffaut, and Godard, to name but five, became stars within this new form of cinema.

So did the film critic. Since the art cinema stressed ambiguity, the meaning of a film was not as explicit as in a straightforward classical Hollywood tale. Some apparatus had to be set up to interpret art films through such publications as the *New York Times* and the *Saturday Review*. The task of the Hollywood reviewer had been to serve as an extension of the industry to promote films and stars. During the 1960s film critics were expected to explain the meaning of films. Gaps were to be filled in, symbols explained, meaning extrapolated. Ingmar Bergman, for a time the most discussed filmmaker in the Western world, understood this; in his *Now About These Women* (1964) he inserted a title after a shot of a man running down a corridor waving fireworks warning critics not to interpret this shot symbolically.[48]

With the art house market now accepted as a permanent part of the moviegoing world, new institutions were created. For example, New York theatre owner Walter Reade, Jr. stepped forward to develop a national chain of art theatres and then became a major foreign film distributor. Reade owned a number of houses in the New York area. In 1953 he began to build a circuit of art houses throughout the United States based on his theatres in New York and the Maury A. Schwartz theatres in San Francisco. Reade then planned to move into Chicago, Los Angeles, Cleveland, St. Louis, Philadelphia, and Boston. The circuit would also distribute films and share the profits among the theatres in conjunction with Continental Distributing, in which Reade had a share of ownership. In 1953 Reade had some forty theatres in New York and New Jersey.[49]

Don Rugoff, who owned a number of important New York art theatres, began booking for others in the late 1950s. In 1963, with backing of a syndicate headed by composer Richard Rogers, his company formally became Cinema 5, a distribution outlet with the first effort *Heavens Above!* (1963), starring Peter Sellers and Cecil Parker, directed by the Boulting brothers. In time Cinema 5 introduced Costa-Gravas' *Z* (1969), Shirley Clarke's *The Cool World* (1963), Francois Truffaut's *Soft Skin* (1964), Werner Herzog's *The Mystery of Kasper Hauser* (1974), and Nicholas Roeg's *The Man Who Fell To Earth* (1967). But the money was made with *Morgan* (1966), *Endless Summer* (1966), and *Elvira Madigan* (1967). Cinema 5 boldly took on the distribution of films about subjects concerning African-Americans such as *One Potato, Two Potato* (1964), a story of interracial marriage.

In the hip, late 1960s, Cinema 5 stood for the art film, distributing Joseph Losey's *Accident* (1967), Milos Forman's *The Fireman's Ball* (1968), and Robert Downey's *Putney Swope* (1969). Rugoff was noted for his promotions, including a thirty-five-thousand-dollar party he staged for Dusan Makaveyev at the Plaza Hotel for the opening of WR: *Mysteries of the Organism*. Cinema 5 was known for its distinctive advertisements and created its own designs. Rugoff would retain control of the Cinema 5 operation until February 1979, when shares of the company, which were traded on the American Stock Exchange, were acquired in a takeover battle by the Forman interests of Pacific Theatres.[50]

In 1960 came yet another force in this business who would eventually turn to distribution, Dan Talbot and his New Yorker Theatre. This theatre played revivals and art films, a mixture to please the film fan on New York's Upper West Side. The neighborhood was gentrifying, and many a New Yorker became addicted to eclectic tastes. In 1965 Talbot branched into film distribution, and his New Yorker company became one of the most important suppliers of hot art house titles to theatres and campus film societies.[51]

By the 1980s Talbot had become a major force in New York exhibition. In 1981 he opened the new Lincoln Center Plaza Triplex, on Broadway at Sixty-third Street opposite Lincoln Center, with Federico Fellini's *City of Women* (1979), Michel Deville's *Voyage en Douce* (1979), and Jacques Doillon's *La Drolesse* (1979). With his duplex Cinema Studio up the street (which he acquired in 1977) Talbot single-handedly made the west side a force in the art cinema world of New York. Many of his New Yorker films played at his theatres. *The Marriage of Maria Braun* (1979) ran for a full year at the Cinema Studio and grossed over two and a half million dollars nationally.[52]

The art cinema and its increased popularity led to the demise of the legal barriers of censorship in the United States. In 1952, for the first time since 1915, the United States Supreme Court agreed to hear a case involving a movie, and on 26 May 1952 in the case involving Roberto Rossellini's *The Miracle* (1948) the Court reversed its precedent and recognized that movies deserved equal protection for free speech. The film had originally been passed, and on 12 December 1950 it opened at the Paris Theatre in New York City. Eleven days later the theatre license commissioner of New York City ordered the film removed from the screen and the film's distributor took the issue to court.

In 1951, when a lower court let the film play, *The Miracle* became a hit at the Paris. Catholic War veterans, under direct encouragement from Cardinal Spellman, marched in front of the theatre. But in March the full New York State Board met and revoked the license for showing *The Miracle*. The controversy then moved to the courts and within a year the case was settled and then the film could be shown again.[53]

The Hollywood-sponsored Production Code Administration never seemed to know what to do about serious art films; often it treated them as simple smut and banned them from cooperating theatres. But there were many disputes. One of the greatest early art film hits, *The Bicycle Thief* (1948), would help break the back of the Production Code Administration. Distributor Joseph Burstyn pushed to have the whole film shown rather than cut two short scenes. Even the Catholic Legion of Decency did not condemn the film. Still the industry's trade association, the Motion Picture Producers and Distributors Association, insisted on the cuts and the subsequent furor made the film into something of a minor cause. By mid-April 1949 the film was running in nearly fifty theatres around the United

States, advertised as "Please come and see me before they cut me out. . . *Bicycle Thief*, the uncensored version."[54]

Art theatres in general saw no reason to cooperate with the Production Code Administration. During the 1950s local censorship boards tried to step in and ban offensive films. In the era of Joseph McCarthy and his Red scare, local censorship boards were hailed for standing up to outside agitators. Alain Resnais's *Hiroshima mon amour* (1959) was banned for its controversial look at the effects of the atomic bomb; Jack Clayton's *A Room at the Top* (1959) was suppressed in several communities for its frank sexuality.

But by the 1960s Hollywood itself had begun to tackle controversial themes it once considered taboo. The traditional theatre began to show films that before could be shown only at the art house. In a test case in 1966 Michelangelo Antonioni's *Blowup* (1966) was denied a seal of approval from the Production Code Administration. MGM, which financed the film, refused to cut it and subsequently released the film through a subsidiary. MGM up to this point had never released a film not approved by the code.[55]

But the legal effects in the world of censorship were hardly the beginning of the changes wrought by the art cinema. The style and appeal of the art cinema led to what many called a "new Hollywood" in the late 1960s and early 1970s. As David Bordwell has noted: "Everything from freeze frames and slow motion to conventions of gapping and ambiguity has been exploited by filmmakers like [Stanley] Donen (*Two for the Road*, 1967), [Richard] Lester (*Petulia*, 1968), [Dennis] Hopper (*Easy Rider*, 1968), [Francis Ford] Coppola (*The Rain People*, 1969), [Mike] Nichols (*Catch-22*, 1973), and [Robert] Altman (*Images*, 1972, *Three Women*, 1977)." Directors of the "new Hollywood" even went on to parody classic Hollywood genres. Westerns like Arthur Penn's *Little Big Man* (1970) and Robert Altman's *MacCabe and Mrs. Miller* (1971) offer telling examples. By the 1970s, Francois Truffaut and Michelangelo Antonioni, valued members of the European art cinema filmmaking community, had journeyed to work in Hollywood.[56]

The new legal framework and new trends in filmmaking led to changes in the business of Hollywood as well. Foreign film distribution had long been the province of small, independent entrepreneurs such as Joseph Burstyn, Don Rugoff and his Cinema 5, and Ilya Lopert and Lopert Films. The operation usually consisted of a New York City office with a handful of employees. The major film companies sought to co-opt the art film and the art theatre became less specialized. With five hundred art houses in the early 1960s, out of some eleven thousand theatres, the art house had become far less marginal.[57]

The case of United Artists and UA Classics provides a typical experience. In the early 1960s Ilya Lopert, a force in the art cinema field, was lured to become a subsidiary of United Artists. Independently Lopert Films had distributed such films as *Shoeshine* (1946), *Richard II* (1956), and *Nights of Cabiria* (1957) and helped open the DuPont Circle Theatre in Washington, D.C., and the Plaza in New York. With United Artists, Lopert attempted to bring the art film into the mainstream, handling such films as *Never on Sunday* (1961), *Electra* (1962), *Persona* (1967), *Hour of the Wolf* (1968), and *Shame* (1969). But this integration of the art cinema into Hollywood would prove a short-lived phenomenon.[58]

The art house movement helped peak interest in the study of cinema in the United States. Film studies departments appeared everywhere during the late 1960s and early 1970s. Students began to write seriously about film in such publications as the *Velvet Light Trap* (the University of Wisconsin) and the *Film Reader* (Northwestern University). By 1975, there were thousands of film majors in institutions from the smallest junior college to the hallowed halls of the Ivy League.[59]

THE END OF THE ART HOUSE

Nonetheless, the peak of the pure art house came sometime in the 1960s. No event more underscored the downturn than when the Walter Reade chain, one of the pioneers of the art house, sought the protection of Chapter XI of the bankruptcy laws. It was just not possible in the climate of the early 1970s for Walter Reade, Inc. to operate a miniconglomerate based on the ownership and operation of art theatres and the distribution of art films. Once Walter Reade, Inc. reorganized, the company transformed itself into a mainstream first-run theatre chain. With this policy Walter Reade, Inc. did so well that it was taken over by Columbia Pictures in 1985.[60]

By 1980, the universe of theatres in the United States that regularly ran foreign films was down to less than one hundred. The core market had shrunk to theatres in New York City, Los Angeles, Boston, San Francisco, Seattle, and Washington, D.C. Art houses in the secondary markets of Chicago, Philadelphia, St. Louis, Santa Fe, Houston, and Dallas struggled to make money consistently with non-Hollywood films.

Examples abounded. In Los Angeles it was Laemmle Theatres; Mel Novikoff dominated San Francisco with the Surf, Lumière, Cannery, and Castro; in Washington, D.C., it was the Circle chain. One film could make or break a struggling art house chain. For example, in February 1987 the Fine Arts of Kansas City ended an eighty-four-week run of *The Gods Must Be Crazy*, yet the total gross for this run added up to less than three hundred thousand dollars or about three thousand dollars per week.[61]

New York City continued to set trends, and by the late 1980s that trend was art films playing nearly exclusively in nonprofit venues. In 1988 the *New York Times* listed twenty-six alternatives for art house exhibition. Topping the list were museums, including the long-standing theatre in the Museum of Modern Art, as well as theatre spaces in the American Museum of the Moving Image, the American Museum of Natural History, the Brooklyn Museum, the Jewish Museum, and the Metropolitan Museum of Art. Local New York City universities continued long-standing film series, principally at New York University and Columbia University.

There were foreign language associations like the Asia Society, the French Institute, the Japan Society, and the Goethe House. And finally there were institutions devoted to the art of the cinema as nonprofit organizations, including Anthology Film Archives, the Collective for Living Cinema, the Film Forum, the Kitchen, Millennium Film Workshop, and the Whitney Museum of American Art. The profit-seeking art theatre had become part of the museum and educational establishment.[62]

Certain trends seemed promising. One was the repertory film movement. Slowly, as film was increasingly considered an art form, societies were created to rerun film classics. The origins of the repertory cinema began in the 1950s, often with a film society connected with a university. By 1960 there were more than 250 film societies around the United States showing in classrooms from Dartmouth to Antioch College, from the University of Wisconsin–Madison to the University of Florida. In a small, select number of cities theatres would be converted to repertory houses during the 1960s.[63]

The apex of the repertory cinema came with the phenomenon of the midnight movie of the 1970s. Beginning in New York at the Elgin, St. Marks, Waverly, and Eighth Street Playhouses, films such as Alexandro Jodorowsky's *El Topo* (1970), George Romero's modern horror classic, *Night of the Living Dead* (1968), and John Waters' *Pink Flamingos* (1971) were shown after hours, at midnight on weekends, repeatedly. The most successful was *The Rocky Horror Picture Show* (1975), which bowed at the

Waverly in the spring of 1976. Fans came regularly every Saturday night, dressed up as characters in the film, ready to mouth their favorite lines. A cult was born.[64]

For a time *The Rocky Horror Picture Show* as a midnight movie even moved to the American heartland. In Austin, Texas, it sold out at the Presido; in Lubbock, Texas, William D. Kerns of the local *Avalanche-Journal* and Pat Shellenbarger of the *Detroit News* both called for the film to be withdrawn because of vandalism and the negative effect on the local youth. In Tucson, Arizona, a young man left the New Loft Theatre, sporting a plastic bubble headdress, screaming: "I've seen it eighty-two times and I love it, love it!" The college and high school students of Oklahoma City and Milwaukee lined up.[65]

With the coming of the conservative 1980s, coupled with the rise of home video, the art house phenomenon came to an end. Home video made it too easy to see foreign films at home. Repertory houses, without the midnight movie attraction, began to close. The Coolidge in Boston ended its older-films policy after ten years. The Seattle Seven Gables chain closed its repertory house. And in New York, the Regency, the Studio, the Bleeker Street, and the Thalia, long *the* trend-setting repertory houses of the nation, shut their doors. The art house movement, begun in the late 1940s, ended in the late 1970s with the cessation of the repertory movie houses.[66]

NEW ETHNIC MOVIE HOUSES

Throughout the art house movement ethnic movie theatres never disappeared. If the population was large enough, the ties to the native language strong enough, and the discretionary income sizable enough, foreign language movie houses remained available. In the 1980s, for example, Hispanic-Americans began to see special theatre circuits. With an increasingly affluent Hispanic population that topped thirty million, and formidable concentrations of Hispanic-Americans in Miami, Florida; New York City; San Antonio, Texas; Detroit, Michigan; Los Angeles; and San Jose, California it was estimated that three hundred to five hundred cinemas were playing Spanish-language films on some sort of regular basis.

On the Upper West Side of New York, for example, a vital pocket of Hispanic America extends from 100th to 110th streets, between Broadway and Central Park West. During the late 1980s, as the area became more and more middle class, the Noevo Edison Cinema, which had been showing Spanish-language films on Broadway between 103rd and 104th, was transformed into the Columbia Cinema, a sleek, six-hundred-seat theatre with Dolby stereo that ran first-run Hollywood films in Spanish as well as fare from Mexico and South America. But the heart of Spanish-language cinemas in the United States of the 1980s could be found on another Broadway, three thousand miles away in downtown Los Angeles. There, the former great movie palaces from another era—the Los Angeles, the United Artists, the Million Dollar, the Orpheum—had been running Spanish films (and live acts) for nearly thirty years, to increasing crowds.[67]

Hollywood even began to recognize the potential dollars that could be extracted from Spanish-language theatres. In the late 1980s major movie companies began to release such films as *La Bamba* (1987), *The Milagro Bean Field War* (1988), and *Stand and Deliver* (1988) simultaneously in English and Spanish versions. For *La Bamba* it was estimated that of the total United States gross at the box office (fifty-three million), some two million dollars was taken from Spanish-language dubbed prints in the United States. In the long run Hollywood may not stand as a regular supplier of films for Hispanic America, but the indication of interest signals the vitality of the theatres showing films in Spanish.[68]

Whether for ethnic Americans interested in films from back home or the educated looking for art films from Europe, entrepreneurs have long sought to serve special markets for movie shows. And nothing indicates that this will not continue. Entrepreneurs will seek to devise special theatres for special audiences as long as going to the movies continues to hold its sway over Americans. We cannot be sure where this might take place, but the entrepreneurial history of movie exhibition should prepare us for nothing less. In fact, there is some evidence that the new art theatre of the 1990s will be found in specialized video stores. Indeed, that leads to the new consideration of the transformation of technical change.[69]

17. *Lining up for a show restricted to blacks in Dallas, Texas*

18.   A *movie house for blacks in Memphis, Tennessee*

19.   A *beautiful theatre in small-town America, the Augusta in Augusta, Kansas*

20.   *The Waikiki Theatre in Hawaii in 1944*

21. *The Telenews Theatre in Milwaukee, Wisconsin; note the advertisement for television offered in the lobby*

22.　*A typical marquee of a 1930s newsreel theatre*

23. *Grauman's Million Dollar Theatre near opening day in 1918*

24. *The Million Dollar Theatre as a present-day movie house for Hispanic Americans*

25. *The interior of the Progresso Theatre in San Antonio in the 1930s*

26. A German-language movie theatre in Milwaukee, Wisconsin

27. *Foreign films at the Apollo in New York City in the mid-1960s*

28.   *Two early drive-in theatres*

29.   *Inventor Ray Dolby (right) on the roof of the company's headquarters in*
San Francisco

30. *The hybrid of a movie palace, the Southtown of Chicago, opened in 1932,
with a parking lot for automobiles*

31. *One of the two largest "screens" of the Cineplex Odeon Universal City Cinema complex*

PART III

Technological Transformations

TEN

Sound

Technology forms the movie show. The introduction of silent, black-and-white 35 mm images drove the first experiments in showing films to mass audiences (chapter 1), the development of the nickelodeon (chapter 2), and the advance of the picture palace (chapter 3). But technological invention and innovation hardly stopped with the ideas of the first scientists. The coming of mechanical sound to the movies constituted the first major technological change in the history of film. Later came color and wide-screen images. The history of these two significant redefinitions of the movie show constitute this and the following chapters.

The greatest addition to the technology of the movie show emerged with the innovation of television. Indeed by the 1970s more people in the United States were watching motion pictures on television than in theatres. Historians too often ignore the impact of television on the movie show. To seek the economic and social impact of television on the presentation of motion pictures, chapter 13 will examine the effect of over-the-air television, chapter 14 will analyze the innovation of cable television, and chapter 15 will detail the enormous influence of the coming of home video.

This final section of *Shared Pleasures* moves beyond the usual definition of the presentation of motion pictures in a theatrical setting. We must accept that television, during the final third of the twentieth century, dominates as the means of movie presentation. To understand the influence of television forms the final chapters, in a continual process of technical change begun in the 1920s with the introduction of talkies.

215

THE COMING OF SOUND

As we have seen, film exhibition in the United States was a big business with set patterns and institutions by the mid-1920s. By 1925 some twenty thousand movie houses were operating in the United States. The exact number is impossible to pin down because many stayed open only a few months each year, as in resort towns, for example. On the margin of the industry, several thousand small theatres in neighborhoods and rural towns did the best they could, and hundreds went in and out of business in any one year. Although the trend was up, the best guess is that there were fifteen thousand full-time theatres, with five thousand more operating on the fringes.[1]

Three-quarters of America's twenty thousand movie theatres were located in small towns. They numbered nearly fifteen thousand but took in less than a quarter of the box-office dollars. They drew less (because of capacity) and charged less (thus collecting less proportionally of the money). The bigger, fancier picture palaces were all located in urban America. They totaled about a quarter of all theatres, but these five thousand houses (at most) accounted for three-quarters of the monies. By 1925 the movies had become an urban phenomenon as a business, and the picture palace set the ideal for the movie show.[2]

Picture palaces always presented more than "silent" movies. Music accompanied all films; the problem of how best to select music was widely discussed and debated. The biggest picture palaces had orchestras upwards of fifty or more, but all houses, however small, had some music, at a minimum one piano player. If there was an average for a neighborhood house, it was five to ten members of a small house orchestra. An overture to the show was common in picture palaces; selections surveyed the standard repertory from the *William Tell* Overture by Rossini to the *1812* Overture by Tschaikowsky.[3]

The house conductor, who doubled as an arranger, had to prepare a new score every time the program changed, at least once a week and more often twice a week. The largest of the picture palaces built up and maintained vast libraries of sheet music, and small-town house leaders had guidebooks to assist their selections. Work was indexed so that players could jump quickly from a First World War battle scene to an intimate meeting between two lovers. By the mid-1920s, movie theatres were the foremost employer of musicians in the nation, almost as many as all other live orchestras combined.[4]

Picture palaces also offered stage shows for one's admission price. Indeed, by the mid-1920s formulae had been established for live show presentations. There came to be certain accepted standards. The picture palace show, of about two- to two-and-a-half hours, opened with music from the house orchestra. Then came the live presentation of usually twenty minutes, followed by a series of shorts, almost always including a set of newsreels. Next came the climax of the show, the feature film. It was the job of the chain to establish the mixture of these shows (music and live acts) and film materials (shorts and features) to appeal to the audiences of that particular city.[5]

There existed three dominant stage show formulae. For the "pure presentation," the theatre would mount a revuelike spectacle with a troupe of female dancers and perhaps specialty vaudeville acts. This is what we associate today with the Radio City Music Hall. In the "prologue" the theme of the live show was linked to the feature film, so, for example, a nautical show (with singers costumed as divers suspended from cables) preceded Buster Keaton's *The Navigator* (1925). Finally there was the "vaudeville show" in which several acts of vaudeville were simply grouped together. This latter strategy survived into the 1930s with swing bands (Benny Goodman or Tommy Dorsey) and noted singers (Bing Crosby or Frank Sinatra).[6]

But there was also more than the feature film and the stage show. Most theatres presented shorts—comedies and newsreels. In the silent era, animated cartoons, travelogues, and other assorted shorts were commonplace. It was up to the theatre manager to program each house slightly different to maximize the appeal to that local audience. The feature film was only one part of the mix, and often it was run faster than normal or even cut to make sure the show included all the attractions and did not run too long. Indeed, until talkies it was not necessary to run a film at one constant speed.[7]

The innovation of sound by Warner Bros. and Fox Film was carefully planned. The film industry of the 1920s had millions invested in its system, and so it was not interested in simply adopting the unproven talkies. Any innovator had to sell a set of significant advantages for talkies vis-à-vis current movie house programming and make the argument that the innovation would be cost effective as well. That is, the innovation would be adopted only if the theatre owner could be convinced it might lead to greater profits. This is precisely what Warner Bros. and Fox demonstrated.

With the backing of Wall Street, Warner Bros. sought to use the new sound technology offered it by AT&T to tender *on film* the stage show attractions so vital to picture palaces. Warner Bros. recorded the greatest vaudeville and musical talents on film and presented them as *substitutes* for the stage shows. Its initial targets were medium-sized theatres that could not afford the more expensive vaudeville performers as live attractions. With talkies substituting for vaudeville, exhibitors could program the best—albeit on film. In short, the medium-sized independent house could have afforded Al Jolson performing one or two of his hit songs on film, while it could never have paid the necessary thousands for Jolson to appear live on stage. Only a handful of theatres in the nation's biggest cities could afford Jolson's fee of several thousand dollars per week.

Warner Bros. never initially set out to make talkies as features but rather to provide one or two reel-length recordings of musical and vaudeville acts that theatre owners could offer as "stage shows." This innovation of sound was not easily accomplished, but after the 6 August 1926 successful premiere of *Don Juan*, with a package of sound shorts plus an orchestra on a recorded disc, Warner Bros. was able to convince theatre owners to try their sound film strategy. The centerpiece of the Warner Bros.' strategy was the regular production and release of vaudeville shorts. Warner Bros. paid Al Jolson twenty-five thousand dollars for his recordings and Eddie Cantor twice that amount. Indeed, the Warner Bros.' threat grew so real that the long-time vaudeville theatre operators began to insert clauses into agreements with stars preventing them from recording on Vitaphone.[8]

Warner Bros. set out to make its Vitaphone brand name as well known in its field as Victor's Red Seal was in the phonograph record business of the mid-1920s. *Variety*, then the leading vaudeville and movie trade paper in the United States, began to review the Vitaphone "acts" on 23 March 1927 and treated them as "canned" vaudeville. Warner Bros.' list of acts would have made any stage show entrepreneur proud. Even Weber and Fields, the comics, who for a time declared they were above Vitaphone, eventually signed up; the money was too good for simply performing a routine one had been doing all one's life.[9]

By April 1927, more than one hundred movie houses around the United States signed up; more than a third were in the East, but at least half of the then forty-eight states had at least one "Vitaphoned" movie house. And these were not minor league theatres; the Stanley circuit and Finkelstein and Rubin, from Minneapolis, both inked contracts. But the important news that spring was when Samuel Rothaefel (Roxy) signed up; exhibitors in all sectors took notice. Roxy was then the most famous movie house impresario in the nation.[10]

By April 1927 Warner Bros.' Vitaphone division had recorded all the popular stars of the day. Nonscientific surveys found patrons preferred Al Jolson and operatic tenor Giovanni Martinelli. In turn, for the second set of recordings of these two stars Warner Bros. paid five thousand dollars each. Warner Bros. soon "ran out" of stars and had to devise something new. What the company did was add Vitaphoned segments to feature films. They believed that if Jolson did so well in short subjects, he could do even better in a feature film designed and written especially for him. The film would be silent as the necessary narrative moved along, but as soon as the Jolson character was required to break into song, the sound technology would be utilized. This strategy represented a merger of the new with the old, designed not to offend theatre owners or filmgoers but simply to attract new patrons.

The first such Vitaphoned feature was *The Jazz Singer* (1927), which opened the 1927–28 movie season, premiering early in October 1927. What Warner Bros. did over the summer months of 1927 was publicize *The Jazz Singer* and thus convince several hundred more theatres to install sound equipment.

The success of *The Jazz Singer* (including accompanying vaudeville shorts) encouraged the brothers Warner and their financial advisors, Wall Street's Goldman Sachs, to exploit their innovation further. By the spring of 1928 *The Jazz Singer* package was being held over in certain theatres for an extraordinary four weeks. (One week during the 1920s was considered normal; a two-week stay usually set a house record.) Warner Bros. followed up *The Jazz Singer* with *Glorious Betsy*, and, for example, during the summer of 1928 the eight-hundred-seat Tudor Theatre in New Orleans broke all house records with this partial talkie.[11]

But the feature that convinced all doubters did not come until September 1928 with Warner Bros.' *The Singing Fool*. From opening day (20 September 1928) on, *The Singing Fool* moved quickly to the top of the box-office charts. The premiere, held in a rented Broadway theatre, the Winter Garden, gave a hint of what was to come. Eleven-dollar opening night tickets (the equivalent of more than fifty dollars today) were being scalped for well in excess of twenty-five dollars (more than one hundred dollars today) by Broadway sharpies outside the doors of the Winter Garden.[12]

By Thanksgiving Day of 1928 Warners knew that *The Singing Fool* had broken some seventy box-office records throughout the United States. In New York City, the movie registered the heaviest business in Broadway history. The advance sales exceeded more than one hundred thousand dollars (more than a half million dollars in present currency) *before* the film had played three full weeks. *The Singing Fool* reached such proportions that every big ticket agency in Manhattan departed from their strict policy of not handling movie shows to broker blocks of seats.

Throughout the United States theatres owned by Warner Bros.' rivals (such as Paramount and Loew's) scrambled to book the film. They ignored the fact that they were making business for a rival producer. Theatres by the dozens ordered sound equipment just to play *The Singing Fool*. The manager of the Great Lakes Theatre in Buffalo, New York, reported that more than 150,000 patrons saw *The Singing Fool* during the first two weeks it was booked.

In Mansfield, Ohio, *The Singing Fool* played to capacity for two weeks, when four days had been the town's previous record for a motion picture. In Menominee, Michigan, the equivalent of one and one-half times the entire population of the town paid to see *The Singing Fool* at one of the town's smaller theatres during its week run. In Albany, New York, the film exceeded the record box-office take of both *The Big Parade* and *Ben Hur*.[13]

The Warner Bros.' strategy of replacing the stage show with vaudeville shorts did not represent the sole innovation of sound meant to tempt exhibitors. Fox Film brought to the marketplace a sound-on-film system by creating newsreels with sound. By adding this realistic touch to a core part of the program in theatres, Fox made its newsreel operations the top in the film business. Indeed Courtland Smith, head of Fox Newsreels in 1926, pushed the company to innovate sound news.[14]

Initially, William Fox's coupling with the experimental work of scientist Theodore Case and patent's power AT&T commenced as a minor part of Fox's attempt to vault into the top echelons of the American motion industry. In 1925 Fox increased the budgets of its feature films, began building a chain of impressive picture palaces in America's major cities, and also started to experiment with talking newsreels. Two years later Fox had a chain of theatres that dominated the West Coast, and he had achieved important footholds in such cities as St. Louis, Detroit, and Milwaukee.

The premiere of Fox Movietone News came on 30 April 1927 at the Fox-owned Roxy Theatre in the form of a record of marching West Point cadets. Lasting but four minutes, this first newsreel with sound drew enthusiastic response from commentators in the mainstream New York press as well as the trade papers of the motion picture industry. Within a month Fox was able to exploit the flight of Charles Lindbergh to thrill the audiences at the Roxy with a newsreel of Lindbergh's takeoff and tumultuous reception upon returning to the United States.[15]

Theatre owners clamored to obtain the equipment that could play such footage. But Fox at first provided only "exclusives" to Fox-owned theatres, as it built up regular releases and soaked the advantages they offered theatre managers. At the same time, Fox purchased and constructed more theatres to milk the advantage it had fully. As competitors switched to talkies in 1928, Fox took the lead with Movietone News, increasing its releases to two per week. As indicated in chapter 7, Fox opened the first newsreel theatre in the United States and sat back and watched the profits roll in.[16]

TRANSFORMING THEATRES TO TALKIES

With the successes of Warner Bros. and Fox the major Hollywood movie companies, and their attendant theatre chains, rapidly shifted to talkies in order to maintain their profits and reap the maximum return from their sizable investments. Paramount, Loew's/MGM, and United Artists, followed quickly by the other Hollywood companies, signed up for sound in May 1928. The diffusion of the technology was on. The conversion shook the movie exhibition business during the remainder of 1928 and was completed by the end of 1930.[17]

Since immediate access to the new "talkies" nearly guaranteed greater profits for the chosen theatre, the Hollywood companies as part of their initial agreements with Western Electric penned guarantees that their houses would be wired first. And they were. This hurt the status of the wavering independent theatre, which had to struggle to float a bank loan. Chain-owned movie houses, in contrast, easily absorbed the costs of wiring and even saved money by jettisoning live acts and using the newfound savings to help with the costs. Daily operation costs, without the stage shows, actually went down.

In the short run, the independent movie house had little to do but wait. For a time in 1929 some took up more vaudeville talent in order to differentiate their products. That is, while the biggest theatres were moving from live to recorded talent, many independent theatres took on more live shows. But they could not continue for long and in time, when it finally became their turn to get installations, they converted to talkies as well.

In this transitional era the biggest problem for the small-town exhibitor was the owners of the new model T automobiles driving on new roads in the Midwest and South. These persons, invariably better off than their neighbors and usually bigger movie fans, began to drive to the nearest city, with its wired theatres, rather than stay at home and enjoy the fare at the local theatre. For example, in Paris, Texas, made immortal by Wim Wenders more than fifty years later, the local Chamber of Commerce even lent money to the owner of the local theatre, the Dent, so that he could install a Movietone sound system rather than wait for the loan to be approved. Folks were driving to Dallas to see the show and this was hurting the Paris economy.[18]

Indeed Paris, Texas, proved typical and so, with many complaints, Hollywood began to take notice of what could become an embarrassing public relations fiasco. Through their trade association, the Motion Picture Producers and Distributors Association, they established a committee to arbitrate disputes over which theatre was wired in what order. Since they could not force Western Electric to make the necessary equipment any faster, the committee served principally to listen to complaints and act as if real decisions were being made. In fact, the majors were still wired first and competitors later.[19]

For most of the more than fifteen thousand theatres in the United States, the selling season in the spring of 1929 proved the most complicated of times. Hollywood had some talkies and some silent films; exhibitors who were wired wanted only the talkies while the others had to be satisfied with silent motion pictures, at least until they were wired. By late in 1929 and into 1930 the transition was by and large completed, although a small number of theatres continued to use the disc system until some months into 1931. Talkies had become the norm, and sound on film systems were even replacing the sound on disc systems installed earlier. Warner Bros., the last holdout, gave up on discs in 1930.[20]

A number of small companies, risking patent suits, tried to perfect sound apparatus quickly, which they offered to small theatres at low cost. Nearly all were sound on disc. There were at least thirty such companies with names like Biophone, Dramaphone, Qualitone, and Filmfone. A few (Biophone and Dramaphone, in particular) had national sales forces. Most only operated in regional markets; for example, the sales force for Han-O-Phone prowled only in upper New York State, those for Paratone invaded only southern Illinois, the Syncrotone sales staff was active in Louisiana, and only theatres in Iowa were sold Talkaphone equipment. Even the most successful could not legitimately claim more than twenty-five real installations.[21]

Some theatres, principally in the smallest markets, the last in line, became desperate, and turned to nonsynchronous sound equipment. This was a simple record player with a loudspeaker system, which to the un-initiated could present the illusion of talkies. Their cost was a fraction of the monies the major theatres had to pay out to Western Electric. The most widely selling of this type was the Theatrephone, which also provided a range of Columbia phonograph music discs with its installations. Most were promoted by fly-by-night technicians looking to make money off the lack of knowledge in the field.[22]

Western Electric and RCA dominated the field for exhibitors' equipment. Nonetheless other companies tried to compete, and their efforts afford illuminating insights into the process of theatre transformation.

Lee DeForest's Phonophone technology was ready in 1923 in the laboratory—before the apparatus of Western Electric and RCA. But DeForest was no businessman, and by 1927 he was far behind installations of the pioneering Vitaphone and Movietone systems. Despite deals with Powell Crosley, who would later make his name in the radio industry, and Pat Powers, who had made a name in the movie business a decade earlier, Phonofilm, even with a newsreel of Charles Lindbergh's historic flight, was out of business before the May 1928 contract was signed.[23]

There was an attempt to save the company from outside. The Schlesinger family interests, representing among other things a large theatre combine in South Africa and the United Kingdom, took over the company in August 1928. Schlesinger formed from the DeForest assets the General Talking Picture Company, but with more than two million dollars in backing the new company was still only able to convince four exhibitors in the United States to take on the equipment. It made an inroad by tendering a "junior" system, at five thousand dollars total cost, for the whole package. While the system could show all types of Hollywood films, it never proved truly reliable, and in the end General Talking Pictures became much more famous for its patent suits, challenging the hegemony of Western Electric's monopoly patent position.[24]

Bristolphone did not lack the necessary financial resources. Millionaire industrialist William H. Bristol first demonstrated his sound-on-disc system at Philadelphia's prestigious Franklin Institute late in 1927. He claimed a number of superior features, including automatic synchronization to make operations much simpler for projectionists. Moreover, Bristolphone was portable; equipment unpacked and set up in an afternoon. Best of all, it cost only one thousand dollars.[25]

Even with these advantages for the small-time exhibitor waiting patiently for a Western Electric installation, Bristol was unable to interest exhibitors.

He formed an alliance with the small-time Gotham Pictures Company in September 1928 and announced twenty features and more than fifty shorts for the 1929–30 season. The one-thousand-seat Academy Theatre in downtown Hagerstown, Maryland, installed the first Bristolphone in October 1928. Still, within a year the whole operation was bankrupt; Bristol's millions were not enough against giants RCA and AT&T. When William Bristol died in June 1930, his heirs refused to revive the failing operation.[26]

Engineer/businessman Louis Gerard Pacent also targeted the small exhibitor with a cheap (only twenty-five hundred dollars) system, announced in January 1929. Equipped for both sound on film and sound on disc, the Pacent system was backed by Pacent's electrical companies and Warner Bros. Indeed, in 1929 Warner installed ninety systems in its expanding theatre operation. Pacent was, with this alliance, able to convince more than four hundred independent theatre owners to sign up and install Pacent equipment during the first six months of 1929. Finally a competitor to Western Electric and RCA emerged. Pacent was so successful that Western Electric sued on 1 April 1929 for eight particular patent violations. Pacent was identified as a significant economic threat, and the case dragged on well into the 1930s, when it did not matter who won since Western Electric had already made its millions installing its sound equipment.[27]

What Western Electric tried to do was force exhibitors into a box by requiring producers not to rent films to theatres with non–Western Electric equipment. But exhibitors balked. In July of 1928 many booked Pathé's *King of Kings* (directed by Cecil B. DeMille) with a soundtrack recorded on RCA Photophone equipment. The two major systems were compatible. Indeed, many of the smaller systems noted also did a fine job playing back movies made by Western Electric. The issue of interchangability would fester, but the damage was already done. The Western Electric and RCA systems had such a head start that few conservative theatre owners were willing to do anything but wait their turn to install one or the other.[28]

A greater set of transitional problems for theatres came with unions, particularly those representing the projectionists and the musicians. The International Alliance of Theatrical and Stage Employees and Moving Picture Operators (hereafter labeled simply IA) demanded more jobs for the talkies. In part they were justified and in part this was a ploy to gain more employment opportunities. Through pressure and threatened theatre closings, the projectionists were able to double the number of union-required jobs and substantially increase their earnings. There is no doubt that projectionists benefited from the coming of sound.[29]

The struggle was more protracted, and far less successful, for the musicians. One of the sales pitches to theatre owners by Western Electric and RCA was that part of the cost of installing sound could be instantly covered by eliminating house orchestras. Even before the majors signed for sound in the summer of 1928 there had been isolated labor disputes. For example, in St. Louis the local chapter of the American Federation of Musicians demanded that a newly constructed theatre, the Grand Central, hire fifteen musicians even though it was built for and would only present talkies. After protracted negotiations, the theatre agreed to hire five featherbedders.[30]

Late in June 1928, the American Federation of Musicians held its annual convention, and nearly the only item of discussion was the loss of jobs due to talkies. The more than 150,000 members contributed $1.5 million for a "defense fund." A position paper declared the nation's culture was in jeopardy from the "mechanization" of the live art of music with silent films.[31]

But the lack of true power by the Musicians Union became apparent in the summer of 1928. In case after case the union saw jobs eliminated, salaries lowered, and contractual guarantees reduced. The union took its stand in Chicago, a powerful union community and one of the strongest American Federation of Musicians chapters. Contracts expired Labor Day of 1928; Balaban & Katz, the heart of the nationwide Paramount Publix theatre chain, refused to give in; all geared up for a protracted strike.[32]

The strike commenced on 4 September 1928 and the whole film industry looked to Chicago, knowing the results of this action would probably set precedents for the nation's theatre circuits. By 5 September Chicago's theatres had no music for the silent films that still formed the core of the offerings. Projectionists prepared to honor the picket lines. The walkout lasted but three days, and both sides claimed victory. It had been agreed that on average only four musicians had to be employed in a theatre (depending on size and run status) and then only for a year henceforth at lower, not higher, wages. Only the power of the support by IA's projectionists guaranteed that much. The end was in sight for musicians playing en mass with motion pictures.[33]

Soon moviegoers saw orchestras disappear. In November 1928 Loew's in New York City eliminated all orchestras and organists. By May 1929 only one theatre in Minneapolis and St. Paul, Minnesota, for example, had any live music. Thousands of musicians had lost their jobs, moving into radio and even journeying to the West Coast to try their luck in movie production. An era was over. Only the elite theatre used live music at all.[34]

INNOVATION TO DOLBY SOUND

The *coming* of sound in the late 1920s did not end changes in theatrical film sound. Indeed, through the following decades innovations were tested constantly. For example, in 1940, when the Disney studio (with RCA) released *Fantasia*, Disney picked the occasion to introduce the first stereophonic sound in specially equipped theatres with ninety-six separate speakers. When the movie unspooled in theatres, there were actually two pieces of film running in synchronization, one with the picture and the other with the four-track stereo sound. Dubbed "Fantasound," this was not a success and did not change the optical theatrical sound.[35]

Optical sound recording was state of the art until after World War II. With technology adapted from German scientific work, Hollywood filmmakers innovated magnetic tape for sound recording in moviemaking by 1950. But because of the tremendous transformation cost involved, in an era when business was declining in the 1950s, the film industry did not, over the long haul, introduce and absorb magnetic sound for use in theatres.[36]

The patron did not, on a consistent basis, experience stereo sound of magnetic quality because of the limitations at the level of the theatre. In particular, high costs of prints and sound track maintenance kept the range of theatre sounds limited. But there were attempts at innovation. In the 1950s magnetic tape was applied to film, with the possibility of films being played back in theatres on projectors equipped with magnetic sound heads. Magnetic sound provided high fidelity and stereo sound, which were not possible at the time with optical sound. With *This Is Cinerama* (1952) came six discrete magnetic tracks. There were five sources behind the screen as well as speakers throughout the auditoria for "surround" effects. But with four separate projectors (three for the picture and one for the sound) CineramaSound was no long-term solution to providing stereo in every American movie house.[37]

Of the various magnetic systems introduced, two received wide adoption. The six-track Todd-AO system for 70 mm films was first used with *Around the World in Eighty Days* (1956). Todd-AO was a spectacular widescreen 70 mm system, with its six sound tracks placed directly on the print. The other, the four-track CinemaScope system for 35 mm films first used with *The Robe* (1953), was much ballyhooed. The four small magnetic tracks were placed directly on the theatrical print of the film, just outside the picture frame. This system offered tracks for right front, center, left front, and surround, similar to the Dolby system of the 1980s. But since most theatres were still mono-optical, most prints went out in "normal" fashion.[38]

The other film companies fought back. For example, Warner Bros. resurrected the Disney-RCA system of 1940, replacing the four optical tracks with magnetic ones, for its WarnerPhonic in 1953. For *House of Wax* (1953) advertisements read: "3-D Action! 3-D Color! 3-D Sound!" Thousands of theatres were equipped in the 1950s, although the playback equipment was expensive. A significant number of films were released in magnetic formats, although such release prints cost about twice as much as a conventional optical print. In the end, the relative expense did not seem worth it. The cost, the comparatively short life of each print, plus the extra investment for installation and maintenance of equipment caused magnetic sound tracks to be coupled only with big road show releases—a handful, each year.

There were experiments. For example, in the 1970s, into a nearly completely optical sound track world of theatrical exhibition, came Sensurround. With *Earthquake* (1974), Universal decided to add to the seven-minute sequence in which Los Angeles is destroyed. By adding low-frequency sound waves to the sound track during the dubbing process engineers produced a rumblelike effect. Theatre owners rented (for five hundred dollars per week) special speakers and an amplifier to add the effect. Sixty units were built, and they helped the film be one of the top box-office attractions of that year. The Sensurround system won a special Academy Award, and through the 1970s the system was used for such films as *Midway* (1976), *Rollercoaster* (1977), and *Battlestar Galactica* (1979).

In 1977 Universal president Sidney J. Sheinberg declared: "Sensurround is as big a star as there is in the movie business today." He was wrong. The problem was that Sensurround worked best in a stand-alone theatre. In multiplex situations the rumble poured through the walls into the other auditoria. Moreover, the latter three films were hardly major box-office attractions, and thus the added expense and trouble seemed wasted. The system was abandoned, although Universal still held onto the patents.[39]

In the 1970s came more interest in theatre sound. This was a way theatre owners could compete with television since most sets at that point had tinny, four-inch speakers. The introduction of new sound coalesced around Dolby sound, first introduced in 1975. Dolby is a high-fidelity stereo sound that provides clear, lifelike reproduction of the entire musical range and accurate reproduction of the volume range.

Dolby-release prints have 35 mm stereo optical tracks. The optical system was maintained because Dolby prints cost no more to produce; they last the needed time under the wear and tear of constant use; and the theatre equipment requires little in the way of special upkeep. Dolby noise reduction is a means of electronically reducing the background noise inherent in all recording media while not disturbing the sounds one is supposed to hear. Dolby noise reduction is at the heart of the Dolby stereo process because it paved the way for improvements in the range of sound.[40]

Dolby Laboratories was founded in 1965 by physicist Ray M. Dolby to develop noise reduction techniques for the music industry. Through the late 1960s, Dolby developed noise reduction techniques for the record industry that eventually made their way to improved home tape recorders, cassette decks, and FM receivers. Indeed Dolby helped bring about high-fidelity cassettes, which were hampered by problems inherent in low recording speeds.[41]

Dolby turned to the film industry in the 1970s. Although Stanley Kubrick did all the premixes and masters of his *A Clockwork Orange* (1971) with Dolby noise reduction, the film was released on conventional optical sound systems. With *Callan* (1974) came the first Dolby-encoded mono sound track in general release. The first true Dolby stereo came with the release of the rock opera *Tommy* in 1975. The sound track in that multi-sensuous experience impressed the young audience, but Ken Russell was hardly the household name to impress moguls in Hollywood. Indeed in the first years, the films with Dolby seemed relegated to musicals: Ken Russell's *Lisztomania* (1975), Robert Altman's *Nashville* (1976), and John Badham's *Saturday Night Fever* (1978).

It was with George Lucas's megahit, *Star Wars* (1977), and Steven Spielberg's *Close Encounters of the Third Kind* (1978) that filmmakers took advantage of the new recording techniques. The films scored at the box office, in part, because of this improved vital sound. In a survey reported in July 1977, the month after *Star Wars* opened, 90 percent of those phoned claimed that Dolby sound made a difference. By 1979 there were twelve hundred equipped theatres in the United States.[42]

The cost to convert a theatre in the late 1970s, depending on how sophisticated the owner wanted the house to be, was under ten thousand dollars. By late in 1984, Dolby could claim some six thousand installations in forty-five countries around the world, with the bulk in the United States. In other words, about one-quarter of theatres in the United States in the mid-1980s had this special advantage, principally all first-run, suburban theatres, often in the center and biggest auditorium in a sixplex or eight-plex. In the mid-1980s nearly 90 percent of all Hollywood films were being released in Dolby, with the common four channels of left front, center, right front, and surround.[43]

In the 1980s improvements in film sound took place on a number of fronts. First, theatre speakers featuring more robust construction, wide sound range, and smoother response were installed, especially in the thousands of new auditoria opened in the late 1980s. Lucasfilm's THX system combined these attributes with specific installation configuration. The THX system is a patented design incorporating auditorium acoustics, a special screen speaker installation, an improved surround system, and other technical improvements. THX promises better audience coverage, improved dialogue intelligibility, and increased dynamic range of sound. In addition, solid state power amplifiers, capable of reproducing a wide volume range, became universal. Finally, there was an increased effectiveness in surround techniques so that audiences felt they were in the middle of the movie.[44]

Sound in movie theatres will surely continue to be improved and transformed. Digital sound systems will make movie theatre sound the equal of any; multi-directional sound systems will make the theatre superior to home systems. Many experts argue today that the sounds in a multiplex auditorium are too good; the sound is superior to reproduction of images and often spills into adjacent auditoria. But this problem will only be solved as a new generation of multiplexes are constructed.

ELEVEN

Color and Wide-Screen Images

Another great change in films presented in theatres came in the 1950s with the emergence of wide-screen and color images. As with the coming of sound, though, this did not happen virtually overnight. The burst of technological innovation in the 1950s took place as the theatrical film industry in the United States struggled for more than a decade to regain its hegemony. Once suburbanization had significantly altered the marketplace for moviegoing in America (as described and analyzed in chapter 4), theatre owners tried a succession of "new" technologies to differentiate their theatrical product.

This process of innovation often took bizarre twists. For example, at various points in the 1950s and early 1960s, before the industry settled on Eastman Color and Panavision wide-screen images, which would define the standards of theatrical moviegoing to the present day, theatre owners toyed with adding more to movies than simply sounds and images. Indeed at one point in October 1959 there existed a battle to bring "smellies" (to use *Variety*'s term) to the theatre business.

Two systems were tendered. Mike Todd, Jr., son of the noted impresario, offered Smell-O-Vision, while Walter Reade, Jr., son of the pioneer of the art theatre, presented AromaRama. Smell-O-Vision spread its odors through the air conditioning system; AromaRama piped them individually to each seat. The former cost a theatre fifteen thousand dollars to install; the latter came in at a third of that price. The problem was that neither system provided for the rapid evaporation of the odors, and by the end of *Scent of Mystery* and *The Great Wall* the auditorium offered the scents of

230

a garbage dump. Smellies would thereafter be subjected to the list of failed technological inventions of film history.[1]

TELEVISION FOR MOVIE THEATRES

Once World War II ended, the initial serious innovation by the American motion picture industry was the attempt to take over television. The Hollywood movie moguls had been interested in television since the late 1930s. Indeed, in 1938 Paramount took the lead by purchasing a significant interest in DuMont, a manufacturer of television equipment and an applicant for experimental television licenses in New York and Washington, D.C. In 1940 Paramount created a television station in Chicago; in 1943 it established another in Los Angeles.

With DuMont's stations in New York and Washington, Paramount had an interest in four of the first nine television stations in the United States. At the end of the war Paramount's vertically integrated rivals all began to seek television licenses. Twentieth Century-Fox sought to establish stations in Los Angeles, New York, Boston, Seattle, Kansas City, and St. Louis. Warner Bros. tried for stations in Los Angeles and Chicago; Loew's sought stations in New York City, Los Angeles, and Washington D.C.[2]

But the Big Five Hollywood corporations would never become major players in television station ownership because of their mounting record of antitrust convictions. The 1934 Communications Act authorized the Federal Communications Commission (hereafter FCC) to refuse licenses to any concern convicted of monopolistic practices in wire or broadcast communication. The FCC of the late 1940s took this dictum one step further and decreed that it would not grant a television license to *any* corporation convicted of monopolistic practices. In 1946, when the Big Five lost at the district court level in the *Paramount* case, the FCC ceased processing their television license applications. With the negative decision in 1948 by the United States Supreme Court, the FCC permanently stopped considering any convicted movie company for a television license.

The Big Five turned to a plan suggested by the Academy of Motion Picture Arts and Sciences committee a decade earlier. They would place television directly in their wholly owned movie houses. Led again by Paramount, they would keep the features on film but offer newsreels and live sporting events on theatre television. Paramount, through DuMont, owned a system that harkened back to the early days of mechanical television. But like other earlier mechanical television technology, the Scophony method only produced faint and grainy images at best.[3]

There were only two serious competitors. RCA expanded the same technology of the home set into a barrel two-and-one-half feet in diameter and three feet long plus a reflection mechanism to magnify the image. Picture quality and brightness were acceptable in a large theatre but hardly up to the standard of a 35 mm movie image. RCA recognized these limitations and sought theatre situations of no more than one hundred people. Warner Bros. and Twentieth Century-Fox allied with RCA.[4]

Paramount's Intermediate Film System used television technology to distribute images and sounds to a theatre but at that point inscribed them onto motion picture film. Thus a theatre used standard television equipment to receive a video signal, and in a minute plus six seconds the Paramount Intermediate Film System turned that electronic information into standard motion picture images and sounds. At the theatre were two cathode ray tubes, one that served as a monitor, and another—a special aluminum-backed, flat-faced screen with reversed polarity—that functioned as the recording screen. A special movie camera recorded the electronic messages, and the exposed 35 mm film then passed directly through a chute into a high-speed processing unit, where it was developed, washed, dried, and projected on standard equipment.

Although the Paramount Intermediate Film System was not totally electronic television, it could take advantage of the speed and immediacy of the television technology to capture live sporting events or breaking news stories. The images were superior to the two aforementioned electronic theatre television methods but not nearly as good as a typical 35 mm film image. Most commentators of the days compared the quality of the Paramount Intermediate Film to a "fair" newsreel image.[5]

As World War II drew to a close, movie entrepreneurs began to issue announcements about possible plans for theatre television; the only impediment seemed to be its high cost of from five to twenty-five thousand dollars per theatre installation. Transmission added further expense. Demonstrations commenced. Warner Bros., in May 1948, presented its version of RCA's system to three thousand invited guests at the Burbank Studio. That summer Twentieth Century-Fox presented to the world its variant of the RCA system at the Fox Theatre in Philadelphia with the telecast of the Joe Louis verses Jersey Joe Walcott heavyweight fight.

But Paramount took the lead. Barney Balaban reasoned that theatre television represented the first step in Paramount's full participation in the television business. In April 1948 Paramount demonstrated its Intermediate Film System to a full house at the Paramount Theatre on Broadway. Commentators hailed the picture quality, arguing that it was nearly the equal of newsreels in tone, depth, and brilliance. During this period, Paramount began to formulate plans for a national chain of theatres using television. Since Paramount owned and operated a television station as well as the dominant movie chain (Balaban & Katz) in Chicago, that city was chosen to serve as the cornerstone of Paramount's initial forays into theatre television.[6]

To launch theatre television Paramount organized a spectacular show for 16 June 1948 at its flagship house, the Chicago Theatre. Television cameras recorded various vaudeville acts in a studio across the street, the signals were then broadcast to the Chicago Theatre, and the Intermediate Film System reconstructed them as filmic images and presented them on the theatre's massive screen. A capacity audience of nearly five thousand viewed themselves entering the theatre, recorded electronically and then presented on film. Paramount figured that theatre television might also bring back the former glory and profit production of the stage show at the Chicago Theatre; they were wrong. Live sporting events quickly came to constitute the core programming: baseball's World Series, Big Ten football, and championship boxing matches.

Balaban & Katz's massive neighborhood houses all took on theatre television equipment, and what would be the greatest test of theatre television was on. By 1951 all Balaban & Katz theatres had canceled theatre television. Throughout the experiment, additional revenues rarely exceeded additional costs. For example, the State-Lake Theatre in Chicago's Loop lost nearly twenty thousand dollars with the Big Ten football games and several thousand dollars more on nonheavyweight championship prize fights.[7]

During 1952 more than one hundred movie theatres, from coast to coast, presented some form of theatre television. One consortium, headed by theatre magnate Si Fabian, envisioned "head-to-head" bidding against home television for professional football, college football, professional wrestling, and Broadway shows. Spyros Skouras, president of Twentieth Century-Fox, announced a deal that would present stage shows from Grauman's Chinese Theatre in Hollywood, regular telecasts of the Metropolitan Opera, and top Broadway's attractions, including the long-running "South Pacific."[8]

But all of these plans remained just that—plans. In 1953 theatre television disappeared. In part this was due to the separation of the Big Five

Hollywood producers from their theatre circuits. Also it was due to the lack of business because of suburbanization and the baby boom. But mostly it was due to the adoption of alternative new technologies. The year 1953 saw the widespread attempt to innovate 3-D and CinemaScope and the march toward a long-lasting alternative to classic four-by-three, black-and-white images.

MOVIES IN COLOR

If the Big Five failed using theatre television, they already had at hand a technology that clearly differentiated their films from any imagery on television at the time—movies in color. Although through the 1930s and 1940s the bulk of any theatre's presentations were in the standard black-and-white system, Technicolor was available. To understand how this one corporation gained its domination of America's movie screens during the 1930s and 1940s requires an examination of the process of invention and innovation.

In 1915, Technicolor, Inc. was formed in Boston by Herbert T. Kalmus, Daniel F. Comstock, and W. Burton Wescott to develop a process for color motion picture production. Comstock and Kalmus were professors of physics at the Massachusetts Institute of Technology, while Wescott was a private inventor and consultant. All had gone to MIT. Indeed nearly all scientists associated with Technicolor at this point had MIT backgrounds, and many were former Kalmus and Comstock students. The "Tech" in Technicolor name honors the corporation's debt to MIT.[9]

It was a limited, two-color subtractive process that gave Technicolor, Inc. its first taste of commercial success. During the early 1920s all the major American movie corporations tried two-color Technicolor in some limited way. Metro-Goldwyn released *Toll of the Sea* (1922); Famous Players released *Wanderer of the Wasteland* (1924). Douglas Fairbanks' *The Black Pirate*, released by United Artists in 1926, represented the initial box-office smash. (Four of the eleven Technicolor cameras in existence were used for filming this latter spectacle.) But not many movie companies wanted to risk the expense of producing a whole film in Technicolor, so during the mid-1920s color sequences became the rage in a handful of movie spectacles: MGM's *Ben Hur* (1926), Fox's *Irene* (1926), Cecil B. De-Mille's independent production of *King of Kings* (1927), and Universal's *The Phantom of the Opera* (1925).[10]

It seemed that the prosperity of the late 1920s might lead to a permanent place for Technicolor movies. The corporations new imbibition process absorbed one color on the top of another, making possible crisp, clear images on the screen. By 1927 Technicolor had readied the imbibition process for use by Hollywood, but with the coming of sound, few moviemakers adopted the new Technicolor technology. But in 1929, with sound successfully innovated, the major Hollywood movie corporations turned seriously to Technicolor to differentiate their products further. Flush with money made by pioneering the coming of sound, Warner Bros. figured Technicolor might help them make even more money. In May 1929 Warner Bros. released *On With the Show*, the first *all-talking* Technicolor feature. Soon thereafter the nation's movie screens were awash with features and shorts in color.

As a result, Technicolor, Inc. experienced a temporary boom; its processing plant was booked ten months in advance. It seemed that color would become a significant part of the Hollywood production. But the timing could not have been less favorable; the decline in movie admissions associated with the Great Depression took away the Hollywood's interest in technological change. Within two years the corporate bottom line of Technicolor had turned from millions on the plus side to millions in the red. To attract more business Technicolor readied a *three*-color imbibition process (using three color-separation negatives, three separate gelatin-relief color-separation transparencies, and the imbibition process to apply the images of the relief transparencies to form the color positive). The three-color Technicolor process provided color fidelity not possible with the previous two-color process. Technicolor hoped this invention would bring back business and finally make Hollywood a color film factory.[11]

The Hollywood majors had too many problems with their floundering theatre circuits to take on the task of innovating three-part Technicolor. Thus it took the tiny Walt Disney operation to bring the three-color process to America's movie screens. Disney set about differentiating the studio's cartoons by scrapping a black and white Silly Symphony, *Flowers and Trees*, already in production and redoing it in Technicolor. *Flowers and Trees* did well at the box office and won the studio its first Academy Award.

What Technicolor, Inc. needed, however, was action by a major studio. This would occur in a roundabout manner. Young millionaire John Hay Whitney wanted to make a name in the movies. In the early 1930s his Pioneer Pictures produced the first three-color feature film, *Becky Sharp* (1935), and released it through one of the Hollywood major studios, RKO.

Becky Sharp did well enough at the box office, but it precipitated no immediate rush to Technicolor. But it did interest David O. Selznick, who first created *A Star Is Born* (1937), released through United Artists, and then *Gone With the Wind* (1939), distributed by MGM, in three-color Technicolor. *Gone With the Wind* went on to gross more money than any film in history, and only then did Hollywood line up to regularly make movies in color.[12]

Technicolor, Inc. had invested two decades and millions to get to this point. Thus, once it convinced Hollywood it did all it could to corner the market. During the 1930s and 1940s, Technicolor, Inc. firmly grasped onto 90 percent of the market for color movies. As such it carefully allocated its equipment and charged top dollar for its use. Color films amounted to only one film in ten. Technicolor, Inc.'s virtual monopoly resulted in substantial sales (about ten million dollars per year), profit accumulation (about one million dollars per year), and a profit rate higher than any movie company. This situation would have remained the status quo unless an outside force intervened.[13]

The United States government recognized Technicolor's monopoly and in 1947, as part of its antitrust campaign against the American film industry, charged Technicolor, Inc. with a conspiracy to monopolize the production of color movies. The United States Department of Justice found that the basis for this power was a series of agreements between Eastman Kodak and Technicolor, Inc., whereby existing patents and any newly developed technologies would be reserved exclusively for Technicolor in the field of 35 mm moviemaking in color.

Technicolor, in league with its film stock supplier Eastman Kodak, had acted as a traditional monopolist: keeping supply low, extracting "monopoly," and earning a rate of profits far higher than the average. Technicolor, Inc. always kept a backlog. The major Hollywood film corporations put up with the inconvenience because in limiting its output Technicolor, Inc. served them first and exclusively; in the process it regularly denied access to independent producers.[14]

The Technicolor monopoly ended in 1948, when Eastman Kodak signed a consent decree. Eastman Kodak had seen the lack of success the major Hollywood firms had in fighting the Justice Department in the *Paramount* case and took the best deal it could. The company developed a color system to rival Technicolor, based on the German Agfacolor process. Eastman Kodak announced Eastman Color in 1950, and soon thereafter it moved to the top of the market. Eastman Kodak did not need Technicolor as much as Technicolor needed Eastman Kodak. In 1950 Technicolor signed its consent decree and agreed to license ninety-two patents on a royalty-free basis to all comers. No longer did movie producers have to hire Technicolor cameras, consultants, and camera operators. The market for movies in color was now wide open.[15]

The economic consequences of the government's action proved dramatic. Suddenly color filmmaking fell in cost, and with the need to differentiate its product from the all black-and-white television images, through the 1950s Hollywood gradually created more and more films in color. The number rose from 115 in 1952 to 163 in 1953 to 170 in 1956. "New" color systems were developed; actually, all were variations of inferior technology that had languished because of the Hollywood-Technicolor monopolistic arrangement.

For example, Cinecolor marketed itself to low-budget independent film companies based on its low price. Consolidated Film Laboratories, a subsidiary of Republic Pictures, brought out Trucolor. Neither Cinecolor nor Trucolor rivaled the clear, luscious images of Technicolor, but their emergence in the early 1950s did demonstrate that the market for movies in color was now wide open and competitive, not the closed shop of the Technicolor days.

Indeed, Technicolor soon lost its dominant position. By the mid-1950s the Eastman Color negative, used in a standard black-and-white camera, not special Technicolor equipment, had become the industry leader. WarnerColor, MetroColor, DeLuxe Color, Pathé Color were, in fact, all shot on Eastman Color stock. The different names referred only to the studio that used them (and their style of color production), and/or the processing plant that developed and printed the film. By 1960 Technicolor was just another corporation that could process color film and best remembered as the pioneer in the field.[16]

Yet as long as television images remained in black and white, Hollywood continued to release cheap black-and-white films. But during the 1960s, as American television moved to become full color, Hollywood did the same. By the late 1960s all Hollywood movies were made in color; by 1969 a black-and-white film was an oddity. (Thirty years earlier fewer than 5 percent of all Hollywood films had been in color.) In 1971, when The Last Picture Show was released in black and white, director Peter Bogdanovich was hailed for his "throwback" to the old days, to the Hollywood masters of the past. Black-and-white images were forever clearly identified with Hollywood's golden age. The coming of color, unlike sound, had taken nearly four decades to become fully diffused.

WIDE-SCREEN MOTION PICTURES

Color features certainly differentiated Hollywood's offerings in movie theatres of the 1950s from the grainy black-and-white images then available on television. But Hollywood went one step further and sought to make its movies "bigger" and thus supposedly even better. This innovation process had actually started in the 1920s. In a burst of enthusiasm with the coming of sound the Hollywood moguls tried wide-screen images, such as Magnascope of Fox, as well. The attempts were short-lived and failed to make any noticeable impact. More serious attempts at technical change toward "bigger" images would wait until the 1950s.

Possibly in the 1950s wide-screen images would catch the public's attention and draw the "lost audience" back to the theatres. The renewed innovation of wide-screen images, unlike the transformation to color, required considerable change in movie theatre equipment. In the late 1940s the average neighborhood movie house had a screen that was twenty by sixteen feet, framed in the proscenium arch. Wide-screen images would go beyond that traditional frame as well as require new projector equipment.[17]

The innovation process commenced in 1952 when Cinerama offered spectacular wide-screen effects by melding images from three synchronized projectors on a vast (specially designed) curved screen. To add to the sense of overwhelming spectacle, Cinerama also included multi-track stereo sound. Theatres that contracted for the new process were required to employ twelve to sixteen projectionists as well as invest thousands of dollars for new projectors, special sound equipment (including nineteen speakers), and a semicircular screen. Projectors also required huge reels holding eight thousand feet of film, running at twenty-six frames per second to "eliminate flicker." The theatres, principally the large downtown picture palaces, had to undergo extensive facelifts; often the proscenium arches were chipped away and dozens of seats were torn out.[18]

The Cinerama process was not new. Fred Waller first developed it as "Vitarama" for the 1939 New York World's Fair, though it was not displayed there. Backed at various stages of its innovation by one of the Rockefeller brothers, *Time* magazine founder Henry Luce, radio star Lowell Thomas, former MGM studio boss, Louis B. Mayer, and noted Broadway producer Michael Todd, Waller's creation repremiered as Cinerama on 30 September 1952 at the Broadway Theatre in New York.

This Is Cinerama, a two-hour travelogue, contained scenes ranging from a gripping roller coaster ride at New York's Rockaway Amusement Park to a plane flying through the Grand Canyon to renditions of Handel's oratorio, *The Messiah*. Prices ranged from ninety cents for a weekday matinee to two dollars and eighty cents for an evening show. Because it cost between fifty and one hundred thousand dollars to install Cinerama at the handful of installations in picture palaces in major cities backers consciously followed the model of the theatrical road show: advance ticket purchase, reserved seating, two shows a day, admission prices far above the normal first-run feature films, and extended runs.[19]

At first the backers of Cinerama seemed to have made an astute judgment. *This Is Cinerama* went on to gross more than twenty million dollars. In New York City it played for more than two years, the longest movie run in Broadway history. Runs in Detroit, Chicago, Philadelphia, Washington, D.C., Pittsburgh, San Francisco, Boston, St. Louis, Minneapolis, Hollywood, and Dallas were nearly as long. *Cinerama Holiday* (1955), the company's second production, proved nearly as popular. But with the third effort, *Seven Wonders of the World* (1956), Cinerama seemed to fade, experiencing poor box-office returns. *Search for Paradise* (1957) and *Cinerama—South Seas Adventure* (1958) signaled the end of the innovation. Although there would be efforts to revive the company, the miracle of Cinerama did better at the box office when it had the wide-screen market to itself.[20]

In the long run, Cinerama, Inc. could not solve certain fundamental flaws to be fully adopted as a permanent system in America's thousands of movie houses. The dollar investment to convert a single theatre (fifty to one hundred thousand dollars) understated the true investment. Hundreds of seats were lost to the massive size of the projection equipment and extra screen. In the initial New York run, one-third of the Broadway theatre's nineteen hundred seats were lost to projection booths.

There also were union problems. In Chicago, for example, the local projectionist's union at first demanded seventeen projectionists be hired, each with a weekly salary of two hundred dollars—nearly twice what the normal projectionist earned. But most important, Cinerama, Inc. was never able to develop a formula for a steady, continuous flow of attractive films. Given the special economics of Cinerama, runs of six months were required, on average, to break even. Another system, innovated by a Hollywood company and attractive to mainstream theatre owners, was needed.[21]

The 3-D process was innovated because of the initial success of Cinerama's premiere. Three-dimensional movies, or simply 3-D, had been around since the 1920s. One premiere had taken place on 27 September

1922 with *The Power of Love*, heralded as "Plasticon." In 1924 came a series of shorts in 3-D advertised as "Plastigrams." In the 1930s came a series of Pete Smith 3-D shorts from Metro-Goldwyn-Mayer. The next "premiere" came in November 1952, when Milton L. Gunzburg, a Hollywood-based entrepreneur, George Schafer, former president of RKO, and Arch Oboler, a veteran radio producer, launched *Bwana Devil*, a crude African adventure story of railroad building in Africa, starring Robert Stack. The narrative and stars may not have been top drawer, but the 3-D process, labeled "Natural Vision," caused quite a stir. Box-office take at various premieres around the United States proved double normal expectations and so United Artists agreed to distribute *Bwana Devil*.[22]

For a continuous screening of a 3-D movie without interruption for rewinding, a theatre needed four projectors instead of the standard two. The 3-D system worked best on a metallic screen, when normal theatres used porous screens so they could set speakers behind them. The exhibitor had to invest thousands to insure a continuous supply of cardboard spectacles (five to ten cents a pair). Patrons hated them, particularly the half of the population who already wore glasses. These spectacles proved so costly that neighborhood theatre owners sat back and watched picture palaces deal with the problems. That 3-D was even tried on a significant scale demonstrated how desperate exhibitors of the early 1950s were for something new in the face of the changes wrought by suburbanization and the baby boom.[23]

Nonetheless during 1953 and into the early months of 1954, 3-D movies were hailed as the savior of the American film industry. The Hollywood majors jumped in head first. In April 1953, Warner Bros. issued what was to remain the most successful of these efforts, *House of Wax* (1953), starring Vincent Price. *House of Wax* grossed one million dollars during its first week of release. Each genre seemed to have its 3-D studio sponsor: Metro-Goldwyn-Mayer released a musical, *Kiss Me Kate* (1953); Columbia tried a crime tale in *Man in the Dark* (1953); Universal contributed the science fiction efforts *It Came from Outer Space* (1953) and *The Creature From the Black Lagoon* (1954).

The innovation of 3-D was over almost before it began. By mid-1954 it was clear that with all the expense involved with special attachments to projectors and glasses issued to patrons, the added revenues from 3-D never proved worth the investment. For example, late in 1953 *Those Redheads from Seattle* (1953) was yanked after just twelve days at the Loew's flagship theatre, the State. The Loew's corporate hierarchy, in their offices in the floors above the theatre, saw receipts dwindling. There would be efforts to revive 3-D in the 1970s and 1980s, but nothing—not pornography, not more horror films, not even a sequel to *Jaws*—would make 3-D a money maker at America's movie houses.[24]

CinemaScope had more of an impact. Backed by the major studio, Twentieth Century-Fox, CinemaScope had its premiere on 16 September 1953 with the biblical spectacle, *The Robe*. The CinemaScope process presented a wide-screen technology that utilized an anamorphic lens that could expand the image by being added to a standard projector; thus the investment involved was relatively small. The screen required a slight curvature of one inch of depth for each foot of width and was made with a cotton base overlaid with plastic and surfaced with aluminum embossed in a pattern like tiny mirrors.

Twentieth Century-Fox initially invested twenty-five million dollars in eleven films; *The Robe*, costing four million and starring Richard Burton and Jean Simmons, broke box-office records. Throughout 1953 and into 1954 the executives of Twentieth Century-Fox, led by President Spyros Skouras, sought to convince exhibitors that CinemaScope was not a system limited to only special uses (such as Cinerama), or simply another fad (such as 3-D), but a technology that would serve as a foundation for regular, ongoing exploitation of feature films that would draw Hollywood out of the "box-office blues."[25]

Like its predecessors, the technological basis for CinemaScope was not new. French inventor Henri Chrétien had begun working on an anamorphic lens process in the 1920s, but repeatedly he failed to interest any major movie company. Spyros Skouras learned of the Chrétien system in 1952 and signed the inventor to fashion a lens that could be fitted to existing equipment. Skouras, a top salesman and a former theatre executive, understood the perspective of the exhibitors. He would not invest in a process that required more than the normal crew of projectionists or cost more than twenty thousand dollars for a theatre to convert.

Six months before the premiere of *The Robe*, Skouras had orders for more than seven hundred installations. Imitators arose: Warner tried its own version of an anamorphic lens system, WarnerSuperScope; RKO invested in SuperScope. But by and large the Hollywood majors were forced to take out a license for CinemaScope from Twentieth Century-Fox. By the end of 1953 every major studio—save Paramount with its VistaVision process—had jumped on the CinemaScope bandwagon. By November 1954 it was reported that nearly half the existing theatres in the United States had facilities to show CinemaScope.[26]

By 1954 experience had taught theatre owners a cruel lesson. Equipping theatres proved more expensive than anticipated. The special screen cost twice as much as a conventional screen of the day. Projected images never seemed bright enough; the anamorphic lens seemed to distort the size and shape of figures. Drive-ins experienced the most trouble. To equip an average drive-in with CinemaScope cost about twenty-five thousand dollars, principally to add new speakers, to convert the projectors, and to extend the screen.

To cut costs, many theatre owners abandoned the stereophonic sound component that had come with all original installations. In 1954 Twentieth Century-Fox made monaural sound optional. Since stereo apparatus accounted for more than half of the total cost of the package, when small- and medium-sized theatre owners argued that stereo made little difference, Twentieth Century-Fox had to agree to drop it. In particular, drive-ins never really embraced the stereo component of CinemaScope. By late in 1954 Twentieth Century-Fox had begun regularly to release non-stereo prints of CinemaScope features. In 1955 Metro-Goldwyn-Mayer announced that it would discontinue releasing CinemaScope versions to foreign theatres. The regular coupling of CinemaScope with color was dropped by Twentieth Century-Fox when it released *Teenage Rebel* (1956). The added expense, in particular at the theatrical level, never seemed to justify the added cost.[27]

VistaVision was Paramount's direct answer to Twentieth Century-Fox's CinemaScope, as can easily be seen by comparing the similar construction of the two brand names. VistaVision utilized a camera through which traditional 35 mm film traveled horizontally rather than vertically. This resulted in an image three times the size of the normal four-by-three negative. The VistaVision film was processed in the normal manner and then optically reduced to be run in the normal vertical sequence.[28]

The first demonstration of VistaVision was held on 2 March 1954 in Hollywood. VistaVision premiered on 27 April 1954 at New York's Radio City Music Hall with a major Paramount film, *White Christmas*, starring Bing Crosby. *White Christmas* set an opening day receipts record of twenty-five thousand dollars when released in October. All major Paramount films for the following years were shot in VistaVision, including Cecil B. De-Mille's *The Ten Commandments* (1956). Other filmmakers used it as well, including Anthony Mann for *Strategic Air Command* (1955), John Ford for *The Searchers* (1956), and Alfred Hitchcock for *To Catch a Thief* (1955).[29]

The drawbacks to a single studio's system that required thousands of dollars in new equipment were obvious after the CinemaScope example. It was widely publicized that Paramount itself had to spend more than one hundred thousand dollars to convert a Times Square flagship house to VistaVision. With Paramount's backing VistaVision remained in play until the early 1960s, but even Paramount finally abandoned this wide-screen alternative in 1961, with the final film released being *One Eyed Jacks*, starring Marlon Brando.[30]

Cinerama, 3-D, CinemaScope, and VistaVision proved that, if carefully used, a new wide-screen technology could increase the profits of America's ailing movie theatres. Through the remainder of the decade innovation continued. Technicolor, Inc. offered up Technirama, using an anamorphic lens plus 35 mm film traveling horizontally through the camera. Technirama's premiere came in 1956 with *The Monte Carlo Story*. A 70 mm version of Technirama was then developed and labeled Super Technirama. This version received its most famous exposition with Stanley Kubrick's *Spartacus* (1960).

Cinemiracle, developed by National Theatres, the former Twentieth Century-Fox theatre chain, employed three projectors and three cameras but joined the images through a complicated set of mirrors. The three projectors could be run side by side, not requiring the separate booths of Cinerama. Both New York's Roxy and Grauman's Chinese in Hollywood were refurbished and premiered the one and only film in Cinemiracle, *Windjammer*, in April of 1958.[31]

Todd-AO alone seemed to generate a sustainable possibility. This wide-screen system, developed by Brian O'Brien of the American Optical Company, utilized a single camera with four lenses and a single projector. The coverage of the lenses was from a huge 128-degree bug-eye down through 64-degree, 48-degree, and 37-degree lenses. Todd-AO used 65 mm film in the camera and 70 mm film for projection onto a curved wide screen. Todd-AO was demonstrated to the movie trade in Hollywood on 22 June 1954 and promised a true hit in its first film, Rogers and Hammerstein's *Oklahoma!*[32]

Mike Todd, a partner in the original Cinerama company, and producer Joseph M. Schenck, founding partner in Twentieth Century-Fox, sought to exploit Todd-AO for a filmed version of *Oklahoma!* Richard Rogers and Oscar Hammerstein II were so impressed with Todd-AO they at last agreed to have their hit play filmed, after turning down many previous offers. (Indeed Oscar Hammerstein II became a partner in Todd-AO.) *Oklahoma!* was shown at "special" admission prices and sold on a reserved seat basis.

The second Todd and Schenck production became *Around the World in Eighty Days*, which won the Academy Award for Best Picture of 1956. Both *Oklahoma!* and *Around the World in Eighty Days* cost five million dollars to make but proved true smashes at the box office. But then Mike Todd died and the necessary highly skilled promoter was gone. Theatre owners would not invest in the extra cost for a Todd-AO projector, however flexible it promised to be, without the promise of a continuing stream of hit films.[33]

PANAVISION AND EASTMAN COLOR

The common problems of all attempted innovations of wide-screen systems (and the dozens of minor systems not mentioned) prompted the film industry—producers and exhibitors—to seek a single, flexible standard. Some sort of permanent, low-cost, "simple-to-operate" technology was needed to project wide-screen images in color, providing theatrical filmgoing with an edge over its smaller television rival. As early as February 1953 *Variety* symbolized the frustration by pointing out the "Need for Uniform 3-D."[34]

The long-term solution would come from Panavision lenses and Eastman Color film stock. In the 1950s Panavision, Inc. was simply one among many smaller suppliers of lenses for the new wide-screen technologies; owner Robert E. Gottschalk had developed the MGM Camera 65, an anamorphic system, for *Raintree County* (1957). MGM used Gottschalk's Panavision innovations to even greater advantage with *Ben Hur* (1959). Panavision anamorphic projection attachments differed from the ones Bausch and Lomb made for Twentieth Century-Fox's CinemaScope in that the optics were prismatic rather than cylindrical, thereby allowing a change in the anamorphic power of the lens with a simple turn of a knob. Panavision attachments soon became the most popular in the world, setting the industry standard.[35]

In 1957 Gottschalk tried to form his own movie company, but in the end he settled for being the innovator of the most widely used system of lenses in the world. Panavision lenses eliminated the distortion, parallax, perspective, and close-up problems associated with superior wide-screen systems. By the late 1960s Panavision became the standard for lenses and camera equipment for Hollywood films, usually employing an aspect ratio of 1:1.85. The typical theatre might have CinemaScope lenses for some special occasion, but other equipment was shelved and long forgotten.[36]

Panavision provided a superior but standardized product for wide-screen images, one that continued to be used well into the 1980s. In the 1970s it revolutionized the filmmaking business again with hand-held cameras of superior quality. With Warner Communication's acquisition of the Panavision corporate enterprise, Panavision became the de facto supplier of all moviemaking equipment in Hollywood. By the 1980s Panavision's system was used to shoot three-quarters of television shows shot on film as well.[37]

Eastman Color's negative and color print film stock was introduced by the Rochester giant in 1950 to rival Technicolor. The first color motion picture using the entire Eastman Color process, negative, and prints, was *Royal Journey* (1951), produced by the National Film Board of Canada. In a mono-pack form Eastman Color signaled the end of the three-pack (three different strips of film) Technicolor system. The Eastman stock's great advantage was ease of handling. The single strip negative achieved the consistency and brilliance of Technicolor and was far cheaper and easier to deal with. Technicolor wanted to maintain control; Eastman Kodak was happy to serve new customers and expand its business.[38]

Eastman Color was immediately successful and by the mid-1950s had become the industry standard. Since the mid-1950s the majority of Hollywood films have used Eastman color. The name may read Metrocolor (owned by MGM), WarnerColor, or Color by Deluxe (owned by Twentieth Century-Fox), but the basic stock nearly always comes from Eastman Kodak. Only the processing was (and is) different. Indeed Color by Technicolor came to mean only that Technicolor had developed the negative using Eastman color stock.

In the long run, Eastman Color's unstable dyes tended to make the negatives susceptible to permanent fading. A new process was introduced in the 1980s, but not before many films were lost forever. Still, the 1950s Hollywood industry had not anticipated the problem. The film industry was happy that Panavision plus Eastman color enabled it, at a relatively low cost, to provide a product quite superior to the black-and-white images offered by America's television networks.[39]

To differentiate the theatre experience from television, a number of movie houses in the United States, beginning in the 1960s, installed equipment to project in 70 mm film. (Indeed today there are nearly one thousand such screens in the United States.) But, although the practice of making films in 70 mm reached a peak in the 1960s, the projection equipment is still utilized when producers blow up 35 mm features to 70 mm. Since the 1960s, two dozen or so films have actually been made in 70 mm, while more than two hundred have been blown up to be shown in 70 mm.[40]

Standardization of wide-screen images in color did not cause the end of technical change in the movie-watching experience. Indeed, one of the most significant technical innovations of the twentieth century—the coming of television—radically transformed the movie show. How television became the principal means by which most Americans watched their Hollywood film favorites provides the subject for the final three chapters.

TWELVE

Movies on Television

The most significant change in the way Americans viewed films during the latter half of the twentieth century came with the advent of television presentations of motion pictures. By the mid-1950s it had become clear that Hollywood would not directly own and operate television stations (or networks) but rather supply programs. With the coming of "The Late Show" in the mid-1950s and "Saturday Night at the Movies," in the early 1960s, feature film showings became one of television's dominant programming forms.

Actually the movie show on television began in a minor way. In the late 1940s British film companies, in particular the Ealing, Rank, and Korda studios, which had never been able to break into the American theatrical market significantly, willingly rented films to television. Monogram and Republic, long able to take only what the major Hollywood corporate powers left them, jumped on board the television bandwagon with a vengeance. This multitude of small producers, all eager for the extra money, delivered some four thousand titles to television before the end of 1950. Typical fare included "B" westerns (Gene Autry and Roy Rogers from Republic, for example) and thrill-a-minute serials (for example, Flash Gordon, also from Republic). But the repeated showings of this fare only served to remind longtime movie fans of the extraordinary number of treasures still resting comfortably in the vaults of MGM, Paramount, Twentieth Century-Fox, and Warner Bros.[1]

To understand how and why the long-dominant Hollywood studios finally agreed to rent (or sell) their vast libraries of film titles to television, one must go back to May 1948, when eccentric millionaire Howard Hughes purchased control of the ailing RKO. In five years, Hughes ran RKO into the ground. Debts soared past twenty million dollars; few new productions were approved to generate needed new revenues. By late 1953, it was clear even to Hughes that he had to do something, so few industry observers were surprised in 1954 when he agreed to sell RKO to the General Tire & Rubber Company for twenty-five million dollars. General Tire wanted the RKO back titles to present on its independent New York television station, WOR (today WWOR), along with other films it had acquired. In 1955 WOR regularly programmed its "Million Dollar Movie," often rerunning the same title several times a week. Any number of later moviemakers cited the repetitive screenings of "Million Dollar Movies" as inspiration for a moviemaking career. George Romero, famous for making *Night of the Living Dead* (1968), for example, told an interviewer that seeing a screening of *The Tales of Hoffman* (1951), directed by Michael Powell, on "Million Dollar Movie" made him take up a career in film.[2]

To gain more cash from its deal, General Tire then peddled rights to RKO's seven hundred features and one thousand short subjects to C&C Television, which in turn rented them to stations throughout the United States in markets in which General Tire did not own stations. Overnight, this brought General Tire an additional fifteen million dollars. In one year General Tire realized a profit of nearly ten million dollars from Hughes's fire sale.[3]

These profit figures impressed even the most recalcitrant Hollywood movie mogul. Within the space of the following twenty-four months all the remaining major companies released their pre-1948 titles to television. (Pre-1948 titles were free from paying residuals to performer and craft unions; post-1948 titles were not.) For the first time in the sixty-year history of film a national audience was able to watch, at their leisure, a broad cross section of the best and worst of Hollywood talkies. Silent films were only occasionally presented, usually in the form of compilations of the comedies of Charlie Chaplin and Buster Keaton.

From the sale or lease to television of these libraries of films, Hollywood was able to tap a significant source of pure profit. This infusion of cash came precisely at a time when Hollywood needed money to support innovation of wide-screen spectacles. Television deals followed one after the other. Columbia Pictures, which had entered television production early on, quickly aped RKO's financial bonanza. In January 1956 Columbia announced that Screen Gems would rent packages of feature films to television stations. The initial package consisted of 104 films. Columbia realized an instant profit of five million dollars.

In March Warner Bros. followed suit. On 1 March 1956 it sold its pre-1948 library of 850 features and 1,500 short subjects to Associated Artists productions. This twenty-one-million-dollar deal enabled Warner Bros. to announce its best "year" in a decade. Two months later Twentieth Century-Fox engineered a similar deal. MGM followed in August with a thirty-four-million-dollar contract with CBS, which tendered the rights to the most famous feature regularly shown on television, *The Wizard of Oz* (1938).[4]

Paramount held out the longest because its management still thought the company had a chance to establish an independent presence in television, at this point in pay television. Finally, disappointed with its failed forays and experiments, in February 1958 Paramount *sold* rather than rented its pre-1948 library. The initial monies were substantial—fifty million dollars. But in the long run the buyer, MCA, then a talent agency, collected far more, so much so that MCA would later turn around and purchase an ailing studio of its own, Universal, and join the ranks of the Hollywood major studios.[5]

The pre-1948 largely black-and-white films functioned as the mainstay of innumerable "Early Shows," "Late Shows," and "Late, Late Shows." Irregular screenings of "reissues" were rare in theatres in the early 1950s. A decade later found more than one hundred different films aired each week on New York City television stations, with smaller numbers in less populous cities. In particular, the owned and operated stations of CBS invested in choice titles (including many from MGM). Each film was rotated: it was shown, then rested for three to six months, and then repeated again. The three television networks booked feature films only as occasional specials, such as CBS's ratings hit *The Wizard of Oz*, not as regular programming.[6]

But with color television a coming reality, the three television networks wanted to show *post*-1948 Hollywood features, principally those in color, in lucrative, attractive, prime-time slots. This required agreements from the Hollywood craft unions, including the American Federation of Musicians, the Screen Actors Guild, the Screen Directors Guild, and the Writers Guild of America. In a precedent-setting action, the Screen Actors Guild, led by its then president, Ronald Reagan, went on strike and won guaranteed residuals for televised airings of post-1948 films. This would set the stage for movie showings to become staples of prime-time television.[7]

The NBC network premiered the first prime-time series of recent films in September 1961 with *How to Marry a Millionaire* (1953), starring Marilyn

Monroe, Betty Grable, and Lauren Bacall. Ratings were high, and of the thirty-one titles shown during this initial season, fifteen were in color and all were post-1948, Twentieth Century-Fox, big-budget releases. All had their television "premiere" on "Saturday Night at the Movies." NBC especially liked the color titles. RCA, a pioneer in television color, owned NBC and used the network to spur sales of color television sets.[8]

The other two major networks, CBS and ABC, seeing how their shows (CBS's "Have Gun, Will Travel" and "Gunsmoke" and ABC's "Lawrence Welk") fared against "Saturday Night at the Movies," quickly moved to negotiate their own "Nights at the Movies." ABC, generally a distant third in the ratings during the 1960s, moved first. A mid-season replacement, "Sunday Night at the Movies," commenced in April 1962. CBS, the long-time ratings leader in network television, remained aloof and did not set in place its own "Night at the Movies," until September 1965.[9]

But with CBS joining the fray at the beginning of the 1965–66 television season, the race was on. Television screenings of recent Hollywood movies became standard practice. In 1968 nearly 40 percent of all television sets in use at the time tuned in to Alfred Hitchcock's *The Birds* (theatrical release date 1963). *The Bridge on the River Kwai* (1957), shown in 1966, and *Cat on a Hot Tin Roof* (1958), shown in 1967, achieved ratings nearly as high. Clearly, recent feature films could be shown on television to blockbuster ratings; when *Gone With the Wind* (1939) was shown in two parts in early November of 1976, half the nation's television sets were tuned to that particular offering. By the fall of 1968, "Nights at the Movies" on ABC, NBC, and CBS covered every night of the week. By the early 1970s, overlapping permitted ten separate movie nights each week. Throughout this period NBC remained the most committed network, in part because it wanted to use recent Hollywood features to help stimulate demand for RCA's color television sets.[10]

This success of movie showings on the networks significantly affected affiliated stations. The number of "Late" and "Early" shows fell by 25 percent. Independent stations, not affiliated with one of the three television networks, continued to rely on pre-1948 features. Indeed films on independent channels accounted for one-quarter of their schedules. With such rediscovered hits as Warner Bros.' *Casablanca* (1943) and RKO's *King Kong* (1933) spaced judiciously throughout the viewing year, regular screenings of movies on television drew large audiences, but routine "B" thrillers and wacky, low-budget war musicals spent their drawing power after one or two screenings.

This unprecedented wave of movie programming quickly depleted the stock of attractive features that had not played on television. On the network level, the rule was to run a post-1948 feature twice ("premiere" and "rerun") and then release it into syndication so that it then could be used by local stations for their "Late" or "Early" shows. Network executives searched for ways to maximize the audiences for repeated showings of blockbuster films.[11]

It soon became clear that there were too many scheduled movie showings on television and too little new product to fill future slots with new theatrical films. Hollywood knew this, and the studios began to charge higher and higher prices for television screenings. Million-dollar price tags became commonplace, first for films that had done well at the box office and then for those that might have not done so well but won some sort of an award, in particular an Academy Award. For the widely heralded September 1966 telecast of *The Bridge On the River Kwai* the Ford Motor Company put up nearly two million dollars as the sponsor. The film attracted some sixty million viewers against formidable competition. Hollywood insiders speculated ten-million-dollar price tags would appear shortly.[12]

MOVIES MADE FOR TELEVISION

Network executives found a solution: make movies aimed for a television premiere. The networks could monitor production costs and guarantee fixed future rentals in the three-hundred- to five-hundred-thousand-dollar range. Moreover, the networks could use these made-for-television movies to test new shows that might then be "down-sized" to appear as regular series. The networks were used to paying the complete cost of pilot programs, so it was not a huge step to fashion them into stand-alone, made-for-television films.

Experiments began as early as 1964. In October 1964 NBC aired *See How They Run* (1964), starring John Forsythe, Senta Berger, Jane Wyatt, Franchot Tone, Leslie Nielsen, and George Kennedy. Labeled "Project 120," in honor of its length in minutes, the experiment proved a modest success. But this was no regular effort. The next entry, *The Hanged Man* (1964), came six weeks later. The idea was to do an anthology series to help NBC overtake CBS in the ratings war.[13]

Early in 1966, NBC contracted with Universal to create a regular series of "World Premiere" movies made for television. The initial entry of this continuing effort was *Fame Is the Name of the Game* (1967), starring minor luminaries Jill St. John and Tony Franciosa, presented on a Saturday night in November 1966. NBC specified all films had to be in color, again to reinforce its leadership in that area. Their agreement with Universal dictated that once the television movie was shown twice on the network, rights reverted back to Universal, which could release the made-for-television movies in theatres in the United States (a rare occurrence), then to foreign theatres (more common), and finally to American television stations for their "Early" and "Late" shows (also common).[14]

Made-for-television motion pictures took only five years to become a mainstay of American network television programming. By early in the 1970s, movies made for television outnumbered theatrical fare in network "Nights at the Movies." Once NBC led the way, ABC, once it saw a successful trend, followed close behind. CBS, again smug with years of constant ratings leadership with traditional series, eventually joined in.

Profits proved substantial. A typical movie made for television cost three-quarters of a million dollars, far less than what Hollywood was demanding for rental of its recent blockbusters. And the ratings were phenomenal. Few expected that millions upon millions would tune in for *The Waltons' Thanksgiving Story* (1973), *Night Stalker* (1972), *A Case of Rape* (1974), and *Women in Chains* (1972). Such fare regularly outdrew what were considered the biggest films of the era: *The Graduate* (1967; 1973 premiere on network television), *West Side Story* (1961; 1972 premiere on network television), and *Goldfinger* (1964; 1972 premiere on network television). With the help of the movie made for television, network executives moved "Nights at the Movies" to a full quarter share of all prime-time programming.[15]

One film in particular signaled that the made-for-television movie had come of age. During the 1971–72 television season, the ABC "Movie of the Week" series, which was composed entirely of movies made for television, finished as fifth highest series of the year. On 30 November 1971, ABC presented a little-publicized made-for-television movie, *Brian's Song* (1971). One-third of the households in the country watched, and half the people watching television that Tuesday night selected that movie (about a football player who dies of cancer) over the fare offered on CBS and NBC. The "ABC Movie of the Week" had premiered in the fall of 1969, sponsored by Barry Diller, then head of prime-time programming at ABC and later founder of the Fox network. In the first five years the "ABC Movie of the Week" accounted for four of the top twenty-five made-for-television movies of all time for the period 1965 through 1980.[16]

Brian's Song vaulted to tenth place in all-time movie screenings on television. With the *Wizard of Oz* accounting for five of the top nine ratings of television screenings of motion pictures up to that November night, *Brian's Song* joined *The Birds, Bridge On the River Kwai,* and *Ben Hur* (1959) in that elite grouping. It demonstrated that movies made for television could win Emmys (five), prestigious George Foster Peabody awards, and citations from the NAACP and the American Cancer Society. When then President Richard M. Nixon declared *Brian's Song* one of his all-time favorite films, ABC reaped an unexpected publicity bonanza.[17]

Brian's Song included no special features from other early ABC movies made for television. Producer Paul Junger Witt had worked with ABC before with his "Partridge Family" series; director Buzz Kulik was a seasoned director of television series fare. *Brian's Song* even proved that success on the small screen could be translated to theatrical features. Billy Dee Williams, who played football star Gale Sayers, had been around Hollywood for years with little success. *Brian's Song* projected him into major roles in *Lady Sings the Blues* (1972) and *Mahogany* (1975). James Caan, as the other leading figure in *Brian's Song,* moved on to stardom in *The Godfather* (1972).[18]

Brian's Song cost less than a half million dollars to make. Stock footage from National Football League games kept production expenses at a minimum. Shooting lasted only two weeks. But the impact of the first-run of *Brian's Song* nearly equaled the publicity bonanza associated with a successful feature film. Books about the film's hero became best-sellers. The movie's music moved onto *Billboard's* charts. The success of *Brian's Song* signaled that the networks must be ready to react to unexpected hits, by preparing publicity campaigns to take advantage of turns in public opinion and even to shape public opinion as only theatrical films had done in the past.[19]

By the late 1970s, the made-for-television motion picture was a staple. One study found that for the three networks during the 1979–80 television season, there were 430 runs of movies of which 40 percent were telecasts of theatrical fare and 60 percent made-for-television films. The three television networks booked just about the same number of theatrical features (about 60), but CBS and NBC scheduled 50 percent more made-for-television films than rival ABC.[20]

The state of theatrical and made-for-television movies was healthy in the 1980s. Both were able to fill enormous amounts of programming time and generate high ratings. Indeed in 1989 CBS recommitted its network to running theatrical features by signing a deal worth sixty million dollars with Universal Pictures. This seemed to say more about the lethargic state of CBS than the ratings power of theatrical films presented by NBC, ABC, or CBS. In the 1980–81 television season there were more than two hundred theatrical films shown, with *Hooper* gaining the top rating in nearly 30 percent of households. Ten seasons later the number of aired theatricals had dropped nearly in half, and *Lethal Weapon*, the top-rated theatrical run of 1989–90 television season, drew only 18 percent of households.[21]

Made-for-television movies made it possible to deal with topical or controversial material not deemed appropriate for regularly scheduled network series, particularly those that would go into syndication and thus, as "evergreens", not wish to be dated. Serious and celebrated actors who did not wish to work in series television could be featured in television movies. But in the 1980s, Hollywood was producing fewer and fewer features. The disadvantage, as we shall see in the next chapter, was that theatrical features had so much exposure in the 1980s (via pay per view and pay cable) that they ceased to be as valuable on network evening showcases. Even as early as 1983 the statistics point to an average network rating during sweeps of 1978–79 of twenty-four and only a sixteen in 1982–83.[22]

Made-for-television films filled the gap. In 1987 these films shown on the three networks outnumbered theatricals and consistently drew higher ratings. When series were shelved, movies were used as a replacement. Indeed when the writers went on strike in the spring of 1988 the networks went to their stockpile of movies. It must be repeated that a successful made-for-television film can attract an audience of from forty to seventy million, while only twenty to thirty million persons attend all theatrical screenings of a movie in an average week.[23]

The number of independent television stations doubled in the 1980s, and all relied heavily on movies. Independents developed movie libraries by contracting with Hollywood studios for five-year rentals and then running these acquired titles as many times as possible during that period. Researchers told executives of independent stations that movies tended to draw a larger than average share of female watchers, in particular those in age groups so valued by advertisers, from eighteen to thirty-four and eighteen to forty-nine.

Strategies called for the development of theme weeks ("John Wayne week" or "Action Theatre"). Managers of independent stations dreamed up clever groupings. For example, KSAS-TV of Wichita, Kansas, in 1987 ran "Women with Strange First Names Week," which included films featuring Farrah Fawcett, Sissy Spacek, and Sigourney Weaver. WGBO-TV of Chicago had "Love Slave Week," with the movies *Little Ladies of the Night*, *The Burning Bed* (1984), *Mistress of Paradise* (1981), *Making Love* (1982), and *Revenge of the Stepford Wives* (1980). Experts claimed well-promoted groupings could add from two to eight rating points to a movie's expected performance. On weekends independent stations stacked movies, playing them from morning through late at night. A typical Saturday would start at 9 A.M. with a movie for kids; one and a half hours later would come a science fiction film for teens then out of bed (as the theory goes); at noon would commence a western for adults; and a former Hollywood blockbuster, with name stars, would be saved for prime time.[24]

Independent television stations, in the face of rising competition from cable and home video in the 1980s, even began to show R-rated films, nearly in their entirety. These ranged from violence-filled serious works such as Martin Scorsese's *Taxi Driver* (1976) and Sam Peckinpah's *Straw Dogs* (1971) to exploitation thrillers such as *The Texas Chain Saw Massacre* (1974) to gory, sexy melodramas such as *The Seduction* (1982) to the titillating *Private Lessons* (1981). Some independents saved the more controversial films for postmidnight unreelings, but most simply trimmed a word or two and then aired them with "parental discretion notices" up front.[25]

A major change in movie programming came in the mid-1970s with the rise of the miniseries. Running over a different number of nights such examples as *Holocaust* (1978), *Shogun* (1980), *Thorn Birds* (1982), *Fresno* (1986), and *Lonesome Dove* (1989) drew high ratings during key rating measurement periods. In 1983 ABC presented *Winds of War* on six successive February evenings, for a total of eighteen hours, at a production cost of nearly forty million dollars. This miniseries required more than two hundred days to shoot, from a script of nearly one thousand pages. *Winds of War*, starring Robert Mitchum and Ali McGraw, more than returned its sizable investment in this key "sweeps" month by capturing half the total viewing audience and selling out all its advertising spots at a third of a million dollars per minute. *The Thorn Birds* (1983) had nearly a sixty share; *Roots* (1977), still considered the progenitor of the form, attracted nearly two-thirds of Americans when it was shown.

Indeed it was *Roots* that in a single week in January 1977 drew an estimated 130 million households to tune into at least one episode on the eight consecutive nights. Eighty million watched the final and eighth episode of this docudrama, breaking the record held by *Gone With the Wind* (1939). In a variety of follow-up studies it seems that black viewing was higher than that of whites. *Roots* was a controversial show, provoking debate and even, some studies found, rare interracial discussions. Television found an event that was the equal of a blockbuster theatrical film.[26]

The origins of the miniseries went back to 1971, when NBC invested more than two million dollars in *Vanished* (1971), a four-hour made-for-television movie planned for showing on two nights in March 1971. The ratings breakthrough came with NBC's *The Blue Knight*, broadcast in four one-hour segments between 13 and 16 November 1983. Starring William Holden, this tale of an aging policeman earned high ratings and critical acclaim, proving that a miniseries could make a difference in crucial rating sweeps months.

Miniseries typically commence on the night of highest viewing, that is, Sunday. If the series goes more than three nights, it invariably skips certain evenings—those with the top regular shows of that network. In the 1980s the costs were so high that with the thirty-hour *War and Remembrance* (1988) production hit a peak and began to fall off, leading to "shorter" (less than six hours) miniseries in the early 1990s.[27]

The trends of miniseries during the late 1980s are reflected in the production, release, and reception of *Amerika* (1987). Indeed early in 1987 ABC covered all possible media with unprecedented hype to sell its fourteen-and-a-half-hour, thirty-five-million-dollar story of a future Soviet occupation of the United States. ABC promoted *Amerika* as provocative, interesting, different, and fresh; the public decided otherwise. Most reviewers summed up public opinion by declaring it "not at all entertaining"; some declared it right-wing propaganda. The United Nations objected to its name being used in connection with troops occupying the United States. Political critics (including star Kris Kristofferson) felt the show would undermine United States–Soviet Union relations. The Chrysler Corporation withdrew planned advertising dollars.

The ratings of *Amerika* started out with a bang; millions of the curious (about a quarter of the nation's households) tuned in on Sunday, 15 February 1987. Then the bottom dropped out; with each succeeding telecast fewer and fewer stay tuned. ABC would have done better with its regular series such as "Moonlighting." Pundits estimate the fiasco cost the network about twenty million dollars in paybacks (in industry jargon, "makegoods") for the ratings advertisers were promised.[28]

Why take such a risk? ABC was inspired three years earlier by a November 1983 presentation of *The Day After* (1983). That two-hour-and-twenty-minute made-for-television movie, depicting a nuclear doomsday in Kansas, attracted a record audience—nearly half the nation's homes with televisions at the time. The impact of *The Day After* was considerable. In the capital of news junkies, Washington, D.C., trendy restaurants reported business was off by half as potential viewers stayed home, glued to their television sets.[29]

Initially ABC had trouble selling *The Day After* to advertisers, who wanted to steer clear of a film depicting the horror of a nuclear attack. But advertisers who stuck it out reaped an enormous bargain. At a discounted price of only one hundred thousand dollars per standard thirty-second advertisement, they were able to reach audiences most advertising executives only dreamed of. Those companies that benefited were Commodore Computers, Dollar Rent-a-Car, Certs breath mints, Orville Redenbacher's popcorn, and English Leather cologne. ABC did make one concession. The twenty-five national advertisements appeared within the first hour to avoid advertisers hawking their wares between scenes of carnage. The key was to present controversy, but as *Amerika* demonstrated, only an acceptable level of controversy.[30]

TELEVISION REDEFINES MOVIE WATCHING

The coming of the movies to television has meant more than simply telecasting the best and worst of (sound) motion pictures from Hollywood's past and repeating presentations of television movies. Television changed the way Americans consumed films. Consider the changes in the reviewing and promotion of motion pictures. By the 1980s film critics on television had begun to play an inordinate role in the praise and criticism of films.

One duo set all this in motion, proving that television reviewing and promotion would be taken seriously and, if correctly timed, yield millions of additional dollars at the box office. Gene Siskel is the tall, thin critic who has been described by his partner as having a "cold and detached" on-camera presence. Roger Ebert, on the other hand, is shorter and a bit more rotund, and he frequently gets outrageously excited about a film. Their pithy weekly critiques of the latest in cinematic fare reach more potential movie viewers (some eight to ten million per week) than any who ply the trade of movie reviewing in a newspaper or magazine. In the 1980s and into the 1990s the major Hollywood studios pored over every word of Siskel's and Ebert's; by 1988 the duo were working for the Disney studio.[31]

In the small world of film reviewing, Roger Ebert and Gene Siskel often seem to be everywhere. They film a nationally syndicated television show ("Siskel & Ebert & the Movies" for Disney), they appear regularly in print (Gene Siskel in the *Chicago Tribune* and Roger Ebert in *Chicago Sun-Times*), and they make appearances as in-house reviewers for the ABC and CBS network-affiliated Chicago television stations.[32] Yet Roger Ebert and Gene Siskel are hardly unique. Every major newspaper and television station in the United States has its "star" movie reviewer; radio stations (even public radio) offer regular analyses of the latest filmic fare.[33]

During the latter half of the 1970s, with Ebert and Siskel in the lead, television began to change movie reviewing by borrowing techniques from Hollywood itself. "Roger and Gene" became a team like Burns and Allen or Laurel and Hardy, stars unto themselves. Currently each is paid in excess of one million dollars per year. Skillfully using television to promote themselves, they were seen by the studios simply as a means to air promotional clips for upcoming motion pictures. By the middle of the 1980s the film industry had begun "helping" the now hundreds of "Roger and Gene" clones throughout the United States by feeding television stations pre-selected clips, forcing even harsh reviewers to show the portions of the film the studios preferred. The Hollywood studios coordinated their national advertising campaigns (more and more on television) with the release of these video press kits. Furthermore, it also became common practice for major studios to fly reviewers to special previews and parties to celebrate the latest blockbuster opening.[34]

Martin Levy, as a vice-president for Columbia Pictures, summed up the film industry's opinion: "We look upon [Roger and Gene] as on the top of the list [of available critics]. They tell the viewer straight off whether to see the film or not. That sells tickets."[35] Thus, two formerly obscure Chicago-based critics were thrust into movie advertisements in type sizes sometimes equal to the stars of the film. Specialty films in particular are especially dependent on a favorable (or any) notice by Gene Siskel and Roger Ebert. One publicist, who handled the account for *My Dinner with Andre* (1981), remembered that the weekend after the duo gave the film a "thumbs up" (Ebert calling it the best film of the year), the grosses for the film increased 300 percent. Indeed by the time *My Dinner with Andre* closed in 1982 it had grossed nearly five million dollars, and Roger Ebert and Gene Siskel were invited to the closing celebration.[36]

Increased movie reviewing hardly represented the lone transformation of the world of movie presentation. In terms of screenings the movie fan of the latter third of the twentieth century seemed never to have had it so good. Indeed movie showings in the 1980s on television seemed a never-ending stream. For example, by the late 1980s the James Bond films had aired more than seventy-five times on network television. And it seems that they will continue to unspool forever.

Similarly, through a loophole in the copyright law that made the film public domain, Frank Capra's *It's a Wonderful Life* (1946) would be shown around the clock in the weeks preceding Christmas. Indeed many public domain films can be shown on television for the simple price of a print. Such film classics as Howard Hawks's *His Girl Friday* (1940), Carol Reed's *The Third Man* (1949), Jean Renoir's *The Southerner* (1945), Roger Corman's *The Little Shop of Horrors* (1960), and Alfred Hitchcock's original *The Man Who Knew Too Much* (1934) are available to new generations of viewers. There are also any number of foreign classics in public domain such as Jean Renoir's *Rules of the Game* (1939), Jean-Luc Godard's *Breathless* (1959), Alain Resnais' *Last Year at Marienbad* (1962), and virtually all the major works of Italian neorealism.[37]

Reliance on television for the presentation of motion pictures has extracted a high price in terms of viewing conditions. The television image ratio is four by three, while the standard image for motion pictures is much wider. To accommodate the larger image, the wide-screen film is cut off at the sides to fit onto the smaller video screen. Using the techniques of panning and scanning the wide-screen film is re-edited so the "action" shifts to the center of the frame. Consider the case of Ernie Hudson, one of the members of the exorcism quartet in *Ghostbusters* (1984). Unfortunately the television image was able to encompass only three ghostbusters, and on television Hudson's character did not appear until the second half of the film. When the film was panned and scanned Hudson was eliminated so the television viewer could see the figures of Dan Aykroyd, Bill Murray, and Harold Ramis.[38]

There are other examples. Compare John Boorman's *Point Blank* (1967) and Milos Forman's *Amadeus* (1984). The television print of *Point Blank* contains cramped compositions with characters on the screen one moment and then off the next. On television the film is a jumbled, confusing mess, because the wide-screen compositions have been reedited to place the action on the center of the television screen. *Amadeus* on the other hand looks far better: there is no jumble and no missing characters. Both films were made in Panavision wide screen; both were panned and scanned. The difference is that John Boorman made his film with no eye toward television; theatrical revenues constituted the bulk of any film's gross in the mid-1960s. Milos Forman, nearly twenty years later, realized millions could be made for television and shot his film accordingly. He directed *Amadeus* with an eye toward panning and scanning. Indeed, by the 1980s most cinematographers making "theatrical" films placed marks on their camera's viewfinders so they could frame the action for *both* the theatre wide screen and the more limited television image.[39]

Of course, films do not need to be panned and scanned. The image can be reduced for television until all of it fits; in practice, this technique of "letterboxing" fills the empty space above and below with a black matte. In the 1980s, a great deal of lip service was paid to letterboxing, but movie watchers en masse do not care for it. Indeed, back in the 1960s, as Hollywood studios tested their film to video transfers, letterbox prints were made to check the total quality of a widescreen movie's negative or master positive *before* it was transferred to video. These were element tests and the home viewer never saw them. Instead the studio filled the television frame with the center of the film and then panned and scanned to capture "all" the action. Today technicians can hide the panning and scanning, making them look "natural" in the course of the film, but still these "additions" were never part of the original viewing experience.[40]

Refitting the spoken language of a theatrical film for television presents yet another problem. In *Planes, Trains, and Automobiles* (1987) John Candy's character entones to Steve Martin's character: "God, you're a tight ass." For the broadcast version the character states: "Gosh, you're a whiner." Eliminating offensive language was once requested by the networks, but prescrubbed versions are routinely prepared by the Hollywood studios to make sure their video versions are acceptable. For redubbing, engineers go to other parts of the sound track and remix what they need. Or sometimes the actors are called back to redo lines. One system, complete with a computer program to locate and substitute lines, is called Automatic Dialogue Replacement System, or ADRS, and has been in place since the late 1970s. And so with little trouble and expense, "shits" routinely become "shoots" and "fuckings" become "freakings."[41]

Computer technology has enabled feature films to be redone. The transformation of black-and-white films into color movies for television (colorization) caused a major outcry in the late 1980s. (With all the hoopla it ought to be noted that colorization does not destroy an original film; all transformation is done on video.) In March of 1985 Norman and Earl Glick of Toronto, Ontario, Canada, acquired the old Hal Roach film library and colorized *Topper* (1937), Laurel and Hardy in *Way Out West* (1937), and *It's a Wonderful Life*. The cost was minimal, only about two thousand dollars per minute to create a "completely new product." For Christmas of 1985 *Miracle on 34th Street* (1947) was colorized and broadcast in 176 television markets. It attracted some twenty million viewers and earned more than a half million dollars, as much as in all its previous years on television.

It was the screening of *It's a Wonderful Life* that set off a storm of objections. Originally director Frank Capra consented to colorization, then he protested. Directors from Steven Spielberg to Federico Fellini issued public denunciations of the new technology for desecrating modern cinematic classics. In 1986, when Ted Turner purchased MGM, he announced a deal to convert more than one hundred films. He declared that he owned them and could do whatever he liked to them, indeed threatening to colorize *Citizen Kane* (1941). The Directors Guild of America took their case to the United States Congress. Hearings were held; stars and filmmakers paraded up to Capital Hill. But after all the smoke had cleared, the owners of the films were still free to colorize whatever they wished.[42]

The biggest complaint from the average television viewer of motion pictures has long been interruption of movies by advertisements. To fit the formulaic slots of television a station allocates only ninety minutes for a two-hour show. This means that in a ninety-minute slot the movie had to be trimmed to seventy-eight minutes. Cutting to fit the allotted time has been commonplace since the early 1950s.

Stories of how television stations accomplished this heinous task are legendary. It is said that Fred Silverman, when he was a lowly film editor at WGN in Chicago, solved the problem of fitting the ninety-six-minute *Jailhouse Rock* (1957) into a seventy-eight-minute afternoon movie block by cutting all of Elvis's musical numbers. (Indeed, musicals are regularly seen on television without the full complement of musical numbers.) In the 1980s apparatus was developed that mechanically condensed the running time of a film by a sixth by speeding up the entire film. More commonly over-the-air television stations shelve theatricals for made-for-television movies to avoid the problem. Since television movies were designed to fit prescribed time blocks, there is no need for editing or speeding up.[43]

The coming of television forever changed moviegoing in America. Before television rural citizens supported fewer movie houses than their urban neighbors. Cities not only had more Hollywood films unspooling at neighborhood theatres but also a selection of newsreel theatres, art houses, and theatres for ethnic audiences. Rural Americans had to wait for whatever came. But television signals raced over urban/rural boundaries. Everyone could watch films day and night.

But motion pictures shown on television hardly constituted a perfect show. They were continually interrupted by advertising messages; they were trimmed to fit into television's prescribed slots. Since television could not rid itself of advertisements and time slots, a market arose for uninterrupted screenings of features on television. As more and more films were shown on television, entrepreneurs developed two solutions to this particular problem: uninterrupted screenings on a premium pay-cable channel and presentation on home video. These are the subjects of the following two chapters.

THIRTEEN

Cable Television's Movie Channels

Over-the-air television served as the principal second-run showcase for Hollywood films through the late 1950s, all of the 1960s, and into the 1970s. The number of stations in any one market was limited. Most of the nation had but three channels, which served up only network fare. The bigger cities did have independent stations that could counter-program, often with movies. But no where could the movie fan see his or her favorites as in theatres. Most annoying was that television stations sanitized the presentations of theatrical films and cut them to fit into prescribed time slots. The emergence of cable television, principally through its pay channels, would take advantage of the frustrations of millions of Americans who watched most of their movies on television.

Cable television movie channels come in two versions: basic (one fee per month for a series of channels) and premium (a special monthly fee for one separate channel, showing uncut, uncensored feature films). Ted Turner's SuperStation (as part of the basic package) and Home Box Office, HBO (as the premium pay-cable movie channel) would become the very symbols for the successes of the cable television industry. Indeed it is fair to say that cable television has become a prime outlet for rerunning motion pictures while movie theatres function mainly as first-run showcases.

THE RISE OF PAY TELEVISION

It was Time, Inc.'s subsidiary, Home Box Office, that innovated a profitable strategy during the 1970s. Into the 1990s HBO continues to be the

263

dominant pay network, functioning as the second-run at the home "neighborhood" movie house. In retrospect HBO's success is not surprising. In one survey taken over twenty-five years ago, in the days before cable television became widespread, sample respondents were asked what they most disliked about film showings on television networks. There were only two significant answers: constant advertisement interruptions and the long wait for blockbusters to appear. HBO would solve both these problems—and more.[1]

HBO began as a microwave service in 1972, and it was not until 1975, when HBO went to satellite distribution, that it sparked the interest in cable television. In one of the most productive investments in television history Time gambled seven and a half million dollars on a five-year lease to put HBO on RCA's satellite, Satcom I, even before the satellite had been launched. HBO commenced satellite national distribution on 30 September 1975, and from a base of three hundred thousand subscribers moved, within five years, to six million subscribers. By giving its subscribers uncut, uninterrupted movies a few months after they had disappeared from theatres, HBO witnessed a growth during the late 1970s and into the early 1980s that proved nothing less than spectacular. By 1983 the company could claim twelve million subscribers. Indeed Time, Inc. proved so successful with its cable operations (read: HBO) that the video arm of the company surpassed the publishing activities in terms of profits generated.[2]

In 1976, Viacom International, a major television program supplier and owner of cable systems, created a rival to HBO with Showtime. This new competitor went to satellite distribution in 1979. Also in 1979, Warner Cable joined with its then partner American Express to create the Movie Channel. In 1980 Time created Cinemax as an all-movie complement to HBO, to appeal to younger audiences, in particular yuppies. To differentiate its product further, during the 1980s, Cinemax regularly scheduled more films than the competition, an average of eighty-five per month. The Movie Channel followed with an average of seventy-eight per month; Showtime had fifty-five, and HBO only fifty. But this was understandable since HBO and Showtime had contracted more of the blockbuster, star-laden titles, which the two repeated regularly.[3]

By the late 1980s nearly every cable system in the United States had at least one HBO-like service, with over 90 percent carrying two or more. If a system had only one pay channel, the odds were that it was HBO since this was in three-quarters of the nation's cable systems. Most of the pay services operated around the clock.

HBO certainly ranked as the healthiest of the pay-cable movie services in the late 1980s, as the home video industry began making inroads into the business of watching uncut, uncensored films outside theatres. Indeed HBO and its sister service Cinemax garnered about two-thirds of all subscriber growth in pay services from 1984 through 1988. Consequently by the close of the 1980s Time-Warner's two pay services controlled some 60 percent of the pay television market, while Showtime and the Movie Channel had to settle for 30 percent. Others gathered up the remaining 10 percent.[4]

But the news in the late 1980s was not all good for HBO. In 1988, HBO had to pull the plug on Festival, the company's year-long experiment to program a family movie channel of all G- and R-rated movies. Festival targeted audiences who complained loudly of the excess sex and violence on HBO and its rivals. Although prices were kept a dollar or two below HBO, the subscriber base never grew large enough to make it profitable.

To maintain its strength in the 1980s HBO continued to sign exclusive agreements with studios in an effort to catch a future hit. In 1988 it signed a deal with Twentieth Century-Fox and had a similar arrangement with Paramount. The contract with Twentieth Century-Fox called for three hundred million dollars in fees and would run for three years. It replaced a nonexclusive agreement then in operation. The agreement was rightly seen as a victory for HBO in its war for market share with Viacom.

Prior to 1985, HBO and Showtime each purchased movies from all the studios and then aired them. Each network looked the same, with the same hit films. Only the mix of lesser products differentiated one from another. Then in 1985 Showtime decided to try for product exclusivity, or what economists call product differentiation; it tried to make its product distinguishable and promoted that advantage accordingly. This was effectively brand-name warfare—a classic example learned from movie theatres that block booked the films of a single studio.[5]

In 1985 Showtime signed exclusive agreements with Paramount and Disney. In response, HBO became more aggressive with the remaining studios as their nonexclusive contracts expired, outbidding Showtime in two cases. For example, when Paramount's contract with Showtime came up for renegotiation in 1987, HBO offered the studio significantly more money to switch to HBO. That gave HBO a stronger product salability at the same time it undercut the sole rival. It was a classic case of two-handed, high-stakes poker.[6]

In 1987 HBO also signed a long-term agreement with Warner Communication's Warner Bros. studio. While that contract was nonexclusive, providing Showtime the right to buy Warner product as well, the realities of this deal changed significantly in March 1989 when Warner and Time announced their merger. This vertical merger offered the ultimate exclusivity deal. Under this arrangement HBO and Warner Bros. Pictures, Inc. would be part of the same company. In 1985 HBO pioneered an advertising campaign, complete with heavy direct marketing efforts and discount offers to subscribers. At the end of the 1980s HBO initiated a wide-ranging, image-boosting media campaign, spending fifty million dollars on over-the-air and cable advertising placements.[7]

The Hollywood studios also tried to establish their own pay-cable movie channel, Premiere. The major Hollywood studios argued that through the 1970s HBO prospered from Hollywood movies. The studios claimed they received insufficient income from the showings on HBO and Showtime because those two, and those two alone, controlled the marketplace. To gain the upper hand, in April 1980 Columbia Pictures, MCA/Universal, Paramount, and Twentieth Century-Fox announced a joint deal with the Getty Oil Company to create Premiere as their pay-television channel to rival HBO. They would withhold their films, and then only after they had played on Premiere would they be released for screening on HBO.[8]

HBO and Showtime asserted a violation of antitrust law and the United States Department of Justice, near the end of the administration of President Jimmy Carter, agreed and filed suit. There was much objection, but in the end the four Hollywood companies backed off and Premiere never went into business. Ironically, if they had tried a few years later, the administration of Ronald Reagan probably would have given the go ahead.[9]

A significant, long-term challenge to HBO would come from Viacom. This media conglomerate combined Showtime and the Movie Channel in 1983, and although they are not as powerful as Time's HBO plus Cinemax combination, they do offer an alternative. In 1988 Showtime, the principal service, added one million subscribers, giving it about ten million subscribers at the end of the year (versus nearly twenty million at HBO). When Sumner Redstone's National Amusements bought Viacom in June of 1987, Redstone instituted changes in the two pay services. He brought in Frank Biondi, former chief executive of HBO, to head the operation and allocated millions for a marketing blitz. The Movie Channel used hosts and packaged movies in groupings such as "Film Festivals," "Movie Marathons," and "Double Features." To contrast with HBO it would start films at 7 P.M. and 9 P.M. rather than 8 P.M. and 10 P.M. But Viacom stuck with it as a pay service, and by 1988 saw the Movie Channel gain a small number of subscribers per month.[10]

To match HBO, Showtime pursued exclusive agreements with studios. For example, in March 1989 Showtime signed an exclusive agreement with Disney's Touchstone Pictures. Since this was the hot movie studio of the late 1980s, with such blockbusters as *Three Men and a Baby* and *Who Framed Roger Rabbit?*, Showtime gained a sizable edge for five years (1989–94). In 1989 the terms of the contract called for Disney to be paid in relationship to the box-office performance; if the film had done well at the box office, Showtime would pay more. Richard Frank, president of the Walt Disney Studios, told the *Wall Street Journal*: "Had HBO been able to corner the whole market, it would have been tough slogging for Showtime and there ultimately wouldn't have been competitive services in the market."[11]

Disney's agreement with Showtime hinged on one other factor. Disney itself operated a pay-cable television network aimed at children, and the company understood that if HBO got too much of an edge it might enter and effectively compete in marketing children's fare. Boosting Showtime meant HBO would continue to have effective competition and thus stay out of the Disney Channel's turf. The Walt Disney Corporation had launched its pay-cable channel in 1983, and soon the Disney Channel became the fastest-growing pay service, based in part by repeating the classic feature films in the Disney library. After only twenty months on line, the Disney Channel began to turn a profit, and by the late 1980s was making more than fifty million dollars per year.[12]

Showtime was bolstered in yet another significant way in 1989 when Tele-Communications, Inc., the national's largest cable holder of subscribers, purchased half interest and infused the corporation with new financial capital. The key to the $225 million deal was the fact that Tele-Communications, Inc., which served more than 23 percent of the nation's homes with cable television, would carry Showtime and the Movie Channel. This pact insured the survival of a competitor, indeed a strong one, for HBO well into the foreseeable future. Tele-Communications, Inc. pursued the deal because it realized that after the 1989 Time-Warner merger HBO possessed a direct link to the second largest MSO (multi-system operator) in the nation. Tele-Communications, Inc. purchased an interest in Showtime and the Movie Channel as an insurance policy against the growing corporate power of Time-Warner.[13]

By the late 1980s the two major pay-television camps had divided up the feature films from the major studios. HBO had signed exclusive deals with Paramount (through 1994), Warner (contractually through 1991, but in reality forever now that Time and Warner are one company), and Twentieth Century-Fox (through 1991). Showtime had lined up Disney, Orion, Carolco, Cannon, Atlantic, Weintraub, and Imagine.[14]

Moving into the 1990s all pay-cable movie channels functioned similarly. Local cable systems charged subscribers about ten dollars per month per pay-cable movie channel. That revenue was then split between the local franchise (which kept about two-thirds) and the pay-cable channel (the other one-third). HBO pioneered the scheduling of movies for pay-television to create an attractive package each month, so that subscribing households would be willing to pay each month. The average pay-television service offered between twenty and fifty movies per month, a handful of first-runs, but mostly "encores" from previous months.[15]

During the course of the month the movies were scheduled from four to six times on different days and at different times of the daily schedule. The idea was to give the viewer several opportunities to watch each film but not to exhaust the movies the pay service has to offer too quickly. Thus, the success of a pay-cable movie channel was determined not by ratings for a single program but by the general appeal and satisfaction level for the month as a whole. The real test was whether the customers kept on writing their monthly checks.[16]

With all the changes and programming variations in this marketplace, the big winners have been the Hollywood studios. Precise figures vary from deal to deal, but reliable estimates suggest that the major studios gain from five to seven million dollars per film from a deal with HBO/Cinemax or Showtime/the Movie Channel. For a single year, this means each of the six major studios stands to gain on average one hundred million extra dollars.

Movie viewers gained as well. For twenty years over-the-air television had brought the best and worst of Hollywood into the home but with significant disadvantages: constant interruptions for advertisements, the sanitization of the movie stories to please television's moralist critics, and a wait of several years for hits to appear. Pay-cable movie channels jettisoned the advertisements and ran the films intact only months after they had disappeared from movie theatres. For theatrical failures, the "clearance time" could be a matter of weeks.[17]

But with all the successes and failures of HBO, Cinemax, Showtime, the Movie Channel, and the Disney Channel, it should not be forgotten that there were also challengers who tried something different. Many corporate casualties have fallen before Time, Viacom, and Disney, but a case for the difficulty of starting and maintaining an alternative pay-cable institution can best be made with a look at the experiences of the Z Channel of Los Angeles. From its founding in the early 1970s, through five owners, to its demise in 1989, the Z Channel drew national attention for its eclectic mix of movie blockbusters, classic motion pictures, foreign films, and even student films from area universities.

The Z Channel wielded a great deal of influence because of its location in the moviemaking capital of the United States. For example, more than 70 percent of the members of the Academy of Motion Picture Arts and Sciences subscribed, so frequent play on the Z Channel could propel a film to multiple Academy Awards as was the case with Woody Allen's *Annie Hall* (1977). Actor James Woods praised the Z Channel: "Yes, it has made my career. *Fast Walking* (1982)—it *debuted* on Z Channel!" [18]

At ten dollars per month, Z Channel subscribers saw an uncut version of *Heaven's Gate* (1980), Orson Welles's cut of *Touch of Evil* (1958), and the studio release and director's cut of *Once Upon a Time in America* (1982). Film buffs lobbied to have a fully restored version of *The Big Trail* (1930) shown. The Z Channel regularly unspooled silent films. But it could never attract more than one hundred thousand subscribers. It calculated it needed three times that to break even. The Z Channel began on 1 April 1974, when only HBO was in business. It was able to survive on the margin even with the introduction of three other pay-cable channels. It could not survive the exclusive contracts Time and Viacom signed in the mid-1980s. By 1989 the Z Channel experiment was over. [19]

THE INNOVATION OF THE SUPERSTATION

Just as important as the innovation of HBO and its premium channel cousins was the arrival of the "superstation," a cable television network fashioned from the widespread presentation of an independent station not affiliated with any network. [20] A superstation serves as an extension of the familiar independent, over-the-air station discussed in the previous chapter. Led by Ted Turner's WTBS, channel 17 from Atlanta, all superstations offer movies for approximately one-half of their broadcast day. WTBS was the first SuperStation and is inextricably linked with the term. Movie showings in the morning, afternoon, and many evenings have always been at the core of the SuperStation programming strategy. If, through the 1980s, one wanted to view the best and worst of Hollywood's sound film past, one tuned to a superstation.

Indeed, Ted Turner purchased an entire movie studio to acquire movies for WTBS. In the spring of 1986 Kirk Kerkorian, long-time head of MGM/ UA in one form or another, sold MGM to Ted Turner for nearly one and a half *billion* dollars. (The stock was selling for nine dollars per share and Kerkorian asked and got twenty-eight dollars per share from Turner.) But Turner soon learned that he had been fleeced, and by that summer was looking for a buyer of MGM—minus the film library. In the end, Kerkorian bought back MGM for three hundred million dollars, which left Turner owning more than four thousand movies for more than one billion dollars (or about four hundred thousand dollars per title). In 1987, Turner purchased the rights to some eight hundred RKO films not covered in the original MGM/UA deal a year earlier, giving him exclusive license to *Citizen Kane* (1941), *King Kong* (1933), and the Astaire-Rogers films.[21]

By late in 1989 WTBS ranked as one of the largest of the cable services, reaching in excess of fifty million homes. Even before Turner temporarily took over MGM, his WTBS was using up to forty feature films per week, or about two thousand films per year. As such, its movie screenings, at times, could reach into ratings that were more than the typical 1 percent that most cable programs strived for. For example, on 13 December 1989 WTBS's cablecast of *Gone With the Wind* (1939) generated the highest household delivery for any feature film in WTBS history. Sent out in its entirety, *Gone With the Wind* was watched in 8 percent of American homes—a phenomenal rating for a superstation.[22]

Because of its presence on nearly every cable system in the United States, Turner's SuperStation ranked among the most watched of all basic cable networks. For example, in November of 1986 WTBS had eleven of the top fifteen rated cable shows, including the top show, the film *The Dirty Dozen* (1967). To insure that the repeat showings of some classics would remain high, Turner pulled some from syndication, and so in the late 1980s one could only see *Captains Courageous* (1937) or *The Red Badge of Courage* (1951) on a Turner channel. Turner also led the way to colorization so that he could use his massive film library more fully on his channel.[23]

Turner's SuperStation hardly represented the only superstation with a nationwide audience. In the late 1980s the line included WWOR from New York, owned by Hollywood's MCA, Inc., the parent company of Universal Studios. MCA purchased this independent in the number-one television market in the United States in 1987 for nearly four hundred million dollars. A glance at a typical Sunday WWOR schedule in the late 1980s revealed that the bulk of that day's offerings were feature films, frequently from parent company Universal's vast film library. WWOR functions as a nationwide outlet for a major Hollywood studio, a classic example of vertical integration.[24]

There are other superstations. WGN, owned by the Tribune Corporation, has long supplied watchers of independent stations in Chicago with movies. WGN was launched on a satellite in October 1978, and within three years was fed to more than ten million cable homes, primarily in the midwestern United States. As an independent station in the 1950s and 1960s, WGN originated theme movie weeks and at one time had Basil Rathbone do the introductions for old Sherlock Holmes movies in which he appeared. Indeed, the Tribune Company of Chicago did so well with WGN that in 1984 it put another of its stations, WPIX from New York, onto the satellite and created yet another superstation. These became the Big Four of the superstation business: WTBS from Atlanta, WGN from Chicago, WWOR from New York, and WPIX from New York.[25]

MOVIES ON BASIC CABLE

In the late 1980s premium pay channels such as HBO and superstations such as Turner's WTBS hardly defined the universe of movie screenings on cable television. Dozens of basic channels had also come to rely heavily on movies. For example, Pat Robertson originated his Christian Broadcasting Network (CBN) in 1977 to spread the message of fundamentalist Christian religion. But since CBN moved to a broad-based service in 1981 as a fully taxed, for-profit institution, more and more movies have appeared, principally Hays Code–approved titles from the 1930s and 1940s.[26] The network was propped up in 1989 when Tele-Communications, Inc. purchased a one-sixth stake in the Family Channel, thus guaranteeing presentation of the Family Channel on Tele-Communication, Inc.'s millions of subscriber homes. As part of that deal Pat Robertson insisted that Tele-Communications, Inc. not force R-rated films on "his" network.[27]

In the late 1980s American Movie Classics (AMC) presented older films with the film buff in mind. AMC, a subsidiary of Cablevision, the giant multiple system operator, was half owned by giant Tele-Communications, Inc. In addition to regular movies, AMC also cablecasted interview segments entitled "Classic Stories from Classic Stars," which were biographical sketches on its "Star Facts," and fascinating minidocumentaries packaged as "Making a Classic." Like the Family Channel, AMC was offered as part of basic cable service in about half the nation's cable systems.[28]

Bravo functioned as the art house cable network of the 1980s, showing foreign films, documentaries, and experimental cinema. As a pay service, Bravo, owned by Cablevision, targeted highly educated, well-off audiences. In July of 1988 Bravo canceled the television premiere of Jean-Luc Godard's controversial film *Hail Mary* (1985) after receiving complaints from around the nation. In earlier years Bravo might have taken a chance on this modern-day version of the tale of Joseph and Mary, but during the late 1980s the station grew less bold so as not to offend its affluent, educated, "sophisticated" audience. The strategy seems to work, since in 1988 Bravo for the first time was able to turn a profit. (During the preceding seven years Bravo had racked up an estimated ten million dollars in losses.) In addition, during 1988 Bravo began to shed its pay status, save in selected upscale situations. By 1989 nearly three-quarters of Bravo's nearly one and a half million subscribers received the channel as part of their basic package. However, Manhattan Cable TV charged nearly thirteen dollars per month for Bravo, and in Montgomery County, Maryland, outside the nation's capital, it was almost ten dollars extra per month.[29]

In the late 1980s there were several other basic cable services that relied heavily on motion pictures. Arts & Entertainment, owned by the Hearst Corporation, Capital Cities/ABC, and NBC, regularly presented movies as a small portion of its service. It was launched in February 1984 and competes with Bravo for upscale cable television viewers. Black Entertainment Television, headquartered in Washington, D.C., featured programs for black Americans including movies made by blacks or for blacks. Launched in January 1980, BET reached more than twenty-three million households. The Nostalgia Channel, launched in May of 1985, programmed classic movies. Aimed at viewers forty-five and older, it relied on older films, but unlike TNT it had no exclusive right to any films. Thus the Nostalgia Channel had to program from the same pool as every other independent station.[30] The Nashville Network regularly cablecasted motion pictures of Roy Rogers and Gene Autry. TNN was launched in March of 1983 and was one of the most widely seen services, particularly in the Southeast.

The USA Network ranked as one of the most far reaching of these other cable channels. Owned by Paramount Communications and MCA/Universal, USA offered a superstation-like schedule. Movies flowed in prime time on USA just like the counter-programming of an independent or the superstations discussed above. USA regularly, for example, programmed Woody Allen "festivals," grouping together titles such as *Manhattan* (1979), *Love and Death* (1975), *Bananas* (1971), and *Everything You Always Wanted to Know About Sex But Were Afraid to Ask* (1972). In the late 1980s USA was aggressive in purchasing films and commissioning made-for-television movies. On the former front, late in 1989 USA agreed to pay some fifty million dollars for twenty-six films from Walt Disney's Touchstone for runs before the films would be released to over-the-air stations. This marked a first and gave USA a way to differentiate its product. As for made-for-television films, USA presented (as the 1990s began) two such features per month. Indeed when *The China Lake Murders* premiered on USA on 31 January 1990 it made cable television history as the highest rated original film ever to go out on a basic cable network. About 4 percent of the nation's households watched.[31]

The biggest success in the market for basic cable channels based on movie screenings came with the introduction of Ted Turner's new Turner Network Television, or TNT, launched in October of 1988. TNT served as a showcase for the older films Turner acquired from Kirk Kerkorian three years earlier: the Warner Bros., RKO, and MGM packages. Reel after reel of rare films, unseen since the 1950s on television and only available in archives, appeared at the rate of nine or ten a day. Despite all-too-frequent breaks for per-inquiry advertisements, film buffs rearranged their schedules, and TNT's rating grew to among the highest in the cable television business.[32]

In the fall of 1989 TNT did begin to add NBA professional basketball to its all-movie schedule, but for the twelve months before that, TNT had been a movie lover's dream come true. For that special year the TNT "day" began at 9 A.M. with romance films ("Love Affairs"). Reruns of the old television series "Medical Center" offered a one-hour chance for a quick bath, aerobics, jog, and/or meal. Then at noon came old musicals ("Song and Dance"), at 2 P.M. a comedy ("Just for Laughs"), at 4 P.M. "Hollywood Legends," then another two-hour break for Jim Henson and the Muppets, and at 8 P.M. and 10 P.M. "Big Pictures," the blockbusters with the best-known stars. From midnight through dawn came an overnight of rare treats—the most obscure of feature films.

Lisa Mateas, TNT's director of program acquisitions and scheduling, and Terry Segal, TNT's vice-president and general manager, held a power rarely matched by any exhibitor in United States film history. They selected the actual offerings from the thousands of choices. Mateas, who had trained at the Los Angeles independent television station KTLA, became famous for her imaginative couplings. One night she presented *He Couldn't Say No* (1938), *She Couldn't Say No* (1954), and *She Had to Say Yes* (1933). Late in 1988 and early in 1989 there came a double bill of the two rare *Trader Horn* (1931 and 1973) films. One could catch seldom-seen Joan Crawford classics from her early flapper phase, such as *Torch Singer* (1933) and *A Woman's Face* (1941). The films, with few exceptions, were gorgeous; the original negatives and master prints, stored in vaults in Kansas City, were remastered onto one-inch videotape in Los Angeles and then sent to TNT headquarters in Atlanta.[33]

THE PAY-PER-VIEW ALTERNATIVE

Premium services and basic cable channels charge viewers for groups of movies, either by subscription or as part of a basic cable package fee. To extract the maximum amount of monies, it would make sense to follow the theatrical box-office model literally and charge a separate fee for each movie watched, just as one pays an admission fee *before* entering a movie theatre. The cable television equivalent of the theatrical box office is called Pay-Per-View, or PPV, and was innovated in the late 1980s.

On a serious level PPV began on a national basis in November 1985, and by the late 1980s it was available on at least a quarter of cable systems. PPV represented one of the faster-growing segments of the cable business as the industry turned into the 1990s. Entrepreneurs sought to offer PPV to customers tired of waiting so long to see blockbuster films. Just as pay-cable services had come into the marketplace because of the limitations of movies presented on over-the-air television, so PPV sought its niche based on the perceived failure of HBO and Showtime. PPV is sold as a convenience service, rotating screenings of the same "new" blockbuster film around the clock as soon as it becomes available. In 1988 PPV became a serious alternative; the number of homes equipped to receive PPV doubled in that year, from five to ten million.[34]

The basic PPV technology of the late 1980s worked this way. The movie was transmitted by satellite to cable MSO, which in turn delivered it to a single home by an addressable converter, a computer-activated technology that unscrambles the signal only for the consumer who has ordered.[35] As of the early 1990s ordering was usually done by phone; in the future the order might be placed through a computer device or a remote control hooked into the television set.[36]

In the late 1980s three networks dominated PPV movie channels: Request Television, Viewer's Choice, and Cable Video Store. Launched in 1985, Request Television has been the greatest success; it stands as the largest and as of the early 1990s was distributed via satellite. It offered a menu of four movies each week on a two-week cycle on each of two channels. For Request Television, one had to order ahead of time and then pay from four to five dollars per viewing for a film (more for professional boxing and wrestling special events). Movies generally reached PPV from a month to two months after their release in a video store. Movie revenues for all PPV in 1989 totaled only about $140 million.[37]

The future of PPV revolves around one question: When should the major Hollywood studios release films to PPV? Should it be soon after the film leaves the theatres? Before home video? Before television? As of the end of the 1980s the release schedule has yet to be firmed up, but most think it will eventually come a month or so after the end of the theatrical run. The Hollywood studios of the late 1980s worried about off-PPV taping. How could they stop the viewer from simply taping the PPV showing and then building up a tape library without buying the tape in the store? In 1989 Macrovison and Eidak began to encode PPV transmissions so that when copied on a video cassette recorder the copy became distorted. This could be overridden but only at considerable expense to the home viewer.

Still, the future seems bright for PPV because it alone offers the Hollywood movie companies and cable companies a method by which to extract the maximum in consumer surplus for movie fans who do not want to pay for a theatre ticket but want to see the film before its debut on tape. PPV could become a new window for motion picture release. Yet some argue that homes would best be served not by cable at all but through direct broadcast satellites or wireless cable.[38] In the 1990s the debate rages on.[39]

In the end, the pay-cable industry, however constituted, has grown and thrived for one reason—its ability to deliver uncut, uncensored, uninterrupted screenings of feature films. Indeed with all the technological change and skilled marketing, the most important point is that the true demand rests not with new technology but with interest in seeing feature films. The extraordinary side of all this innovation is that Americans in record numbers wish to watch their favorite motion pictures repeatedly. The new technologies of pay-cable television simply seek the most profitable way to satisfy that demand. However, during the 1980s pay cable ceased to be the only show in town; a revolution in watching movies at home took place; home video would transform movie watching as nothing had since the introduction of the movie show itself.

FOURTEEN

Home Video

The most important transformation in movie watching in the second half of the twentieth century has been the innovation of the video cassette recorder, usually known as the VCR. Home video, represented by the VCR and its tapes, enables the movie fan to program his or her own theatre. No one is dependent on the desires of a theatre owner or television station programmer. In the convenience of one's home, a movie fan can choose from thousands of the best films ever made. With such freedom (and falling equipment prices), the VCR stimulated movie watching to new heights during the 1980s.

In little more than a decade after the 1976 introduction of the Betamax and the VHS alternative, rentals and sales of movies on tape surpassed the theatrical box-office take in the United States. Although sales of video cassette machines leveled off at the start of the 1990s, home video represents the largest (in terms of number of plays) component of movie watching, movie collecting, and movie participation by the fan on the street.

Home video combines the best of the box-office approach of movie economics (voting for one's favorites directly with dollars rather than indirectly through ratings) and the convenience of television watching at home. Unlike advertising-based television, in which the presentation of films is geared to the desires of advertisers, home video is geared to the desires of the individual fan. For as little as a dollar a video—after the investment of approximately three hundred dollars for the machine—the home theatre is up and running. This assumes that the purchaser of a VCR already has a television set, which is a safe assumption in a nation where more homes

276

have television sets than indoor plumbing. A theatre's location near the home was brought to its ultimate conclusion by moving the theatre into the home.

Home video is superior to the best alternatives discussed, including pay television's Home Box Office. With the HBO system of monthly payment collection, films are shown over and over again until the new month begins. HBO's brand of choice is better than the advertising-driven world of over-the-air television but hardly as optimal as a world in which one can choose the movies (on tape) and the viewing time.

The home video world is not perfect, however. The major Hollywood studios are still dominant, always figuring out ways to maximize their take. What this means is that the concentration of rentals and sales, as in theatres for decades, rests with a handful of titles. These are the blockbuster selections made at the theatrical box office. Thus, for current hits, it requires more effort than simply going to the local video store and picking up a copy. In the first few weeks of a hit film's release, luck is required as well, but within the span of a month or so, nearly any title can be gotten at any time and played at one's convenience. And that is the key point. For the best and worst of Hollywood's past (as well as films from around the world) the VCR enables a repertory movie theatre at home.

Tape viewing generally requires a well-stocked video store nearby. Here location matters in the classic urban/rural split so important to movie watching since its beginnings with the nickelodeon craze of 1905. Video stores stocked with thousands of titles have appeared only on corners of middle-class neighborhoods in the biggest cities. That is where the greatest possible profits can be made. Small communities, poorer communities (even in parts of major cities), and rural communities have stores with less selection. There is some activity through mail rental, but this is less convenient and more costly.

Still, for the majority of Americans, the ability to watch movies on tape has provided a cornucopia of film choices. In the world prior to home video rental one had to wait until a theatre or television station decided to book the movie. It was not legally possible (in all but a handful of cases) or financially possible to own films and the necessary equipment with which to see them. Copies on 8 mm hardly provided an optimal viewing experience and required upkeep and expense. Copies of 16 mm films were expensive, and in some cases owning them was outside the law. Only outright thieves privately stored and showed 35 mm films.

In the 1980s all that changed. Home video added positively to the choices of the movie fan. The venues of the movie theatre, pay television, and over-the-air television all still exist, but home video simply has added a new and important "window" (in industry terms). With home video we now have greater participation in movie watching than at any point in history, albeit at home and not in theatres. Home video represents the ultimate extension of the age of viewing films by way of over-the-air television, which began in the 1950s.

THE INVENTION AND INNOVATION OF HOME VIDEO

The invention of the equipment for watching videotapes (and recording off the air) at home made the marketplace for home video possible. The easy-to-use movie show at home had been the dream of many an inventor. The Kodak Corporation innovated and sold a 16 mm projector for home use in the 1920s. Later, Kodak and others developed an 8 mm projector for home use. But both were relatively expensive, complicated to use, and only ten-year-old (or older) titles were ever available in those forms. Dedicated film buffs bought an 8 mm or 16 mm projector and invested hundreds and often thousands of dollars in a collection of films. But this market was always relatively small.[1]

In 1956 came videotape recording, developed by the Ampex Company of California. The first videotape recorders were bulky, expensive devises, using two-inch tape. Indeed the first machines were the size of a side-by-side washer-dryer. Engineers were required to thread the two twelve-inch diameter tape reels and run them. Such machines were used only for studio work. Later, one-inch and then three-quarter-inch machines came into use, but these were still reel-to-reel formats.

The breakthrough for simple home use came in the early 1970s with smaller equipment (one-half-inch tape) enclosed in its own cassette. These machines could record off the air (the popular "time-shifting") as well as play prerecorded movies. In 1972 Sony of Japan introduced the first video cassette recorder for educational and business uses; it was equipped with three-quarter-inch tape. In 1975 came the Betamax, with the smaller one-half-inch tape at an initial price of thirteen hundred dollars. This was expensive, but it did give the owner the ability to tape off the air and watch the program (often a movie) whenever he or she wanted.[2]

Sony's monopoly was short-lived; in 1977 Matsushita of Japan introduced a technically incompatible system, the Video Home System, or

VHS. Matsushita charged less for the machinery, although it admitted its picture quality was not that of a top Beta system. By as early as 1978 VHS outsold Beta by two to one. Although engineers hailed Beta, the public wanted VHS.

Home VCRs were not an instantaneous success. The idea had to be sold to the public. At first, only true buffs bought machines at high prices. From the initial cost of twelve hundred dollars in the late 1970s, the average price fell steadily. By 1981 VCRs sold for less than one thousand dollars; by mid-decade the price was less than three hundred dollars and held at that figure despite persistent inflation of about 5 percent per year.[3]

In 1980 only two of every one hundred homes in the United States had a VCR. But with the prices decreasing and movies becoming available, sales of the apparatus picked up considerably. Buyers in out of the way places such as Anchorage and Fairbanks, Alaska, led the way. This was expected, for they had long had little access to numerous over-the-air television stations. Surprisingly, however, millions in the nation's largest cities (Chicago, New York, Washington, D.C.) also began to purchase VCRs. This baffled observers initially, for these citizens had the greatest over-the-air television choices. Observers seemed to forget the convenience associated with the use of the VCR versus going out to the movies.

Soon it was clear that the wealthy were the most interested in the new technology. This was vividly illustrated at the other end of the income scale, where citizens of poorer cities, such as Loredo, Texas, Sioux Falls, South Dakota, and Greenwood, South Carolina, were least likely to buy a new VCR. By the late 1980s a profile of the average video household had emerged: a head of household who was well off (more likely to own a home) and well educated (at least some college education).[4]

In terms of the war between Beta and VHS, price and the possibility of longer tapes won out, and by the end of the 1980s the VHS system had virtually captured the market. While the original invention was not instantly accepted, the VCR became an "overnight" success in the 1980s. From a penetration of less than 1 percent of the nation's households in 1978, the climb was steady, reaching half the nation's households by 1988, and two-thirds by the close of the decade. Americans adopted the VCR as quickly as they did television itself.[5]

The new buyers of VCRs voted their favorite uses for this new attachment to the television set. Initially the preference was for taping a program off the air for viewing at another time ("time shifting"). But soon another motivation, watching recent feature films, uncut, uncensored, and at any time one chose, emerged as primary. The remote control gave one control of the movie theatre in the home, and soon movies were watched in record numbers.

Hollywood was slow to catch on to the use of the VCR as an exhibition venue. At first the moguls loathed the machine. Early on, Jack Valenti, head of the Motion Picture Association of America, representing the major Hollywood studios, declared that the VCR was a parasitical instrument pilfering Hollywood's rightful take at the box office. Valenti asserted that the VCR would kill moviegoing in the United States, and this new evil machine from Japan would cripple the ability of Hollywood to make top-flight movies.[6]

Without the sponsorship of the major studios, the system by which millions of new VCR owners obtained movies for their machines was worked out thousands of miles from Southern California—through the rental of tapes. In 1977 Andre Blay proposed that the movie studios release their films on tape. All save Twentieth Century-Fox ignored him; he had to settle for a handful of titles including *Patton* (1970), *The French Connection* (1971), and *The King and I* (1956). He sold them for about sixty dollars, and by 1978 he was so successful that his Magnetic Video was bought by Twentieth Century-Fox for more than seven million dollars.

It was not until November 1979 that the next studio, Paramount, released its films on tape. In 1980 Warner Bros., Universal, Columbia, and Disney followed. Indeed, in 1980 the major Hollywood studios commenced forming video distribution subsidiaries. But they seized not on the model of rental but on the model of sales. The tape, they thought, should be sold like a hardcover book, bought for a relatively high price and then shelved for repeated use over an extended period of time.

Hollywood fully expected that in the same way one purchased a reference book to consult occasionally, one would buy a tape of a motion picture to view infrequently. Only the most dedicated movie buffs would be interested. In retrospect it is not surprising that few buyers emerged. In the end Blay and the Hollywood studios were proven wrong. The public did not want to purchase and collect movies at sixty dollars each but rather rent them for a couple of dollars for single viewings.[7]

Dozens of innovators, not connected with Hollywood, took to renting tapes during the early 1980s. Their repeated success throughout the United States would transform how Americans watched subsequent-run movies. Consider the case of a particularly successful entrepreneur, Erol Oranan of Washington, D.C. Oranan, a decade later head of one of the largest chains of video rental stores in the United States, remembered the beginnings of his new business this way:

> When the [VCR] machine came out, it made sense, but I don't think anybody thought it would be this widely used a tool or toy. And the approach then was for studios to try to sell the movies, not to rent them. I honestly didn't believe people would buy movies, but studios insisted 'no rentals,' which they tried to enforce, or they made two kinds of movies—one for sale, one for rent.[8]

Erol Oranan started from a modest base. The Erol's video chain, by the late 1980s one of the five largest in the business, developed from a single television repair shop in Washington, D.C. Oranan's native Turkey did not have television when he left in the early 1960s, and so his career there had been built on repairing tape recorders and radios. Upon completing a degree at the Technical Engineering Institute of Washington, D.C., Oranan switched to the more lucrative profession of television repair. He worked for others until he opened his own shop in 1963 and repaired sets for the upper middle class. Oranan prospered by repairing (and selling) the then new color television sets; when the VCR appeared in the mid-1970s Erol's moved into that market.

From that base Oranan started selling movies to his VCR customers. The first rentals were kept on a single shelf in a manager's office in suburban Arlington, Virginia. But soon consumer demand forced an expansion of that part of Erol's business. In 1981 the company recorded thirty thousand rentals; over four years Erol's recorded eighteen million separate rentals. The number of outlets increased accordingly. In 1982 there were seven stores; by 1985 fifty; a year later the figure had doubled and reached three figures. Gross revenues for tape rentals increased from zero to $100 million in six years. By the fiscal year for 1988 Erol's had revenues of more than $150 million dollars.

By the end of the 1980s Erol's stood for nearly two hundred Video Clubs (most of them in the mid-Atlantic Region) and one million Video Club members, adding up to nearly a million rentals per week, served by four thousand employees. Not surprisingly late in 1989 Erol's exited the television and VCR hardware sales and service business all together.[9]

Erol's achieved its success based on several important business strategies. First, Oranan sought the then familiar family and suburban trade (as he had in his repair and hardware sales business). For example, in contrast to many who looked for a quick buck in the early days, Erol's never rented

X-rated tapes. Indeed in the early days of rentals, there were more X-rated tapes rented than Hollywood features. In 1980 X-rated tapes, by some estimates, accounted for three-quarters of all videotape rentals. Erol's foresaw a broader market and so refused to trade in the X-rated tapes that might have alienated the suburban trade.

Responding to tedious delays at checkout counters, the company pioneered the computerized retail bar code system that grocery stores used. Erol's developed a computer program to deal with bar codes and special printers to handle the bills. The company also manufactured its own hard-shell cassette cases so the customer could pull the titles directly off the shelf rather than choose an empty box and ask a clerk to find the actual tape from a storehouse behind the counter. Erol's used its cases to advertise the films, promoting them with the same bold graphics that had long been a part of the packaging of hardcover books.

Erol's was one of the first to embrace the superstore concept, in which inventories of seven to ten thousand titles filled a store with classics, art films, children's films, and all sorts of Hollywood features. Its Springfield, Virginia, warehouse, which with the nearby corporate headquarters employs about seven hundred people, is a self-contained industry, manufacturing everything from signs, advertising sheets, monthly magazine, and tape cartons. The heart of the operation is the IBM computer found at the Springfield office, a system that handles one hundred thousand transactions per day. From the beginning Erol's pursued a volume business.[10]

Erol's certainly typified the transformation of the video rental business from a "mom-and-pop" operation into vast regional powerhouses. But economic logic dictated that a national chain, to take full advantage of the business strategies Erol's and others had developed, ought to be in place. This would be accomplished by Blockbuster Entertainment, a Florida-based company, which symbolically overtook Erol's as the nation's number-one video chain sometime in late 1988 or early 1989.

Blockbuster's growth had been spectacular. In 1986 it had only seventeen stores, and by 1988 it had nearly three hundred. With the acquisition of Major Video (once the fourth largest chain), Blockbuster had nearly six hundred outlets nationwide. By 1990 Blockbuster had more than one thousand stores and more than four hundred million dollars in revenue, and it even began to hire away Erol's top executives. Profits topped forty million dollars.[11]

Blockbuster's strategy differed from Erol's. Franchised on a national basis, Blockbuster planned big, brightly lit stores with ten thousand or more tapes in stock (versus about four thousand at an average Erol's). These so-called superstores offered three-day rentals (versus Erol's overnight policy). Whereas Erol's was only known to the inhabitants of its market region, Blockbuster opened the 1990s with a twenty-five-million-dollar national advertising campaign, including joint promotions with Domino's Pizza and McDonalds. Blockbuster not only sought to become the McDonald's of the video rental business in the United States but like its fast-food counterpart, it also began to open stores in Great Britain, Australia, and Western Europe.[12]

Near the end of 1990 Blockbuster purchased Erol's. The franchising of home video rental operations on a national basis—in the manner of McDonald's—promises to be the wave of the future. For consumers the acquisition meant a greater selection for rental at higher prices. The new Blockbuster will lead the way to a concentrated industry in the same manner as the movie theatre industry. That is, Blockbuster and its significant rivals will capture the greatest share of the market in America's cities and suburbs, leaving rural and poorer markets to "mom-and-pop" operations.[13]

In short, the innovation of the business of video rental has moved through the familiar stages of the development of a big business, from regional chains to national operations. (This compares to the business developments in the movie theatre marketplace, analyzed in chapters 1, 2, and 3.) By the late 1980s, more people watched more movies than ever, and the theatrical box office reached record numbers. By the mid-1980s, as singled by the cover of *Time* magazine, it was clear that this had become a national phenomenon. "Everybody" had a tape machine; millions of dollars in tape rentals were generated; the United States Supreme Court had decided in the notorious *Betamax* case that home taping was legal; and the innovation that seemed so risky in the late 1970s turned into a solid part of the industry.[14]

THE DIFFUSION OF HOME VIDEO

By the late 1980s the diffusion of the VCR was ongoing, and watching recent Hollywood features on tape was at its heart. By the mid-1980s more than two-thirds of households in the United States had a VCR, and that penetration figure was rising steadily toward three-quarters of all households. By 1986 receipts for rentals and sales of prerecorded tapes (principally movies) for the first time exceeded the box-office take in the United

States. As the 1980s drew to a close, there were a record twenty-five thousand movie theatres in the United States, but an astonishing one hundred thousand outlets renting video tapes of films.[15]

Tapes could be rented anywhere and everywhere. By the late 1980s prerecorded movies could be rented at convenience stores, gas stations, country stores, and dry cleaners. In some locales, one was able to rent a tape and have it delivered with a pizza. Indeed one video and pizza delivery service in Washington, D.C., promised four thousand titles with two-dollar per day rentals. By 1989 the average convenience store did four thousand dollars per year in video rentals. In Soap-a-Rama near Boston University it was possible to wash one's clothes, get an indoor tan, buy a snack, or rent a videotape. For those in small-town America, Home Film Festival rented hard-to-find art films or cult films through the mail from Scranton, Pennsylvania.[16]

And while in the early 1980s it took Oscar-winning pictures years to make it to the shelves of a video store, the window of release by the late 1980s had been reduced to several months. *Batman* was in the stores for Christmas rental and sale, even though the film had played in theatres as late as the previous September. The typical hit feature film release was rented an average of 110 times per rental store. This figure was good for rental stores which indicated in a 1987 survey that the average "A" title cost about $90 and generated more than $250 in rentals, compared with less than $200 the year before. The average rental stayed at about $2.50. Less popular titles, the so-called "B" titles, were rented about half as often but still took in more than $150 on average while costing the dealer less than $70.[17]

Rentals totaled close to ten billion dollars per year by the end of the decade. The owners and operators in the video rental industry of the late 1980s loved holidays, weekends, and bad weather. It was easy and convenient to grab a couple of tapes of one's favorite films and snuggle up at home. But success led to a vexing problem. "Everybody" wanted to rent the same tape at the same time. Copies needed to be made with hundreds of "slave" VCRs in real time, demanding a large investment in equipment. Moreover, once Hollywood sold a tape copy to an entrepreneur, the studio did not share in the rentals paid by the consumers, reducing its incentive to produce many copies quickly.

Indeed the First Sale Doctrine stated that once a videotape was sold, the second party owned the material and could do with it what he or she wished, save make additional copies. That is, once a tape was bought from a Hollywood studio, the owner could rent that tape until it wore out—about two hundred runs on a reasonably well-kept machine.[18]

The demand to rent a "hot" title peaked during the first weeks of its videotape release and then declined significantly thereafter. The video store did not need or want, several weeks after the release, a vast inventory. Thus, it is not surprising that in a survey taken by the Fairfield Group in 1987, more than half the video rental customers polled were unable to rent the title of their first choice when visiting a video store. Although four-fifths rented a title (their first choice or a substitute), fully a fifth actually walked out of the store empty handed. Thus the "inventory problem." Video stores sought to abide by the First Sale Doctrine, but they stocked only enough tapes to satisfy about a quarter of customers during the first month of a film's release on videotape. No store owner wanted to buy so many copies that after a month he or she had a roomful of unrentable tapes.

It is unlikely that the First Sale Doctrine will be changed soon. One solution to consumer dissatisfaction put forth has been labeled Pay-Per-Transaction (PPT); that is, the Hollywood studios would rent the tapes to the store, supplying the maximum needed copies and sharing in the revenue. Supplying copies would eliminate inventory problems, and sharing in rental revenues would create a system similar to theatres. Monitoring would be done by computer. PPT is a logical strategy for Hollywood and the video rental industry.[19]

A second solution to the inventory problems created by the First Sale Doctrine could be found in "Sell Through," that is, selling the film on tape at a low enough price so the public bypasses rental. Experiments with this tactic began in the mid-1980s. For example, Paramount's *Top Gun* (1986) brought in $82 million to the parent company in theatrical rentals. But this tape, priced at $26.95, sold more than two and a half million copies in its initial thrust onto the market, pushing Paramount's revenues from that source to some $40 million. At a price of $19.95 many believe that those figures might have been reversed.[20]

The ultimate test in the development of mass sales of home video came during the October 1988 sale of *E.T.* In mid-1987 Pepsi approached MCA and a deal was worked out. Steven Spielberg, the creator of *E.T.*, embraced a low-priced, sales rather than rental strategy so he could be assured that pirated copies would not appear. To minimize this further and thus convince Spielberg to release *E.T.* years after its theatrical play, MCA spent more than one million dollars to place special symbols on the boxes and guards at the warehouses storing the tapes, and they took extra precautions when the tapes were moved. Dubbing the cassette into a dozen different languages and releasing them on a single day also held down the incentive for piracy.[21]

By Labor Day of 1988, MCA Home Video confirmed that it had orders for eight million units of *E.T.*. Stores had begun to take orders the previous July. The average store ordered nearly two hundred units a month even before *E.T.*'s October release. On 27 October 1988 *E.T.* was shipped in more than eleven million cartons, breaking the record for video sales and adding to the more than seven hundred million dollars that the film generated in worldwide ticket sales. The less than twenty-five-dollar official sales price for the video was the lowest yet for a major blockbuster. Many customers paid less than fifteen dollars after a Pepsi-sponsored rebate. The sales of *E.T.* videotapes proved so extraordinary that one in five U.S. households reportedly owned the video.[22]

MCA's net take from *E.T.* from sales in the United States and Canada came to more than $150 million, a figure almost four times the box-office gross on the film's 1985 rerelease. *E.T.* signaled that the Hollywood studios could earn more for tape sales, but with billions involved in the established rental market and few films of the drawing power of *E.T.*, Hollywood did not move to convert to a sales-only policy. The top ten all-time best-sellers as of mid-1990 were *E.T.* (Universal Studios, 12.5 million units shipped), *The Little Mermaid* (Disney, 10.0 million), *Batman* (Warner, 9.5 million), *Bambi* (Disney, 8.5 million), *Cinderella* (Disney, 7.5 million), *Who Framed Roger Rabbit?* (Disney, 6.8 million), *The Wizard of Oz* (MGM/UA, 6.7 million), *Honey, I Shrunk the Kids* (Disney, 4.5 million), *Indiana Jones and the Last Crusade* (Paramount, 4.0 million), *The Land Before Time* (Universal, 3.6 million) and *Top Gun* (Paramount, 3.5 million).[23]

Thus as the 1990s began, the market for purchasing movies on video remained far smaller than the rental market. Even with average tapes falling in price, approaching the fifteen-dollar level, total sales increased only slowly. Many were entering this market, from grocery stores to American Express, but the future of tapes for sale remained cloudy by the end of the 1980s. Would titles that appealed only to adults sell as well as *The Little Mermaid* or *The Land Before Time?*[24]

The future of sales versus rental will depend on what the old Hollywood called the "clearance"—the time between a theatrical run and the appearance of the film on video. Consider the case of *Batman* (1989). This film was one of the more expensive films made up to that point, at an estimated cost of fifty-five million dollars. It was also one of the more successful, accumulating over a quarter of a million dollars in domestic rentals before 1989 was up. But the film will be remembered longer for converting a blockbuster summer theatrical release into a Christmas video release. The short window proved a mixed blessing. After an initial buying frenzy during the two weeks after its 15 November 1989 release, sales of *Batman* fell. Still, the tape sold thirteen million units.[25]

Hollywood began to sell advertisements at the front of feature films on tape in 1983. This practice started simply enough. The Hollywood studios, which had gained control of the release of their features on tape, began adding previews or trailers to the ends of the tapes. Some said this was just like the theatres. Then companies moved this form of advertising to the front of the tape, where they would more likely be watched.

The use of advertisements on a widespread level commenced in 1987 with the release of Paramount's *Top Gun* (1986), which featured a Diet Pepsi advertisement tied to the theme and images of the feature that followed. Then came advertisements for Jeep vehicles in *Platoon* (1986), Hershey's Kisses candy in *The Princess Bride* (1987), Snicker's candy bars for *Moonstruck* (1987), and Pepsi Cola before *Innerspace* (1987). In some cases the deal involved a "trade-out"; in *Top Gun*, for example no money exchanged hands but Paramount received promotional "plugs" on posters and packages placed in 7-Eleven and grocery stores throughout the United States by Pepsi. More and more advertisers, though, began simply to pay the required millions of dollars for the placement of an advertisement on a videotape.[26]

CAUSES AND CONSEQUENCES FOR MOVIE WATCHING

VCRs have caused numerous important changes in movie watching in the United States. The highly influential tradepaper *Variety* summed it up correctly when it labeled the coming of the VCR as "the biggest boon to the movie biz since the advent of celluloid."[27] Consider the staggering numbers: By the mid-1980s households with VCRs rented more than one hundred million cassettes per month, or an average of almost a movie a week. By the beginning of the 1990s revenues from tape rentals in the United States were moving well past ten billion dollars per year. Some one hundred thousand outlets rent tapes. Movies on tape ranks with the innovation of the nickelodeon, the picture palace, and the multiplex in shaping the movie-watching habits of Americans.[28]

VCRs boosted interest in movie watching, and by successfully exploiting video sales and rentals the Hollywood movie companies were able to reach a position of prosperity unseen since the days of World War II. Hollywood features, not independent films, captured the bulk of the rentals and sales. Two-thirds of video monies goes to studio-controlled companies: Time-Warner, Disney, Paramount, CBS/Fox, MCA, MGM/UA, and RCA/Columbia. The two largest independents of the early 1980s, Vestron and Karl, were out of business by the close of the decade. Vestron was unable to match its lone hit, *Dirty Dancing*. Karl could not make a company based on Jane Fonda workout tapes.[29]

More and more the video audience resembles the theatrical audience for movies. Although the ownership of a VCR seems nearly universal, it is not. In one survey nearly 80 percent of households earning more than forty thousand dollars per year in 1987 owned a VCR, while fewer than 10 percent of the households with incomes under ten thousand dollars per year owned one. The statistics are similar in terms of educational attainment: only about a third of those households headed by a person who had not graduated from high school had a VCR, while nearly three-quarters of those headed by college graduates had home video. In the end, those who were already heavy consumers of magazines, books, and newspapers were heavy renters of movies on tape.[30]

There is no doubt about the vitality and importance of the rental market for movies on tape. And the implications of millions renting movies on tape each week are being felt. Quietly, small films are discovered in home video. Few found it surprising that in the youth-driven theatrical box office of the late 1980s *A Nightmare on Elm Street, Part 4* (1989) did four times the business of *Mystic Pizza* (1989). What was surprising was that the latter did twice the business for video rental. Indeed the top movie rental on tape in 1989 was not one of the expected blockbusters (such as *Die Hard* or *Coming to America*) or an honored feature (such as the Academy Award–winner *Rain Man*) but *A Fish Called Wanda* (1988), a modest success at the theatrical box office at best. Properly this was also due to a successful promotion for *A Fish Called Wanda* sponsored by Cadbury Schweppes. The refreshment manufacturer advertised *A Fish Called Wanda* in grocery stores ten weeks after the video hit the stores, and rentals increased dramatically.[31]

All this has had important implications for Hollywood's filmmakers. Video rights to a feature command five million dollars and up. In other words, it is expected that a good film at the box office will add a minimum of five million to its revenues from sales of tapes to video stores and individuals. It was the night of 31 March 1987, when *Platoon* won the Oscar, that home video was singled out as the driving force behind the biggest film of 1986. When Oliver Stone accepted the film's four Academy Awards that night (including Best Picture) he unabashedly acknowledged that it was only a video company, Vestron, and the potential moneys from home video, that made his film possible. *Variety* called the new monies available from home video "the most important entertainment development of the last ten years, . . . the film industry's safety net."[32]

Home video has also changed the market for adult films. The porno theatre has all but disappeared because those who want to see X-rated material prefer the price and privacy that home video offers. By the late 1980s the market for X-rated videotapes accounted for up to a fifth of some stores' business, about four hundred million dollars worth of tapes at the wholesale level. This has meant, however, that conservative forces, led by religious groups, and liberal forces, led by outraged feminists, have sought to limit the rental of adult videotapes. As the 1990s commensed instances of harassment increased. In Denton, Texas, two employees of TK Video were sentenced to a year in jail for promoting obscenity because they sold adult tapes to undercover police. In Woodbury County, Iowa, the county prosecutor, armed with a newly expanded antipornography law, raided two video stores and seized their inventory in order to "review" the material to see if it was in violation. In Nassau County, New York, just outside New York City, the owner of the county's only all-adult video and bookstore was arrested for selling a copy of *My Name Is Paula* (1989), a nonexplicit bondage film.[33]

In one particularly controversial case, ten Kansas City adult video stores agreed to follow a local prosecutor's suggested guidelines in order to prevent two clerks, arrested on obscenity charges, from going to jail. Bills in state legislatures would prevent minors from obtaining "unsuitable material" by prohibiting the sale or rental of videotapes without the Motion Picture Association of America rating clearly displayed on the package. The Hollywood motion picture industry opposes this form of legislation on the grounds that video dealers ought to regulate themselves.[34] In 1989 in Missouri the legislature passed the so-called Movie Slasher Law, which required video retailers to isolate explicitly violent tapes in a separate room that would be off limits to minors.

Increasingly, in state after state, the battle lines have been drawn. No matter what state capital is considered, the same terms of debate can be found. Supporters favor stiff legal penalties to compel retailers to keep "harmful" movies out of the hands of minors; detractors favor the status quo, free speech. In the 1990s the battle for videotape morality will continue to be fought. A case in Michigan may foreshadow the future. The head of the Michigan Decency Council, a conservative group monitoring the mass media, was able to pressure state legislators to introduce more than twenty bills in 1989 designed to "combat" offensive home videos, but none passed. Yet it seems only a matter of time before a series of laws are put into effect and then tested in the courts.[35]

Finally it must be noted that not all films make it onto videotape. As of 1 January 1990 *The Last Picture Show* (1971), *Annie Get Your Gun* (1950), *The King of Marvin Gardens* (1972), and *Children of Paradise* (1944) had not been released onto home video. The question of clearing musical and literary rights often provides an insurmountable constraint. Indeed to release *Desperately Seeking Susan* (1985) on tape, one song on the sound track, Foreigner's "Urgent," was replaced by a cover version. As more and more homes obtain VCRs, in the United States and around the world, it must be assumed that such problems will be overcome and virtually every film will be released on tape.[36]

FUTURE TECHNICAL CHANGE

What of the future of the technology of home video? Certainly by the early years of the next century the current VHS and Beta hardware will have been replaced by 8 mm home video. Although VHS was the dominant system in American homes in the early 1990s, in the late 1980s the dominant Japanese manufacturers innovated a *single* standard for the 8 mm system. This will eliminate the confusion that Beta versus VHS caused with half-inch taping. For now the Japanese manufacturers will slowly begin to sell 8 mm while they complete their marketing of VHS and Beta half-inch machines.

By the early 1990s 8 mm had begun to gain a niche in the world dominated by VHS, after only several years in the marketplace. The 8 mm video system has been innovated through the camcorder, a portable means for producing video images. Introduced to a mass market in 1980, in essence the camcorder (for *camera recorder*) is nothing more than an old super-8 mm film camera designed to use video instead of super-8 mm film. In the first half of the 1980s half-inch camcorders were costly and complex to operate, because they consisted of a ten- to fifteen-pound video camera, propped on the shoulder like a bazooka, plus a separate recorder, dangling under the arm by a strap. The 8 mm system compresses all the equipment into one lightweight camera.

Making movies on 8 mm tape has tempted many to pay the several thousand dollar price. The plan is that once a number of 8 mm camcorders are in place and the market for half-inch equipment has been saturated, the Japanese manufacturers will begin to sell the 8 mm as a substitute for current home video movie watching. In the early 1990s Sony had taken the lead in promoting movies on 8 mm. There were some fifteen hundred movie titles available on 8 mm, but once Sony had taken over Columbia Pictures, one of the major Hollywood movie studios, it became clear Sony would use its RCA/Columbia home video titles to tempt consumers to try 8 mm home video. In early 1990 Sony announced it would issue *Casualties of War* (1989), *Roxanne* (1987), and thirty other titles in 8 mm at less than thirty dollars each.

Sony hardly constituted the lone interested seller. In 1989 Video Yesteryear, a leading nostalgia company based in Connecticut, began to offer all of its nearly one thousand titles in 8 mm. Feature films on 8 mm were priced less than thirty dollars, with the anticipation that 8 mm purchase, not rental, will be the principal form of participation in this format. Only the future will tell whether the Japanese manufacturers and the Hollywood studios are correct in their marketing plans.[37]

Predicting even further into the future is risky and even dangerous. Some pundits predict home video will be improved with giant video screens hung from the wall. Presently any screen more than thirty-five inches simply magnifies the distance between the standard 525 television lines. Larger images, however beautifully housed and marketed, simply present fuzzier and fuzzier images. The invention of a preferable large-screen video image awaits us.[38]

Nearer on the horizon is the possibility of a better picture for conventional-sized images. This includes a screen size that would match the aspect ratio of the current wide-screen theatrical movie image. This package of innovations is labeled high-definition television, or HDTV. Many HDTV systems are currently touted, but the two that seem the most likely to be widely adopted are the MUSE system from Japan (1,125 lines) and the EUREKA system from Europe (1,050 lines), both far superior to the NTSC system of 525 lines. Both of these "improved" images come in a wide-screen format. MUSE, delivered to the home by satellite, began on a limited basis in Japan in 1989, while the EUREKA system, also delivered by satellite to home, is scheduled to be in place in Europe in the early 1990s.

Many issues must be considered before an ideal system is chosen as standard, and these considerations surely will delay introduction in the United States until well into the 1990s. Few doubt that the Japanese are ahead of the pack. Japanese Broadcasting (NHK) has developed a satellite-based system, which made its debut in Japan in the late 1980s. They began in 1970 with the pooled efforts of Sony, Toshiba, NEC, and other technology leaders to work on a market-oriented HDTV system. It was, in part, Japan's efforts in this area that gave the world inexpensive VCRs in the late 1970s.[39]

Many questions remain unanswered about improved television images (capable of carrying movies on tape) as we approach the twenty-first century. Undecided is the question of whether HDTV should be carried over the air, by cable, from satellites, or only as video cassettes? Certainly HDTV could be innovated into the United States for home video. By acquiring a new television set and a new VCR, any movie buff could see movies closer to the 35 mm image on MUSE or EUREKA. But this would be very expensive, three thousand dollars per set at a minimum, and thus only available to the rich. With questions of foreign ownership and compatibility unresolved, HDTV seems to be a home video addition of the next century and not the 1990s.[40]

Finally, lost in all the excitement and growth of a tape-based home video industry, has been the video disk. It was thought in the early 1980s that discs might rival tape as a home medium for movie watching. Indeed, RCA spent more than fifty million dollars on its SelectaVision system, a crude disc system with low-priced discs of movies. The public was given a clear choice between SelectaVision and VHS. Since VHS could tape movies off the air as well as provide the apparatus for playing pre-recorded movies it won the day—despite being 25 percent more expensive.[41]

But laser discs could play back far superior images and theoretically never wear out. However, there was no standard (indeed three were touted in the early 1980s), and an average system cost thousands of dollars. Thus the laser disc failed as home video in the United States. Laser discs found their way into the homes of only the purest of film collectors. No one doubts that laser discs provide a better picture and sound. They are simply not as convenient or as cheap. Into the 1990s sales to home video enthusiasts remain small when compared to the VCR, and it appears that the laser disc will remain a specialized medium, principally used by archives and libraries and not for movie watching on a mass scale.[42]

For now, and into the foreseeable future, the preferred choice for watching movies at home will be the video cassette recorder. Sometime before the twenty-first century nearly 90 percent of American homes will own a VCR (many will own two or three). And Hollywood will be proffering movies but with all the attendant problems discussed in this chapter. That is, until HDTV is innovated, watching movies on a VCR will mean a panned, scanned, and limited image. Watching a film on a VCR is surely convenient and cheap, but the theatrical experience remains the purer aesthetic form.

EPILOGUE

The institutions of motion picture presentation in the United States have undergone many economic, social, and technological changes since the beginnings of the movie show in 1895. But looking back from the early 1990s, there have been several constants throughout this history. Powerful movie show institutions have united with the major Hollywood producers to dominate the industry. During the golden age of the 1930s and 1940s the Hollywood majors owned the key movie theatres; in the 1980s they reacquired direct control. But in other decades Hollywood has been able to hold sway over the movie presentation marketplace, through the coming of sound and the coming of color and wide screen, through a Great Depression and a World War, through the adoption of television, and the VCR. The very term *Hollywood* should embrace not only an image of movie production but also the history described in the first section of *Shared Pleasures*.[1]

How has this control been maintained? Through price discrimination, the major Hollywood companies—in cooperation with theatre owners and, since the 1950s, in league with the owners of the new forms of television technology—have long sought to discriminate among potential customers and have them pay as much as possible for viewing a film. In the United States this was ensured by theatres having set runs and then charging top price for first run, less for the second run, and even less down the line. But in fact this principle, separating markets and charging different prices to maximize revenues, continues today.

Consider a simple contrast. Even as late as the early 1970s the process of payoff for a Hollywood feature film seemed simple, based on principles that had been little adapted since the 1920s. A big-budget opus opened with a lavish premiere and attendant promotion. Publicity filled newspapers, magazines, and radio. A film earned the bulk of its money from playing theatres. Television, even with a sale for presentation on one of the three major networks, and then years of "Late Shows" and "Early Shows," accounted for little in the way of revenues—usually no more than a tenth. These repeated screenings on television simply replaced the matrix of neighborhood theatres that existed in the 1930s and 1940s.

This long-established pattern of release began to change in 1975. Universal Pictures fundamentally altered film marketing with *Jaws*, the first major film to employ saturation advertising on network television. This use of television was considered an adventuresome marketing maneuver in 1975; today it is standard practice. During the final six months of that year this one film earned more than one hundred million dollars. The success of *Jaws* led to today's constant barrage of television advertisements for upcoming films, television reviews by critics such as Siskel and Ebert, and promotion shows such as Paramount's "Entertainment Tonight."[2]

The major Hollywood companies were the big winners in the world of the new television technologies. They learned to take advantage of all possible television windows of release, extracting monies from their feature films as they had done exclusively through theatrical showings. The Hollywood majors have done this quietly and efficiently, with little fanfare outside the Wall Street community of analyists. As the major Hollywood corporations entered the final decade of the twentieth century, they held more economic power and profits than ever before.

Feature films still begin their marketing life in theatres. To make enormous amounts of money through the later television-based ancillary markets, a feature film must do well at the theatrical box office. What has changed is that today the first (and only)-run movie theatre has turned into a make-or-break advertising display venue. A theatrical blockbuster guarantees millions of additional dollars from the home video and pay television arenas. That is why the major Hollywood companies work so hard to craft a hit in the theatres, for once they have a proven commodity there the rest of the way is smooth sailing to millions of dollars.

The continuing importance of theatres has only become obvious in the last few years. At the beginning of the 1980s some industry observers predicted that there would be no need for movie theatres by 1990. Everybody could stay home and view films on the coming new television technologies. Instead, during the 1980s more new movie theatres were built, creating more theatrical screens in the United States than at any time in history. Theatrical release requires more and more theatre screens so Hollywood can take full advantage of the economies of television advertising. Even though the cost of marketing a film can often exceed ten million dollars, as it is spread over more and more theatres, marketing costs per theatre per film remain relatively low.

Then the popular feature enters pay cable television and home video, where the potential millions to be extracted *exceed* the theatrical box office. Only after playing on pay cable and home video does a film in the 1980s finally show up on NBC, ABC, and CBS and then the independent television stations. Indeed, with repeated showings on pay cable and home video, the ratings for theatrical features shown on network television have fallen to a low unmatched since Twentieth Century-Fox and NBC introduced "Saturday Night at the Movies" in the early 1960s. Now "Saturday Night at the Movies" (or a counterpart on another night, depending on the schedule and the season) means a series of films that premier on television, the ubiquitous made-for-television movies.

The final run for a Hollywood movie is its presentation on a nonnetwork-affiliated television station. Today such independent stations, whether delivered over the air or through cable, represent a very important market. It usually takes a couple of years for important feature films to make it to independent television (less for box-office failures), but once released the film is shown repeatedly. Turner Broadcasting Service's SuperStation, WTBS from Atlanta, and its cable-only TNT are among the most watched of all cable channels in the United States, reaching some forty million households. Fully half of WTBS's time is filled with old films; three-quarters of the time on TNT see movies unspooling.

Movies on independent stations are not only cablecast. Through the 1980s over-the-air independent stations increased their power and reach. They became connected to the very heart of Hollywood itself. Rupert Murdoch may be more famous for his Fox network or his ownership of a major studio, Twentieth Century-Fox, but it is his cluster of television stations that support all these operations. His six former Metromedia stations are located in New York City (the largest United States' television market), Los Angeles (the second largest), Chicago (third), Dallas (eighth), Washington, D.C. (ninth), and Houston (tenth). In toto, nearly 20 percent of all households in the United States with televisions are able to view one of these stations, providing the largest reach for any set of stations outside of those owned by the three networks.

Murdoch does not lack for rivals in a quest for valuable television outlets. Paramount Communications owns a string of independent stations, Disney owns a major station in Los Angeles, and MCA/Universal has a valuable station in the New York City market. More than two hundred other independent stations vie for programming, double the number only seven years ago. Wall Street observers believe that the prospects of finding enough independent station outlets for a fourth network appear to be promising. Prior to 1980 only the top twenty or thirty cities had independent stations. The latest survey indicates that independents exist in all markets down to the sixty-seventh media market—and at that point 75 percent of American homes with television have been reached. A network of independent stations could provide an adequate basis for selling national advertising time. These may offer a further opportunity for movie viewing.

Price discrimination, as can be seen from numerous examples, is best accomplished if one owns the means of presentation. This involves another basic principle—vertical integration. The creation of the Time-Warners and the Twentieth Century-Foxes in the 1980s seeks to take advantage of the same economic motivations that drove Sam Katz to create a vast theatre chain in the 1920s. First, corporations desire to take full advantage of the power that integration offers to reduce costs of sales and transactions. The vertically integrated corporation sells films to "itself" and does not have to go through the costs associated with bidding for films. It can thus have smaller sales and accounting departments.

Second, vertically integrated corporations possess greater market control. A vertically integrated firm need not worry about being shut out of key markets. For example, in the early 1970s Twentieth Century-Fox had to convince television stations to buy its films; Universal had to persuade a theatre chain to book its films. With Twentieth Century-Fox's acquisition of television stations in the 1980s and Universal's takeover of Cineplex Odeon, these two Hollywood companies need not worry that their marginal films will fail for the lack of proper exposure in one or more major city markets.

Motion picture companies have long understood the need to reduce costs and control the outlets through vertical integration. The major Hollywood companies during the golden age of the 1930s and 1940s produced films, distributed them throughout the world, and owned and operated theatres in major cities in the United States, Canada, Australia, and several

European countries. The United States Department of Justice successfully sued the major movie corporations (including Fox) to force them to sever ownership and control of their theatres. But the administration of Ronald Reagan permitted the studios to purchase theatres and television stations.

Over and over the films play, with Hollywood extracting profits all the way down the line. The basic principles of motion picture presentation economics of today are the same as those of the 1930s and 1980s—price discrimination and vertical integration.

Throughout the 1980s the American motion picture industry has gained increasingly more economic power because of its skillful manipulation of the new television technologies. In the early 1970s there was some hope that with the advent of new technologies Hollywood would lose its long-held central place in American popular entertainment. Critics argued that this would change the structure of the mass entertainment industry and hence its conduct. More and more small companies could begin to offer alternative films and television programs. This has not happened.

Instead Hollywood has gained even more power and profits. The major Hollywood studios not only control movies that we see in theatres; they successfully exploit them. What is different in the 1980s is that Hollywood makes far more from recently innovated venues of pay cable and home video than its former pots of gold, network screenings and repeated showings on local television stations. Hollywood controls movie presentation as never before and with growing power in television production as well; it has surpassed the television networks in the race to dominate the new television technologies.

But this does not mean total control. We have seen in Part II aspects of the history of alternative forms of movie presentation. None ever made as much as the aforementioned Hollywood system, but all made enough to become available to millions. Surely the newsreel theatre will never reappear, but marginal operations will. Into the 1990s, the equivalent of the marginal operation of the past is the specialized cable television channel with movies unspooling in different languages (Spanish), for certain audiences (Black Entertainment Television), or for an art house policy (Arts and Entertainment Channel). Despite the cries that too much power resides in the hands of Hollywood, the worry that Hollywood will take over *completely* is unjustified. Too many niche markets will continue to be exploited.

Surely more change in the watching of motion pictures will take place in the 1990s, as economic, social, and technological relations continue to be transformed. Nothing better symbolizes further transfigurations as we approach the twenty-first century than the announcement in March of 1990 that Time-Warner, the largest media enterprise in the world, would join with the Soviet film industry to construct American-style movie complexes in Moscow and Leningrad. The two multiplexes, expected to cost nearly thirty million dollars, will take the experience of contemporary movie-going in the United States and transfer it to the "new" USSR. The two Soviet complexes—one with ten screens and the other with nine—will take credit cards for payment, offer soft drinks, and introduce popcorn to Soviet moviegoers. They are scheduled to be the first air conditioned theatres in the Soviet Union. Innovations that have come over the past decades in the United States will emerge "instantly" for the Soviet filmgoer.[3]

NOTES
SELECTED BIBLIOGRAPHY
INDEX

NOTES

INTRODUCTION

1. See my "Film and Business History: The Development of an American Mass Entertainment Industry," *Journal of Contemporary History*, vol. 19, no. 1 (January 1984): 89–103 and "Film Culture and Industry: Recent Formulations in Economic History," *IRIS*, vol. II, no. 2 (Spring 1985): 17–19.

2. Scott Heller, "Once-Theoretical Scholarship on Film Is Broadened to Include History of Movie-Industry Practices," *The Chronicle of Higher Education*, 21 March 1990, p. A6.

3. For more on the economic study of the cinema see my "Thinking About Motion Picture Exhibition," *The Velvet Light Trap*, no. 25 (Spring 1990): 3–11 and "The Economics of Film: What Is the Method?" *Film/Culture: Explorations of Cinema and Its Social Practice* (Metuchen, N.J.: The Scarecrow Press, 1982), pp. 81–94.

4. For more on method see Robert C. Allen and Douglas Gomery, *Film History: Theory and Practice* (New York: Alfred A. Knopf, 1985).

5. John F. Kasson, *Rudeness & Civility: Manners in Nineteenth-Century Urban America* (New York: Hill and Wang, 1990), pp. 252–255.

6. I do not want to leave the impression that nothing has ever been written about the presentation of movies in the United States. Far from it. The interested reader is referred to issue 25 of *The Velvet Light Trap*, Spring 1990. The bibliography therein demonstrates, I think, the need for a systematic historical overview.

7. For one outline of how a broader study might function see Robert C. Allen, "From Exhibition to Reception: Reflections on the Audience in Film History," *Screen*, vol. 31, no. 4 (Winter 1990): 347–356.

8. David Bordwell, Janet Staiger, and Kristin Thompson, *The Classic Holly-*

wood Cinema: Film Style & Mode of Production to 1960 (New York: Columbia University Press, 1985), p. xiv.

9. For a fascinating study of a separate institution that grew up alongside network radio see Rudolf Arnheim and Martha Collins Bayne, "Foreign Language Broadcasts over Local American Stations," in *Radio Research–1941*, ed. Paul F. Lazarfeld and Frank N. Stanton (New York: Duell, Sloan and Pearce, 1941), pp. 3–64.

CHAPTER 1: THE MOVIE SHOW BEGINS

1. Understanding late nineteenth-century American profitably begins by reading Irwin Unger and Debi Unger, *Twentieth Century America* (New York: St. Martin's, 1990), pp. 1–68; Jonathan Hughes, *American Economic History* (Glenview, Ill.: Scott Foresman, 1983), pp. 282–449; Oliver Zunz, *The Changing Face of Inequality: Urbanization, Industrial Development, and Immigrants in Detroit, 1880–1920* (Chicago: University of Chicago Press, 182), pp. 1–199; Garth Jowett, *Film: The Democratic Art* (Boston: Little, Brown, 1976), pp. 1–22.

2. For more on the late nineteenth-century revolution in American business see Alfred D. Chandler, Jr., *The Visible Hand: The Managerial Revolution in American Business* (Cambridge: Harvard University Press, 1977), pp. 209–285; Richard S. Tedlow, *New and Improved: The Story of Mass Marketing in America* (New York: Basic Books, 1990), pp. 3–21; Susan Porter Benson, *Counter Cultures: Saleswomen, Managers, and Customers in American Department Stores, 1890–1940* (Urbana: University of Illinois Press, 1986), pp. 12–30.

3. For more on this issue see Bruce A. McConachie, "Pacifying American Theatrical Audiences, 1820–1900," pp. 47–70 and Robert W. Snyder, "Big Time, Small Time, All Around the Town: New York Vaudeville in the Early Twentieth Century," pp. 118–135, both in Richard Butsch, ed., *For Fun and Profit: The Transformation of Leisure into Consumption* (Philadelphia: Temple University Press, 1990); John F. Kasson, *Rudeness & Civility: Manners in Nineteenth Century Urban America* (New York: Hill and Wang, 1990), pp. 215–256.

4. To capture a flavor of the debate of who was first see George C. Pratt, "Firsting the Firsts," in Marshall Deutelbaum, ed., *"Image" on the Art and Evolution of the Film* (New York: Dover, 1979), pp. 20–22; Geoffrey Bell, "The First Picture Show," *California Historical Quarterly*, vol. 54, no. 2 (Spring 1975): 125–138; and Gene G. Kelkres, "A Forgotten First: The Armat-Jenkins' Partnership and the Atlanta Projection," *Quarterly Review of Film Studies*, vol. 9, no. 1 (Winter 1984): 45–58.

5. Many other inventors around the world were working to create moving pictures. See the most recent claim in Christopher Rawlence, *The Missing Reel: The Untold Story of the Lost Inventor of Motion Pictures* (New York: Atheneum, 1990)

for Louis Aime Augustin Le Prince. I do not claim Edison was the first. But with his power and prestige Edison surely led the way in the United States.

6. Alfred O. Tate, *Edison's Open Door* (New York: Dutton, 1938), p. 285; Gordon Hendricks, *The Kinetoscope* (New York: The Beginnings of the American Film, 1966), pp. 50–57.

7. This account is based on Hendricks, *The Kinetoscope* pp. 9–70.

8. Hendricks, *The Kinetoscope*, p. 62; *Washington Star*, 1 October 1894, p. 11; 6 October 1894, p. 10; 8 November 1894, p. 15.

9. Blake McKelvey, *The Quest for Quality: Rochester, 1890–1925* (Cambridge: Harvard University Press, 1956), p. 222.

10. Frederick A. Talbot, *Moving Pictures: How They Are Made and Worked*, rev. ed. (Philadelphia: J. B. Lippincott, 1912), pp. 43–49.

11. Washington, D.C., was a segregated city and thus there was a separate downtown for black citizens. See Sandra Fitzpatrick and Maria R. Goodwin, *The Guide to Black Washington* (New York: Hippocrene, 1990), pp. 21–25.

12. *Washington Star*, January 1897, passim; February 1987, passim.

13. See Alan Williams, "The Lumière Organization and 'Documentary Realism,'" *Film Before Griffith*, ed. John Fell (Berkeley: University of California Press, 1983), pp. 153–161.

14. *New York Daily Tribune*, 23 April 1896, p. 9; *Dramatic Mirror*, 2 May 1896, p. 19 and 11 July 1896, p. 17.

15. For the complete history of Edison's dealings with Raff and Gammon efforts see Robert C. Allen's pathbreaking Ph.D. dissertation, "Vaudeville and Film 1895–1915: A Study in Media Interaction," reprinted in 1980 by Arno Press. Franchising was in its early stages of development at this point. By midway through the twentieth century franchising had become commonplace. See John F. Love, *McDonald's: Behind the Arches* (London: Bantam Press, 1987), pp. 48–65.

16. *New Orleans Daily Picayune*, 26 July 1896, p. 7; 2 August 1896, p. 9; 8 August 1896, p. 7; 9 August 1896, p. 7; 21 September 1896, p. 4; 7 February 1897, pp. 7, 11; 9 February 1987, p. 5.

17. *Washington Star*, 1 October 1898, p. 10; 31 December 1898, p. 12.

18. *Portland Telegram*, 21 June 1896, p. 4; *Portland Sunday Telegram*, 12 July 1896, p. 13; Gregory A. Waller, "Introducing the 'Marvellous Invention' to the Provinces: Film Exhibition in Lexington, Kentucky, 1896–1897," *Film History*, vol. 3, no. 4 (Winter 1989–1990): 223–234.

19. The literature on the history of the amusement park too often simply consists of nostalgic picture books. But one can learn a great deal from reading John F. Kasson, *Amusing the Million: Coney Island at the Turn of the Century* (New York: Hill & Wang, 1978); Brooks McNamara, "Come On Over: The Rise and Fall of the American Amusement Park," *Theatre Crafts*, vol. 11, no. 9 (September 1977): 33, 84–86; Al Griffin, *"Step Right Up Folks"* (Chicago: Henry Regency Company, 1974); Gary Kyriazi, *The Great American Amusement Parks: A Pictorial History*

(Secausus, N.J.: Citadel Press, 1976); Lee O. Bush, Edward C. Chukayne, Russell Allon Hehr, and Richard F. Hershey, *Euclid Beach Park* (Mentor, Ohio: Amusement Park Books, 1977).

20. *New Orleans Daily Picayune*, 21 June 1896, section 1, p. 7; section 3, p. 13.

21. *New Orleans Daily Picayune*, 14 March 1897, p. 5; 5 September 1897, p. 7.

22. *New Orleans Daily Picayune*, 26 June 1897, pp. 5, 10; 16 September 1897, p. 7; 1898, 1899, 1900, 1901, and 1902, passim.

23. Robert Kirk Headley, Jr., *Exit: A History of the Movies in Baltimore* (University Park, Md.: Privately published, 1974), pp. 5–6; *Moving Picture World*, 15 July 1916, p. 372.

24. Gregory A. Waller, "Situating Motion Pictures in Pre-Nickelodeon Period: Lexington, Kentucky, 1897–1906," *The Velvet Light Trap*, no. 25 (Spring 1990): 19–23.

25. *Variety*, 14 July 1906, p. 12; 23 June 1906, p. 13; 27 January 1906, p. 12; 22 September 1906, p. 11; 21 April 1906, p. 12; 17 February 1906, p. 11. The best account of the history of this phase of the movie business can be found in Raymond Fielding, "Hale's Tours: Ultrarealism in the Pre-1910 Motion Picture," most easily found in an anthology edited by John Fell, *Film Before Griffith* (Berkeley: University of California Press, 1983), pp. 116–130.

26. *Variety*, 23 June 1906, p. 13.

27. *Variety*, 28 April 1906, p. 12 and 4 April 1908, p. 13; *Moving Picture World*, 18 September 1909, p. 374; Abel Green and Joe Laurie, Jr., *Show Biz: From Vaude to Video* (New York: Henry Holt and Company, 1951), pp. 73–74; Christine Grenz, *Trans-Lux: Biography of a Corporation* (Norwalk, Conn.: Trans-Lux Corporation, 1982), pp. 30–33.

28. For a sense of what life in rural America was like at the turn of the century see Wayne E. Fuller, *RFD: The Changing Face of Rural America* (Bloomington: Indiana University Press, 1964). See also Howard Rusk Long, "Rural Communication Patterns: A Study in the Availability and Use of Print, Radio and Film in Shelby County, Missouri," unpublished Ph.D. dissertation, University of Missouri, 1948.

29. For more on the European experience see Mark E. Swartz, "An Overview of Cinema on the Fairgrounds," *Journal of Popular Film and Television*, vol. 15, no. 3 (Fall 1987): 102–108.

30. *Motion Picture News*, 15 April 1911, p. 18; *Moving Picture World*, 15 July 1916, p. 371. Charles Musser has promised us a book about this important figure, *High Class Moving Pictures: Lyman H. Howe and the Traveling Exhibitor*, listed as forthcoming from Princeton University Press. I have not seen this manuscript.

31. Quoted in Edward Lowery, "Edwin J. Hadley: Traveling Film Exhibitor," *Journal of the University Film Association*, vol. 28, no. 3 (Summer 1976): 6. This summary of Hadley's activities covers pp. 5–12.

32. For more on the background see Calvin Pryluck, "The Itinerant Movie

Show and the Development of the Film Industry," *Journal of the University Film and Video Association*, vol. 25, no. 4 (Fall 1983): 11–22; Charlotte Herzog, "The Archeology of Cinema Architecture," *Quarterly Review of Film Studies*, vol. 9, no. 1 (Spring 1984): 17–21.

33. Charlotte Herzog, "The Motion Picture Theatre and Film Exhibition—1896–1932," 2 vols. unpublished Ph.D. dissertation, Northwestern University, pp. 11–12, based on primary documents at the Ringling Museum in Baraboo, Wisconsin.

34. *Motion Picture News*, 15 April 1911, p. 18; *Moving Picture World*, 15 July 1916, p. 371; Benjamin Hampton, *A History of the Movies* (New York: Civici Friede, 1931), p. 25; *Motion Picture Herald*, 25 April 1936, p. 58 and 1 May 1937, p. 59; interview with Marilyn Moon about her grandfather, Clarence Johnson, who set up and assisted traveling exhibitors who regularly made their way to Enterprise, Kansas.

35. *Motion Picture Herald*, 3 October 1942, p. 23; *New York Times*, 12 September 1943, p. 23; Gene Fernett, "Itinerant Roadshowmen and the Free Movie Craze," *Classic Images*, no. 88, (October 1982): 12–13; Mark E. Swartz, "Motion Pictures on the Move," *Journal of American Culture*, vol. 9, no. 3 (Fall 1987): 1–7.

36. Robert C. Allen, "Vaudeville and Film 1895–1915: A Study in Media Interaction," unpublished Ph.D. dissertation, University of Iowa, 1977, pp. 23–66; Myron Matlow, ed., *American Popular Entertainment* (Westport, Conn.: Greenwood Press, 1979), pp. 11–18; Joe Laurie, Jr., *Vaudeville: From Honky Tonks to the Palace* (New York: Henry Holt and Company, 1953), pp. 337–407; Bill Smith, *The Vaudevillians* (New York: Macmillan, 1976), pp. 7–18; Snyder, "Bigtime, Small-time, All Around the Town," pp. 118–135; Robert W. Snyder, *The Voice of the City: Vaudeville and Popular Culture in New York* (New York: Oxford University Press, 1989), pp. 130–154.

37. Alfred L. Bernheim, "The Facts of Vaudeville," *Equity*, vol. 8, no. 9 (September 1923): 9–13, 32–35, 37.

38. *New York Times*, 28 June 1896, pp. 10–11 and 13 September 1896, p. 18; *New York Daily Tribune*, 13 October 1896, p. 7; *New York Times*, 81 October 1896, p. 11.

39. Robert C. Allen, "Vaudeville and Film 1895–1915: A Study in Media Interaction," unpublished Ph.D. dissertation, University of Iowa, 1977, pp. 134–144.

40. *New Orleans Daily Picayune*, 22 February 1897, p. 7; 11 February 1897, p. 14; 8 February 1897, p. 9; 6 March 1897, pp. 10–11; 11 March 1897, p. 8; 5 May 1898, p. 7; 26 June 1898, p. 8; 10 June 1898, p. 8; *New Orleans Times Democrat*, 9 August 1898, p. 8.

41. Waller, "Situating Motion Pictures in Pre-Nickelodeon Period," 13–18.

42. I have adapted this five-stage historical description from Charles Musser, "The 'Chaser Theory,' Another Look at the 'Chaser Theory'," *Studies in Visual Communication*, vol. 10, no. 4 (Fall 1984): 24–44.

CHAPTER 2: THE NICKELODEON ERA

1. *Moving Picture World*, 15 July 1916, p. 371; *Variety*, 14 December 1907, p. 33; *Moving Picture World*, 17 August 1907, p. 376 and 4 May 1907, p. 140; *Variety*, 28 March 1908, p. 13; *Moving Picture World*, 11 January 1908, p. 21; C. Francis Jenkins and Oscar B. DePue, *Handbook for Motion Picture and Stereopticon Operators* (Washington, D. C.: Knega, 1908), pp. 89–90; Joseph Medill Patterson, "The Nickelodeons, the Poor Man's Elementary Course in Drama," *Saturday Evening Post*, 23 November 1907, pp. 10–11; *Variety*, 17 March 1906, p. 4; *Moving Picture World*, 4 May 1907, p. 140 and 1 February 1908, p. 76; *Variety*, 29 February 1908, p. 6 and 11 January 1908, p. 2.

2. David S. Hulfish, *Motion Picture Work* (Chicago: American School of Correspondence, 1913), pp. 176–177; *Moving Picture World*, 15 July 1916, p. 371 and 17 August 1907, p. 376. Often sign painters entered the business, as we shall see with the Saxe brothers, who dominated movie shows in Milwaukee from 1905 until 1928, when they sold out to Fox.

3. *Motion Picture News*, 6 December 1913, pp. 35–36 and 18 March 1911, p. 13; Roger Brett, *Temples of Illusion* (Bristol, R.I.: Brett Theatrical, 1976), p. 154; *Variety*, 6 November 1907, p. 6; *Moving Picture World*, 28 December 1907, p. 702; *The Nickelodeon*, July 1909, p. 12–13.

4. *Moving Picture World*, 4 May 1907, reprinted in Gerald Mast, ed., *The Movies in Our Midst* (University of Chicago Press, 1982), p. 44; Lucy France Pierce, "The Nickelodeon," *The World Today*, October 1908, p. 1052; *Exhibitor's Herald* and *Moving Picture World*, 18 February 1928, p. 9; *Motion Picture News*, 19 July 1913, p. 8; *Moving Picture World*, 4 May 1907, p. 140; John J. Klaber, "Planning the Motion Picture Theater," *Architectural Record*, vol. 38, no. 5 (November 1915): 550; Robert Grau, *The Theatre of Science* (New York: Benjamin Blom, 1914), p. 334; *Motion Picture News*, 6 December 1913, pp. 19–20.

5. *Variety*, 14 December 1907, p. 33.

6. Many try to claim the first. See the case for Harry Davis and Pittsburgh in Eugene Lemoyne Connelly, "The First Motion Picture Theater," *Western Pennsylvania Historical Magazine*, vol. 23, no. 1 (March 1940): 2 and a note in *Boxoffice*, 4 June 1955, p. 20. Indeed Davis began promoting his "discovery" as early as 1907, as in *Moving Picture World*, 11 May 1907, p. 629. But the more important point is not who was first, but the remarkable speed and acceptance after 1905. See John Collier, "Cheap Amusements," *Charities and the Commons*, April 1908, p. 74.

7. *Variety*, 27 April 1906, p. 8; 31 March 1906, p. 13; 14 December 1907, p. 33; *The Nickelodeon*, March 1909, p. 67; *Boyd's Directory of the District of Columbia*, 1909, (Washington, D.C.: R. L. Polk and Company, 1910), p. 126; *Boyd's Directory of the District of Columbia*, 1912 (Washington, D.C.: R. L. Polk, 1912), p. 130.

8. *Moving Picture World*, 26 July 1908, pp. 61–62. From inspecting various *Moving Picture Worlds* and *Varietys* of the day, these figures seem typical. For another detailed example, from slightly past the nickelodeon era, see Robert K. Headley, Jr., "Nickelodeon Finances and Operations, 1909–1911: The Horn Theatre, Baltimore, Maryland," *Marquee*, vol. 13, no. 1 (First Quarter 1981): 21–22.

9. *Moving Picture World*, 17 August 1907, p. 376. *Variety*, 14 December 1907, p. 12 and 33; *Moving Picture World*, 5 October 1907, p. 487; *Variety*, 1 February 1908, p. 11.

10. *Moving Picture World*, 5 October 1907, p. 487.

11. Barton W. Currie, "The Nickel Madness," *Harper's Weekly*, 24 August 1907, p. 1246; *Moving Picture World*, 26 December 1908, p. 523.

12. For a fascinating contemporary analysis of the influence of overall economic prosperity see *Moving Picture World*, 26 October 1907, p. 541. The history of the flood of immigrants into America's cities at the turn into the twentieth century has been the subject of many books. One might profitably start learning about United States urban history by reading Charles N. Glabb and A. Theodore Brown, *A History of Urban America*, 2d ed. (New York: Macmillan, 1976); Alexander B. Callow, Jr., *American Urban History* (New York: Oxford University Press, 1969); and Maxine Seller, *To Seek America: A History of Ethnic Life in the United States* (New York: Jerome S. Ozer, 1977).

13. *Variety*, 6 October 1906, p. 5; 26 January 1907, p. 12; 6 April 1907, p. 18; 27 April 1907, p. 8; *Moving Picture World*, 4 May 1907, p. 140; *Variety*, 14 December 1907, p. 30.

14. *Moving Picture World*, 11 July 1908, p. 26.

15. Robert C. Allen emphasizes this complaint in his "From Exhibition to Reception: Reflections on the Audience in Film History," *Screen*, vol. 31, no. 4 (Winter 1990): 348–352.

16. *Variety*, 26 January 1907, p. 12.

17. The following account is indebted to Robert C. Allen's "Motion Picture Exhibition in Manhattan 1906–1912: Beyond the Nickelodeon," *Cinema Journal*, vol. 18, no. 2 (Spring 1979): 2–15. In this provocative piece of scholarship Allen cites some of my earlier work. I have revised my thinking since then and thus do not completely agree with the conclusion of Allen's article. But Allen's pioneering research led me to rethink my basic ideas and to valuable data sources. See also *Motography*, April 1911, pp. 27–30 and Michael M. Davis, *The Exploitation of Pleasure: A Study of Commercial Recreation in New York* (New York: Sage, 1911).

18. *Moving Picture World*, 5 October 1907, p. 487.

19. Quotation is from *Moving Picture World*, 5 October 1907, p. 487. See also Gilbert Osofsky, *Harlem: The Making of a Ghetto, Negro New York City, 1890–1930* (New York: Harper & Row, 1966).

20. Robert Kirk Headley, Jr., *Exit: A History of the Movies in Baltimore* (University Park, Md.: privately published, 1974), pp. 2–20; Headley "Nickelodeon

Finances and Operations 1909–1911," pp. 21–22; *Moving Picture World*, 15 July 1915, pp. 383–385.

21. *Milwaukee Sentinel*, 30 July 1911, p. 10; *Wisconsin News*, 16 July 1936, p. 12; *Milwaukee Sentinel*, 27 June 1927, p. 30; *Motography*, 7 November 1914, pp. 615–616; *Motion Picture News*, 7 April 1923, p. 1656; *Exhibitor's Herald*, 11 June 1927, p. 66.

22. See *Moving Picture World*, 17 October 1908, p. 298 for the quotation. See also *Billboard*, 16 March 1907, p. 116; *Evening Wisconsin*, 10 November 1906, p. 11; *Motion Picture News*, 7 April 1923, p. 1656.

23. Larry Widen and Judi Anderson, *Milwaukee Movie Palaces* (Milwaukee County Historical Society, 1986), pp. 5–57.

24. *Milwaukee Sentinel*, 12 December 1909, p. 34; *The Nickelodeon*, 1 February 1910, p. 61; *Moving Picture World*, 22 October 1910, p. 928; *Milwaukee Sentinel*, 12 December 1909, p. 32; Rowland Haynes, *Recreation Survey* (Milwaukee: Milwaukee Bureau of Economy and Efficiency 1911), bulletin number 17, pp. 8–10, 28–29; *Moving Picture World*, 23 September 1911, p. 432; 26 September 1914, p. 1799; 9 December 1911, p. 808.

25. *New Orleans Daily Picayune*, 4 November 1906, section 3, p. 3; *New Orleans Times Democrat*, 28 October 1906, p. 14; *New Orleans Daily Picayune*, 28 October 1906, p. 13.

26. *New Orleans Daily Picayune*, 20 October 1907, section 2, p. 7 and 21 October 1907, p. 2; 29 December 1907, section 2, p. 7; 3 November 1907, section 2, p. 7; 31 October 1907, p. 4.

27. This account is drawn from Roy Rosenzweig, *Eight Hours For What We Will: Workers and Leisure in an Industrial City, 1870–1920* (Cambridge: Cambridge University Press, 1983), pp. 192–215.

28. Joseph Fraizer Wall, *Iowa* (New York: W. W. Norton, 1978), pp. 127–144.

29. *Waterloo Times-Courier*, 6 January 1905, p. 7; *Des Moines Leader*, 8 January 1905, p. 5; 17 June 1905, p. 5; 2 July 1905, p. 5; 5 November 1905, p. 5; 12 November 1905, p. 5. Quotation is from *Des Moines Leader*, 3 September 1906, p. 5.

30. *Moving Picture World*, 12 October 1907, p. 503.

31. *Variety*, 5 October 1907, p. 5; *Des Moines Leader*, 8 July 1907, p. 5; August 1907, p. 7; 5 October 1907, pp. 5, 9.

32. This following account is based on information gathered for Douglas Gomery, "The Story of the Augusta Theatre," *Marquee*, vol. 21, no. 2 (Second Quarter 1989): 3–8. This was found from records at August City Hall and the city's Historical Museum. Also the *Augusta Daily Gazette* was consulted from 1906 through the 1980s.

33. In order of the communities noted see Paul E. Glase, "The Motion Picture Theatre in Reading: Silent Drama Days—1905–1926," *Historical Review of Berks County*, January 1948, pp. 35–44; Helen Brophy Geary, "After the Last Picture

Show," *Chronicles of Oklahoma*, vol. 61, no. 1 (Spring 1983): 4–27; Joe E. Smith, "Early Movies and their Impact on Columbia," *Missouri Historical Review*, October 1979, pp. 72–85; Mike Burch, "The Robey Theatre, Spencer, West Virginia," *Marquee*, vol. 13, no. 1 (First Quarter 1981): 17–18; Roger Brett, *Temples of Illusion* (Providence: Brett Theatrical, 1976), pp. 147–174.

34. *Variety*, 17 March 1906, p. 4; 31 August 1907, p. 6.

35. Compare this to similar tactics used by the emerging department store industry as discussed in William R. Leach, "Transformations in a Culture of Consumption: Women and Department Stores, 1890–1925," *Journal of American History*, vol. 71, no. 3 (September 1984): 319–342 and Susan Porter Benson, *Counter Cultures: Saleswomen, Managers, and Department Stores, 1890–1940* (Urbana: University of Illinois Press, 1986), pp. 75–122.

36. Since this initial phase of innovation of the movie house would later be recalled with a nostalgic innocence, some historians have been seduced into thinking that the nickelodeon offered a haven for the working class. Democracy's theatres lasted only as long as it took entrepreneurs to find a broad based middle-class patronage (a few years in most locations), one which would guarantee higher stable profits.

37. Adolph Zukor, *The Public Is Never Wrong* (New York: G. P. Putnam's Sons, 1953), pp. 29–53; Jack Warner, *My First Hundred Years in Hollywood* (New York: Random House, 1964), pp. 32–59; *Motion Picture News*, 30 January 1926, p. 563; *Motion Picture Herald*, 5 February 1955, p. 32; *Moving Picture World*, 15 July 1915, pp. 420–421; *Motion Picture Herald*, 17 May 1952, pp. 25, 28.

38. Fox tells his version of the story in Joseph P. Kennedy ed., *The Story of the Films* (Chicago; A. W. Shaw, 1927), pp. 301–315 and Upton Sinclair, *Upton Sinclair Presents William Fox* (Los Angeles: Published by the author, 1933), pp. 32–45. See also *Variety*, 15 August 1908, p. 6; 12 December 1908, p. 12; 19 December 1908, p. 13; 1 October 1910, p. 10; 29 February 1908, p. 6.

39. Marcus Loew tells his version of the story in Kennedy, ed., *The Story of the Films* pp. 285–300. See also *Moving Picture World*, 11 September 1927, p. 2 and Bosley Crowther, *The Lion's Share* (New York: E. P. Dutton, 1957), pp. 23–39.

40. *Variety*, 14 December 1907, p. 33; *Moving Picture World*, 1 June 1907, p. 227.

41. For more on the audience of the nickelodeon see David Nasaw, *Children of the City: At Work and at Play* (Garden City, New York: Anchor Press, 1985), pp. 121–122; Jane Addams, *The Spirit of Youth and the City Streets* (New York: Macmillan, 1909), pp. 86–87; *Moving Picture World*, 16 May 1908, p. 433; 26 December 1908, p. 523; 29 August 1908, p. 152; *The Nickelodeon*, January, 1909, pp. 7–10.

42. *Moving Picture World*, 28 August 1909, p. 280.

43. *Variety*, 14 December 1907, p. 33; *Motography*, 18 October 1913, p. 264.

44. *Motography*, October 1911, pp. 159–160.

CHAPTER 3: THE RISE OF NATIONAL THEATRE CHAINS

1. Alfred D. Chandler, Jr., *The Visible Hand: The Managerial Revolution in American Business* (Cambridge: Harvard University Press, 1977), pp. 209–284; Richard S. Tedlow, *New and Improved: The Story of Mass Marketing in America* (New York: Basic Books, 1990), pp. 1–21.

2. Walter S. Hayward and Percival White, *Chain Stores*, 3d ed. (New York: McGraw Hill, 1928), pp. 1–14.

3. *The Visible Hand*, pp. 233–237; Thomas C. Cochran, *200 Years of American Business* (New York: Delta, 1977), pp. 116–117; Geoffrey M. Lebher, *Chain Stores in America, 1859–1962* (New York: Chain Store Publishing Corporation, 1962), pp. 24–64; Tedlow, *New and Improved* pp. 186–214.

4. *Variety*, 30 March 1907, p. 6; *Moving Picture World*, 6 February 1907, p. 88; Arthur Prill, "The 'Small Time' King," *Theatre Magazine*, vol. 19 (March 1914): 139–140, 145.

5. *Variety*, 28 August 1909, p. 8; 10 September 1910, p. 2; Bosley Crowther, *The Lion's Share* (New York: E. P. Dutton, 1957), pp. 23–30; Marcus Loew, "The Motion Picture and Vaudeville," in *The Story of the Films*, ed. Joseph P. Kennedy (Chicago: A. W. Shaw, 1927), pp. 286–287.

6. Crowther, *The Lion's Share*, pp. 32–33; Loew, "The Motion Picture and Vaudeville," pp. 287–288; Robert C. Allen, *Vaudeville and Film: 1895–1915: A Study in Media Interaction* (New York: Arno Press, 1980), pp. 274–298.

7. Abel Green and Joe Laurie, Jr., *Show Biz: From Vaude to Video* (New York: Henry Holt and Company, 1951), pp. 162–163; Crowther, *The Lion's Share*, pp. 40–42; John Sherman Porter, ed., *Moody's Manual of Industrials* (New York: Moody's Investor Service, 1920), p. 2736. Quotation is from *Motography*, 22 April 1916, p. 931.

8. *Moving Picture World*, 13 March 1920, p. 1765.

9. Bosley Crowther, *Hollywood Rajah: The Life and Times of Louis B. Mayer*, (New York: Holt, Rinehart and Winston, 1960), pp. 50–53; Crowther, *The Lion's Share*, pp. 43–46, 124–133; *Exhibitors Herald*, 17 January 1920, p. 47. For information on the mergers that led to MGM see Jackson Schmidt, "On the Road to MGM: A History of Metro Pictures Corporation, 1915–1920," *The Velvet Light Trap*, no. 19 (1982): 50–51. For more information on the architect responsible for many of Loew's theatres see Robert A. M. Stern, Gregory Gilmartin, and Thomas Mellins, *Architecture and Urbanism Between the Two World Wars* (New York: Rizzoli, 1987), pp. 246–252.

10. We need more on the development of the great theatre circuits but see my work on the Saxe brothers in particular, "Saxe Amusement Enterprises: The Movies Come to Milwaukee," *Milwaukee History*, vol. 2, no. 1 (Spring 1979): 18–28, and on the Skouras brothers in St. Louis see "The Skouras Brothers: Bringing the Movies to St. Louis and Beyond," *Marquee*, vol. 16, no. 1 (Second Quarter

1984): 18–21. For what is still the best account of the creation of First National, see Benjamin B. Hampton, A *History of the Movies* (New York: Covici Friede, 1931), pp. 176–196 as well as *Variety*, 21 April 1926, p. 26.

11. *Film Daily Yearbook*, 1928, p. 920. The name of this important yearbook, begun in the 1920s, has many different variations in titles and editors. To keep the matter simple the single title, *Film Daily Yearbook*, followed by the year, will be used.

12. Richard J. Beamish, "The Acorn and the Oak," *Exhibitor*, 30 August 1926, p. 27; *New York Times*, 8 December 1926, p. 27; *Exhibitor's Herald*, 18 December 1926, p. 23; *Variety*, 14 September 1907, p. 2; 19 October 1907, p. 6; 23 November 1907, p. 9; 25 April 1908, p. 13; *Moving Picture World*, 12 September 1908, p. 195 and 30 January 1909, p. 6; *Variety*, 19 June 1909, p. 6.

13. *Film Daily Yearbook*, 1926, pp. 244, 569–570; *Variety*, 8 December 1926, p. 5; *Exhibitor's Herald*, 18 December 1926, pp. 23–24; Irving Glazer, "The Philadelphia Mastbaum," *Marquee*, vol. 7, no. 1 (First Quarter 1975): 3–16; M. J. McCosker, "Philadelphia and the Genesis of the Motion Picture," *Pennsylvania Magazine of History and Biography*, October 1941, p. 419.

14. Hampton, A *History of the Movies*, pp. 176–177; *Moving Picture World*, 19 August 1916, p. 1284.

15. *Federal Trade Commission v. Stanley Booking Corporation*, *Federal Trade Commission Decisions*, 1 FTC 212 (1918); Hampton, A *History of the Movies*, pp. 252–253.

16. *Exhibitors Herald* and *Moving Picture World*, 2 June 1928, p. 77 and 20 October 1927, p. 27; *Moving Picture World*, 15 February 1919, p. 872; *Motion Picture News*, 23 March 1918, pp. 1712–1713; *Wall Street Journal*, 30 June 1927, p. 8; *Motion Picture News*, 18 December 1926, p. 2323; *Exhibitor's Herald*, 12 September 1925, pp. 23, 35; *Moving Picture World*, 5 September 1925, p. 33.

17. *Motography*, June 1912, p. 247; *Exhibitor's Film Exchange*, 1 July 1915, p. 28; 21 August 1915, p. 4; 2 October 1915, p. 5; *Exhibitor's Herald*, 26 February 1916, p. 7; *Motion Picture News*, 15 July 1916, p. 315; *Motography*, 7 April 1917, p. 704.

18. *Motography*, March, 1912, p. 105 and 17 April 1915, p. 620; *Exhibitor's Film Exchange*, 9 October 1915, p. 23; *Motography*, 2 December 1916, p. 1220; Joseph P. Kennedy, ed., *The Story of Films* (Chicago: A. W. Shaw, 1927), pp. 349–350; *United States of America v. Motion Picture Patents Co. et al.*, 225 F. 800 (1915), record, vol. V, p. 2737.

19. *Exhibitor's Herald*, 24 November 1917, p. 23 and 15 December 1917, p. 217; *Motion Picture News*, 22 December 1917, p. 4426 and 1 June 1918, pp. 3327–3328; F. Cyril James, *The Growth of Chicago Banks* (New York: Harper Bros., 1938), p. 1304; Melchoir Palyi, *The Chicago Credit Market* (Chicago: University of Chicago Press, 1937), p. 71; John Sherman Porter, ed., *Moody's Manual of Industrials* (New York: Moody's Investor Service, 1920), p. 1514.

20. *Who's Who in Chicago and Illinois* (Chicago: A.N. Marquis, 1917), pp. 75, 584; *Who's Who in Chicago and Illinois* (Chicago: A.N. Marquis, 1926), pp. 107, 625; Paul M. Angle, *Philip K. Wrigley* (Chicago: Rand McNally, 1975), pp. 11–41; M. R. Werner, *Julius Rosenwald* (New York: Harper, 1938), pp. 20–22; "Paramount Pictures," *Fortune* 15 (March 1937): 87–96; Tedlow, *New and Improved*, pp. 261–300.

21. *Moving Picture World*, 19 October 1918, p. 366; *Exhibitor's Herald*, 7 June 1919, p. 35; *Motion Picture News*, 5 April 1919, p. 4; *Exhibitor's Herald and Motography*, 31 April 1919, p. 37; *Motion Picture News*, 31 May 1919, p. 3574; *Exhibitor's Herald and Motography*, 6 September 1919, p. 46; *Motion Picture News*, 6 December 1919, p. 4065; *Exhibitor's Herald and Motography*, 4 October 1919, p. 47; *Motion Picture News*, 24 January 1920, p. 1038; 26 February 1912, p. 1615; 6 August 1921, p. 759.

22. *Variety*, 26 May 1922, p. 39; *Motion Picture News*, 24 June 1922, p. 3321; *Variety*, 23 June 1922, p. 38 and 7 July 1922, p. 61; *Motion Picture News*, 8 July 1922, p. 178; 15 December 1923, p. 2771; 8 September 1923, p. 1170; *Variety*, 12 July 1923, p. 20; 9 April 1924, p. 16; 23 July 1924, p. 24; *Motion Picture News*, 15 November 1924, p. 2482.

23. *Motion Picture News*, 10 May 1924, p. 2085; *Variety*, 14 January 1925, p. 21; *Motion Picture News*, 14 February 1925, p. 708 and 14 March 1925, p. 1150; *Variety*, 2 September 1925, p. 33; 15 July 1925, p. 23; 4 November 1925, p. 29; 16 December 1925, p. 29; 7 April 1926, pp. 24, 28; Kennedy, *The Story of Films*, p. 75.

24. Barney Balaban and Sam Katz, *The Fundamental Principles of Balaban and Katz Theatre Management* (Chicago: Balaban & Katz, 1926), p. 54.

25. James L. Davis, *The Elevated System and the Growth of Chicago* (Evanston, Ill.: Northwestern University, Department of Geography, 1965), pp. 11–49; Homer Hoyt, *One Hundred Years of Land Values in Chicago* (Chicago: University of Chicago Press, 1933), pp. 1–53.

26. Irving Cutler, "The Jews of Chicago: From Shtetl to Suburb," in *Ethnic Chicago* eds. Melvin G. Holli and Peter d'A. Jones (Grand Rapids, Mich.: William B. Eerdman's Publishing, 1984), pp. 46–69.

27. Chicago Plan Commission, *Forty-Four Cities in the City of Chicago* (Chicago: Chicago Plan Commission, 1942), pp. 27–28; Louis Wirth, *The Ghetto* (Chicago: University of Chicago Press, 1928), pp. 241–252. To capture a flavor of what it was like read Meyer Levin, *The Old Bunch* (New York: The Citadel Press, 1937). Levin based his novel on friends and experiences in this Chicago neighborhood.

28. T. V. Smith and Leonard D. White, eds., *Chicago: An Experiment in Social Science Research* (Chicago: University of Chicago Press, 1929), pp. 113–118; Malcolm J. Proudfoot, "The Major Outlying Business Centers of Chicago," unpublished Ph.D. dissertation, University of Chicago, 1936, pp. 16–50, 100–

224; Hoyt, *One Hundred Years*, pp. 227–231; Balaban and Katz, *The Fundamental Principles*, p. 87.

29. Chicago Plan Commission, *Forty-Four Cities*, pp. 118–119.

30. Michael Conant, *Antitrust in the Motion Picture Industry*, (Berkeley: University of California Press, 1960), pp. 154–155; Chicago Recreation Commission, *The Chicago Recreation Survey*, 1937, vol. II, "Commercial Recreation" (Chicago, 1938), pp. 36–37; Hoyt, *One Hundred Years*, p. 262.

31. Federal Writers Project, *New York City Guide* (New York: Random House, 1939), pp. 226–252; New York Herald, *The New York Market* (New York: New York Herald, 1922), pp. 60, 63; Allan Nevins and John A. Krout, eds., *The Greater City* (New York: Columbia University Press, 1948), pp. 148–172; Walter Laidlow, *Population of the City of New York, 1890–1932* (New York: Cities Census Committee, 1932), pp. 51–58; Harold T. Lewis, *Transit and Transportation*, Regional Survey, vol. IV (New York: Regional Plan of New York, 1928), pp. 19–69.

32. Levin, *The Old Bunch*, p. 58.

33. But not everyone shared this unabashed enthusiasm. H. L. Menckem wrote in 1928: "I advocate hanging architects whose work is intolerably bad. Most of them specialize in the design of movie and gasoline cathedrals." Quoted in "Editorial Comment," *Architecture*, vol. 57, no. 6 (June 1928): 319.

34. For an analysis of Rapp & Rapp see Stern, Gilmartin, and Mellins, *Architecture and Urbanism Between the Two World Wars*, p. 256.

35. Ben M. Hall, *The Best Remaining Seats* (New York: Bramhall House, 1961), pp. 136–142.

36. "Uptown Theatre," *Marquee*, vol. 9, no. 2 (Second Quarter, 1977): 1–27; Theatre Historical Society, *Chicago Theatre* (Notre Dame, Ind.: Theatre Historical Society, 1975), pp. 1–20; "Special Issue on the Balaban & Katz Tivoli Theatre," *Marquee*, vol. 17, no. 4 (Fourth Quarter 1985): 1–36; George L. Rapp, "History of Cinema Theater Architecture," in *Living Architecture*, ed. Arthur Woltersdorf (Chicago: A. Kroch, 1930), pp. 55–64. John W. Landon, *Jesse Crawford* (Vestal, N.Y.: Vestal Press, 1974), pp. 19–44.

37. Arthur Mayer, *Merely Colossal* (New York: Simon and Schuster, 1953), p. 71; Ira Berkow, *Maxwell Street* (Garden City, N.Y.: Doubleday, 1977), p. 201.

38. Balaban and Katz, *The Fundamental Principles*, pp. 14–15, 54–55.

39. Kennedy, *The Story of Films*, pp. 269–273; *Exhibitor's Herald and Motography*, 21 December 1918, p. 25; Balaban and Katz, *The Fundamental Principles*, pp. 20–33.

40. For more on the history of the stage show see Hall, *The Best Remaining Seats*, pp. 200–206 and Charles Beardsley, *Hollywood's Master Showman: The Legendary Sid Grauman* (New York: Cornwall Books, 1983), pp. 42–47, 57–58, 76–77.

41. Compare this with the success of Sid Grauman, who centered his publicity

campaigns around Hollywood-sponsored premieres. Grauman may be credited with the development of the prologue, but his success was due to access to movie stars. Balaban & Katz in distant Chicago (days away by train) had no such means of publicity. See David Karnes, "The Glamorous Crowd: Hollywood Movie Premiers Between the Wars," *American Quarterly*, vol. 38, no. 4 (Fall 1986): 557–560.

42. *Variety*, 22 September 1922, p. 1; Hall, *The Best Remaining Seats*, p. 208; *Variety*, 25 October 1923, p. 18; 14 June 1923, p. 21; 11 March 1925, pp. 39–40; Carrie Balaban, *Continuous Performance* (New York: A. J. Balaban Foundation, 1941), pp. 46–60.

43. Vincente Minnelli, *I Remember It Well* (Garden City, N.Y.: Doubleday, 1974), pp. 52–56; *Variety*, 12 April 1923, p. 30; 12 July 1923, p. 27; 1 November 1923, p. 26; 8 November 1923, p. 21.

44. *Variety*, 8 December 1922, p. 37; 29 March 1923, p. 30; 23 September 1925, p. 32; 18 March 1925, p. 27; 31 January 1924, p. 21.

45. Landon, *Jesse Crawford*, pp. 30–42. See David L. Junchen, *Encyclopedia of the American Theatre Organ*, vol. I (Pasadena, Calif.: Showcase Publications, 1985), pp. 16–22 for a technical history of the remarkable organs manufactured for theatres. The author estimates about seven thousand were made and placed, principally between 1923 and 1929.

46. *Variety*, 22 July 1925, p. 27; 5 August 1925, p. 27; 19 August 1925, pp. 32, 35; 28 October 1925, p. 30; 26 May 1926, p. 23; Hall, *The Best Remaining Seats*, pp. 187–188.

47. Fred Wittenmeyer, "Cooling of Theatres and Public Buildings," *Ice and Refrigeration*, July 1922, pp. 13–14; Fred Wittenmeyer, "Development of Carbon Dioxide Refrigerating Machines," *Ice and Refrigeration*, November 1916, p. 165; R. E. Cherne, "Developments in Refrigeration as Applied to Air Conditioning," *Ice and Refrigeration*, January 1941, pp. 29–30; Walter L. Feisher, "How Air Conditioning Has Developed in Fifty Years," *Heating, Piping and Air Conditioning*, January 1950, pp. 120–122.

48. Barney Balaban, "My Biggest Mistake," *Forbes*, vol. 50 (1 February 1946): 16; Ruth Ingels, *Willis Haviland Carrier: Father of Air Conditioning* (New York: Doubleday, 1952), p. 143.

49. "Air Conditioning System in Motion Picture House," *Ice and Refrigeration*, November 1925, pp. 251–252; "Heating, Ventilating and Cooling Plant of the Tivoli Theatre," *Power Plant Engineering*, 1 March 1922, pp. 249–255.

50. "Air Conditioning," *Ice and Refrigeration*, November 1925, p. 251.

51. *Variety*, 10 June 1925, p. 31 and 9 September 1925, p. 30; Ingels, *Willis Haviland Carrier*, pp. 65–68; Oscar E. Anderson, *Refrigeration in America* (Princeton: Princeton University Press, 1953), pp. 309–311.

52. Lizabeth Cohen, *Making a New Deal: Industrial Workers in Chicago, 1919–1939* (New York: Cambridge University Press, 1990), pp. 121–125 and Lizabeth Cohen, "Encountering Mass Culture at the Grassroots: The Experience

of Chicago Workers in the 1920s," *American Quarterly*, vol. 41, no. 1 (March 1989): 12–16.

53. *Variety*, 28 October 1925, p. 27; Mason Miller, "Famous Players in Transition Period," *The Magazine of Wall Street*, 23 April 1927, p. 1178; *Variety*, 26 June 1929, p. 5; "Review of Operations—Paramount Famous Lasky," *Commercial and Financial Chronicle*, 21 April 1928, p. 2490.

CHAPTER 4: HOLLYWOOD CONTROL

1. *Film Daily Yearbook*, 1931, pp. 823–844; *Variety*, 7 August 1929, pp. 3–10, 50; *Wall Street Journal*, 11 June 1927, pp. 1, 4; *Film Daily*, 26 August 1927, pp. 1, 4.

2. Joseph P. Kennedy, ed., *The Story of the Films* (Chicago: A. W. Shaw, 1927), pp. 275–277; Howard T. Lewis, *Cases in the Motion Picture Industry*, (New York: McGraw Hill, 1930), pp. 516–521; *Variety*, 7 August 1929, pp. 2–10, 189. For the theory behind chain-store, scientific retailing see Richard S. Tedlow, *New and Improved: The Story of Mass Marketing in America* (New York: Basic Books, 1990), pp. 189–199.

3. Arthur Mayer, *Merely Colossal*, (New York: Simon and Schuster, 1953), pp. 106–111; Lewis, *Cases in the Motion Picture Industry*, pp. 516–518; *Variety*, 7 August 1929, pp. 2–8, 189.

4. *Film Daily*, 8 April 1929, p. 1 and 16 April 1929, pp. 1, 4; *Variety*, 26 September 1928, p. 19; 29 May 1929, p. 30; 14 May 1930, p. 4; Ben M. Hall, *The Best Remaining Seats*, (New York: Bramhall House, 1961), pp. 251–253.

5. *Barrons*, 28 October 1929, p. 15; *Variety*, 9 October 1929, p. 6; *Film Daily*, 18 November 1930, pp. 1, 4; 10 April 1931, pp. 1–2; 20 August 1931, p. 1; *Variety*, 18 March 1931, p. 30 and 29 April 1931, p. 7; *Barrons*, 7 November 1932, p. 16.

6. See Douglas Gomery, *The Hollywood Studio System* (New York: St. Martin's Press, 1986), pp. 14–21, where I develop this analysis of the relative importance of a few theatres.

7. Benjamin B. Hampton, *A History of the Movies* (New York: Covici Friede, 1931), pp. 390–413 summarizes the details of these mergers. For more on the general merger movement in the United States of the late 1920s see Ralph L. Nelson, *Merger Movements in American Industry, 1895–1956* (Princeton: Princeton University Press, 1956).

8. This account of Paramount's history is based on Michael Conant, *Antitrust in the Motion Picture Industry* (Berkeley: University of California Press, 1960), pp. 51–54, 94–106, 130–131; United States Temporary National Economic Committee, *The Motion Picture Industry*, Monograph 43 (Washington, D. C.: United States Government Printing Office, 1941), pp. 5–16, 45–48, 68–74; Lewis, *Cases in the Motion Picture Industry*, pp. 30–50, 74–75; Mae D. Huettig, *Economic*

Control of the Motion Picture Industry: A Study in Industrial Organization (Philadelphia: University of Pennsylvania Press, 1944), pp. 65–72, 134–138; Gomery, *The Hollywood Studio System*, pp. 26–40; "Paramount Pictures," *Fortune*, vol. 15 (March 1937): 87–96; "Paramount: Oscar for Profits," *Fortune*, vol. 35 (June 1947): 90–94.

9. The account of Loew's history is based on Conant, *Antitrust in the Motion Picture Industry*, pp. 49–54, 94–106; United States Temporary National Economic Committee, *The Motion Picture Industry*, pp. 8–16, 59–69; Lewis, *Cases in the Motion Picture Industry*, pp. 18–25; Huettig, *Economic Control of the Motion Picture Industry*, pp. 134–136; Gomery, *The Hollywood Studio System*, pp. 51–62; "Loew's, Inc.," *Fortune*, vol. 20 (August 1938): 69–72; Bosley Crowther, *The Lion's Share* (New York: E. P. Dutton, 1957), pp. 167–229.

10. This account of the history of the Warner Bros.' theatre chain is based on Conant, *Antitrust in the Motion Picture Industry*, pp. 49–54, 130–134; United States Temporary National Economic Committee, *The Motion Picture Industry*, pp. 6–16, 60–74; Lewis, *Cases in the Motion Picture Industry*, pp. 22–23; Huettig, *Economic Control of the Motion Picture Industry*, pp. 40–46, 85–89; Gomery, *The Hollywood Studio System*, pp. 101–112; "Warner Brothers," *Fortune*, vol. 16 (December 1937): 110–113.

11. This history of the growth of the Fox theatre chain is based on Conant, *Antitrust in the Motion Picture Industry*, pp. 49–54; United States Temporary National Economic Committee, *The Motion Picture Industry*, pp. 9–15; Lewis, *Cases in the Motion Picture Industry*, pp. 69–79, 208–212; Huettig, *Economic Control of the Motion Picture Industry*, pp. 77–83, 109–111; Gomery, *The Hollywood Studio System*, pp. 76–90; "20th Century-Fox," *Fortune*, vol. 12 (December 1935): 85–93.

12. This account of the history of the RKO theatre chain is based on Conant, *Antitrust in the Motion Picture Industry*, pp. 49–54, 108–109, 138–142; United States Temporary National Economic Committee, *The Motion Picture Industry*, pp. 61–69; Lewis, *Cases in the Motion Picture Industry*, pp. 110–116; Huettig, *Economic Control of the Motion Picture Industry*, pp. 46–49; Gomery, *The Hollywood Studio System*, pp. 124–133; "RKO: It's Only Money," *Fortune*, vol. 47 (May 1953): 122–127; Richard Austin Smith, *Corporations in Crisis* (Garden City, N.Y.: Doubleday, 1966), pp. 43–62.

13. The operation of the distribution in the Hollywood system was well documented in the antitrust case *United States v. Paramount et al.*, 334 U.S. 131 (1948), described and analyzed in Conant, *Antitrust in the Motion Picture Industry*, with an update in Conant's "The Paramount Decrees Reconsidered," *Law and Contemporary Problems*, vol. 44, no. 4 (Autumn 1981): 79–107.

14. I traced this for a Warner Bros. film, *High Sierra* (1941), in an essay that introduced the screenplay in the series for University of Wisconsin Press: *High Sierra: Screenplay and Analysis* (Madison: University of Wisconsin press, 1979), pp. 9–16. With all the various runs of the film, in a city such as Chicago, for in-

stance, *High Sierra* was running, off and on, in that city for more than a year and a half.

15. This admission price discrimination is a modification of well-known principles of microeconomics. See Louis Phlips, *The Economics of Price Discrimination* (Cambridge: Cambridge University Press, 1983).

16. Gregory J. Edwards, *The International Film Poster: The Role of the Poster in Cinema Art, Advertising, and History* (Salem, N.H.: Salem House, 1985), pp. 55–103; John Kobal and V. A. Wilson, *Foyer Pleasure: The Golden Age of Cinema Lobby Cards* (New York: Deliliah, 1983), pp. 9–20; Stephen Rebello and Richard Allen, *Reel Art: Great Posters from the Golden Age of the Silver Screen* (New York: Abbeville Press, 1988), pp. 37–41, 117–119.

17. Rebello and Allen, *Reel Art*, pp. 41–106. The film industry carefully regulated the production of publicity materials: see Mary Beth Haralovich, "Film Advertising, the Film Industry, and the Pin-up: The Industry's Accommodations to Social Forces in the 1940s," in *Current Research in Film: Audiences, Economics, and Law*, vol. 1, ed. Bruce A. Austin (Norwood, N.J.: Ablex Publishing Corporation, 1985), pp. 127–164.

18. *Boxoffice*, March 1986, pp. 22–28; *New York Times*, 4 January 1942, p. 33; *Theatre Catalog*, 1945, pp. 430–439 and 1946–1947, pp. 442–454. The *Motion Picture Herald*, aimed at exhibitors, regularly published tips for promoting upcoming films.

19. *Variety*, 6 August 1980, pp. 1, 32 and 2 April 1980, pp. 6, 48 summarize the detailed work of Theodore E. James and Arthur Murphy, which seeks to pin down the exact decline of box office during the Great Depression. On the effect of substitutes such as radio see J. F. Steiner, "Recreation and Leisure Time Activities," President's Research Committee on Social Trends, *Recent Social Trends in the United States* (New York: McGraw-Hill, 1933), pp. 939–944; 947–954.

20. For a general description of the use of giveaways see Frank H. Ricketson, Jr., *The Management of Motion Picture Theatres* (New York: McGraw-Hill, 1938), pp. 249–255, 260–268.

21. Forbes Parkhill, "Bank Night Tonight," *Saturday Evening Post*, vol. 210 (4 December 1937): 20.

22. These rules to evade lottery laws did not prevent antigambling forces from becoming morally outraged. Bank Night was sued hundreds of times throughout the late 1930s. For examples of the attendant legal controversies see *Motion Picture Herald*, 26 February 1938, p. 30 or 25 June 1938, p. 38.

23. Raymond Kresensky, "Bank Night," *Christian Century*, 14 August 1935, pp. 1034–1035; Forbes Parkhill, "Bank Night Tonight," *Saturday Evening Post*, vol. 210 (4 December 1937): 20–22, 82; *Motion Picture Herald*, 18 May 1935, p. 58 and 21 September 1935, p. 23.

24. *Business Week*, 8 December 1934, p. 24; Gene Fernett, "When Movie Houses Gave Premiums," *Classic Images*, no. 87, p. 27.

25. *Motion Picture Herald*, 7 March 1936, p. 80; 5 December 1942, p. 23;

27 November 1943, p. 16; Alan S. Milward, *War, Economy and Society, 1939–1945* (Berkeley: University of California Press, 1979), pp. 208–244; Richard R. Lingeman, *Don't You Know There's a War On?* (New York: G. P. Putnam's Sons, 1970), pp. 330–380.

26. Ricketson, *The Management of Motion Picture Theatres*, p. 126.

27. *Variety*, 26 September 1928, p. 19; 15 May 1929, p. 40; 29 May 1929, p. 30; 22 October 1930, p. 5; 29 October 1930, p. 43; 30 June 1931, p. 4.

28. *Motion Picture Herald*, 28 November 1953, p. 37; Derek Jewell, *Frank Sinatra* (Boston: Little Brown, 1985), pp. 39–60; George T. Simon, *The Big Bands*, 4th ed. (New York: Schirmer, 1981), passim; Paramount Pictures Corporation, "Listing of State Show Attractions in Chicago, 1941," on file at Theatre Historical Society Archive, Chicago, Illinois.

29. Bob Birchard, "Gene Autry: Back in the Saddle Again," *Westerner*, vol. 6, no. 5 (September–October 1974): 43–46; Douglas B. Green, "Gene Autry," in *Stars of Country Music*, eds. Bill C. Malone and Judith McCulloh (Urbana: University of Illinois Press, 1975), pp. 146–147.

30. Ricketson, *The Management of Motion Picture Theatres*, pp. 1–30; Jane Preddy, *Temples of Illusion: The Atmospheric Theatres of John Eberson*, (New York: The Betha and Karl Leubsdorf Art Gallery, Hunter College, 1988); Norman Morse, "An American Cavalcade of Theatre Architecture," *Theatre Catalog*, 1948–49, pp. 15–18. This is the first citation for the *Theatre Catalog*, an annual yearbook from Jay Emmanuel Publications of Philadelphia issued through the 1940s into the 1950s. Hereafter this publication, with a number of editors and various dates, will be listed as *Theatre Catalog* with the appropriate year.

31. Mark Walston, "The Commercial Rise and Fall of Silver Spring: A Study of the 20th Century Development of the Suburban Shopping Center in Montgomery County," *Maryland Historical Magazine*, vol. 81, no. 4 (Winter 1986): 330–335; *Washington Post*, 27 October 1938, Special Section; *Motion Picture Herald*, 12 November 1938, "Better Theatres," pp. 12–14, 26. See also *Marquee on Main Street* (Minneapolis: University Gallery, 1982), pp. 19–24 and Jane Preddy, "Glamour, Glitz, and Sparkle: The Deco Theatres of John Eberson," *The 1989 Annual of the Theatre Historical Society*, no. 16 (Chicago: Theatre Historical Society of America, 1989), pp. 29–39.

32. See my "The Warner Theatre: Architectural Splendor in Milwaukee," *Marquee*, vol. 12, no. 1 & 2 (Spring 1981): 27–31 for more information about this remarkable design.

33. David Naylor, *American Picture Palaces: The Architecture of Fantasy* (New York: Van Nostrand Reinhold, 1981), pp. 141–172.

34. John Zink was hardly alone in creating art deco theatres. The best-known designer of this style worked out of Los Angeles: S. Charles Lee. See Lee's own take on the new style in his "Influence of West Coast Designers on the Modern Theater," *Journal of the SMPE*, vol. 50, no. 4 (April 1948): 329–336.

35. James M. Goode, *Capital Losses: A Cultural History of Washington's Destroyed Buildings* (Washington, D.C.: Smithsonian Institution Press, 1979), pp. 381–382; Charles Francisco, *The Radio City Music hall: An Affectionate History of the World's Greatest Theater* (New York: E. P. Dutton, 1979).

36. R. E. Cherne, "Developments in Refrigeration as Applied to Air Conditioning," *Ice and Refrigeration*, (1941), pp. 29–30; Oscar E. Anderson, *Refrigeration in America* (Princeton: Princeton University Press, 1953), pp. 309–311; M. G. Harbula, "Air Conditioning Design for Theatres," *Heating and Ventilating*, December 1931, pp. 38–43.

37. Margaret Ingels, *Willis Haviland Carrier: Father of Air Conditioning* (New York: Doubleday, 1952), passim; Carl F. Boester, "New Things in Air Conditioning that Are Bringing Lower Costs," *Motion Picture Herald*, "Better Theatres," 18 March 1939, pp. 6–7; John Eberson, "Theatre Construction Costs Today," *Motion Picture Herald*, "Better Theatres," 15 October 1938, pp. 9–11.

38. Carl Bernstein, *Loyalties: A Son's Memoir* (New York: Simon and Schuster, 1989), pp. 92, 95. Bernstein's mother was active in picketing downtown restaurants that at the time would not serve African-Americans.

39. J. H. Toler, "Air Conditioning Wanted for New and Remodeled Theatres," *Domestic Engineering* 165 (March 1945): 113–114; *Business Week*, 27 June 1953, pp. 43–44, 46; Boester, "New Things in Air Conditioning," pp. 6–7.

40. For more on the relations of the National Recovery Act and the Hollywood film industry see Douglas Gomery, "Hollywood, the National Recovery Administration, and the Question of Monopoly Power," *Journal of the University Film Association*, vol. 31, no. 2 (Spring 1979): 47–52 reprinted in Gorham A. Kindem, ed., *The American Movie Industry* (Carbondale: Southern Illinois University Press, 1982), pp. 205–214.

41. Robert W. Chambers, "The Double Feature as a Sales Problem," *Harvard Business Review*, vol. 16, no. 2 (Winter 1938): 226–230; *Motion Picture Herald*, 14 November 1931, p. 9 and 8 July 1933, p. 9.

42. Chambers, "The Double Feature as a Sales Problem," pp. 229–236; *National Board of Review Magazine*, September 1940, pp. 3–5.

43. *Motion Picture Herald*, 2 November 1935, p. 42; *Business Week*, 5 March 1938, pp. 45–46; *Motion Picture Herald*, 19 February 1938, p. 23; *National Board of Review Magazine*, September 1940, pp. 3–5.

44. *Motion Picture Herald*, 2 November 1935, p. 42; *Business Week*, 5 March 1938, pp. 45–46; *Motion Picture Herald* 19 February 1938, p. 23; 25 June 1938, p. 41; 5 August 1939, p. 28.

45. *Motion Picture Herald*, 2 January 1943, p. 35 and 23 October 1943, p. 17; *Variety*, 22 March 1950, pp. 7, 18; *Motion Picture Herald*, 23 April 1955, pp. 12–13; Bosley Crowther, "Double Feature Trouble," *New York Times Magazine*, 14 July 1940, pp. 8, 20.

46. Ulf Jonas Bjork, "Double Features and B Movies: Exhibition Patterns in

Seattle, 1938," *Journal of Film and Video*, vol. 41, no. 3 (Fall 1989): 44–47.

47. *Motion Picture World*, "Better Theatres," 19 November 1932, pp. 55–56 and 19 October 1935, p. 40; *Motion Picture World*, 4 March 1939, p. 2.

48. Marsha Meyer and Gene Sculatti, *Popcorn: America's Amazing Obsession* (New York: Long Shadow, 1984), pp. 18–20; *Motion Picture Herald*, "Better Theatres," 21 November 1931, pp. 26, 28.

49. *Motion Picture Herald*, 22 March 1952, pp. 55–57; "What's Playing at the Grove?," *Fortune* 38 (August 1948): 94–96; *Film Daily Yearbook*, 1937, p. 37.

50. William J. Baumol and Alan S. Blinder, *Economics: Principles and Policy* (New York: Harcourt Brace Jovanovich, 1979), pp. 355–356, 368–369 and C. E. Ferguson and J. P. Gould, *Microeconomic Theory*, 4th ed. (Homewood, Ill.: Richard D. Irwin, 1975), pp. 58–62.

51. Vassily Aksyonov, *In Search of Melancholy Baby: A Russian in America* (New York: Random House, 1988), p. 124.

52. *Motion Picture Herald*, 24 February 1940, p. 42; *Motion Picture Herald*, "Better Theatres," 11 January 1941, pp. 8–9.

53. Charles E. Buckhead, *Rice, Popcorn, and Buckwheat By States, 1866–1953*, Statistical Bulletin Number 238, United States Department of Agriculture (Washington, D.C.: United States Government Printing Office, 1958), pp. 10–17; Arthur Bartlett, "Popcorn Crazy," *Saturday Evening Post*, 221 (21 May 1949): 36, 141; *Business Week*, 17 June 1944, p. 66.

54. Pat Watters, *Coca-Cola: An Illustrated History* (Garden City, N.Y.: Doubleday, 1978), pp. 171–200; *Beverage World*, December 1982, "Special Issue: 100 Year History," pp. 139–153.

55. Bartlett, "Popcorn Crazy," pp. 36, 141; John J. Riley, *A History of the American Soft Drink Industry, 1807–1957* (Washington, D.C.: American Bottlers of Carbonated Beverages, 1958), pp. 143–152; Richard S. Tredlow, *New and Improved: The Story of Mass Marketing in America* (New York: Basic Books, 1990), pp. 55–68.

56. Bartlett, "Popcorn Crazy," pp. 36, 141; *Business Week*, 17 June 1944, p. 66; *Motion Picture Herald*, 22 March 1952, pp. 55–57; Riley, *A History of the American Soft Drink Industry*, pp. 143–152; "What's Playing at the Grove?," *Fortune* 38, (August 1948): 94–96.

57. *Motion Picture Herald*, 9 May 1953, pp. 46–48 and 5 January 1952, pp. 16, 27; *Boxoffice*, March 1986, pp. 12–14; *Variety*, 24 February 1988, p. 319; *Showman's Handbook* for Plitt Theatres, Inc. (Chicago: Plitt Theatre Corporation, 1977), p. 50.

CHAPTER 5: NEW NATIONAL CHAINS

1. Indeed, Hollywood recognized that there was something wrong and tried to take over television to head off the problem. For more on this subject see Douglas

Gomery, "Failed Opportunities: The Integration of the U. S. Motion Picture and Television Industries," *Quarterly Review of Film Studies*, vol. 10, no 2 (Summer 1984): 219–228.

2. This data on movie attendance is nicely summarized in Michael Conant, *Antitrust in the Motion Picture Industry* (Berkeley: University of California Press, 1960), pp. 10–12. Remember that the year 1946 was the best in movie history not because it climaxed a long-term trend, but because it reflected the artificial inflation of movie audiences during the golden age—for the American film industry—of the Second World War.

3. Christopher H. Sterling and Timothy R. Haight, *The Mass Media: Aspen Institute Guide to Communication Industry Trends* (New York: Praeger, 1978) summarizes the basic financial and audience data for the motion picture and television industries. See pp. 186–189, 206–214.

4. Data for this passage section came from Sterling and Haight, *The Mass Media*, pp. 208–209, 211, and 373.

5. Jonathan Hughes, *American Economic History* (Glenview, Ill.: Scott Foresman, 1983), pp. 540–542; Howard R. Smith, *Economic History of the United States* (New York: The Ronald Press, 1955), pp. 665–666, 705–706; United States Department of Commerce, *National Income and Product Accounts, 1929–1965* (Washington, D.C.: United States Government Printing Office, 1966), pp. 32–33, 40–41 and 78–79; Charles H. Hession and Hyman Sardy, *Ascent to Affluence: A History of American Economic Development* (Boston: Allyn and Bacon, 1969), pp. 805–811; James M. Henderson and Richard E. Quandt, *Microeconomic Theory* (New York: McGraw-Hill, 1958), pp. 26–27, 238–240; Richard Leftwich, *The Price System and Resource Allocation* 6th ed. (Hinsdale, Ill.: The Dryden Press, 1976), pp. 89–93.

6. Hession and Sardy, *Ascent to Affluence*, pp. 780–790.

7. Landon Y. Jones, *Great Expectations: America and the Baby Boom Generation* (New York: Random House, 1981), pp. 43–54; Louise Russell, *The Baby Boom Generation and the Economy* (Washington, D.C.: The Brookings Institution Press, 1982), pp. 8–20; Louis H. Masotti and Jeffrey K. Hadden, eds., *Suburbia in Transition* (New York: New Directions, 1974), pp. 46–70; Philip C. Dolce, ed., *Suburbia* (Garden City, N.Y.: Anchor, 1976), pp. 1–59.

8. The aforementioned history and analysis of the baby boom is based on Jones, *Great Expectations*, pp. 11–78; Paul C. Light, *Baby Boomers* (New York: W. W. Norton, 1988), pp. 19–44; Richard A. Easterlin, *Birth and Fortune: the Impact of Numbers on Personal Welfare*, 2d ed. (Chicago: University of Chicago Press, 1987), pp. 3–33.

9. Robert Sklar, *Movie-Made America* (New York: Random House, 1976), p. 269.

10. C. E. Ferguson and J. P. Gould, *Microeconomic Theory*, 4th ed. (Homewood, Ill.: Richard D. Irwin, 1975), pp. 62–65, 92–93; William J. Baumol and

Alan S. Blinder, *Economics: Principles and Policy* (New York: Harcourt Brace Jovanovich, 1979), pp. 342–343.

11. Sterling and Haight, *The Mass Media*, pp. 203–206.

12. Frederic Stuart, *The Effects of Television on the Motion Picture and Radio Industries* (New York: Arno Press, 1976), p. 120; Erik Barnouw, *The Golden Web: A History of Broadcasting in the United States, 1933–1953* (New York: Oxford University Press, 1968), pp. 285–290.

13. The specific case was titled *United States v. Paramount Pictures et al.*, 334 U. S. 131 (1948). For the reaction of the film industry during the 1950s see Michael Conant's classic study, *Antitrust in the Motion Picture Industry*.

14. Michael Conant, "The Paramount Decrees Reconsidered," *Law and Contemporary Problems*, vol. 44, no 4 (Autumn 1981): 100.

15. For the historical background see Conant, *Antitrust in the Motion Picture Industry*, p. 108; *Variety*, 7 September 1960, pp. 5, 15 and 19 June 1957, pp. 3, 7.

16. Hunt Williams, *Beyond Control: ABC and the Fate of the Networks* (New York: Antheneum, 1989), pp. 37–41; Sterling Quinlan, *Inside ABC: American Broadcasting Company's Rise to Power* (New York: Hastings House, 1979), pp. 23–45.

17. *Wall Street Journal*, 18 October 1973, p. 14; American Broadcasting Companies, Inc., Annual Report, 1978.

18. *Business Week*, 24 March 1986, p. 83; *Variety*, 12–18 April 1989, pp. 1, 4; Peter J. Dekom, "The Motion Picture in 1987: A Study in Turmoil," *American Premiere*, vol. 8, no 1 (Spring 1987), pp. 9–15. For the historical background see Conant, *Antitrust in the Motion Picture Industry*, p. 108; *Moody's Industrial Manual*, 1971, p. 2190; *Wall Street Journal*, 30 March 1973, p. 16.

19. Conant, *Antitrust in the Motion Picture Industry*, pp. 108–109; *Wall Street Journal*, 22 April 1959, p. 18; 7 August 1967, p. 24; 21 August 1967, p. 2; *Moody's Industrial Manual*, 1978, p. 1497.

20. Andrew Horton, "Turning On and Turning Out at the Drive-in: An American Phenomenon Survives and Thrives," *Journal of Popular Film*, vol. 5, nos. 3 and 4 (Fall 1976): 233–244.

21. *Variety*, 13 July 1933, p. 5; *Motion Picture Daily*, 10 June 1933, pp. 1, 15; "Camden's Drive-in Theatre," *Literary Digest*, vol. 116, 22 July 1933, p. 19; Anthony Downs, "Drive-ins Have Arrived," *Journal of Property Management*, vol. 18 (March 1953): 149–153; "Drive-in Movie Holds Four Hundred Cars," *Popular Mechanics*, vol. 60 (September 1933): 326; *Business Week*, 5 August 1933, p. 19.

22. *International Motion Picture Almanac*, 1950–1951, p. 8; *Variety*, 15 June 1949, p. 18; *Film Daily Yearbook–1953*, pp. 1063–1087.

23. *Business Week*, 9 August 1952, pp. 46–48 and 9 May 1953, pp. 129, 131; Frank J. Taylor, "Big Boom in Outdoor Movies," *Saturday Evening Post*, vol. 229 (15 September 1956): 31, 100–102; *Barrons*, 23 June 1958, pp. 3, 17–19.

24. *Theatre Catalog*, 1950–1951, pp. 300–302; Katharine Best and Katharine Hillyer, "Movies Under the Stars," *Cue* 19 June 1948, pp. 18–19; Rodney Luther, "Drive-in Theatres: Rags to Riches in Five Years," *Hollywood Quarterly*, vol. 5 (Summer 1951): 401–411; "Drive-in Film Business Burns Up the Prairies," *Life* 24 (September 1951): 104–106; Al Hines, "The Drive-ins," *Holiday*, July 1952, pp. 6–10; *Barrons*, 23 June 1958, pp. 3, 17–19; *New York Times*, 1 March 1953, p. 6.

25. *Theatre Catalog*, 1947–1948, pp. 180–196; 1948–1949, pp. 125–128; 1953–1954, pp. 77–84; 1954–1955, pp. 76, 83, 87.

26. And for all the analysis of the special films made for drive-ins, most patrons preferred first-run Hollywood films. The majors did not want to cooperate and did all they could to obstruct the new drive-ins from booking anything but subruns. See the evidence in various court cases such as *Milgram et al. v. Loew's, Inc., et al.*, 192 F. 2nd 579, and *Basle Theatres, Inc. v. Warner Bros. Pictures Dist. Corp.*, 168 F. Supp. 553.

27. Edward W. Kellogg, "History of Sound Motion Pictures," *Journal of the SMPTE*, vol. 64, no. 8 (August 1955): 422–437; Kenneth T. Jackson, *Crabgrass Frontier: The Suburbanization of the United States* (New York: Oxford University Press, 1985), pp. 255–256; *New York Times*, 29 January 1950, p. 53 and 20 August 1950, p. 42; *Variety*, 6 June 1949, p. 25; 12 July 1950, p. 7; 2 April 1952, p. 25.

28. J. C. Nichols, "The Planning and Control of Outlying Shopping Centers," *The Journal of Land and Public Utility Economics*, vol. II, no. 1 (January 1926): 17–22; Homer Hoyt, "The Status of Shopping Centers in the United States," *Urban Land*, vol. 19 (1960): 3–6; Yehoshua S. Cohen, *Diffusion of an Innovation in an Urban System* (Chicago: The University of Chicago Department of Geography, 1972), pp. 1–22.

29. Peter O. Muller, *Contemporary Suburban America* (Englewood Cliffs, N.J.: Prentice Hall, 1981), pp. 120–124; Edward T. Thompson, "The Shopping Center Macy's Built," *Fortune*, vol. 61, no. 2 (1960): 195–200; *New York Times*, 16 January 1957, p. 30; *Business Week*, 11 October 1952, pp. 124–128; John C. Van Nostrand, "The Queen Elizabeth Way: Public Utility Versus Public Space," *Urban History Review*, vol. 12, no. 4 (October 1983): 1–23.

30. Thomas Harrison, "The Advent of the Super Regional Shopping Center," *The Appraisal Journal*, vol. 36, no. 1 (January 1968): 90–97; *Wall Street Journal*, 20 February 1969, pp. 1, 21; *Washington Post*, 20 February 1977, pp. 22–23; Jackson, *Crabgrass Frontier*, pp. 257–261.

31. William Severini Kowinski, "The Malling of America," *New Times*, 1 May 1978, pp. 33–34.

32. *Motion Picture Herald*, 16 February 1966, p. 23 and 9 November 1966, p. 22.

33. *Motion Picture Herald*, 27 September 1967, p. 14; *Moody's Industrial Manual*, 1971, p. 421; *Barrons*, 14 October 1974, p. 39 and 10 July 1978, p. 32; *Business Week*, 20 May 1972, p. 31.

34. *Forbes*, 15 April 1968, p. 71; *Barrons*, 18 July 1966, p. 20.

35. *Business Week*, 14 March 1970, p. 29; *International Motion Picture Almanac–1979*, (New York: Quigley Publications, 1979), p. 30A; *Barrons*, 28 June 1971, p. 11; *Wall Street Journal*, 8 February 1977, p. 46.

36. *Variety*, 29 May 1963, p. 17 and 17 July 1963, p. 15.

37. *Boxoffice*, 6 August 1973, p. SE-1 and 27 August 1973, p. 5.

38. *Boxoffice*, 17 June 1974, p. 6.

39. *Boxoffice*, 28 August 1972, p. C-1; 2 January 1972, p. W-1; 20 July 1970, p. 48; *Variety*, 29 December 1976, p. 20. The quotation is from *Boxoffice*, 18 December 1972, p. E-9.

40. *Variety*, 10 November 1982, p. 92.

41. Tino Balio, *United Artists: The Company Built By the Stars* (Madison: University of Wisconsin Press, 1976), pp. 64–65, 130.

42. *Boxoffice*, 10 December 1973, p. 10; *Variety*, 15 December 1976, pp. 7, 41; *Barrons*, 19 January 1970, pp. 21–22; *Film Journal*, February 1980, p. 12.

43. *Wall Street Journal*, 15 July 1986, p. 2; *Cablevision*, 4 August 1986, pp. 48–49; Tom Kerver, "TCI's 'Enfant Terrible'," *Cable Television Business*, 1 May 1987, pp. 24–30; *Business Week*, 28 November 1988, pp. 174–175.

44. By the early 1970s, movie trade papers began to note an increasing number of cities in the United States that had no single-screen cinemas left within their proper borders. New York City, in particular Manhattan, proved the lone exception, with a handful of single-screen cinemas, often functioning as art houses.

CHAPTER 6: CONTEMPORARY MOVIEGOING

1. *Variety*, 25 November 1987, p. 6. As of 1 January 1989 the Motion Picture Association of America estimated there were fifteen hundred drive-ins left. But that was down by one thousand from a couple years earlier. No one is sure where the bottom will come, whereas the number of indoor screens continues to increase. See *Boxoffice*, October 1989, p. 85.

2. *Variety*, 20 January 1988, p. 99; *Boxoffice*, October 1988, p. 46.

3. *Wall Street Journal*, 9 February 1989, p. B1; *Boxoffice*, July 1989, pp. 14–15.

4. *Boxoffice*, August 1988, pp. 18, 20, 24. And the massive multiplex idea has spread abroad. For example, the Decascoop opened in Ghent, Belgium, with twelve auditoria seating thirty-six hundred patrons and the Kinepolis outside Brussels, with over a dozen screens and a fabulously appointed auditoria. Reports in *Washington Post*, 2 January 1987, p. D6 and conversation with David Bordwell, 7 October 1990.

5. For more on this see Douglas Gomery, "Hollywood's Business," *Wilson Quarterly*, vol. 10, no. 3 (Summer 1986): 43–57.

6. Using product differentiation to gain entry into a "closed" market is discussed in F. M. Scherer and David Ross, *Industrial Market Structure and Economic Performance* (Boston: Houghton Mifflin, 1990), pp. 404–407.

7. *Variety*, 18 April 1979, p. 32. Taylor claimed to have originated the first twin cinema in Canada, the Elgin, in Ottawa in 1948.

8. *Variety*, 18 April 1979, pp. 5, 32; *Boxoffice*, 23 April 1979, pp. 10–12.

9. *Wall Street Journal*, 9 November 1981, p. 31; *Variety*, 11 June 1980, pp. 3, 38 and 21 November 1979, p. 51. Indeed the pay television was just then hitting a peak it would never again approach and video discs never took off, save for specialized institutional use.

10. *Wall Street Journal*, 9 November 1981, p. 31.

11. *New York Times*, 22 November 1981, section 10, p. 11.

12. *New York Times*, 22 November 1981, section 10, p. 11 and 27 July 1982, p. C15; *Variety*, 21 July 1982, pp. 5, 25; *Boxoffice*, July 1982, p. 26; October, 1982, p. 20; November 1981, pp. 74–77.

13. Karen Stabiner, "The Shape of Theatres to Come," *American Film*, vol. 7, no. 10 (September 1982): 51–52.

14. Quotation is from *Variety*, 21 November 1984, pp. 62, 84. See also *Variety*, 30 May 1984, pp. 1, 121 and *Wall Street Journal*, 30 May 1984, p. 10.

15. *Variety*, 24 April 1985, p. 7; *Boxoffice*, December 1985, pp. 139–140.

16. *Annual Report*, Cineplex Odeon Corporation, 1985, pp. 2, 3, 20; *Boxoffice*, November 1985, p. 22; *Variety*, 27 November 1985, p. 3; *Variety*, 4 December 1985, p. 86.

17. *Annual Report*, Cineplex Odeon Corporation, 1985, p. 3.

18. *Variety*, 22 January 1986, p. 3; *Wall Street Journal*, 16 January 1986, p. 86. The MCA Cineplex Odeon deal set off a wave of mergers. Columbia Pictures took over Loew's, Inc., while Warner Bros. and Paramount together took over a number of chains and jointly formed the Cineamerica chain.

19. *Annual Report*, Cineplex Odeon Corporation, 1986, pp. 12–16. The quotation is taken from the *Annual Report*, Cineplex Odeon Corporation, 1985, p. 13.

20. *Boxoffice*, February 1988, pp. 10–12; Richard Trainor, "Let's Get Vertical," *American Film*, vol. 13, no. 8 (June 1988): 44–45; *Variety*, 26 April–2 May 1989, pp. 54–60.

21. *Boxoffice*, February 1988, pp. 10–12; Trainor, "Let's Get Vertical," pp. 43–45; *Variety*, 26 April–2 May 1989, pp. 54–60.

22. *Annual Report*, Cineplex Odeon Corporation, 1985, p. 6.

23. *Variety*, 14 December 1983, p. 13; *Chicago Tribune*, 13 May 1986, section III, pp. 1, 6; *Annual Report*, Cineplex Odeon Corporation, 1986, p. 4; *Film Journal*, April 1986, p. 8 and May 1986, p. 4.

24. *Los Angeles Times*, part IV, 30 July 1986, p. 2; *Wall Street Journal*, 31 July 1986, p. 12; *Variety*, 25 March 1987, pp. 7, 35; *Film Journal*, April 1987, p. 6.

25. *Variety*, 30 July 1986, pp. 3, 87 and 12 November 1986, p. 3; *Film Journal*, January 1988, p. 6; *Variety*, 17 February 1988, p. 5 and 23 December 1987, pp. 3, 30.

26. Quotation from *Los Angeles Times*, 7 July 1987, section VI, pp. 1, 10; *Variety*, 29 July 1987, p. 7; *Los Angeles Times*, 16 June 1987, section IV, pp. 1, 8; *Annual Report*, Cineplex Odeon Corporation, 1986, pp. 3–5; *Variety*, 12 July 1986, p. 19 and 15 October 1986, p. 8; *Washington Post*, 26 December 1986, "Weekend Section," p. 26; *Annual Report*, Cineplex Odeon Corporation, 1986, p. 3; *Variety*, 17 December 1986, pp. 5, 105; *Film Journal*, January 1987, p. 6.

27. *Annual Report*, Cineplex Odeon Corporation, 1987, p. 4; *Wall Street Journal*, 7 May 1987, p. 59.

28. *Annual Report*, Cineplex Odeon Corporation, 1987, pp. 2–6; *Los Angeles Times*, 16 June 1987, section, VI, pp. 1, 8 and 7 July 1987, section VI, pp. 1, 10.

29. *Variety*, 24 June 1987, pp. 1, 108; *Film Journal*, January 1988, p. 6; *Variety*, 6 January 1988, p. 6; *New York Times*, 6 January 1988, pp. B1, B2.

30. *Variety*, 10 June 1987, p. 23 and 6 January 1988, p. 6; *Wall Street Journal*, 19 December 1988, p. B3; *Business Week*, 10 October 1988, p. 148.

31. *Wall Street Journal*, 4 December 1989, pp. A3, A9; *Wall Street Journal*, 7 December 1989, p. B10; *Variety*, 6 December 1989, pp. 3, 7 and 28 March 1990, p. 2; *Wall Street Journal*, 29 March 1990, p. A6; *Variety*, 4 July 1990, p. 6.

32. And the company was praised accordingly. See Ron Zemke with Dick Schaaf, *The Service Edge: 101 Companies That Profit from Customer Care* (New York: Plume, 1989), pp. 534–536.

33. As I write this at the end of 1990 there are many predictions of gloom and doom for the movie theatre business. These are due, for the most part, to the anticipated economic recession. But then moviegoing has never been recession proof. The underlying structure of the business seems sound but see *Business Week*, 3 December 1990, pp. 128–129.

34. *New York Times*, 27 April 1988, p. C17; *Variety*, 7 February 1990, p. 169; *New York Times*, 7 March 1988, p. C13.

35. *Boxoffice*, July 1989, pp. 16–17; *Variety*, 22–28 February 1989, p. 342; *Boxoffice*, December 1989, p. 14; *Forbes*, 23 July 1990, pp. 39–40; Harold L. Vogel, *Entertainment Industry Economics: A Guide for Financial Analysis*, 2d ed. (New York: Cambridge University Press, 1990), pp. 34–35.

36. *New York Times*, 28 March 1990, pp. C1, C6; *Washington Post*, 18 April 1990, pp. C1, C2. Some "cinemas" have become restaurants with films. For example, in the Washington, D.C., area two 1930s neighborhood theatres have been turned into Cinemas 'N' Drafthouses. The films are second-run; the admission prices are in the range of a dollar or two; the "theatres" serve beer to individual tables; the money is made exclusively on food, with the movies as an added attraction.

37. For more see Bruce A. Austin, *Immediate Seating: A Look at Movie Audiences* (Belmont, Calif.: Wadsworth Publishing, 1989), in particular pp. 38–43.

38. *Variety*, 29 October 1990, pp. 1, 76.

39. *Boxoffice*, March 1989, pp. 30–31; *Boxoffice*, March 1989, pp. 24, 26; *Film Journal*, February 1990, pp. 82, 84, 94–96 and September 1989, p. 24.

40. *Washington Post*, "Washington Business," 25 December 1989, p. 6; *Boxoffice*, July 1989, pp. 26–27.

41. *Boxoffice*, January 1989, p. 40.

42. *Variety*, 27 December 1989, p. 6; *Boxoffice*, December 1989, pp. 24–26.

43. *Advertising Age* 18 September 1989, p. 14; *Variety*, 28 March 1990, p. 7; *Wall Street Journal*, 9 February 1990, pp. B1, B7; Keith F. Johnson, "Cinema Advertising," *Journal of Advertising*, vol. 10, no. 4 (Winter 1981): 11–19; Kim B. Rotzoll, "The Captive Audience: The Troubled Odyssey of Cinema Advertising," in *Current Research in Film: Audiences, Economics, and Law*, ed. Bruce A. Austin (Norwood, N.J.: Ablex Publishing, 1987), pp. 72–87.

44. *Wall Street Journal*, 23 June 1989, p. B4.

45. *Washington Post*, 3 January 1990, p. B1, B4; *Film Journal*, May 1989, pp. 24, 26.

CHAPTER 7: SPECIALIZED THEATRES

1. *Newsweek*, 20 October 1934, p. 40; *Motion Picture Herald*, 23 October 1934, p. 19.

2. *Motion Picture Herald*, "Better Theatres," 8 February 1936, pp. 10–11.

3. Arthur Mayer, *Merely Colossal* (New York: Simon and Schuster, 1953), pp. 165–186.

4. *Motion Picture Herald*, 11 July 1942, p. 38 and 16 July 1946, p. 17.

5. *New York Times*, 2 February 1947, p. 44.

6. *Motion Picture News*, 13 May 1916, p. 2879; *Variety*, 13 December 1950, p. 4. Richard deCordova in a paper presented to the Society for Cinema Studies Annual Conference on 30 May 1990 in Washington, D. C., "The Hays Office and Saturday Morning Movies for Children," lays out how the Motion Picture Producers and Distributors Association (or the Hays Office) sponsored Saturday morning programs of clean movies to ward off threats of censorship.

7. *Motion Picture Herald*, 3 October 1931, pp. 21–22 and 25 December 1937, p. 57; *Theatre Catalog*, 1946–1947, pp. 476–477.

8. See my "Splendor in Paradise: The Paramount in Palm Beach," which appeared in *Marquee*, vol. 14, no. 4 (Fourth Quarter 1982): p. 3–6, for more about this unique movie theatre.

9. The Palm Beach Paramount was designed by Joseph Urban, noted theatre

and stage designer of Broadway. See Robert A. M. Stern, Gregory Gilmartin, and Thomas Mellins, *Architecture and Urbanism Between the Two World Wars* (New York: Rizzoli, 1987), pp. 235–240.

10. *Moving Picture World*, 30 April 1910, p. 1; *Film Daily*, 10 July 1923, p. 1; *Motion Picture Herald*, 28 December 1946, p. 28; John G. Bitel, "Sound Films for Passenger Trains," *Journal of the Society of Motion Picture Engineers*, January 1948, pp. 64–67; *Theatre Catalog*, 1946–47, pp. 471–474; *Motion Picture Herald*, 19 July 1952, p. 32 and 25 April 1962, pp. 9–10.

11. *Wall Street Journal*, 13 July 1982, p. 20; *Motion Picture Herald*, 12 January 1935, p. 24; *New York Times*, 24 May 1961, p. 47; Howard Coffin, "Films in Flight," *Show*, vol. I, no. 5 (May 1970): 23; *Variety*, 22 April 1981, p. 9. See also Donald William Orr, "The Impact of In-Flight Entertainment Upon Passengers on Selected Flights of a Recognized Commercial Airline," unpublished M.A. Thesis, Temple University, 1966.

12. For more on the history of the newsreel as a form see Raymond Fielding, *The American Newsreel, 1911–1967* (Norman: University of Oklahoma Press, 1972), the first nine chapters, and Adelaide F. Cumming, "A History of the American Newsreel, 1927 to 1950," unpublished Ph.D. dissertation, New York University, 1966, pp. 19–61.

13. *Variety*, 11 May 1927, p. 80 and 4 May 1927, p. 27; *Moving Picture World*, 7 May 1927, p. 28; *Variety*, 8 June 1928, p. 10; *Moving Picture World*, 11 June 1927, p. 433; *Variety*, 29 June 1927, p. 10; *Moving Picture World*, 23 July 1927, p. 1; *Variety*, 7 September 1927, p. 8; *Moving Picture World*, 1 December 1927, p. 8; *Variety*, 30 November 1927, pp. 18–19.

14. Ellen S. Thomas, " 'Scooping the Local Field': Oregon's Newsreel Industry, 1911–1933," *Oregon Historical Quarterly*, Fall 1989, pp. 229–304, describes in loving detail the competition that existed in the local market in and around Portland, Oregon. Examples could (and should) be considered in nearly all major American cities.

15. *Motion Picture News*, 9 November 1929, p. 11; *Exhibitor's Daily Review*, 2 November 1929, p. 4; *Variety*, 10 October 1929, p. 21; *Exhibitors Herald-World*, 9 November 1929, p. 21.

16. *Motion Picture Herald*, 15 April 1938, p. 50 and 28 October 1939, p. 38; Caroline Lejeune, *Cinema* (London: MacLehose, 1931), pp. 208–215; Leslie Wood, *The Miracle of the Movies*, (London: Burke, 1947), p. 190; *Motion Picture Herald*, 2 May 1936, p. 64.

17. *Motion Picture Herald*, 15 May 1937, p. 36.

18. Christine Grenz, *Trans-Lux: Biography of a Corporation* (Norwalk, Conn.: Trans-Lux Corporation, 1982), pp. 3–5.

19. Grenz, *Trans-Lux*, pp. 7–8.

20. Creighton Peet, "The New Movies: Trans-Lux," *Outlook and Independent*, 25 March 1931, p. 442.

21. *Film Daily*, 8 May 1931, pp. 1, 8.

22. Grenz, *Trans-Lux*, pp. 10–11, 28–29.

23. Hans Wirz and Richard Striner, *Washington Deco: Art Deco Design in the Nation's Capital* (Washington, D.C., Smithsonian Institution Press, 1984), p. 81.

24. James M. Goode, *Capital Losses: A Cultural History of Washington's Destroyed Buildings* (Washington, D.C.: Smithsonian Institution Press, 1979), pp. 378–380.

25. Grenz, *Trans-Lux*, pp. 31–32. In 1949 Trans-Lux had fifteen theatres, eight of which were in New York, the others in Philadelphia, Washington, D.C., and Boston.

26. *Motion Picture Herald*, 6 January 1934, p. 12.

27. *New York Times*, 20 November 1949, p. 31; *Motion Picture Herald*, 31 August 1935, p. 41; *New Yorker*, 26 November 1949, pp. 24–25.

28. *New York Times*, 20 November 1949, p. 22.

29. *Motion Picture Herald*, 15 April 1938, p. 50; T. F. Woods, "Headlines in Celluloid," *Saturday Evening Post*, 11 August 1945, p. 66.

30. "The Newsreel Boxoffice," *Fortnight*, 1 September 1952, p. 14.

31. *Motion Picture Herald*, "Better Theatres," 9 March 1940, p. 17.

32. This account of the history of the Telenews is taken from clippings in the morgue file of the *Milwaukee Journal*, in particular unpaginated items dated 22 August 1945, 26 August 1945, 24 March 1946, 18 January 1946, 18 June 1947, 10 July 1947, 11 July 1947, and 20 May 1952.

33. *Motion Picture Herald*, 9 May 1942, p. 49.

34. *Motion Picture Herald*, 4 July 1942, p. 52; 2 May 1942, p. 40; 24 January 1942, p. 21.

35. *Motion Picture Herald*, 24 January 1942, pp. 21, 35.

36. *Motion Picture Herald*, 31 January 1948, p. 15; *Variety*, 12 March 1947, p. 43; Ted Nielsen, "A History of Network Television News," in *American Broadcasting: A Source Book on the History of Radio and Television*, ed. Lawrence W. Lichty and Malachi C. Topping (New York: Hastings House, 1975), p. 426.

37. *New Yorker*, 26 November 1949, p. 24.

38. *New York Times*, 6 November 1949, Section II, p. 6 and 20 November 1949, p. 22; *Motion Picture Herald*, 11 December 1948, p. 42.

CHAPTER 8: MOVIE THEATRES FOR BLACK AMERICANS

1. African-American and black will be used interchangeably in this chapter.

2. There exists no general survey of the laws as applied to motion picture theatres, but that aspect of general recreation is covered in Robert B. McKay, "Segregation and Public Recreation," *Virginia Law Review*, vol. 40, no. 6 (October 1954): 697–731.

3. *Washington Post*, 29 April 1990, p. B12.

4. Derrick A. Bell, Jr., "The Racial Imperative in American Law," in *The Age of Segregation: Race Relations in the South, 1890–1945*, ed. Robert Haws (Jackson: University Press of Mississippi, 1978), pp. 19–20; Charles S. Mangum, Jr., *The Legal Status of the Negro* (Chapel Hill: University of North Carolina Press, 1940), pp. 55–58; Gunnar Myrdal, *An American Dilemma: The Negro Problem and Modern Democracy* (New York: Harper & Row, 1944), pp. 632–639.

5. Max W. Turner and Frank R. Kennedy, "Exclusion, Ejection, and Segregation of Theatre Patrons," *Iowa Law Review*, vol. 32, no. 4 (May 1947): 631–637.

6. Max W. Turner and Frank R. Kennedy, "Exclusion, Ejection and Segregation of Theatre Patrons," *Iowa Law Review*, vol. 32, no. 4 (May 1947): 654–657. The quotation is from p. 636. See also *Motion Picture Herald*, 10 February 1934, pp. 11–12.

7. *Moving Picture World*, 5 March 1910, p. 337.

8. The following analysis can be found in more detail in Robert C. Allen and Douglas Gomery, *Film History: Theory and Practice* (New York: Alfred A. Knopf, 1985), pp. 205–207.

9. Gregory A. Waller, "Another Audience: Black Moviegoing, 1907–1916," a paper presented at the Annual Conference of the Society for Cinema Studies, 30 May 1990.

10. *Moving Picture World*, 16 August 1919, p. 964. See also William M. Tuttle, Jr., *Race Riot: Chicago in the Summer of 1919* (New York: Atheneum, 1975), pp. 32–107 and Allan H. Spear, *Black Chicago: The Making of a Negro Ghetto, 1890–1920* (Chicago: University of Chicago Press, 1967), pp. 206–207.

11. Sharon Scott, "Imitation of Life," *AFI Report*, vol. 4, no. 2 (May 1973): 8.

12. *Motion Picture Herald*, 24 January 1942, pp. 33–34.

13. *Motion Picture Herald*, 15 August 1936, p. 27.

14. *Washington Post*, 7 June 1987, p. B5; Gregory Waller, "Another Audience," pp. 23–24.

15. *Motion Picture Herald*, 24 January 1942, pp. 33–34.

16. Scott, "Imitation of Life," p. 7.

17. Quotation in *Motography*, 30 November 1917, p. 934. See also *Film Daily Yearbook*, 1949, p. 1151.

18. Paul K. Edwards, *The Southern Urban Negro as a Consumer* (New York: Prentice Hall, 1932), pp. 183–184.

19. Quotation is from *Motion Picture News*, 30 August 1924, p. 1134. See also *New York Times*, 16 July 1925, p. 23 and Daniel J. Leab, *From Sambo to Superspade: The Black Experience in Motion Pictures* (Boston: Houghton Mifflin, 1975), p. 94.

20. "Effects of Technological Change Upon Employment in the Motion-Picture Theatres of Washington, D.C.," *Monthly Labor Review*, vol. 33, no. 5 (November 1931): 1005–1018.

21. *Motion Picture Herald*, 24 April 1937, p. 78 and 15 July 1939, pp. 41–42.

22. Thomas Cripps, *Slow Fade to Black: the Negro in American Film, 1900–1942* (New York: Oxford University Press, 1977), pp. 189–192.

23. Joe William Trotter, Jr., *Black Milwaukee: The Making of an Industrial Proletariat, 1915–1945* (Urbana: University of Illinois Press, 1985), p. 201; "Regal Theatre," *Wisconsin Enterprise Blade*, 2 November 1940, p. 1.

24. June Sawyers, "Way We Were," *Chicago Tribune Magazine*, 4 October 1987, p. 10.

25. Mangum, p. 59; *Film Daily Yearbook*, 1949, pp. 1148–1152.

26. *Motion Picture Herald*, 24 January 1942, pp. 33–34.

27. *Motion Picture Herald*, 21 March 1942, pp. 53–54.

28. *Theatre Catalog*, 1950–1951, p. 102.

29. *New York Times*, 29 October 1949, p. 21; *Variety*, 29 November 1967, p. 61.

30. Peter M. Bergman, *The Chronological History of the Negro in America* (New York: Harper & Row, 1969); Constance McLaughlin Green, *The Secret City: A History of Race Relations in the Nation's Capital* (Princeton: Princeton University Press, 1967), pp. 290, 310.

31. Beverly Jones, "Before Montgomery: The Desegregation Movement in the District of Columbia, 1950–1953," *Phylon*, vol. 43, no. 2 (June 1982): 144–154; *Variety*, 7 October 1953, p. 7; Chalmers M. Roberts, *The Washington Post: The First 100 Years* (Boston: Houghton Mifflin, 1977), pp. 292–293.

32. *Variety*, 27 January 1954, pp. 1, 69.

33. *Motion Picture Herald*, 20 June 1953, p. 35; *Variety*, 7 April 1954, p. 5 and 8 January 1958, p. 15; *New York Times*, 18 July 1957, p. 33. Quotation is from *Variety*, 13 April 1955, p. 2.

34. *Variety*, 9 March 1955, pp. 3, 18.

35. *Variety*, 31 August 1960, pp. 3, 21.

36. Marcellus C. Barksdale, "The Indigenous Civil Rights Movement and Cultural Change in North Carolina," unpublished Ph.D. dissertation, Duke University, 1977, pp. 200–206; *Variety*, 9 January 1963, p. 52; Christopher North, "Film History for Exhibitors," *Films in Review*, vol. 21 (October 1970): 477.

37. *Motion Picture Herald*, 6 May 1961, p. 20.

38. Mary Ann Watson, *The Expanding Vista: American Television in the Kennedy Years* (New York: Oxford University Press, 1990).

39. Kim Lacy Rogers, *The Desegregation of New Orleans, 1954–1966* (Minneapolis: University of Minnesota Press, 1982), pp. 14–25. See also John Blassingame, *Black New Orleans* (Chicago: University of Chicago Press, 1973).

40. *Motion Picture Herald*, 20 June 1962, p. 10; *Variety*, 29 May 1963, p. 3.

41. Arthur M. Schlesinger, Jr., *Robert Kennedy and His Times* (Boston: Houghton Mifflin, 1978), pp. 368–371; Carl M. Bauer, *John F. Kennedy and the Second Reconstruction* (New York: Columbia University Press, 1977), pp. 230–320.

42. *Variety*, 5 June 1963, p. 3. Quotation is from *Variety*, 29 May 1963, p. 3.

43. *Variety*, 29 May 1963, pp. 3, 19 and 5 June 1963, p. 3; *Motion Picture Herald*, 26 June 1963, p. 4; *Washington Post*, 23 April 1987, "Maryland Section," p. 1; *Motion Picture Herald*, 7 August 1963, p. 7; *Variety*, 5 June 1963, pp. 3, 20.

44. *Motion Picture Herald*, 11 December 1963, p. 10.

45. *Motion Picture Herald*, 22 July 1964, p. 14 and 29 April 1964, pp. 13, 23.

46. *Variety*, 14 August 1963, p. 5.

47. *Variety*, 29 July 1964, p. 29.

48. *Variety*, 21 June 1967, p. 4; *Report of the National Advisory Commission on Civil Disorders* (New York: Bantam Books, 1968), pp. 42–47.

49. *Variety*, 29 November 1967, pp. 3, 61.

50. *Variety*, 3 January 1973, p. 48; Renee Ward, "Black Films, White Profits," *The Black Scholar*, vol. 7, no. 8 (May 1976): 13–24.

51. *Boxoffice*, 2 January 1978, p. NE-4.

52. *Washington Post*, 7 January 1987, p. A16; *Variety*, 19 November 1986, p. 1.

53. *Newsweek*, 9 January 1988, pp. 26–27.

CHAPTER 9: ETHNIC THEATRES AND ART CINEMAS

1. There has been a great deal written about the immigrants who journeyed to the United States. For a good summary see James Stuart Olson, *The Ethnic Dimension in American History* (New York: St. Martin's, 1979), in particular pp. 345–358.

2. *Moving Picture World*, 2 April 1921, p. 481; 23 April 1921, p. 852; 4 June 1921, p. 501; *Motion Picture News*, 9 April 1921, p. 2470; *New York Times*, 23 December 1920, p. 28.

3. *Moving Picture World*, 21 May 1921, p. 269; 28 May 1921, pp. 388, 396; 4 June 1921, p. 526.

4. A. Scott Berg, *Goldwyn: A Biography* (New York: Random House, 1989), pp. 98–101.

5. *Motion Picture Herald*, 30 March 1935, pp. 75–76; John Larkin, Jr., "The Guild Is Here," *Theatre*, May 1926, pp. 32, 62; Michael Mindlin, "The Little Cinema Movement," *Theatre*, July 1928, pp. 18, 62; *New York Times*, 6 February 1938, p. 21.

6. *Shared Pleasures* explicitly does not deal with nonprofit-seeking film presentation. But it might be noted at this point that in the 1920s and 1930s nontheatrical screenings could be found throughout the United States, particularly in large cities. For example, the Workers International Relief and various affiliate groups sought to build a political constituency through film showings, and in the late 1930s the Museum of Modern Art and its Circulating Film Library helped promote interest in film as an art form.

7. Irving R. Glazer, *Philadelphia Theatres, A–Z* (New York: Greenwood Press, 1986), pp. 195–196.

8. *New York Times,* 8 November 1985, p. C3; *Motion Picture News,* 19 December 1925, p. 3060; *New York Times,* 6 February 1938, p. 19.

9. Donald C. King, "Wardman Park Theatre, Washington, D.C.," *Marquee,* vol. 11, no. 4 (Fourth Quarter 1979): 10.

10. Robert K. Headley, *Exit* (University Park, Md.: Privately printed, 1974), p. 91.

11. *Film Daily,* 16 August 1931, pp. 1, 3.

12. *Motion Picture Herald,* 12 November 1932, p. 18.

13. *Boxoffice,* July, 1987, p. 49.

14. Indeed some small companies began to try to compete with Hollywood by turning out specialized foreign films for selected U.S. markets. Through 1929 and 1930, for example, Empire Films of New York City produced Spanish short subjects.

15. *Variety,* 30 April 1929, p. 6 and 7 August 1929, p. 189; *Business Week,* 9 February 1930, p. 40; *Film Daily,* 23 June 1931, pp. 1, 8.

16. *Variety,* 26 March 1930, p. 10; 9 April 1930, p. 4; 30 April 1930, p. 7; *New York Times,* 27 April 1930, p. 10.

17. *Variety,* 7 January 1931, pp. 7, 78; 19 March 1931, p. 30; 6 August 1930, p. 4; 30 September 1930, p. 6; 24 December 1930, p. 6; 29 October 1930, p. 6; 15 September 1931, p. 17.

18. *Variety,* 3 November 1931, p. 15; 12 April 1932, p. 11; 16 August 1932, pp. 11, 39; 12 July 1932, pp. 13, 36; 1 November 1932, p. 11; 20 June 1933, p. 19; 1 January 1935, p. 29.

19. *Motion Picture Herald,* 15 July 1939, pp. 39–40. These nontraditional theatres also presented documentaries and rarely experimental cinema.

20. For analysis of the reactions of first-generation, working-class Americans to the movies see Lizabeth Cohen, *Making a New Deal: Industrial Workers in Chicago, 1919–1939* (New York: Cambridge University Press, 1990), pp. 122–124 and Lizabeth Cohen, "Encountering Mass Culture at the Grassroots: The Experience of Chicago Workers in the 1920s," *American Quarterly,* vol. 41, no. 1 (March 1989): 14–16.

21. *Film Daily Yearbook,* 1949, pp. 1128–1135.

22. *Motion Picture Herald,* 15 July 1939, pp. 39–40; Martin Quigley, ed., *International Motion Picture Almanac—1947–1948* (New York: Quigley Publishing Company, 1948), p. 596; *Motion Picture Herald,* 8 July 1939, p. 16 and 14 November 1931, p. 12.

23. Frances Blake, "Something New In the Motion Picture," *Close-Up,* vol. 10, no. 2 (June 1933): 155–165; *Motion Picture Herald,* 3 August 1935, p. 17.

24. *Motion Picture Herald,* 23 January 1943, p. 50; 28 September 1940, p. 129; 14 November 1942, p. 40; *New York Times,* 1 February 1942, p. 32.

25. Harris Dienstfrey, "The New American Film," in *The New American Arts*, ed. Richard Kostelanetz (New York: Horizon Press, 1965), pp. 31–49.

26. *New York Times*, 8 February 1948, p. 33; Arthur Mayer, *Merely Colossal* (New York: Simon & Schuster, 1953), pp. 215–218; *Variety*, 5 August 1987, pp. 4, 8; *New York Times*, 8 June 1947, p. 23.

27. Christine Ogan, "The Audience for Foreign Film in the United States," *Journal of Communication*, vol. 40, no. 4 (Autumn 1990): 59.

28. *Motion Picture Herald*, 17 November 1945, p. 17.

29. Thomas Guback, *The International Film Industry: Western Europe and America Since 1945* (Bloomington: Indiana University Press, 1969), pp. 68–90; Tino Balio, *United Artists: The Company that Changed the Film Industry* (Madison: University of Wisconsin Press, 1987), pp. 275–301.

30. *Motion Picture Herald*, 17 November 1945, p. 17; *New York Times*, 30 March 1947, p. 44; *Motion Picture Herald*, 17 January 1948, p. 18.

31. *New York Times*, 8 February 1948, p. 33.

32. *Film Daily Yearbook*, 1949, pp. 65–71.

33. *Motion Picture Herald*, 15 July 1950, p. 12.

34. *Motion Picture Herald*, "Better Theatres," 20 November 1948, p. 25 and 1 January 1949, p. 21; *Variety*, 23 September 1959, p. 3 and 22–28 February 1989, pp. 219, 223, 224.

35. *New York Times*, 6 November 1949, Section II, p. 5.

36. *Motion Picture Herald*, 17 January 1948, p. 18; *New York Times*, 8 June 1947, p. 23 and 8 February 1948, p. 33.

37. *Motion Picture Herald*, 25 June 1949, p. 42; *Chicago Tribune*, 2 February 1990, Section 5, pp. 1–3. By 1990 things had changed considerably and the Esquire was converted into a six-screen multiplex.

38. *Motion Picture Herald*, 1 January 1949, p. 21; *Time*, 17 October 1949, pp. 101–102; *Motion Picture Herald*, 15 July 1950, p. 12.

39. *Motion Picture Herald*, 16 February 1952, p. 24.

40. *Motion Picture Herald*, 15 July 1950, p. 12; Michael F. Mayer, *Foreign Films on American Screens* (New York: Arco, 1964), p. 106; *Motion Picture Herald*, 16 February 1952, p. 24.

41. *Motion Picture Herald*, 16 February 1952, p. 24 and 1 March 1952, p. 16.

42. *Motion Picture Herald*, 16 February 1952, p. 24 and 9 February 1952, p. 46.

43. *Motion Picture Herald*, 16 February 1952, p. 24; 7 June 1952, pp. 8–10; 24 May 1952, p. 47; *New York Times*, 4 May 1952, p. 31.

44. *Newsweek*, 28 May 1962, p. 102; *New York Times*, 21 May 1989, p. H3.

45. Stanley Frank, "Sure-Seaters Discover an Audience," *Nation's Business*, January 1952, p. 34.

46. *Variety*, 17 June 1953, p. 5; 30 September 1953, p. 3; 6 January 1954, p. 5; 29 March 1959, p. 5; 7 February 1962, p. 6; 26 April 1967, p. 41.

47. Kenneth P. Adler, "Art Films and Eggheads," *Studies in Public Communication*, vol. 2 (Summer 1959): 7–15; *Museum & Arts Washington*, November/December 1988, p. 61; *Motion Picture Herald*, 6 August 1955, pp. 24–25, 36.

48. This discussion and example are taken from David Bordwell's insightful discussion of the aesthetics of the art cinema in his *Narration in the Fiction Film* (Madison: University of Wisconsin Press, 1985), pp. 205–233.

49. *Variety*, 23 September 1953, p. 18; 30 September 1953, p. 8; 16 December 1953, p. 3; *Motion Picture Herald*, 3 April 1963, pp. 9, 28 and 27 March 1968, p. 7.

50. *Variety*, 23 September 1959, p. 3; *New York Times*, 29 April 1989, p. 10 and *New York Times*, 21 May 1989, p. H3; *Variety*, 3–9 May 1989, p. 7.

51. Arthur Knight, "A Managerial Revolution," *Saturday Review of Literature*, 18 June 1960, p. 26; *Newsweek*, 15 August 1960, p. 80.

52. *New York Times*, 12 April 1981, Section II, p. 23.

53. Bosley Crowther, "The Strange Case of "The Miracle," *Atlantic*, vol. 187 (April 1951): 35–39; *New York Times*, 8 January 1951, p. 14 and 21 January, 1951, p. 53.

54. Leonard J. Leff and Jerold L. Simmons, *The Dame in the Kimono* (New York: Grove Weidenfeld, 1990), pp. 141–161.

55. *New York Times*, 5 January 1967, p. 51.

56. The quotation is drawn from Bordwell, *Narration in the Fiction Film*, p. 232. See Bordwell's fascinating discussion on pp. 231–233.

57. *Variety*, 24 April 1957, p. 5; Christine Grenz, *Trans-Lux: Biography of a Corporation* (Norwalk, Connecticut: Trans-Lux Corporation, 1982), p. 49.

58. *Variety*, 19 February 1958, pp. 2, 16; 12 May 1965, p. 30; 11 January 1967, pp. 5, 78; 8 May 1968, p. 40.

59. The American Film Institute's *Guide to College Courses in Film and Television* (Washington, D.C.: Acropolis Books, 1973) lists some six hundred universities, four-year colleges, and junior colleges with film courses on the books by 1972. The editors claimed more than twenty thousand students were enrolled.

60. *Variety*, 4 October 1972, p. 6; *Boxoffice*, 2 June 1980, pp. 1, 4; *Variety*, 25 September 1985, p. 5.

61. *Variety*, 7 May 1980, pp. 11, 344; 3 February 1982, pp. 43, 52; 12 December 1984, p. 88; 11 March 1987, p. 23.

62. *New York Times*, 20 May 1988, pp. C1, C10; *Boxoffice*, June 1989, pp. 30–31.

63. *Variety*, 23 March 1955, pp. 3, 61; J. Blair Watson, Jr., "The Dartmouth Film Society," *Films in Review*, November 1953, pp. 467–471; Joseph L. Anderson, "Antioth's Film Activity," *Films in Review*, May 1953, pp. 215–219; *Variety*, 13 February 1980, p. 7; *Boxoffice*, November 1982, pp. 12–13.

64. *Variety*, 5 November 1980, pp. 6, 36; J. Hoberman and Jonathan Rosenbaum, *Midnight Movies* (New York: Harper & Row, 1983), pp. 1–14; Stuart

Samuels, *Midnight Movies* (New York: Collier, 1983), pp. 7–13; *Boxoffice*, February 1990, pp. 107–108.

65. *Boxoffice*, 17 January 1977, p. SW-1; 18 December 1978, p. SW-1; 31 July 1978, p. SE-7; 7 August 1978, p. SW-1; 13 November 1978, p. NC-4; 8 January 1979, p. ME-4.

66. *Variety*, 28 March 1990, p. 7; *Washington Post*, 13 October 1986, p. D1; *Newsweek*, 8 June 1987, pp. 76–77; *Boxoffice*, September 1986, pp. 25–26; *New York Times*, 22 August 1987, p. 9; 13 August 1987, p. C23; 25 March 1990, p. 34; *Variety*, 22 August 1990, p. 26.

67. *New York Times*, 18 July 1987, p. 9 and 11 September 1987, pp. B1, B4; *Boxoffice*, January 1989, p. 22.

68. *Wall Street Journal*, 6 April 1988, p. 30; *Variety*, 25 November 1987, p. 22.

69. Ogan, "The Audience for Foreign Film in the United States," pp. 70–74.

CHAPTER 10: SOUND

1. *Film Daily Yearbook*, 1927, p. 3; Benjamin B. Hampton, *A History of the Movies* (New York: Covici Friede, 1931), pp. 358–368; Jesse L. Lasky, "Hearing Things in the Dark," *Colliers*, 25 May 1929, p. 48.

2. William A. Johnson, "The Structure of the Motion Picture Industry," *Society of Motion Picture Engineers Transactions*, April 1927, pp. 667–675; William A. Johnson, "The Motion Picture Industry," *The Annals of the American Academy*, vol. 127 (September 1927): 100; *Film Daily Yearbook*, 1927, pp. 649–671; *Variety*, 12 May 1926, p. 5.

3. *Motion Picture News*, 25 November 1922, p. 2644; *Film Daily*, 24 October 1926, p. 9; Russell Sanjek, *American Popular Music and Its Business: The First Four Hundred Years*, vol. III, from 1900 to 1984 (New York: Oxford University Press, 1988), pp. 48–50.

4. A typical guidebook of the day is Erno Rapee, *Motion Picture Moods for Pianists and Organists* (New York: Schirmer, 1924). See also George W. Beynon, *Musical Presentation of Motion Pictures* (New York: Schirmer, 1921), the introduction to Gillian B. Anderson, *Music for Silent Films: 1894–1929: A Guide* (Washington, D. C.: Library of Congress, 1988), and E. C. Mills, "The Musician, the Movie, and the Music Tax," *The Metronome*, 15 September 1926, p. 26.

5. *Variety*, 1 April 1926, p. 36; Eric T. Clarke, "An Exhibitor's Problems in 1925, *Transactions of the Society of Motion Pictures Engineers*, January 1926, pp. 47–49.

6. Ben M. Hall, *The Best Remaining Seats* (New York: Bramhall House, 1961), pp. 200–210; Lewis W. Townsend and William W. Hennessy, "Some Novel Projected Motion Picture Presentations," *Society of Motion Picture Engineers Transactions*, June 1928, pp. 345–354; *Variety*, 10 March 1926, p. 35. Indeed *Variety*

regularly reviewed presentation acts from the major theatres in Chicago, New York, and Los Angeles.

7. *Exhibitor's Herald*, 28 August 1926, p. 50; *Motion Picture News*, 25 November 1922, p. 2644; Clarke, "An Exhibitor's Problems in 1925," p. 46.

8. *Variety*, 10 November 1926, p. 9; 17 November 1926, p. 13; 24 November 1926, p. 5; *Moving Picture World*, 11 December 1926, p. 416; 25 December 1926, p. 577; 8 January 1927, p. 93.

9. *Variety*, 20 October 1926, p. 64; 23 March 1927, pp. 14–15; 6 April 1927, pp. 31, 34; 2 May 1927, p. 1; 13 April 1927, p. 30.

10. *Variety*, 9 February 1927, p. 28; *Moving Picture World*, 19 February 1927, p. 566; *Variety*, 2 March 1927, p. 1 and 13 April 1927, p. 5; *Moving Picture World*, 15 January 1927, pp. 1–2; *Variety*, 13 April 1927, p. 14 and 20 April 1927, p. 6; *Moving Picture World*, 2 May 1927, p. 783 and 29 January 1927, p. 1.

11. *The New Orleans Times Picayune*, 29 June 1928, p. 26; 8 July 1928, Section 4, p. 7; 5 August 1928, Section 4, p. 8.

12. *The Jazz Singer* did well at the box office but failed to better records set just a few years earlier by *Four Horsemen of the Apocalypse* (1921), *The Big Parade* (1925), and *Ben Hur* (1926). Appropriately skeptics of the day questioned the staying power of talkies. If features with sound were so great, why didn't *The Jazz Singer* move to the top of the all-time box-office list?

13. *The Singing Fool* spilled over into other popular entertainment markets. Gossett and Dunlap publishers issued a "novelized" version of the film complete with "illustrated scenes" (seven publicity production stills) from the "photoplay starring Al Jolson." Two songs from the film, "Sonny Boy" and "There's a Rainbow 'Round My Shoulder" went on to comprise the first million-selling phonograph record of the talkie era. Both also sold a million copies in sheet music. See Douglas Gomery, "Warner Bros. Innovates Sound: A Business History," in *The Movies in Our Midst*, ed. Gerald Mast (Chicago: University of Chicago Press, 1982), pp. 267–281.

14. *Paramount Publix Corporation v. American Tri-Ergon Corporation*, 292 U.S. 464 (1935), Record, pp. 410–412; In the Matter of William Fox, Bankruptcy Number 24431 (New Jersey, 1936), testimony of William Fox, pp. 117–146; *Altoona Publix Theatres, Inc. v. American Tri-Ergon Corporation*, 294 U.S. 477 (1935), Record, pp. 233–240.

15. *Variety*, 4 May 1927, p. 27; 11 May 1927, p. 80; 25 May 1927, pp. 9, 18; 1 June 1927, p. 25; 15 June 1927, p. 28; *Moving Picture World*, 28 May 1927, p. 248.

16. Altoona Publix Theatres, 294 U.S. 477, Record, p. 243; *Variety*, 17 August 1927, p. 12; 7 September 1927, p. 8; 21 September 1927, pp. 1, 20, and 23; 30 November 1927, pp. 18–19; 16 May 1928, passim; 1 August 1928, pp. 16, 22; 5 December 1928, p. 7.

17. For more on the adoption of talkies by the major studios see Douglas

Gomery, "The 'Warner-Vitaphone Peril': The American Film Industry Reacts to the Innovation of Sound," *Journal of the University Film Association*, vol. 28, no. 1 (Winter 1976): 11–20.

18. *Variety*, 18 July 1928, p. 20; 29 May 1929, p. 30; 17 July 1929, p. 5; 8 May 1929, p. 29; 7 August 1929, p. 185; *The Motion Picture*, September 1928, p. 4.

19. *The Motion Picture*, September 1929, p. 3.

20. *Variety*, 6 February 1929, p. 5; 9 April 1930, p. 2; 14 May 1930, p. 4; 25 June 1930, p. 14; Martin Quigley, ed., *The International Motion Picture Almanac—1931* (New York: Quigley Publishing Company, 1931), p. 294.

21. *Variety*, 20 February 1928, p. 11; 5 December 1928, p. 16; 19 December 1928, p. 15; 17 April 1929, p. 31; 23 January 1929, p. 23; 30 January 1929, p. 7; 27 February 1929, p. 68; 21 August 1929, p. 21.

22. *Variety*, 30 January 1929, p. 17; 3 April 1929, p. 63; 13 June 1928, p. 24; 24 April 1929, p. 25; 20 February 1929, p. 30.

23. *Business Week*, 17 September 1930, p. 23; *Variety*, 16 February 1927, p. 7; *Moving Picture World*, 4 April 1927, p. 10; *Variety*, 19 April 1927, p. 1 and 11 May 1927, p. 73; *Moving Picture World*, 21 May 1927, p. 1; *Variety*, 15 June 1927, p. 19 and 22 June 1927, p. 19.

24. *Variety*, 22 June 1927, p. 7; *Moving Picture World*, 9 April 1927, p. 1; *Variety*, 13 July 1927, p. 55; 14 December 1927, p. 11; 19 September 1928, p. 18; 3 October 1928, p. 7; 14 December 1927, p. 11; 9 January 1919, p. 4; 10 April 1929, p. 28; 6 March 1929, p. 23; 15 May 1929, p. 29; 2 October 1929, p. 29.

25. William H. Bristol, "Talking and Synchronized Motion Pictures, *Journal of the Franklin Institute*, vol. 205, no. 2 (February 1928): 179–196; *Variety*, 4 January 1928, pp. 1, 8; *New York Times*, 15 May 1929, p. 46.

26. *Variety*, 1 August 1928, p. 5 and 15 August 1928, p. 20; *Film Daily Yearbook*, 1929, p. 889; *Variety*, 31 October 1928, p. 5; 17 October 1928, p. 20; 7 November 1928, p. 12; 12 September 1928, p. 23; 15 May 1929, p. 15; 24 October 1929, p. 15; 24 October 1928, p. 4; 7 November 1928, p. 4; 25 December 1929, p. 9.

27. *Variety*, 2 January 1929, p. 28; 23 January 1929, p. 14; 6 February 1929, p. 27; *New York Times*, 2 April 1929, p. 12; *Variety*, 22 May 1929, p. 32.

28. *Variety*, 2 January 1929, p. 28; 23 January 1929, p. 14; 18 July 1929, p. 5; 11 July 1929, p. 7.

29. Francis E. Ziesse, "America's Highest Paid Labor," *American Federationist*, vol. 37, no. 5 (May 1930): 570–575; *Variety*, 30 May 1928, p. 21 and 25 July 1982, pp. 4, 37; "Effects of Technological Changes Upon Employment in Motion Picture Theatres of Washington, D.C.," *Monthly Labor Review*, vol. 33, no. 11 (November 1931): 1007–1111; "Effects of Technological Changes Upon Employment in the Amusement Industry," *Monthly Labor Review*, vol. 33, no. 8 (August 1931): 263–266.

30. *Variety*, 7 March 1928, p. 12 and 22 August 1928, p. 24.

31. *New York Times*, 30 June 1928, p. 24; *Variety*, 13 June 1928, p. 20; *New York Times*, 20 July 1928, p. 21.

32. *Variety*, 18 July 1928, p. 19; 1 August 1928, p. 14; 22 August 1928, pp. 24, 37.

33. *New York Times*, 2 September 1928, Section II, p. 9 and 3 September 1928, p. 14; *Variety*, 12 September 1928, p. 11.

34. *Variety*, 21 November 1928, p. 57; 22 May 1929, p. 6; 9 January 1929, p. 27; 12 September 1928, p. 17; 15 May 1929, p. 64; 8 May 1929, p. 71.

35. *Variety*, 13 February 1985, p. 7; Michael Arick, "In Stereo! The Sound of Money," *Sight and Sound*, Winter 1987/1988, pp. 14–15.

36. For the most comprehensive account of the introduction of magnetic tape technology see William Charles Lafferty, Jr., "The Early Development of Magnetic Sound Recording in Broadcasting and Motion Pictures, 1928–1950," unpublished Ph.D. dissertation, Northwestern University, 1981, in particular pp. 150–219.

37. Hazard E. Reeves, "The Development of Stereo Magnetic Recording for Film: Part I," *SMPTE Journal*, October 1952, pp. 947–953; Hazard E. Reeves, "The Development of Stereo Magnetic Recording for Film: Part II," *SMPTE Journal*, November 1982, pp. 1087–1090.

38. *Variety*, 25 March 1953, pp. 4, 22; *Film Daily Yearbook*, 1954, p. 817; *Motion Picture Herald*, 4 July 1953, "Better Theatres," pp. 11, 13.

39. *New York Times*, 12 April 1977, p. 23; *Premiere*, November 1987, p. 9.

40. *Motion Picture Herald*, "Modern Theatres," 15 November 1976, p. 28; *Boxoffice*, 16 October 1978, p. SE-1; *Film Journal*, September 1980, pp. 23–24; *American Cinematographer*, vol. 56, no. 9 (September 1975): 1032–1033, 1088–1091.

41. *New York Times*, 29 November 1987, p. F6; *Los Angeles Times*, 29 January 1988, Part V, p. 2; Russell Sanjek, *American Popular Music and Its Business: The First Four Hundred Years*, vol. III, From 1900 to 1984 (New York: Oxford University Press, 1988), pp. 551, 598.

42. Rich Warren, "Ray Dolby: Quiet on the Set," *Video*, April 1988, p. 61; *Boxoffice*, 21 August 1978, p. 19; *Film Journal*, April 1980, p. 45.

43. *Boxoffice*, 21 August 1978, p. 19; *Variety*, 5 September 1979, p. 6 and 31 October 1984, pp. 7, 44; *Video*, September 1989, p. 31.

44. *Boxoffice*, December 1985, pp. 118–119; *Film Journal*, August 1984, p. 23 and August 1987, pp. 38–40.

CHAPTER 11: COLOR AND WIDE-SCREEN IMAGES

1. *Variety*, 14 October 1959, pp. 1, 13; Henry Hart, "Aromarama," *Films in Review*, vol. 11, no. 1 (January 1960): 35–36; *Variety*, 2 December 1959, p. 5; Herb A.

Lightman, "The Movie Has Scents!" *American Cinematographer*, February 1960, pp. 92–93, 120.

2. Federal Communications Commission, Docket 10036 et al. Barney Balaban's testimony, pp. 1382–1390; *Broadcasting*, 15 August 1938, p. 77; 15 November 1938, p. 17; 15 January 1939, p. 25; 1 March 1943, p. 79; 18 December 1944, p. 18; *Variety*, 1 May 1938, p. 4 and 24 August 1938, p. 6; *Broadcasting*, 27 November 1944, p. 71 and 2 July 1945, p. 30; *Variety*, 7 November 1945, p. 3; 30 January 1946, p. 32; 24 April, 1946, p. 28; 1 May 1946, p. 34; 12 May 1948, p. 18; 30 June 1948, p. 3.

3. Barton Kreuzer, "Progress Report—Theatre Television," *Journal of the Society of Motion Picture Engineers*, vol. 53, no. 2 (August 1949): 128–136; Theatre Television Committee, "Theatre Television," *Journal of the Society of Motion Picture Engineers*, vol. 52, no. 3 (March 1949): 243–267; William Snyder, "Television Developments," *Film Daily Yearbook*, 1947, p. 89.

4. John E. McCoy and Harry P. Warner, "Theatre Television Today—Part I," *Hollywood Quarterly*, vol. 4, no. 2 (Winter 1949): 160–177; *Motion Picture Herald*, 5 March 1949, p. 32; Roy Wilcox and H. J. Schlafly, "Demonstration of Larger Screen Television in Philadelphia," *Journal of the Society of Motion Picture Engineers*, vol. 52, no. 5 (May 1949): 549–560; Ralph V. Little, "Developments in Larger-Screen Television," *Journal of the Society of Motion Picture Engineers*, vol. 51, no. 1 (July 1948): 37–46.

5. Richard Hodgson, "Theatre Television System," *Journal of the Society of Motion Picture Engineers*, vol. 52, no. 5 (May 1949): 540–548.

6. *Motion Picture Herald*, 8 October 1949, p. 19; *Variety*, 4 February 1948, p. 6; 28 April 1948, p. 3; 26 May 1948, p. 5; 7 July 1948, pp. 5 and 18; 8 March 1950, pp. 7, 20; McCoy and Warner, "Theatre Television Today—Part I," pp. 162–163.

7. Paramount's failure in theatre television is explored in some detail in Timothy R. White, "Hollywood's Attempt to Appropriate Television: The Case of Paramount Pictures," unpublished Ph.D. dissertation, University of Wisconsin, Madison, 1990.

8. *Variety*, 29 December 1948, p. 5; 27 April 1949, pp. 1, 63; 2 November 1949, pp. 4, 5; 11 May 1949, p. 1; 27 June 1951, pp. 1, 63; 24 September 1952, p. 1; 17 December 1952, p. 4.

9. Herbert Kalmus, "Technicolor and New Screen Techniques," in *New Screen Techniques*, ed. Martin Quigley, Jr. (New York: Quigley Publishing Company, 1953), pp. 78–81.

10. Fred E. Basten, *Glorious Technicolor: The Movies' Magic Rainbow* (New York: A. S. Barnes, 1980), pp. 29–46.

11. J. A. Ball, "The Technicolor Process of Three-Color Cinematography," *Journal of the Society of Motion Picture Engineers*, vol. 25, no. 2 (August 1935):

127–138; Basten, *Glorious Technicolor*, pp. 47–52; Rudy Behlmer, "Technicolor," *Films in Review*, vol. 15, no. 6 (June–July 1964): 333–351.

12. Richard Schickel, *The Disney Version* (New York: Simon and Schuster, 1968), pp. 123–125; Bob Thomas, *Walt Disney: An American Original* (New York: Simon and Schuster, 1976), pp. 114–115; *Business Week*, 22 May 1937, p. 49; E. J. Kahn, Jr., *Jock: The Life and Times of John Hay Whitney* (Garden City, N.Y.: Doubleday, 1981), pp. 105–108; Herbert T. Kalmus, "Adventures in Cinemaland," in Raymond Fielding, A *Technological History of Motion Pictures and Television* (Berkeley: University of California Press, 1967), pp. 52–59.

13. Technicolor, Inc.'s total profits hardly matched the millions regularly accumulated by giants Loew's, Warner Bros., Twentieth Century-Fox, or Paramount, but the company did consistently equal the yearly profits established by RKO, Universal, Columbia, and United Artists.

14. *Fortune*, vol. 13 (June 1935): 40, 46, 54; *Motion Picture Herald*, 25 May 1935, pp. 11–13; Roderick T. Ryan, A *History of Motion Picture Color Technology* (London: The Focal Press, 1977), pp. 77–82; F. J. Taylor, "Mr. Technicolor," *Saturday Evening Post*, vol. 222 (22 October 1949): 26–27, 131–135; *Business Week*, 22 May 1947, p. 47; the exhibits in *United States v. Technicolor, Inc., Technicolor Motion Picture Corp., and Eastman Kodak Co.*, No. 7507-WM (S.D. California), 1947–1950.

15. Basten, *Glorious Technicolor*, pp. 137–157; Michael Conant, *Antitrust in the Motion Picture Industry* (Berkeley: University of California Press, 1960), p. 197; testimony and exhibits in *United States v. Technicolor, Inc., Technicolor Motion Picture Corp., and Eastman Kodak Co.*, No. 7507-WM (S.D. California), 1947–1950.

16. *Business Week*, 18 August 1956, p. 146; James L. Limbacher, *Four Aspects of Film* (New York: Brussel and Brussel, 1968), pp. 26–48; Gorham A. Kindem, "Hollywood's Conversion to Color: The Technological, Economic, and Aesthetic Factors," in *The American Movie Industry: The Business of Motion Pictures*, ed. Gorham A. Kindem (Carbondale, Ill.: Southern Illinois University press, 1982), pp. 143–154.

17. *Motion Picture Herald*, 6 August 1955, p. 14.

18. Henry Hart, "Cinerama," *Films in Review*, vol. 3, no. 9 (November 1952): 433–435; John W. Boyle, "And Now . . . Cinerama," *American Cinematographer*, November 1952, pp. 480–481; Walter Beyer, "Wide Screen Production Systems," *American Cinematographer*, May 1962, p. 296, 309; Jack Gieck, "Backstage at Cinerama," *International Projectionist*, May 1954, pp. 16, 30–31; *Variety*, 11 February 1953, p. 3; Michael Z. Wysotsky, *Wide Screen Cinema and Stereophonic Sound* (New York: Hastings House, 1971), pp. 59–61; LeRoy Chadbourne, "1952: A Wonder Year for Progress," *International Projectionist*, January 1953, p. 12.

19. Alden P. Armagnac, "Supermovies Put You in the Show," *Popular Sci-*

ence, vol. 157 (August 1950): 74–78; *Variety*, 12 March 1952, p. 7 and 19 March 1952, pp. 2, 63; *New York Times*, 4 October 1953, p. 53; *Business Week*, 8 November 1952, p. 132; *Variety*, 26 May 1954, pp. 4, 18; 19 November 1952, pp. 5, 21; 22 October 1952, pp. 3, 18; *Hollywood Reporter*, 20 October 1952, pp. 1, 7; *Motion Picture Herald*, 3 January 1953, p. 35; *Variety*, 11 July 1951, p. 7.

20. *Motion Picture Herald*, 8 January 1955, p. 39 and 8 January 1955, p. 39; *Variety*, 22 June 1960, p. 5; *Business Week*, 28 July 1962, p. 128; *Variety*, 16 December 1959, p. 5; *Film Daily Yearbook*, 1966, p. 12; John Belton, "Cinerama: A New Era in the Cinema," *The Perfect Vision*, vol. I, no. 4 (Spring/Summer 1988): 78–90.

21. *Variety*, 22 April 1953, p. 7 and 18 March 1953, p. 7; *Chicago Daily News*, 14 January 1953, p. 35; *Variety*, 28 December 1949, pp. 1, 49; 22 February 1950, p. 7; 4 March 1953, p. 7; *Motion Picture Herald*, 3 January 1953, p. 35 and 26 June 1963, p. 15; *Variety*, 12 June 1963, pp. 3, 17 and 5 August 1953, pp. 3, 18; *Hollywood Reporter*, 5 August 1953, pp. 1, 5 and 7 September 1954, p. 1.

22. Richard C. Hawkins, "Perspective on 3-D," *Quarterly of Film, Radio and Television*, vol. 7, no. 4 (Summer 1953): 325–334; *New York Times*, 28 November 1952, p. 57; *Motion Picture Herald*, 31 January 1953, p. 12; *Variety*, 5 October 1949, pp. 1, 55; *New York Times*, 8 December 1935, p. 55. For a review of the failed attempts at 3-D prior to the 1950s see Edward Connor, "3-D on the Screen," *Films in Review*, vol. 17, no. 3 (March 1966): 159–174.

23. *New York Times*, 3 June 1951, p. 56; *Variety*, 4 February 1953, p. 7 and 18 February 1953, p. 7.

24. *Variety*, 29 April 1953, p. 4; *New York Times*, 18 October 1953, p. 55; *Theatre Catalog*, 1954–1955, pp. 281–284; Alan D. Williams, "3-D System Formats," *American Cinematographer*, July 1983, pp. 24–25; Lenny Lipton, "A Plea for Technical Standards in 3-D," *American Cinematographer*, July 1983, pp. 32–33; *Variety*, 5 August 1981, p. 7; 2 September 1981, pp. 1, 76; 1 December 1982, pp. 5, 28; 17 February 1982, p. 1; Linda Lovely, "Jaws 3-D," *American Cinematographer*, July 1983, pp. 60–61, 92; *Forbes*, 27 September 1982, p. 176; *Boxoffice*, November 1982, pp. 16–17; *Variety*, 9 February 1983, pp. 4, 46; *Boxoffice*, July 1982, pp. 41–42.

25. *Motion Picture Herald*, 28 June 1952, p. 14; *New York Times*, 2 February 1953, p. 57; *Motion Picture Herald*, 7 February 1953, p. 12; 19 September 1953, pp. 13–14; 26 September 1953, p. 16; 2 May 1953, p. 21.

26. *Motion Picture Herald*, 26 September 1953, pp. 18, 20; *New York Times*, 19 March 1952, p. 41 and 21 March 1953, p. 36; *Motion Picture Herald*, 28 March 1953, pp. 12, 14 and 21 November 1953, pp. 13–14.

27. *Film Daily*, 16 November 1953, pp. 1, 11 and 19 November 1953, pp. 1, 11; *Variety*, 21 October 1953, p. 11; *Motion Picture Herald*, 14 November 1953, p. 23; 23 January 1954, p. 19; 15 January 1955, p. 20; *Variety*, 12 March 1952, p. 1; Derek J. Southall, "Twentieth Century-Fox Presents a CinemaScope Pic-

ture," *Focus on Film*, no. 31 (November 1978): 8–26, 47; *Boxoffice*, 24 April 1954, p. 11 and 8 May 1954, pp. 8–10; *Motion Picture Herald*, 22 May 1954, p. 20 and 5 February 1955, p. 19; *Variety*, 13 May 1953, pp. 5, 26 and 21 October 1953, pp. 11, 22.

28. C. R. Daily, "New Paramount Lightweight Horizontal-Movement Vista-Vision Camera," *SMPTE Journal*, vol. 65, no. 5 (May 1956): 279–281; *Boxoffice*, 20 March 1954, p. 12; *Motion Picture Herald*, "Better Theatres," 8 May 1954, pp. 13–14, 80–81.

29. *Theatre Catalog*, 1954–1955, pp. 232–239; *Motion Picture Herald*, 23 April 1955, p. 20; 23 October 1954, p. 23; 1 May 1954, pp. 12–13.

30. *Film Daily Year Book–1955*, p. 59; *Variety*, 31 August 1960, p. 3; *Motion Picture Herald*, 26 March 1955, p. 18.

31. *Film Daily*, 7 April 1958, pp. 5–13; *Cue*, 5 April 1958, p. 12; *International Photographer*, June 1957, pp. 5–8; Henry Hart, "De Rochemont's 'Windjammer,'" *Films in Review*, vol. 9, no. 5 (May 1958): 235–240; *Variety*, 29 June 1955, pp. 7, 20 and 21 May 1958, p. 13.

32. For an encyclopedic survey of the various wide-screen formats and their special sound systems see Robert E. Carr and R. M. Hayes, *Wide Screen Movies: A History and Filmography of Wide Gauge Filmmaking* (Jefferson, N.C.: McFarland & Company, 1988). See also *Film Daily Yearbook–1955*, p. 59; *Variety*, 1 April 1953, p. 29; *Theatre Catalog*, 1955–1956, pp. 250–254.

33. Michael Todd, Jr. and Susan McCarthy Todd, *A Valuable Property: The Life Story of Michael Todd* (New York: Arbor House, 1983), pp. 245–303; Arthur Rowan, "Todd-AO—Newest Wide-Screen System," *American Cinematographer*, (October 1954): 494–496, 526; *Business Week*, 1 October 1955, pp. 176–180.

34. *Variety*, 4 February 1953, p. 3.

35. *Variety*, 24 July 1957, p. 29; 5 November 1958, p. 20; 7 May 1958, p. 13; *Motion Picture Herald*, 14 February 1953, pp. 12, 13 and 24 March 1956, pp. 20–21; *Theatre Catalog*, 1955–1956, pp. 206–207; Ralph H. Heacock, "Wide Screens in Drive-in Theatres," *Journal of the SMPTE*, vol. 64, no. 2 (February 1955): 86–87.

36. *Boxoffice*, 8 August 1977, p. 12; *Film Journal*, 13 May 1983, p. 13.

37. *Los Angeles Times*, 24 January 1985, Section VII, pp. 1, 5; Robert E. Gottschalk, "A History of Anamorphic Photography in Modern Motion Picture Production," in *American Cinematographer Manual*, ed. Charles G. Clarke (Hollywood: American Society of Cinematographers, 1980), pp. 264–265; *New York Times*, 30 October 1957, p. 24; *Los Angeles Times*, 3 September 1987, Part IV, p. 3; Scott Henderson, "The Panavision Story," *American Cinematographer*, (April 1977): 414–415, 422, 423, 432.

38. Wesley T. Hanson, Jr., "Color Negative and Color Positive Film for Motion Picture Use," *SMPTE Journal*, vol. 58, no. 3 (March 1952): 223–238; Wesley T. Hanson, Jr., "The Evolution of Eastman Color Motion Pictures," *SMPTE Jour-*

nal, vol. 90, no. 9 (September 1981): 791–794; Brian Coe, *The History of Movie Photography* (Westfield, N.J.: Eastview Editions, 1981), pp. 138–139.

39. Ryan, *A History of Motion Picture Color Technology*, pp. 148–180.

40. Carr and Hayes, *Wide Screen Movies*, pp. 187–189, 200–206.

CHAPTER 12: MOVIES ON TELEVISION

1. Orton Hicks and Haven Falconer, "MGM Television Survey: Interim Report," 29 April 1955, Dore Schary Collection, Wisconsin Center for Film and Theatre Research, Madison, Wisconsin, pp. 1–11; *Broadcasting*, 17 January 1955, pp. 50–51; the Record in *Gene Autry v. Republic*, 213 F. 2d 667 (1954); *Sponsor*, 2 June 1950, p. 31.

2. Paul R. Gagne, *The Zombies That Ate Pittsburgh: The Films of George A. Romero* (New York: Dodd, Mead, 1987), p. 12.

3. Hicks and Falconer, "MGM Television Survey," pp. 14–25; *Broadcasting*, 15 March 1954, p. 35 and 19 December 1955, p. 40; *Variety*, 1 May 1957, p. 50; *Broadcasting*, 23 April 1956, p. 96; Richard Austin, *Corporations in Crisis* (Garden City, N.Y.: Doubleday, 1966), pp. 64–66.

4. *Broadcasting*, 5 March 1956, p. 42; 23 April 1956, p. 98; *Broadcasting*, 30 August 1954, p. 58; 27 August 1956, p. 68; 25 June 1956, pp. 50–53; *Variety*, 6 March 1957, p. 25; *Business Week*, 1 September 1956, pp. 62–64; *Variety*, 1 May 1957, p. 50.

5. *Broadcasting*, 2 January 1956, p. 7; 23 April 1956, p. 98; 21 May 1956, p. 52; 25 June 1956, p. 48; 27 August 1956, p. 68; 5 November 1956, p. 48; *Variety*, 6 March 1957, p. 25 and 5 June 1957, p. 27; Stanley Brown, "That Old Villain TV Comes to the Rescue and Hollywood Rides Again," *Fortune* (November 1966): 270–272.

6. Hollis Alpert, "Now the Earlier, Earlier Show," *New York Times Magazine*, 11 August 1963, p. 22; *Radio-Television Daily*, 29 July 1960, p. 27.

7. David F. Prindle, *The Politics of Glamour: Ideology and Democracy in the Screen Actors Guild* (Madison: University of Wisconsin Press, 1988), pp. 82–90.

8. *Broadcasting*, 17 December 1956, p. 27; *Television*, January 1956, p. 39.

9. *Radio-Television Daily*, 30 July 1962, p. 32; *Variety*, 21 June 1972, p. 34 and *Variety*, 20 September 1978, pp. 48, 66; Cobbett S. Steinberg, *Reel Facts* (New York: Random House, 1978), pp. 355–357; Tim Brooks and Earle Marsh, *The Complete Directory to Prime Time Network TV Shows, 1946–Present* (New York: Ballantine, 1979), pp. 416–420.

10. *Motion Picture Herald*, 18 January 1967, p. 1; Neil Hickey, "The Day the Movies Ran Out," *TV Guide*, 23 October 1965, pp. 6–9; Steinberg, *Reel Facts*, pp. 355–357; Brooks and Marsh, *The Complete Directory to Prime Time Network TV Shows*, pp. 416–420.

11. Ryland A. Taylor, "The Repeat Audience for Movies on TV," *Journal of Broadcasting*, vol. 17, no. 1 (Winter 1972–1973), pp. 95–100.

12. Ryland A. Taylor, "Television Movie Audiences and Movie Awards: A Statistical Study," *Journal of Broadcasting*, vol. 18, no. 2 (Spring 1974): 181–186.

13. Jon Krampner, "In the Beginning . . . The Genesis of the Telefilm," *Emmy*, vol. 11, no. 6 (December 1989): 30–35; Henry Harding, "First Attempts at Making Movies for TV," *TV Guide*, 4 July 1964, p. 14; Alvin H. Marill, *Movies Made for Television* (Westport, Conn.: Arlington House, 1980), pp. 1–12.

14. *Variety*, 18 August 1971, p. 30 and 14 June 1972, p. 29; *Broadcasting*, 15 January 1973, p. 37; *Washington Post*, 6 October 1974, pp. E1–E2; Douglas Stone, "TV Movies and How They Get That Way," *Journal of Popular Film and Television*, vol. 7, no. 2 (1979): 147–149.

15. Dick Adler and Joseph Finnigan, "The Year America Stayed Home for the Movies," *TV Guide*, 20 May 1972, pp. 6–10; *Broadcasting*, 25 September 1972, p. 61 and 15 January 1973, p. 37; Caroline Meyer, "The Rating Power of Network Movies," *Television*, vol. 25, no. 3 (March 1968): 56, 84; Joseph R. Dominick and Millard C. Pearce, "Trends in Network Prime-Time Programming, 1953–74," *Journal of Communication*, vol. 26, no. 1 (Winter 1976): 74–75.

16. Patrick McGilligan, "Movies Are Better Than Ever—on Television," *American Film*, vol. 5, no. 5 (March 1980): 52–53.

17. Cobbett S. Steinberg, *TV Facts* (New York: Facts on File, 1980), pp. 172, 181; Brooks and Marsh, *The Complete Directory to Prime Time Network Programs*, pp. 419–420; *New York Times*, 28 January 1972, p. 91.

18. *Variety*, 8 December 1971, p. 34; John W. Ravage, *Television: The Director's Viewpoint* (Boulder, Colo.: Westview Press, 1978), pp. 103–112; Christopher Wicking and Tise Vahimagi, *The American Vein: Directors and Directions in Television* (New York: E. P. Dutton, 1979), pp. 27–28.

19. Martin Kasindorf, "Movies Made for Television," *Action*, January/February 1974, pp. 13–15; Eileen Lois Becker, "The Network Television Decision Making Process: A Descriptive Examination of the Process within the Framework of Prime-Time Made-for-TV Movies," unpublished M.A. thesis, University of California at Los Angeles, pp. 19–56; *Variety*, 8 December 1971, p. 34; *New York Times*, 28 January 1972, p. 91; *Variety*, 15 December 1971, p. 29.

20. Peter J. Dekom, ed., *The Selling of Motion Pictures in the '80s: New Producer/Distributor/Exhibitor Relationships* (Los Angeles: Privately published, 1980), pp. 302–312.

21. *Electronic Media*, 30 April 1990, pp. 3, 54.

22. Tom Link, "The Last Picture Format," *Emmy*, May/June 1984, p. 30. In 1990 CBS broke pay cable's decade-long hold on the right of first presenting blockbuster features by signing with Universal for premiere television rights (after home video) for ten films including *Born on the Fourth of July* and *Do the Right Thing*. It is too early to tell if this is a trend or aberration. See *Electronic Media*, 9 April

1990, pp. 1, 89, and *Wall Street Journal*, 9 April 1990, pp. B1, B4.

23. Susan Tyler Eastman, Sydney W. Head, and Lewis Klein ed. *Broadcast/Cable Programming: Strategies and Practices*, 3d ed. (Belmont, Calif.: Wadsworth, 1989), pp. 165–168; *New York Times*, 22 April 1988, p. C38; *Los Angeles Times*, 6 November 1987, Part VI, p. 31.

24. *Broadcasting*, 12 February 1990, pp. 27–29; *Variety*, 7 February 1990, pp. 163–164; Tom Link, "The Last Picture Format," pp. 31–33; Eastman, Head, and Klein, *Broadcast/Cable Programming*, pp. 238–239; *Electronic Media*, 3 April 1987, pp. 1, 27 and 27 October 1987, p. 24.

25. *Electronic Media*, 29 February 1988, pp. 6, 55; *Broadcasting*, 12 February 1990, pp. 27–29.

26. John Howard, George Rothbart, and Lee Sloan, "The Response to 'Roots': A National Survey," *Journal of Broadcasting*, vol. 22, no. 3 (Summer 1978): 279–287; K. Kyoon Hur, "Impact of 'Roots' on Black and White Teenagers," *Journal of Broadcasting*, vol. 22, no. 3 (Summer 1978): 289–307; Stuart H. Surlin, " 'Roots' Research: A Summary of Findings," *Journal of Broadcasting*, vol. 22, no. 3 (Summer 1978): 309–320; Leslie Fishbein, "*Roots*: Docudrama and the Interpretation of History," in *American History/American Film: Interpreting the Video Past*, ed. John E. O'Connor (New York: Frederick Ungar Publishing Company, 1983), pp. 279–305; David L. Wolper, *The Inside Story of TV's "Roots"* (New York: Warner Books, 1978).

27. Eastman, Head, and Klein, *Broadcast/Cable Programming*, pp. 168–169; Richard A. Blum and Richard D. Lindheim, *Primetime: Network Television Programming* (Boston: Focal Press, 1987), pp. 159–163; *Electronic Media*, 4 January 1988, pp. 1, 164.

28. *Variety*, 4 March 1987, pp. 1, 124; *Television/Radio Age*, 16 March 1987, pp. 46–47; *Washington Post*, 15 February 1987, pp. F1, F4.

29. Blum and Lindheim, *Primetime*, pp. 166–167; *Broadcasting*, 28 November 1983, p. 26; Stanley Feldman and Lee Sigelman, "The Political Impact of Prime-Time Television: 'The Day After'," *Journal of Politics*, vol. 47, no. 2 (Spring 1985): 556–578.

30. *Variety*, 14 January 1987, p. 164; see also Gregory A. Waller, "Re-placing *The Day After*," *Cinema Journal*, vol. 26, no. 3 (Spring 1987): 3–20.

31. *Advertising Age*, 19 January 1987, p. S-26; Toni Schlesinger, "Best Enemies," *Chicago*, May 1987, p. 121.

32. In 1990 Gene Siskel began to appear on "CBS This Morning" as well.

33. *Electronic Media*, 31 March 1986, pp. 1, 12; *Variety*, 18 June 1986, pp. 3, 32; *Broadcasting*, 21 April 1986, p. 95. Indeed when, in 1986, Roger Ebert and Gene Siskel moved to "review" movies from a program distributed by a major studio, the ruse was ended. The duo now worked for one of the seven major studios, indeed one of the top studios of the late 1980s. Siskel was relieved of his daily reviewing duties by the *Chicago Tribune*; many asked if they were "reviewers" or simple extensions of the promotion department?

34. *Wall Street Journal*, 5 June 1981, p. 21; *Electronic Media*, 4 January 1987, p. 13; 14 December 1987, p. 42; 3 August 1987, p. 20; *Variety*, 9 April 1986, pp. 2, 44.

35. *Wall Street Journal*, 21 May 1981, p. 1.

36. *Los Angeles Times*, Part VI, 9 July 1987, p. 10; Schlesinger, "Best Enemies," *Chicago*, p. 122; *Variety*, 15 August 1985, pp. 4, 30.

37. Irwin Karp, "The Copyright Trap," *Film Comment*, vol. 26, no. 1 (January–February 1990): 12–15.

38. *Variety*, 9 April 1986, pp. 2, 44; *Premiere*, August 1989, p. 15.

39. Frank Thompson, "The Big Squeeze," *American Film*, vol. 15, no. 5, February 1990, p. 41.

40. Ty Burr, "The Letterbox Dilemma," *Video Review*, February 1990, pp. 40–43.

41. *Electronic Media*, 18 April 1988, p. 40; *Premiere*, March 1988, p. 7.

42. *New York Times*, 6 June 1988, p. C18; *Variety*, 12 August 1987, p. 20; *New York Times*, 11 July 1988, p. C13; *Electronic Media*, 4 July 1988, pp. 3, 4; *Video*, December 1988, pp. 21–22; Susan Linfield, "The Color of Money," *American Film*, vol. 13, no. 5, January/February 1987, pp. 29–35; *Daily Variety*, 30 January 1985, p. 1.

43. John Belton, "The Pan & Scan Scandals," *The Perfect Vision*, vol. I, no. 1 (Summer 1987): 41–49; Michael Kerbel, "Edited for Television," *Film Comment*, vol. 13, no. 3 (May–June 1977): 28–30; Michael Kerbel, "Edited for Television II," *Film Comment*, vol. 13, no. 4 (July–August 1977): 38–40; *Washington Post*, 6 March 1988, pp. G1, G6, G7; Eastman, Head, and Klein, *Broadcast/Cable Programming*, pp. 214–215.

CHAPTER 13: CABLE TELEVISION'S MOVIE CHANNELS

1. Diane Brown, Joseph M. Ripley II, and Lawrence W. Lichty, "Movies on Television: What the Audience Says," *Radio-Television-Film Audience Studies*, Department of Speech, University of Wisconsin, no. 1, March 1966, pp. 1–3.

2. The history of the origins of HBO are vividly told in George Mair, *Inside HBO* (New York: Dodd, Mead, 1988), pp. 1–35, and Curtis Prendergast, *The World of Time Inc: The Intimate History of a Changing Enterprise, 1960–1980* (New York: Antheneum, 1986), pp. 489–512. See also *New York Times*, 7 March 1983, pp. D1, D8; *Broadcasting*, 15 November 1982, p. 48; Robert Lindsey, "Home Box Office Moves in on Hollywood," *New York Times Magazine*, 12 June 1983, pp. 31–33; *Electronic Media*, 30 November 1987, p. 22; *Broadcasting*, 15 November 1990, p. 48.

3. Susan Tyler Eastman, Sydney W. Head, and Lewis Klein, eds., *Broadcast/Cable Programming: Strategies and Programming*, 3d ed. (Belmont, Calif.: Wadsworth, 1989), pp. 333–334. There have been other pay movie channels such as

Spotlight, which was in business from 1981 until 1984, but they were never able to seriously challenge HBO and Cinemax, and Showtime and the Movie Channel.

4. *Multichannel News*, 26 December 1988, p. 1; *Cable World*, 23 October 1989, p. 2.

5. *Channels*, March 1990, pp. 46–47.

6. *Wall Street Journal*, 6 May 1988, p. 26.

7. *Wall Street Journal*, 7 March 1989, pp. B1, B6; *New York Times*, 5 March 1989, pp. 1, 38; *Marketing New Media*, no. 79 (16 October 1989): 1–2; *Channels*, March 1990, pp. 46–47.

8. Dale Pollock and Peter Warner, "Premiere: Studios Tell Why Hollywood Empire Struck Back," *Watch*, July 1980, pp. 36–39.

9. H. Polskin, "Inside Pay-Cable's Most Savage War," *Panorama*, March 1981, pp. 54–58; *Broadcasting*, 5 January 1981, p. 31; *Cablevision*, 19 January 1981, p. 26–27.

10. Lisa Gubernick, "Sumner Redstone Scores Again," *Forbes*, 31 October 1988, pp. 44–45; *Broadcasting*, 14 November 1988, p. 103.

11. *Wall Street Journal*, 16 March 1989, p. B6.

12. Eastman, Head, and Klein, *Broadcast/Cable Programming*, pp. 338–339; Paula Ellis-Simons, "The Disney Channel," *Channels*, October 1987, pp. 43–44; *Cablevision*, 16 February 1986, p. 12.

13. *Cable World*, 31 July 1989, p. 24 and 23 October 1989, pp. 1, 2; *Multichannel News*, 23 October 1989, pp. 1, 4; *Channels*, March 1990, pp. 46–47.

14. *Wall Street Journal*, 6 May 1989, p. 26; Ronald Hawkins, "The Battle for Exclusivity," *Cable Television Business*, 15 June 1989, pp. 47–48; *New York Times*, 20 May 1988, p. D5.

15. The primary services (HBO and Showtime) offer more first-run fare; the secondary services (Cinemax and the Movie Channel) less.

16. Eastman, Head, and Klein, *Broadcast/Cable Programming*, pp. 324–328; *Multichannel News*, 31 July 1989, pp. 1, 50.

17. *Wall Street Journal*, 12 May 1988, p. 28.

18. *Premiere*, December 1989, p. 59; *Multichannel News*, 25 January 1988, p. 6; Ethel Greenfield Booth, "Regional Services: Tailor Made," *Cable Television Business*, 1 December 1986, pp. 31, 34.

19. *Multichannel News*, 9 February 1987, p. 18; *Electronic Media*, 21 September 1987, p. 39; *Los Angeles Times*, 9 September 1987, Part IV, p. 3; *Multichannel News*, 31 August 1987, p. 58.

20. Ted Turner capitalized the term "SuperStation." Hereafter I shall use *SuperStation* to refer to Turner's WTBS cable network and *superstation* to refer to the class of independent television stations presented on cable.

21. *Wall Street Journal*, 5 June 1987, p. 1; Aaron Latham, "Requiem for Leo the Lion," *Manhattan, Inc.* September 1988, pp. 101–102; *Broadcasting*, 14 December 1987, p. 43; Susan Tyler Eastman, Sydney W. Head, and Lewis

Klein, *Broadcast/Cable Programming: Strategies and Practices*, 2d ed. (Belmont, Calif.: Wadsworth, 1985), pp. 302–306.

22. *Variety*, 17 January 1990, p. 39; Eastman, Head and Klein, *Broadcast/Cable Programming*, 2d ed., pp. 310–312.

23. David Carey, "The Confessions of Ted Turner," *Financial World*, 18 April 1989, p. 65; *Cablevision*, 19 January 1987, p. 22.

24. *Television/Radio Age*, 26 October 1987, pp. 45–46.

25. Eastman, Head and Klein, *Broadcast/Cable Programming*, 2d ed., pp. 307–308; *Wall Street Journal*, 4 March 1982, p. 1; *Broadcasting*, 30 November 1987, pp. 47–50; *Electronic Media*, 15 February 1988, pp. 1, 126. It should be noted that the four SuperStations examined here hardly represent the lone attempts at creating a nation cable station. In the late 1970s and early 1980s KTVU from Oakland, California, had been declared a SuperStation. In the late 1980s there was WSKB from Boston and KTLA from Los Angeles. But none even obtained the success of the big four.

26. The standards of Will Hays' Production Code Administration in the 1930s and 1940s roughly equate to the acceptable boundaries for the Family Channel.

27. *Cable World*, 15 January 1990, p. 32; *Multichannel News*, 15 January 1990, pp. 1, 58.

28. *Broadcasting*, 17 October 1988, pp. 55–56; *Multichannel News*, 17 March 1986, pp. 1, 117 and 16 November 1987, p. 11; Alex Ben Block, "Manna from Turner," *Forbes*, 18 May 1987, pp. 126–128.

29. Cecilia Capuzzi, "Will a New Bravo be Too Basic?" *Channels*, January 1989, pp. 42–46; *New York Times*, 27 October 1985, p. H26.

30. *Multichannel News*, 24 July 1989, p. 40 and 7 September 1987, pp. 1, 45.

31. *Cable World*, 9 October 1989, pp. 1, 21; *Wall Street Journal*, 21 July 1988, p. 19; *Multichannel News*, 24 August 1987, p. 24; *Variety*, 7 February 1990, pp. 1, 7; *Electronic Media*, 12 March 1990, pp. 1, 16. USA is not the only cable network commissioning made-for-TV movies. HBO, Showtime, and the Family Channel do it regularly, although as of the early 1990s it is not clear where this genre will lead.

32. *Wall Street Journal*, 3 October 1988, p. B6; *Electronic Media*, 22 February 1988, p. 94.

33. *New York Times*, 12 January 1989, pp. C19, C26; *Electronic Media*, 26 December 1988, p. 20 and 25 December 1989, p. 12; *Variety*, 7 February 1990, pp. 1, 7.

34. *Multichannel News*, 1 January 1990, pp. 9, 11; *Channels*, March 1990, pp. 46–47; *Wall Street Journal*, 2 November 1988, p. B1; Patricia E. Bauer, "Young and Impulsive: Pay-Per-View Projected Growth," *Channels*, May 1987, pp. 50–51.

35. AT&T's Automatic Number Identification (ANI) allows the caller to order PPV movies without talking to a human. By dialing a toll-free number, the system records your telephone number and transmits it to a central facility. The phone

number is then beamed up to the network's satellite (like a long-distance phone call) and then the programming is freed to that home. It is also routed to the computer to bill the home. The whole process takes about six seconds. See Frank Lovace, "Descrambling Pay-Per-View," *Video*, February 1989, pp. 48, 50, 106.

36. Judith Reitman, "Pay-Per-View Inches Along," *Cable Marketing*, November 1986, pp. 18–20; *New York Times*, 14 November 1988, p. D9.

37. *Broadcasting*, 16 July 1990, pp. 40–42; *Wall Street Journal*, 19 December 1989, pp. B6, B8; Eastman, Head, and Klein, *Broadcast/Cable Programming*, pp. 339–345; *Multichannel News*, 5 February 1990, p. 4.

38. Multichannel microwave distribution service (MMDS or "wireless" cable) has yet to develop beyond special niche markets. Wireless cable may pose a challenge if its capacity is expanded beyond fifty channels. Direct broadcast satellites (or DBS) seems logical, but at a thousand-dollar investment (minimum) plus monthly payments to unscramble services, DBS has been chosen by less than two million homes, principally well-off rural citizens to which cable television will never be available. To be competitive DBS will require a generation of new, more powerful satellites. Still many will try to innovate wireless cable and DBS. See *Wall Street Journal*, 22 February 1990, p. B4 and *Broadcasting*, 26 February 1990, pp. 27–31. See also *Washington Post*, 19 January 1989, p. C16; *New York Times*, 9 August 198, pp. C1, C10; *Premiere*, December 1988, p. 134.

39. Terry L. Childers and Dean M. Krugman, "The Competitive Environment of Pay Per View," *Journal of Broadcasting & Electronic Media*, vol. 31, no. 3 (Summer 1987): 335–342; *Broadcasting*, 26 September 1988, pp. 66–67; *Variety*, 18–24 January 1989, p. 43.

CHAPTER 14: HOME VIDEO

1. For more on the history and use of home movies see the work of Patricia R. Zimmermann, for example "Hollywood, Home Movies and Common Sense: Amateur Film as Aesthetic Dissemination and Social Control, 1950–1962," *Cinema Journal*, vol. 27, no. 4 (Summer 1988): 23–44.

2. For a wonderful journalistic account of the invention and innovation of the VCR and Hollywood's reluctance see James Lardner, *Fast Forward: Hollywood, the Japanese, and the Onslaught of the VCR* (New York: W. W. Norton, 1987).

3. *Broadcasting*, 20 August 1984, p. 43; *Variety*, 13 June 1984, p. 37; *Fortune*, 19 August 1985, p. 77.

4. *Variety*, 10 January 1990, p. 31; *Multichannel News*, 13 February 1989, p. 35 and 8 May 1989, p. 61; *Video Flash*, Subscriber Bulletin, no. 13 (5 October 1987): 1–3.

5. *Fortune*, 16 July 1979, p. 110; *Business Week*, 5 December 1983, p. 88 and 5 December 1983, p. 88.

6. For Valenti's efforts see Lardner, *Fast Forward*, pp. 203–217.

7. *Merchandising*, February 1980, p. 58; *Broadcasting*, 24 October 1977, p. 34; *Home Video Yearbook*, 1981–1982 (White Plains, N.Y.: Knowledge Industry Publications, 1982), p. 163; *Video*, September 1988, pp. 74–75; *Wall Street Journal*, 5 June 1980, p. 17; *Variety*, 23 July 1980, p. 1.

8. *Washington Post*, 29 March 1989, p. C4.

9. *Washington Post*, 29 March 1989, pp. C1, C4.

10. *Washington Post*, 6 October 1988, p. C7; 17 November 1988, p. C2; 27 October 1988, p. B7. The 1990s may not be as good to Erol's. Early in the decade the company began to lay off workers, citing a softening market for rentals and increased competition. See *Washington Post*, 2 March 1990, p. F1.

11. *Business Week*, 22 January 1990, p. 47; *Washington Post*, 16 February 1989, p. C13; *Wall Street Journal*, 10 May 1989, pp. C1, C2; *Washington Post*, "Washington Business," 20 August 1990, pp. 1, 24–25.

12. *Business Week*, 22 January 1990, p. 48; *Forbes*, 2 May 1988, pp. 54–56; *Business Week*, 12 June 1989, pp. 72–73; *Washington Post*, "Washington Business," 9 January 1989, p. 30 and 27 August 1988, pp. D10, D15.

13. *Washington Post*, 20 November 1990, pp. A1, A6; *Wall Street Journal*, 20 November 1990, p. B6; *Washington Post*, 21 November 1990, pp. E1, E3.

14. See "Home Truths for Hollywood," *The Economist*, 30 July 1983, pp. 72–73; *Variety*, 1 September 1982, p. 57 and 26 June 1985, p. 84. For a complete discussion of the legal issues involved in taping off the air see Joseph McCann, "Videotape Recorders and Copyright Infringement: The Fair Use Doctrine on Instant Replay," *The Journal of Arts Management and Law*, vol. 13, no. 4 (Winter 1984): 5–30.

15. *Variety*, 24 January 1990, p. 153.

16. Bruce C. Klopfenstein, "The Diffusion of the VCR in the United States," in *The VCR Age: Home Video and Mass Communication*, ed. Mark R. Levy (Newbury Park, Calif.: Sage, 1989), pp. 21–39; *Variety*, 10 January 1990, p. 31; *Washington Post*, "Washington Business," 12 June 1989, p. 6; *New York Times*, 19 March 1989, p. 43; *Washington Post*, "Washington Business," 15 May 1989, p. 3; *New York Times*, 8 October 1989, p. F1.

17. *Washington Post*, 1 September 1988, p. B7. The top-ten rental titles as of mid-1980 read like a list of the top Hollywood hits of the 1980s: *Top Gun, Crocodile Dundee, Dirty Dancing, Three Men and a Baby, Platoon, The Color Purple, Robocop, Die Hard, Fatal Attraction,* and *Lethal Weapon,* in that order.

18. *Barrons*, 21 September 1987, p. 8; *Variety*, 31 January 1990, p. 59.

19. *Video Store*, November 1988, pp. 72–74; *Variety*, 1–7 March 1989, pp. 1, 2; *Video Review*, October 1988, pp. 23–24.

20. *Washington Post*, 9 October 1988, pp. H1, H7; *Wall Street Journal*, 23 September 1988, p. 21; *Variety*, 7 February 1990, pp. 169–170.

21. *New York Times*, 17 May 1988, p. C18.

22. *New York Times*, 27 October 1988, p. C21.

23. *Wall Street Journal*, 6 June 1990, pp. B1, B3.

24. *Variety*, 17 January 1989, p. 35; *Washington Post*, 11 January 1990, p. E7 and 3 January 1990, p. 47; *Video*, September 1988, pp. 79–81, 162; *Washington Post*, 23 October 1988, pp. G1, G4, G5; *Variety*, 24 January 1990, p. 152 and 29 November 1989, p. 41.

25. *New York Times*, 7 January 1990, p. H14; *Variety*, 6 December 1989, p. 47; *Forbes*, 5 February 1990, pp. 39–40.

26. *Video Review*, December 1988, p. 34.

27. *Variety*, 24 January 1990, p. 153.

28. *Electronic Media*, 12 February 1990, p. 14; *New York Times*, 6 May 1990, pp. 1, 34; *Washington Post*, 14 February 1990, pp. D1, D5.

29. Heikki Hellman and Martti Soramaki, "Economic Concentration in the Videocassette Industry: A Cultural Comparison," *Journal of Communication*, vol. 35, no. 3 (Summer 1985): 37; *New York Times*, 19 September 1985, p. D1; *Variety*, 31 October 1984, p. 49 and 10 January 1990, p. 32.

30. Clifford W. Scherer, "The Videocassette Recorder and Information Inequity," *Journal of Communication*, vol. 39, no. 3 (Summer 1989): 94–103.

31. *Variety*, 1 November 1989, p. 47 and 27 December 1989, p. 23.

32. *Variety*, 24 January 1990, p. 153.

33. *Variety*, 17 January 1990, pp. 1, 35, 36 and 1 October 1980, p. 1; *Broadcasting*, 2 September 1985, p. 44; *Variety*, 30 January 1985, p. 37; *Washington Post*, 26 April 1990, p. C7.

34. The American motion picture industry began to encounter opposition to its videos abroad long before trouble brewed in the United States. In Moslem countries restrictions on public viewing have long been enforced, but movies can be seen at home with little fear. So while *E.T.* never showed in Iranian theatres, it was widely available on home video.

35. *Variety*, 21 February 1990, pp. 327–328; *Video Review*, February 1990, pp. 37–38.

36. Frank Lovece, "The Lost Picture Show," *Video*, July 1990, pp. 44–47.

37. Ira Robbins, "8mm How Far, How Fast?," *Video*, February 1990, pp. 56–57; *Video Review*, February 1990, pp. 33–35; *Variety*, 31 January 1990, p. 59.

38. *Forbes*, 5 February 1990, p. 112.

39. *Broadcasting*, 17 October 1988, pp. 38–39; *Fortune*, 24 October 1988, pp. 161–162.

40. *National Journal*, 25 February 1989, pp. 470–473; *Business Week*, 30 January 1989, pp. 56–66; *Wall Street Journal*, 24 August 1987, p. 25.

41. A detailed, fascinating case study of the invention and an attempted, but failed, innovation of SelectaVision can be found in Margaret B. W. Graham, *The Business of Research: RCA and the VideoDisc* (Cambridge: Cambridge University Press, 1986). See also *Video*, March 1990, pp. 39–41, 104.

42. *Wall Street Journal*, 6 December 1988, p. B1; *Video Review*, March 1990, pp. 29–31.

EPILOGUE

1. Although this book does not aim to make predictions, I think the movie show will survive the recession of the early 1990s quite nicely.

2. For more on this see Douglas Gomery, "Jaws," in Christopher Lyon, ed., *Films* (Chicago: St. James Press, 1984), pp. 220–221.

3. *New York Times*, 7 March 1990, p. D8.

SELECTED BIBLIOGRAPHY

PERIODICALS

Action
Advertising Age
American Cinematographer
American Federationist
The Appraisal Journal
Architectural Record
Atlantic

Barrons
Bell Laboratories Record
Beverage World
Billboard
Boxoffice
Broadcasting
Business Week

Cable Marketing
Cable Television Business
Cablevision
Cable World
Channels
Chicago
Chicago Daily News
Chicago Sun Times
Chicago Tribune
Christian Century

Close-up
Colliers
Commercial and Financial Chronicle
Cue
Current Research in Film

Daily Variety
Davenport Democrat and Leader
Des Moines Leader
Domestic Engineering
Dramatic Mirror

Economist
Electronic Media
Emmy
The Exhibitor
Exhibitor's Film Exchange
Exhibitor's Herald
Exhibitor's Herald and Motography
Exhibitor's Herald-World

Film Comment
Film Daily
Film Daily Yearbook
Film Journal
Films in Review
Financial World
Focus on Film
Forbes
Fortune

Harvard Business Review
Holiday
Hollywood Reporter
Home Video Yearbook

Ice and Refrigeration
International Motion Picture Almanac
International Photographer
International Projectionist
International Sound Technician

Journal of the Franklin Institute
Journal of Land and Public Utility Economics
Journal of the Society of Motion Picture Engineers
Life
Literary Digest

Los Angeles Times
The Magazine of Wall Street
Manhattan, Inc.
Marketing New Media
Merchandising
The Metronome
Milwaukee Journal
Milwaukee Sentinel
Monthly Labor Review
Moody's Industrial Manual
The Motion Picture
Motion Picture Daily
Motion Picture Herald
Motion Picture News
Motography
Moving Picture World
Multichannel News
Museum & Arts Washington

National Journal
National Real Estate Journal
Nation's Business
New Orleans Daily Picayune
New Orleans Times Democrat
Newsweek
New York Clipper
New York Daily Tribune
New Yorker
New York Times
Nickelodeon

Outlook and Independent

Panorama
Popular Mechanics
Popular Science
Power Plant Engineering
Premiere

Quarterly of Film, Radio and Television

Radio-Television Daily
Review of Reviews

Saturday Evening Post
Saturday Review of Literature
Show

Sight and Sound
SMPTE Journal
Society of Motion Picture Engineers Transactions
Television
TV Guide
Television/Radio Age
Theatre
Theatre Catalog
Time
Transactions of the Society of Motion Picture Engineers
Urban History Review
Urban Land
Variety
Video
Video Flash
Video Review
Video Store
Wall Street Journal
Washington Post
Washington Star
Watch
Waterloo Times-Courier
Wisconsin Enterprise Blade

BOOKS AND DISSERTATIONS

Addams, Jane. *The Spirit of Youth and the City Streets*. New York: Macmillan, 1909.
Aksyonov, Vassily. *In Search of Melancholy Baby: A Russian in America*. New York: Random House, 1988.
Aldridge, Henry Belden. "Live Musical and Theatrical Presentations in Detroit Moving Picture Theatres: 1896–1930." Unpublished Ph.D. dissertation, University of Michigan, 1973.
Allen, Robert C. *Vaudeville and Film: 1895–1915: A Study in Media Interaction*. New York: Arno Press, 1980.
Allen, Robert C., and Douglas Gomery. *Film History: Theory and Practice*. New York: Alfred A. Knopf, 1985.
Allvine, Glendon. *The Greatest Fox of Them All*. New York: Lyle Stuart, 1969.
Anderson, Gillian B. *Music to Silent Films: 1894–1929: A Guide*. Washington, D.C.: Library of Congress, 1988.

Anderson, Oscar E. *Refrigeration in America*. Princeton: Princeton University Press, 1953.

Angle, Paul M. *Philip K. Wrigley*. Chicago: Rand McNally, 1975.

Austin, Bruce A. *The Film Audience: An International Bibliography of Research*. Metuchen, N.J.: The Scarecrow Press, 1983.

Austin, Richard. *Corporations in Crisis*. Garden City, N.Y.: Doubleday, 1966.

Balaban, Barney, and Sam Katz. *The Fundamental Principles of Balaban and Katz Theatre Management*. Chicago: Balaban & Katz, 1926.

Balaban, Carrie. *Continuous Performance*. New York: A. J. Balaban Foundation, 1941.

Balio, Tino. *United Artists: The Company Built By the Stars*. Madison: University of Wisconsin Press, 1976.

Barksdale, Marcellus C. "The Indigenous Civil Rights Movement and Cultural Change in North Carolina." Unpublished Ph.D. dissertation, Duke University, 1977.

Barnouw, Erik. *The Golden Web: A History of Broadcasting in the United States, 1933–1953*. New York: Oxford University Press, 1968.

Basten, Fred E. *Glorious Technicolor: The Movies' Magic Rainbow*. New York: A. S. Barnes, 1980.

Bauer, Carl M. *John F. Kennedy and the Second Reconstruction*. New York: Columbia University Press, 1977.

Baumol, William J., and Alan S. Blinder. *Economics: Principles and Policy*. New York: Harcourt Brace Jovanovich, 1979.

Benson, Susan Porter. *Counter Cultures: Saleswomen, Managers, and Customers in American Department Stores, 1890–1940*. Urbana: University of Illinois Press, 1988.

Berg, A. Scott. *Goldwyn: A Biography*. New York: Random House, 1989.

Berkow, Ira. *Maxwell Street*. Garden City, N.Y.: Doubleday, 1977.

Bernstein, Carl. *Loyalties: A Son's Memories*. New York: Simon and Schuster, 1989.

Beynon, George W. *Musical Presentation of Motion Pictures*. New York: Schirmer, 1921.

Blassingame, John. *Black New Orleans*. Chicago: University of Chicago Press, 1973.

Blum, Richard A., and Richard D. Lindheim. *Primetime: Network Television Programming*. Boston: Focal Press, 1987.

Bordwell, David. *Narration in the Fiction Film*. Madison: University of Wisconsin Press, 1985.

Bordwell, David, Janet Staiger, and Kristin Thompson. *The Classic Hollywood Cinema: Film Style & Mode of Production to 1960*. New York: Columbia University Press, 1985.

Bowers, Q. David. *Nickelodeon Theatres and Their Music*. Vestal, N.Y.: The Vestal Press, 1986.

Brett, Roger. *Temples of Illusion*. Providence, R.I.: Brett Theatrical, 1976.

Brooks, Tim, and Earle Marsh. *The Complete Directory to Prime Time Network Programs, 1946–Present*. New York: Ballantine, 1979.

Bush, Lee O., Edward C. Chukayne, Russell Allon Hehr, and Richard F. Hershey. *Euclid Beach Park*. Mentor, Ohio: Amusement Park Books, 1977.

Butsch, Richard, ed., *For Fun and Profit: The Transformation of Leisure into Consumption*. Philadelphia: Temple University Press, 1990.

Carlson, Marvin. *Places of Performance*. Ithaca, N.Y.: Cornell University Press, 1989.

Carmen, Ira H. *Movies, Censorship and the Law*. Ann Arbor: University of Michigan Press, 1966.

Carr, Robert E., and R. M. Hayes. *Wide Screen Movies: A History and Filmography of Wide Gauge Filmmaking*. Jefferson, N.C.: McFarland & Company, 1988.

Chandler, Alfred D., Jr. *The Visible Hand: The Managerial Revolution in American Business*. Cambridge: Harvard University Press, 1977.

Cochran, Thomas C. *200 Years of American Business*. New York: Delta, 1977.

Coe, Brain. *The History of Movie Photography*. Westfield, N.J.: Jersey: Eastview Editions, 1981.

Cohen, Lizabeth. *Making a New Deal: Industrial Workers in Chicago, 1919–1939*. New York: Cambridge University Press, 1990.

Conant, Michael. *Antitrust in the Motion Picture Industry*. Berkeley: University of California Press, 1960.

Cripps, Thomas. *Slow Fade to Black: The Negro in American Film, 1900–1942*. New York: Oxford University Press, 1977.

Crowther, Bosley. *Hollywood Rajah: The Life and Times of Louis B. Mayer*. New York: Holt, Rinehart and Winston, 1960.

Crowther, Bosley. *The Lion's Share*. New York: E. P. Dutton, 1957.

Cumming, Adelaide F. "A History of the American Newsreel, 1927 to 1950." Unpublished Ph.D. dissertation, New York University, 1966.

Dittmer, John. *Black Georgia in the Progressive Era, 1900–1920*. Urbana: University of Illinois Press, 1977.

Dolce, Philip C., ed., *Suburbia*. Garden City, N.Y.: Anchor, 1976.

Donahue, Suzanne Mary. *American Film Distribution*. Ann Arbor, Mich.: UMI Research Press, 1987.

Easterlin, Richard A. *Birth and Fortune: the Impact of Numbers on Personal Welfare*, 2d ed. Chicago: University of Chicago Press, 1987.

Eastman, Susan Tyler, Sydney W. Head, and Lewis Klein, eds. *Broadcast/Cable Programming: Strategies and Practices*, 3d ed. Belmont, Calif.: Wadsworth, 1989.

Edwards, Gregory J. *The International Film Poster: The Role of the Poster in Cinema Art, Advertising, and History*. Salem, N.H.: Salem House, 1985.

Edwards, Paul K. *The Southern Negro as a Consumer*. New York: Prentice Hall, 1932.

Erffmeyer, Thomas Edward. "A History of Cinerama: A Study of Technological Innovation and Industrial Management." Unpublished Ph.D. dissertation, Northwestern University, 1985.

Fell, John, ed. *Film Before Griffith*. Berkeley: University of California Press, 1983.

Ferguson, C. E., and J. P. Gould. *Microeconomic Theory*, 4th ed. Homewood, Ill.: Richard D. Irwin, 1975.

Fielding, Raymond. *The American Newsreel, 1911–1967*. Norman: University of Oklahoma Press, 1972.

Fishman, Robert. *Bourgeois Utopias: The Rise and Fall of Suburbia*. New York: Basic Books, 1987.

Francisco, Charles. *The Radio City Music Hall: An Affectionate History of the World's Greatest Theatre*. New York: E. P. Dutton. 1979.

Franklin, Harold B. *Motion Picture Theatre Management*. New York: George H. Doran Company, 1927.

Gagne, Paul R. *The Zombies That Ate Pittsburgh: The Films of George A. Romero*. New York: Dodd, Mead, 1987.

Glazer, Irving R. *Philadelphia Theatres, A–Z*. New York: Greenwood Press, 1986.

Gomery, Douglas. *High Sierra: Screenplay and Analysis*. Madison: University of Wisconsin Press, 1979.

Gomery, Douglas. *The Hollywood Studio System*. New York: St. Martin's Press, 1986.

Goode, James M. *Capital Losses: A Cultural History of Washington's Destroyed Buildings*. Washington, D.C.: Smithsonian Institution Press, 1979.

Graham, Margaret B. W. *The Business of Research: RCA and the Videodisc*. Cambridge: Cambridge University Press, 1986.

Grau, Robert. *The Theatre of Science*. New York: Benjamin Blom, 1914.

Green, Abel, and Joe Laurie, Jr. *Show Biz: From Vaude to Video*. New York: Henry Holt and Company, 1951.

Grenz, Christine. *Trans-Lux: Biography of a Corporation*. Norwalk, Conn.: Trans-Lux Corporation, 1982.

Griffin, Al. *"Step Right Up Folks."* Chicago: Henry Regency Company, 1974.

Guback, Thomas. *The International Film Industry: Western Europe and America Since 1945*. Bloomington: Indiana University Press, 1969.

Hall, Ben M. *The Best Remaining Seats*. New York: Bramhall House, 1961.

Hampton, Benjamin B. *A History of the Movies*. New York: Covici Friede, 1931.

Handel, Leo A. *Hollywood Looks at Its Audience*. Urbana: University of Illinois Press, 1950.

Haralovich, Mary Beth. "Motion Picture Advertising: Industrial and Social Forces and Effects, 1930–1948." Unpublished Ph.D. dissertation, University of Wisconsin, Madison, 1984.

Hayes, R. M. *3-D Movies: A History and Filmography of Stereoscopic Cinema.* Jefferson, N.C.: McFarland & Company, 1989.

Hayward, Walter S., and Percival White. *Chain Stores,* 3d ed. New York: McGraw Hill, 1928.

Headley, Robert Kirk, Jr. *Exit: A History of the Movies in Baltimore.* University Park, Md.: Privately published, 1974.

Henderson, James M., and Richard E. Quandt. *Microeconomic Theory.* New York: McGraw Hill, 1958.

Hendricks, Gordon. *The Kinetoscope.* New York: The Beginnings of the American Film, 1966.

Herzog, Charlotte. "The Motion Picture Theatre and Film Exhibition—1896–1932." Unpublished Ph.D. dissertation, Northwestern University, 1980.

Hession, Charles H., and Hyman Sardy. *Ascent to Affluence: A History of American Economic Development.* Boston: Allyn and Bacon, 1969.

Hoberman, J., and Jonathan Rosenbaum. *Midnight Movies.* New York: Harper & Row, 1983.

Holli, Melvin G., and Peter d'A. Jones, eds. *Ethnic Chicago.* Grand Rapids, Mich.: William B. Eerdmans Publishing, 1884.

Hoyt, Homer. *One Hundred Years of Land Values in Chicago.* Chicago: University of Chicago Press, 1933.

Hughes, Jonathan. *American Economic History.* Glenview, Ill.: Scott Foresman, 1983.

Hulfish, David. *Motion Picture Work.* Chicago: American School of Correspondence, 1913.

Ingels, Ruth. *Willis Haviland Carrier: Father of Air Conditioning.* New York: Doubleday, 1952.

Jackson, Kenneth T. *Crabgrass Frontier: The Suburbanization of the United States.* New York: Oxford University Press, 1985.

Jenkins, C. Francis, and Oscar B. DePue. *Handbook for Motion Picture and Stereopticon Operators.* Washington, D. C.: Knega, 1908.

Jenkins, Reese V. *Images and Enterprise: Technology and the American Photographic Industry, 1839 to 1925.* Baltimore: The Johns Hopkins University Press, 1975.

Jewell, Derek. *Frank Sinatra.* Boston: Little Brown, 1985.

Jones, Landon Y. *Great Expectations: America and the Baby Boom Generation.* New York: Random House, 1981.

Jowett, Garth. *Film: The Democratic Art.* Boston: Little Brown, 1976.

Junchen, David L. *Encyclopedia of the American Theatre Organ,* vol. I. Pasadena, Calif.: Showcase Publications, 1985.

Kahn, E. J., Jr. *Jock: The Life and Times of John Hay Whitney.* Garden City, N.Y.: Doubleday, 1981.

Kasson, John F. *Amusing the Million: Coney Island at the Turn of the Century.* New York: Hill & Wang, 1978.

Kasson, John F. *Rudeness & Civility: Manners in Nineteenth Century America.* New York: Hill and Wang, 1990.

Kennedy, Joseph P., ed. *The Story of the Films.* Chicago: A. W. Shaw, 1927.

Kenney, Roy Wallace. "The Economics of Block-Booking." Unpublished Ph.D. dissertation, University of California at Los Angeles, 1979.

Kerr, Paul, ed. *The Hollywood Film Industry.* London: Routledge & Kegan Paul, 1986.

Kobal, John, and V. A. Wilson. *Foyer Pleasure: The Golden Age of Cinema Lobby Cards.* New York: Deliliah, 1983.

Kyriazi, Gary. *The Great American Amusement Parks: A Pictorial History.* Secaucus, N.J.: Citadel Press, 1976.

Lafferty, William Charles, Jr. "The Early Development of Magnetic Sound Recording in Broadcasting and Motion Pictures, 1928–1950." Unpublished Ph.D. dissertation, Northwestern University, 1981.

Landon, John W. *Jesse Crawford.* Vestal, N.Y.: Vestal Press, 1974.

Lardner, James. *Fast Forward: Hollywood, the Japanese, and the Onslaught of the VCR.* New York: W. W. Norton, 1987.

Laurie, Joe, Jr. *Vaudeville: From Honky Tonks to the Palace.* New York: Henry Holt and Company, 1953.

Leab, Daniel J. *From Sambo to Superspade: The Black Experience in Motion Pictures.* Boston: Houghton Mifflin, 1975.

Lebher, Geoffrey M. *Chain Stores in America, 1859–1962.* New York: Chain Store Publishing Corporation, 1962.

Leftwich, Richard. *The Price System and Resource Allocation,* 6th ed. Hinsdale, Ill.: The Dryden Press, 1976.

Lejeune, Caroline. *Cinema.* London: MacLehose, 1931.

Levin, Meyer. *The Old Bunch.* New York: The Citadel Press, 1937.

Levy, Mark, ed., *The VCR Age: Home Video and Mass Communication.* Newbury Park, Calif.: Sage, 1989.

Lewis, Howard T. *Cases in Motion Picture Industry.* Harvard Business Reports. New York: McGraw Hill, 1930.

Lewis, Howard T. *The Motion Picture Industry.* New York: D. Van Nostrand, 1933.

Leyda, Jay, and Charles Musser, eds., *Before Hollywood.* New York: American Federation of Arts, 1986.

Liebs, Chester. *From Main Street to the Miracle Mile: American Roadside Architecture.* New York: New York Graphic Society, 1985.

Light, Paul C. *Baby Boomers.* New York: W. W. Norton, 1988.

Limbacher, James L. *Four Aspects of Film.* New York: Brussel and Brussel, 1968.

Lingeman, Richard R. *Don't You Know There's a War on?* New York: G. P. Putnam's Sons, 1970.

Mangum, Charles S., Jr. *The Legal Status of the Negro.* Chapel Hill: University of North Carolina Press, 1940.

Mair, George. *Inside HBO.* New York: Dodd, Mead, 1988.

366 / Selected Bibliography

Malone, Bill C., and Judith McCulloh, eds. *Stars of Country Music.* Urbana: University of Illinois Press, 1975.

Marx, Arthur. *Goldwyn: A Biography of the Man Behind the Myth.* New York: W. W. Norton, 1976.

Masotti, Louis H., and Jeffrey K. Hadden, eds., *Suburbia in Transition.* New York: New Directions, 1974.

Mast, Gerald, ed. *The Movies in Our Midst.* Chicago: University of Chicago Press, 1982.

Matlow, Myron, ed. *American Popular Entertainment.* Westport, Conn.: Greenwood Press, 1979.

Mayer, Arthur. *Merely Colossal.* New York: Simon and Schuster, 1953.

Mayer, Michael F. *Foreign Films on American Screens.* New York: Arco, 1964.

Milward, Alan S. *War, Economy and Society, 1939–1945.* Berkeley: University of California Press, 1979.

Minnelli, Vincente. *I Remember It Well.* Garden City, N.Y.: Doubleday, 1974.

Muller, Peter O. *Contemporary Suburban America.* Englewood Cliffs, N.J.: Prentice Hall, 1981.

Myrdal, Gunnar. *An American Dilemma: The Negro Problem and Modern Democracy.* New York: Harper and Row, 1944.

Nasaw, David. *Children of the City: At Work and at Play.* Garden City, N.Y.: Anchor Press, 1985.

Naylor, David. *American Picture Places: The Architecture of Fantasy.* New York: Van Nostrand Reinhold, 1981.

Nelson, Ralph L. *Merger Movements in American Industry, 1895–1956.* Princeton: Princeton University Press, 1956.

Olson, Stuart. *The Ethnic Dimension in American History.* New York: St. Martin's, 1979.

Osofsky, Gilbert. *Harlem: The Making of a Ghetto, Negro New York City, 1880–1930.* New York: Harper & Row, 1966.

Phlips, Louis. *The Economics of Price Discrimination.* Cambridge: Cambridge University Press, 1983.

Peiss, Kathy. *Cheap Amusements: Working Women and Leisure in Turn-of-the-Century New York.* Philadelphia: Temple University Press, 1986.

Prendergast, Curtis. *The World of Time, Inc.: The Intimate History of a Changing Enterprise, 1960–1980.* New York: Antheneum, 1986.

Proudfoot, Malcolm J. "The Major Outlying Business Centers of Chicago." Unpublished Ph.D. dissertation, University of Chicago, 1936.

Quinlan, Sterling. *Inside ABC: American Broadcasting Company's Rise to Power.* New York: Hastings House, 1979.

Randall, Richard S. *Censorship of the Movies: The Social and Political Control of a Mass Medium.* Madison: University of Wisconsin Press, 1968.

Rapee, Erno. *Motion Picture Moods for Pianists and Organists.* New York: Schirmer, 1924.

Ravage, John W. *Television: The Director's Viewpoint*. Boulder, Colo.: Westview Press, 1978.

Rawlence, Christopher. *The Missing Reel: The Untold Story of the Lost Inventor of Motion Pictures*. New York: Atheneum, 1990.

Rebello, Stephen, and Richard Allen. *Reel Art: Great Posters from the Golden Age of the Silver Screen*. New York: Abbeville Press, 1988.

Reddick, David Bruce. "Movies Under the Stars: A History of the Drive-in Theatre Industry, 1933–1983." Unpublished Ph.D. dissertation, Michigan State University, 1986.

Ricketson, Frank H., Jr. *The Management of Motion Picture Theatres*. New York: McGraw Hill, 1938.

Riley, John J. *A History of the American Soft Drink Industry, 1807–1957*. Washington, D.C.: American Bottlers of Carbonate Beverages, 1958.

Roberts, Chalmers M. *The Washington Post: The First 100 Years*. Boston: Houghton Mifflin, 1977.

Rogers, Kim Lacey. *The Desegregation of New Orleans, 1954–1966*. Minneapolis: University of Minnesota Press, 1982.

Rosenzweig, Roy. *Eight Hours For What We Will: Workers and Leisure in an Industrial City, 1870–1920*. Cambridge: Cambridge University Press, 1983.

Russell, Louise. *The Baby Boom Generation and the Economy*. Washington, D.C.: The Brookings Institution Press, 1982.

Ryan, Roderick T. *A History of Motion Picture Color Technology*. London: The Focal Press, 1977.

Samuels, Stuart. *Midnight Movies*. New York: Collier, 1983.

Sanjek, Russell. *American Popular Music and Its Business: The First Four Hundred Years*, vol. III, From 1900 to 1984. New York: Oxford University Press, 1988.

Schickel, Richard. *The Disney Version*. New York: Simon and Schuster, 1968.

Schlesinger, Arthur M., Jr. *Robert Kennedy and His Times*. Boston: Houghton Mifflin, 1978.

Simon, George T. *The Big Bands*. 4th ed. New York: Schirmer, 1981.

Sklar, Robert. *Movie-Made America*. New York: Random House, 1976.

Smith, Bill. *The Vaudevillians*. New York: Macmillan, 1976.

Smith, Howard R. *Economic History of the United States*. New York: The Ronald Press, 1955.

Snyder, Robert W. *The Voice of the City: Vaudeville and Popular Culture in New York*. New York: Oxford University Press, 1989.

Spear, Allan H. *Black Chicago: The Making of a Negro Ghetto, 1890–1920*. Chicago: University of Chicago Press, 1967.

Spehr, Paul C. *The Movies Begin: Making Movies in New Jersey, 1887–1920*. Newark: The Newark Museum, 1977.

Spellerberg, James Edward. "Technology and the Film Industry: The Adoption of CinemaScope." Unpublished Ph.D. dissertation, University of Iowa, 1980.

Steinberg, Cobbett S. *Reel Facts*. New York: Random House, 1978.

Sterling, Christopher H., and Timothy R. Haight. *The Mass Media: Aspen Institute Guide to Communication Industry Trends.* New York: Praeger, 1978.

Stern, Robert A. M., Gregory Gilmartin, and Thomas Mellins. *Architecture and Urbanism Between the Two World Wars.* New York: Rizzoli, 1987.

Stuart, Frederic. *The Effects of Television on the Motion Picture and Radio Industries.* New York: Arno Press, 1976.

Talbot, Frederick A. *Moving Pictures: How They Are Made and Worked*, rev. ed. Philadelphia: J. B. Lippincott, 1912.

Tate, Alfred O. *Edison's Open Door.* New York: E. P. Dutton, 1938.

Tedlow, Richard S. *New and Improved: The Story of Mass Marketing in America.* New York: Basic Books, 1990.

Thomas, Bob. *Walt Disney: An American Original.* New York: Simon and Schuster, 1976.

Todd, Michael, Jr., and Susan McCarthy Todd. *A Valuable Property: The Life Story of Michael Todd.* New York: Arbor House, 1983.

Trotter, Joe William, Jr. *Black Milwaukee: The Making of an Industrial Proletariat, 1915–1945.* Urbana: University of Illinois Press, 1985.

Tuttle, William M., Jr. *Race Riot: Chicago in the Summer of 1919.* New York: Antheneum, 1975.

Unger, Irwin, and Debi Unger, *Twentieth Century America* (New York: St. Martin's, 1990).

Vogel, Harold L., *Entertainment Industry Economics: A Guide For Financial Analysis*, 2d ed. (New York: Cambridge University Press, 1990).

Wagenknecht, Edward. *The Movies in the Age of Innocence.* New York: Random House, 1971.

Warner, Jack. *My First Hundred Years In Hollywood.* New York: Random House, 1964.

Watson, Mary Ann. *The Expanding Vista: American Television in the Kennedy Years.* New York: Oxford University Press, 1990.

Watters, Pat. *Coca-Cola: An Illustrated History.* Garden City, N.Y.: Doubleday, 1978.

Werner, M. R. *Julius Rosenwald.* New York: Harper, 1938.

White, Timothy R. "Hollywood's Attempt to Appropriate Television: The Case of Paramount Pictures." Unpublished Ph.D. dissertation, University of Wisconsin, Madison, 1990.

Wicking, Christopher, and Tise Vahimagi, *The American Vein: Directors and Directions in Television.* New York: E. P. Dutton, 1979.

Williams, Hunt. *Beyond Control: ABC and the Fate of the Networks.* New York: Antheneum, 1989.

Wirth, Louis. *The Ghetto.* Chicago: University of Chicago Press, 1928.

Wirz, Hans, and Richard Striner. *Washington Deco: Art Deco Design in the Nation's Capital.* Washington, D.C.: Smithsonian Institution Press, 1984.

Wood, Leslie. *The Miracle of the Movies*. London: Burke, 1947.

Wysotsky, Michael Z. *Wide Screen Cinema and Stereophonic Sound*. New York: Hastings House, 1971.

Zukor, Adolph. *The Public Is Never Wrong*. New York: G. P. Putnam's Sons, 1953.

Zunz, Oliver. *The Changing Face of Inequality: Urbanization, Industrial Development, and Immigrants in Detroit, 1880–1920*. Chicago: University of Chicago Press, 1982.

ARTICLES

Adler, Kenneth P. "Art Films and Eggheads." *Studies in Public Communication*, vol. 2 (Summer 1959): 7–15.

Agostino, Donald E., Herbert A. Terry, and Rolland C. Johnson. "Home Video Recorders: Rights and Ratings." *Journal of Communication*, vol. 30, no. 3 (Autumn 1980): 28–35.

Allen, Robert C. "Motion Picture Exhibition in Manhattan, 1906–1912: Beyond the Nickelodeon." *Cinema Journal*, vol. 18, no. 2 (Spring 1979): 2–15.

Andrew, Dudley. "Film and Society: Public Rituals and Private Space." *East West Film Journal*, vol. I, no. 1 (Winter 1988): 7–22.

Arnheim, Rudolf, and Martha Collins Bayne. "Foreign Language Broadcasts over Local American Stations: A Study of a Special Interest Program." in *Radio Research—1941*, edited by Paul F. Lazarfeld and Frank N. Stanton, 3–64. New York: Duell, Sloan and Pearce, 1941.

Arnold, Robert F. "Film Space/Audience Space: Notes Toward a Theory of Spectatorship." *The Velvet Light Trap*. no. 25 (Spring 1990): 44–52.

Austin, Bruce A. "Cinema Screen Advertising: An Old Technology with New Promise for Consumer Marketing." *Journal of Consumer Marketing*, vol. 3, no. 4 (Winter 1986): 45–56.

Belton, John. "CinemaScope: The Economics of Technology." *The Velvet Light Trap*, no. 21 (Summer 1985): 35–43.

Belton, John. "CinemaScope and Historical Methodology." *Cinema Journal*, vol. 28, no. 1 (Fall 1988): 22–44.

Belton, John. "Cinerama: A New Era in the Cinema." *The Perfect Vision*, vol. I, no. 4 (Spring/Summer 1988): 78–90.

Bernheim, Alfred L. "The Facts of Vaudeville." *Equity*, vol. 8, no. 9 (September 1923): 9–13, 32–35, 37.

Bjork, Ulf Jonas. "Double Features and 'B' Movies: Exhibition Patterns in Seattle, 1938." *Journal of Film and Video*, vol. 41, no. 3 (Fall 1989): 44–47.

Brown, Diane, Joseph M. Ripley II, and Lawrence W. Lichty. "Movies on Television: What the Audience Says." *Radio-Television-Film Audience Studies*. Department of Speech, University of Wisconsin, no. 1 (March 1966): 1–3.

Burch, Mike. "The Robey Theatre, Spencer, West Virginia." *Marquee*, vol. 13, no. 1 (First Quarter 1981): 17–18.

Childers, Terry L., and Dean M. Krugman. "The Competitive Environment of Pay Per View." *Journal of Broadcasting & Electronic Media*, vol. 31, no. 2 (Summer 1987): 335–342.

Cohen, Lizabeth. "Encountering Mass Culture at the Grass Roots: The Experience of Chicago Workers in the 1920s." *American Quarterly*, vol. 41, no. 1 (March 1989): 6–33.

Conant, Michael. "The Paramount Decrees Reconsidered." *Law and Contemporary Problems*, vol. 44, no. 4 (Autumn 1981): 79–107.

Connelly, Eugene Lemoyne. "The First Motion Picture Theatre." *Western Pennsylvania Historical Magazine*, vol. 23, no. 1 (March 1940): 1–12.

Dienstfrey, Harris. "The New American Film." in *The New American Arts* edited by Richard Kostelantez, 31–49. New York: Horizon Press, 1965.

Dominick, Joseph R., and Millard C. Pearce. "Trends in Network Prime-Time Programming, 1953–74." *Journal of Communication*, vol. 26, no. 1 (Winter 1976): 70–80.

Downs, Anthony. "Drive-ins Have Arrived." *Journal of Property Management*, vol. 18 (March 1953): 149–153.

Erffmeyer, Thomas E. "20th Century-Fox Introduces CinemaScope: A Study of Technological and Organizational Innovation." *Film Reader 6* (April 1985): 27–32.

Feisher, Walter L. "How Air Conditioning Has Developed in Fifty Years." *Heating, Piping and Air Conditioning*. January 1950, 120–122.

Feldman, Stanley, and Lee Sigelman. "The Political Impact of Prime-Time Television: 'The Day After'." *Journal of Politics*, vol. 47, no. 2 (Spring 1985): 556–578.

Fernett, Gene. "Itinerant Roadshowmen and the 'Free Movie' Craze." *Classic Images*, no. 88 (October 1982): 12–13.

Fernett, Gene. "When Movie Houses Gave Premiums." *Classic Images*, no. 87, 27.

Gaines, Jane. "From Elephants to Lux Soap: The Programming and 'Flow' of Early Motion Picture Exploitation." *The Velvet Light Trap*, no. 25 (Spring 1990): 29–43.

Geary, Helen Brophy. "After the Last Picture Show." *Chronicles of Oklahoma*, vol. 61, no. 1 (Spring 1983): 4–27.

Glase, Paul E. "The Motion Picture Theatre in Reading: Silent Drama Days—1905–1926." *Historical Review of Berks County*. January 1948, 35–44.

Glazer, Irving. "The Philadelphia Mastbaum." *Marquee*, vol. 7, no. 1 (First Quarter 1975): 3–16.

Gomery, Douglas. "The Coming of Television and the 'Lost' Motion Picture Audience." *Journal of Film and Video*, vol. 37, no. 3 (Summer 1985): 5–11.

Gomery, Douglas. "Failed Opportunities: The Integration of the U.S. Motion Picture and Television Industries." *Quarterly Review of Film Studies*, vol. 10, no. 2 (Summer 1984): 219–228.

Gomery, Douglas. "Hollywood's Business." *Wilson Quarterly*, vol. 10, no. 3 (Summer 1986): 43–57.

Gomery, Douglas. "Hollywood, the National Recovery Administration, and the Question of Monopoly Power." *Journal of the University Film Association*, vol. 31, no. 2 (Spring 1979): 47–52.

Gomery, Douglas. "Movie Audiences, Urban Geography, and the History of the American Film." *The Velvet Light Trap*, no. 19 (Spring 1982): 23–29.

Gomery, Douglas. "Saxe Amusement Enterprises: The Movies Come to Milwaukee." *Milwaukee History*, vol. 2, no. 1 (Spring 1979): 18–28.

Gomery, Douglas. "The Skouras Brothers: Bringing Movies to St. Louis and Beyond." *Marquee*, vol. 16, no. 1 (Second Quarter 1984): 18–21.

Gomery, Douglas. "Splendor in Paradise: The Paramount in Palm Beach," *Marquee*, vol. 14, no. 4 (Fourth Quarter 1982): 3–6.

Gomery, Douglas. "The Story of the Augusta Theatre." *Marquee*, vol. 21, no. 2 (Second Quarter 1989): 3–8.

Gomery, Douglas. "Theatre Television: A History." *SMPTE Journal*, vol. 98, no. 2 (February 1989): 120–123.

Gomery, Douglas. "Theatre Television: The Missing Link of Technological Change in the U. S. Motion Picture Industry." *The Velvet Light Trap*, no. 21 (Summer 1985): 54–61.

Gomery, Douglas. "Thinking about Motion Picture Exhibition." *The Velvet Light Trap*, no. 25 (Spring 1990): 3–11.

Gomery, Douglas. "U. S. Film Exhibition: The Formation of a Big Business," in *The American Film Industry*, rev. ed., edited by Tino Balio, 218–228. Madison: University of Wisconsin Press, 1985.

Gomery, Douglas. "The Warner Theatre: Architectural Splendor in Milwaukee." *Marquee*, vol. 12, no. 1 & 2 (Spring 1981): 27–31.

Gomery, Douglas. "The 'Warner-Vitaphone Peril': The American Film Industry Reacts to the Innovation of Sound." *Journal of the University Film Association*, vol. 28, no. 1 (Winter 1976): 11–20.

Gottschalk, Robert E. "A History of Anamorphic Photography in Motion Picture Production." in *American Cinematographer Manual*, edited by Charles G. Clarke, 264–265. Hollywood: American Society of Cinematographers, 1980.

Haralovich, Mary Beth. "Film Advertising, the Film Industry, and the Pin-up: The Industry's Accomodations to Social Forces in the 1940s." in *Current Research in Film: Audiences, Economics, and Law*, vol. 1, edited by Bruce A. Austin, 127–164. Norwood, N.J.: Ablex Publishing Corporation, 1985.

Headley, Robert K. Jr. "Nickelodeon Finances and Operations, 1909–1911: The Horn Theatre, Baltimore, Maryland." *Marquee*, vol. 13, no. 1 (First Quarter 1981): 21–22.

Hellman, Heikki, and Martti Soramaki. "Economic Concentration in the Videocassette Industry: A Cultural Comparison." *Journal of Communication*, vol. 35, no. 3 (Summer 1985): 35–44.

Hincha, Richard. "Selling CinemaScope: 1953–1956." *The Velvet Light Trap*, no. 21 (Summer 1985): 44–53.

Hollyman, Burnes St. Patrick. "The First Picture Shows: Austin, Texas, 1894–1913." *Journal of the University Film Association*, vol. 29, no. 3 (Summer 1977): 3–8.

Howard, John, George Rothbart, and Lee Sloan. "The Response to 'Roots': A National Survey." *Journal of Broadcasting*, vol. 22, no. 3 (Summer 1978): 279–287.

Hoyt, Homer. "The Status of Shopping Centers in the United States." *Urban Land*, vol. 19 (1960): 3–6.

Hur, K. Kyoon. "Impact of 'Roots' on Black and White Teenagers." *Journal of Broadcasting*, vol. 22, no. 3 (Summer 1978): 289–307.

Jenkins, Henry III. " 'Shall We Make It for New York or for Distribution?': Eddie Cantor, *Whoopee*, and Regional Resistance to the Talkies." *Cinema Journal*, vol. 29, no. 3 (Spring 1990): 32–52.

Johnson, Keith F. "Cinema Advertising." *Journal of Advertising*, vol. 10, no. 4 (Winter 1981): 11–19.

Jones, Beverly. "Before Montgomery: The Desegregation Movement in the District of Columbia, 1950–1953." *Phylon*, vol. 43, no. 2 (June 1982): 144–154.

Kalmus, Herbert. "Technicolor and New Screen Techniques," in *New Screen Techniques*, edited by Martin Quigley, Jr., 78–81. New York: Quigley Publishing Company, 1953.

Karnes, David. "The Glamorous Crowd: Hollywood Movie Premiers Between the Wars." *American Quarterly*, vol. 38, no. 4 (Fall 1986): 553–572.

Kelkres, Gene G. "A Forgotten First: The Armat-Jenkins Partnership and the Atlanta Projection." *Quarterly Review of Film Studies*, vol. 9, no. 1 (Winter 1984): 45–58.

Kindem, Gorham A. "Hollywood's Conversion to Color: The Technological, Economic, and Aesthetic Factors," in *The American Movie Industry: The Business of Motion Pictures*, edited by Gorham A. Kindem, 143–154. Carbondale, Ill.: Southern Illinois University Press, 1982.

Kmet, Jeffrey. "Milwaukee's Nickelodeon Era: 1906–1915." *Milwaukee History*, vol. 2, no. 1 (Spring 1979): 2–7.

Kowinski, William Severini. "The Malling of America." *New Times*, 1 May 1978, 33–44.

Krampner, Jon. "In the Beginning . . . The Genesis of the Telefilm." *Emmy*, vol. 11, no. 6 (December 1989): 30–35.

Leach, William R. "Transformations in a Culture of Consumption: Women and Department Stores, 1890–1925." *Journal of American History*, vol. 71, no. 3 (September 1984): 319–342.

Lee, S. Charles. "Influence of West Coast Designers on the Modern Theatre." *Journal of the SMPE*, vol. 50, no. 4 (April 1948): 329–336.

Leff, Leonard, and Jerold L. Simmons. "No Trollops, No Tomcats." *American Film*, vol. 14, no. 3 (December 1989): 43, 52–54.

Linfield, Susan. "The Color of Money." *American Film*, vol. 13, no. 5 (January/February 1987): 29–35.

Lowery, Edward. "Edwin J. Hadley: Traveling Film Exhibitor." *Journal of the University Film Association*, vol. 28, no. 3 (Summer 1976): 5–12.

Luther, Rodney. "Drive-in Theatres: Rags to Riches in Five Years." *Hollywood Quarterly*, vol. 5, no. 3 (Summer 1951): 401–411.

McCann, Joseph. "Videotape Recorders and Copyright Infringement: The Fair Use Doctrine on Instant Replay." *The Journal of Arts Management and Law*, vol. 13, no. 4 (Winter 1984): 5–30.

McConachie, Bruce A. "Pacifying American Theatrical Audiences, 1820–1900," in *For Fun and Profit: The Transformation of Leisure into Consumption*, edited by Richard Butsch, 47–70. Philadelphia: Temple University Press, 1990.

McElwee, John P. "Theatrical Re-Issues." *Films in Review*, Part I. December 1989, 593–596; Part II, January/February 1990, 21–25.

McGilligan, Patrick. "Movies Are Better Than Ever—on Television." *American Film*, vol. 5, no. 4 (March 1980): 52–55.

McKay, Robert B. "Segregation and Public Recreation." *Virginia Law Review*, vol. 40, no. 6 (October 1954): 697–731.

Musser, Charles. "The 'Chaser Theory,' Another Look at the 'Chaser Theory'." *Studies in Visual Communication*, vol. 10, no. 4 (Fall 1984): 24–44.

Neupert, Richard. "A Studio Built of Bricks: Disney and Technicolor." *Film Reader* 6 (April 1985): 33–40.

Nielsen, Ted. "A History of Network Television News," in *American Broadcasting: A Source Book on the History of Radio and Television*, edited by Lawrence W. Lichty and Malachi C. Topping, 421–428. New York: Hastings House, 1975.

Ogan, Christine. "The Audience for Foreign Film in the United States." *Journal of Communication*, vol. 40, no. 4 (Autumn 1990): 58–77.

Pratt, George C. "Firsting the Firsts," in *"Image" on the Art and Evolution of the Film*, edited by Marshall Deutelbaum, 20–22. New York: Dover, 1979.

Preddy, Jane. "Glamour, Glitz and Sparkle: The Deco Theatres of John Eberson." *The 1989 Annual of the Theatre Historical Society*, no. 16. Chicago: Theatre Historical Society, 1990, 1–39.

Pryluck, Calvin. "The Itinerant Movie Show and the Development of the Film Industry." *Journal of the University Film and Video Association*, vol. 25, no. 4 (Fall 1983): 11–22.

Rotzoll, Kim B. "The Captive Audience: The Troubled Odyssey of Cinema Advertising," in *Current Research in Film: Audiences, Economics, and Law*, edited by Bruce A. Austin, 72–87. Norwood, N. J.: Ablex Publishing Corporation, 1987.

374 / Selected Bibliography

Scherer, Clifford W. "The Videocassette Recorder and Information Inequality." *Journal of Communication*, vol. 9, no. 3 (Summer 1989): 94–103.

Schmidt, Jackson. "On the Road to MGM: A History of Metro Pictures Corporation, 1915–1920." *The Velvet Light Trap*, no. 19 (1982): 46–52.

Schneider, Donald. "The Controversy over Sunday Movies in Hastings, 1913–1929." *Nebraska History*, vol. 69, no. 1 (Summer 1988): 60–72.

Scott, Sharon. "Imitation of Life." *AFI Report*, vol. 4, no. 2 (May 1973): 6–10.

Snyder, Robert W. "Big Time, Small Time, All Around the Town: New York Vaudeville in the Early Twentieth Century," in *For Fun and Profit: The Transformation of Leisure into Consumption*, edited by Richard Butsch, 118–135. Philadelphia: Temple University Press, 1990.

Southall, Derek J. "Twentieth Century-Fox Presents a CinemaScope Picture." *Focus on Film*, no. 31 (November 1978): 8–26, 47.

Stabiner, Karen. "The Shape of Theatres to Come." *American Film*, vol. 7, no. 10 (September 1982): 34–38.

Staiger, Janet. "Announcing Wares, Winning Patrons, Voicing Ideals: Thinking about the History and Theory of Film Advertising." *Cinema Journal*, vol. 29, no. 3 (Spring 1990): 3–31.

Streible, Dan (coordinator). "The Literature of Film Exhibition: A Bibliography on Motion Picture Exhibition and Related Topics." *The Velvet Light Trap*, no. 25 (Spring 1990): 80–119.

Surlin, Stuart H. " 'Roots' Research: A Summary of Findings," *Journal of Broadcasting*, vol. 22, no. 3 (Summer 1978): 309–320.

Swartz, Mark E. "Motion Pictures on the Move." *Journal of American Culture*, vol. 9, no. 3 (Fall 1987): 1–7.

Swartz, Mark E. "An Overview of Cinema on the Fairgrounds." *Journal of Popular Film and Television*, vol. 15, no. 3 (Fall 1987): 102–108.

Taylor, Ryland A. "The Repeat Audience for Movies on TV." *Journal of Broadcasting*, vol. 17, no. 1 (Winter 1972–1973): 95–100.

Taylor, Ryland A. "Television Movie Audiences and Movie Awards: A Statistical Study." *Journal of Broadcasting*, vol. 18, no. 2 (Spring 1974): 181–186.

Thomas, David O. "From Page to Screen in Small Town America: Early Motion Picture Exhibition in Winona, Minnesota." *Journal of the University Film Association*, vol. 33, no. 3 (Summer 1981): 3–13.

Thomas, David O. "Winona Nickelodeon Theatres 1907–1913: The Battle for Local Control." *Marquee*, vol. 13, no. 1 (First Quarter 1981): 12–16.

Thompson, Frank. "The Big Squeeze." *American Film*, vol. 15, no. 5 (February 1990): 40–43.

Toler, J. H. "Air Conditioning Wanted for New and Remodeled Theatres." *Domestic Engineering* 165 (March 1945): 113–114.

Trainor, Richard. "Let's Get Vertical." *American Film*, vol. 13, no. 8 (June 1988): 43–48.

Turner, Max W., and Frank R. Kennedy. "Exclusion, Ejection, and Segregation of Theatre Patrons." *Iowa Law Review*, vol. 32, no. 4 (May 1947): 631–654.

Waller, Gregory A. "Introducing the 'Marvellous Invention' to the Provinces: Film Exhibition in Lexington, Kentucky, 1896–1897." *Film History*, vol. 3, no. 3 (Fall 1989): 223–234.

Waller, Gregory A. "Re-placing *The Day After*." *Cinema Journal*, vol. 26, no. 3 (Spring 1987): 3–20.

Waller, Gregory A. "Situating Motion Pictures in the Pre-Nickelodeon Period: Lexington, Kentucky, 1897–1906." *The Velvet Light Trap*, no. 25 (Spring 1990): 12–28.

Walston, Mark. "The Commercial Rise and Fall of Silver Spring: A Study of the 20th Century Development of the Suburban Shopping Center in Montgomery County." *Maryland Historical Magazine*, vol. 81, no. 4 (Winter 1986): 330–335.

Ward, Renee. "Black Films, White Profits." *The Black Scholar*, vol. 7, no. 8 (May 1976): 13–24.

Wittenmeyer, Fred. "Cooling of Theatres and Public Buildings." *Ice and Refrigeration*, July 1922, 13–14.

Wittenmeyer, Fred. "Development of Carbon Dioxide Refrigerating Machines." *Ice and Refrigeration*, November 1916, 165–166.

Zimmermann, Patricia R. "Hollywood, Home Movies, and Common Sense: Amateur Film as Aesthetic Dissemination and Social Control, 1950–1962." *Cinema Journal*, vol. 27, no. 4 (Summer 1988): 23–44.

INDEX

A & P (grocery store chain), 35–36, 58
"ABC Movie of the Week," 252–253
ABC television network, 89–90
Advertising, 117
Air conditioning, 53–54, 75–76; photograph, 130
Amadeus (1984), 259–260
American Federation of Musicians, 225
American Movie Classics, 271–272
American Multi-Cinema (AMC), 97–98, 99, 104, 114
Amerika (1987), 256, 257
Ampex Company, 278
Amusement parks, 8–10
Animation, 137
Architecture, 47–49, 95, 100, 109, 113, 115
AromaRama, 230
Art cinemas, 180–195
Art Deco, 74–75, 108
Arts & Entertainment cable channel, 272, 298
Ash, Paul, 52–53, 72
AT&T, 217
Audience behavior, 117–118
Augusta, Kansas, 28–29; photograph, 199

Baby boom, 86–87, 113

Balaban, Abraham Joseph (A. J.), 41, 52
Balaban, Barney, 41, 53, 61, 232–233
Balaban & Katz, 34, 40–56, 162, 225; photographs, 123, 124, 128
Baltimore, Maryland, 9, 24–25, 175
Bank Night, 70–71
Baronet Theatre, 187
Beekman Theatre, 187–188
Benjamin, Robert, 167
Betamax, 278–279
Bethesda, Maryland, 167
Beverly Center, 107
Black Entertainment Television, 272, 298
Blockbuster, 282–283
Bordwell, David, xix, 192
Boston, Massachusetts, 179
Bravo cable channel, 272
Brecker, Leo, 174
Brian's Song (1971), 252–253
Bridge On the River Kwai, The (1957), 251, 253
Bristol, William H., 223–224
Brownie Club, 139
Burger, Alfred A., 150–151

Cabinet of Dr. Caligari, The (1919), 173
Cable television, 263–275
Candy, 79–80

377